Able, Gifted and Talented Underachievers

Able, Gifted and Talented Underachievers

Second Edition

Edited by Diane Montgomery

A John Wiley & Sons, Ltd, Publication

This second edition first published 2009
© 2009 John Wiley & Sons Ltd

Edition history: Whurr Publishers Ltd (1e, 2000).

Wiley-Blackwell is an imprint of John Wiley & Sons, formed by the merger of Wiley's global
Scientific, Technical, and Medical business with Blackwell Publishing.

Registered Office
John Wiley & Sons Ltd, The Atrium, Southern Gate, Chichester, West Sussex, PO19 8SQ, UK

Editorial Offices
The Atrium, Southern Gate, Chichester, West Sussex, PO19 8SQ, UK
9600 Garsington Road, Oxford, OX4 2DQ, UK
350 Main Street, Malden, MA 02148-5020, USA

For details of our global editorial offices, for customer services, and for information about how to
apply for permission to reuse the copyright material in this book please see our website at
www.wiley.com/wiley-blackwell.

Library of Congress Cataloging-in-Publication Data

Able, gifted and talented underachievers / edited by Diane Montgomery. – 2nd ed.
    p. cm.
  Rev. ed. of: Able underachievers.
  Includes bibliographical references and index.
  ISBN 978-0-470-74097-2 (cloth) – ISBN 978-0-470-77940-8 (pbk.)   1. Underachievers–Great
Britain.   2. School failure–Great Britain.   3. Gifted children–Education–Great Britain.
I. Montgomery, Diane.   II. Able underachievers.
  LC3969.A25 2009
  371.2′8–dc22

                                    2008049822

A catalogue record for this book is available from the British Library.

Set in Minion 10.5/13pt by Aptara Inc., New Delhi, India.
Printed in Singapore by Fabulous Printers Pte Ltd.

Contents

Preface   vii

Biographies   xi

I THE NATURE AND IDENTIFICATION OF
   UNDERACHIEVEMENT AND THE GENERAL PRINCIPLES
   AND PRACTICES IN RAISING ACHIEVEMENT

1 Why Do the Gifted and Talented Underachieve? How Can
   Masked and Hidden Talents Be Revealed?   3
   Diane Montgomery

2 Literacy, Flexible Thinking and Underachievement   41
   Joan Freeman

3 What Do We Mean by an 'Enabling Curriculum' That
   Raises Achievement for All Learners? An Examination of
   the TASC Problem-Solving Framework: Thinking Actively
   in a Social Context   59
   Belle Wallace

4 How Can Inclusive and Inclusional Understandings of
   Gifts/Talents Be Developed Educationally?   85
   Jack Whitehead and Marie Huxtable

5 Effective Teaching and Learning to Combat
   Underachievement   111
   Diane Montgomery

 6 Changing the Teaching for the Underachieving Able
    Child: The Ruyton School Experience   155
    Lee Wills and John Munro

II IDENTIFYING AND MAKING PROVISION FOR DIFFERENT
    GROUPS OF UNDERACHIEVERS

 7 Understanding and Overcoming Underachievement in
    Women and Girls – A Reprise   185
    Carrie Winstanley

 8 Understanding and Overcoming Underachievement
    in Boys   201
    Barry Hymer

 9 Improving the Quality of Identification, Provision and
    Support for Gifted and Talented Learners from
    Under-Represented Communities through
    Partnership Working   219
    Ian Warwick

10 Gifted and Talented Children with Special Educational
    Needs – Underachievement in Dual and Multiple
    Exceptionality   265
    Diane Montgomery

11 Using Assistive Technologies to Address the Written
    Expression Needs of the Twice-exceptional Student   303
    William F. Morrison, Tara Jeffs and Mary G. Rizza

12 Case Studies of Three Schools Tackling Underachievement   327
    Diane Montgomery

    Index   345

Preface

In a summary of international research on gifted education Passow (1990), former founding president of the World Council for Gifted and Talented Children, wrote that as we neared the end of the twentieth century we still did not know of what good provision for the highly able should consist or how to motivate and include those who were socially disadvantaged, nor how to include the able culturally and linguistically disadvantaged.

In the first edition of this book in 2000, we wrote about what forms of teaching and learning did work for the gifted and talented; the reasons for underachievement (UAch) in boys and girls from a range of backgrounds and methods for helping them, and the impact of particular literacy difficulties on achievement and how to overcome them. It was a time when the education climate in the United Kingdom was not receptive to investigating the needs of its most able pupils, to find if they were not achieving sufficiently well. There were other pupils who needed help more and standards across the board to be driven up.

The government initiative on the 'Gifted and Talented' (DfEE, 1999) was just beginning to take effect, but without major funding and no clear policy on effective teaching and learning it was a fringe activity encouraging summer schools and master classes. It seemed to many teachers that it was being imposed in direct contradiction of inclusion policies and excellence for all children. As the 'G and T' initiative gathered impetus, effective teaching and learning policies focusing on more stretch and challenge were developed, and these coincided with what was being recommended at Key Stage 3 in foundation subjects – challenging questioning, teaching thinking skills and assessment for learning.

The accumulated data from national testing over a decade seemed all of a sudden in about 2003 to 'discover' that boys were underachieving and something serious must be done. Within a year or two, in the wake of this concern, underachievement was on the schools' and research agenda, at last!

This new edition of the book contains much new material, but also some from the previous edition that is still relevant today. It shows that we do know now what needs to be done in the education of the gifted and talented, how UAch can be identified and lifted and how disadvantaged groups may be helped.

Part I opens with a chapter on the nature and identification of the complex phenomenon of UAch, showing how schools can and do identify their underachievers and can remove some of the causes. Chapter 2 by Joan Freeman examines research from an international perspective on the development of high ability in an 'e literacy age' and the developmental constraints that may be placed upon it in different cultural environments.

The next four chapters deal with effective teaching and learning to motivate and include the gifted and talented underachievers. Although these are written from different perspectives, they also represent the personal learning journeys of the authors. Belle Wallace describes her development of TASC (Thinking Actively in A Social Context) and of which she is now the international director. Detailed evaluations of TASC's impact on current practice in the United Kingdom are also presented.

Jack Whitehead and Marie Huxtable in Chapter 4 use the metaphor of 'living theory' to show how this impacts upon their practice and that of their teachers working with gifted pupils and using TASC. It is then we see this metaphor was operative in the development of Belle's work with TASC and with Montgomery's work in Chapter 4. It shows how their 'living theories' were constructed and over time become developed into formal theories in the field, and are taken up by government, practitioners and researchers as the basis for effective teaching and learning.

Chapter 6 describes the 'living theory' of John Munro and the work of Lee Wills as she implements the ideas with him in the Ruyton School. This Australian approach based upon learning codes seems to me to be more theoretically sound than one based on the notion of multiple intelligences, although the learning outcomes for underachievers might be equally effective.

Part II of the book is devoted to identifying the needs and provision for different underachieving groups. Chapter 7 by Carrie Winstanley deals with the current position in the United Kingdom of gifted and underachieving girls. They are now performing better in school than boys, but not in the 'afterlife' in their later careers. Chapter 8 by Barry Hymer restates and updates the position of boys and the origins of their underachievements in comparison with girls. It provides an overview of what had been found to work in the Cumbrian project.

Chapter 9 by Ian Warwick presents a wealth of new material on underachieving learners from different cultural and linguistic groups in six areas in inner London and Northern England. The Realising Equality and Achievement for Learners (REAL) Project shows how teachers with advisers and coordinators have identified the needs and made effective provision for Black and Minority Ethnic (BME) and English as Additional Language (EAL) learners. Again, it exemplifies the 'living theory' approach.

Chapter 10 by Diane Montgomery summarises the identification and needs of twice- and multiply-exceptional learners, and focuses in the final section on the writing problems so often encountered by many gifted and talented underachievers, suggesting ways based on case studies in which the difficulties may be overcome. Bill Morrison's Chapter 11 with Mary Rizza and Tara Jeffs, reports in detail how assistive technologies may be used to support those with written language difficulties.

The final short chapter by Montgomery returns the discussion to the developmental perspective, and shows how three case study schools from widely different settings have lifted the underachievement of their pupils and how they were inclusive and more similar than different.

Two themes run throughout the book, and these are 'living theory' and personalising learning.

References

Passow, A. H. (1990) Needed research in development in teaching high ability children. *European Journal of High Ability*, **1**, 15–24.

DfEE (1999) *Excellence in Cities* London: DfEE.

Biographies

Professor Joan Freeman is a world expert in the lifetime development of gifts and talents. She is a Fellow of the British Psychological Society, a chartered psychologist, and 2007 winner of the Society's lifetime achievement award. She is the founding president of the European Council for High Ability (ECHA) and visiting professor at Middlesex University, London. Joan has published 16 books for scholars and parents, and hundreds of academic and non-academic publications and addresses given in most parts of the world.

See www.JoanFreeman.com

Marie Huxtable is a senior educational psychologist, working within an English local authority where she coordinates and develops the inclusive gifts, talents and education project. Her work rests on her belief that all learners have the capacity for extraordinary achievement, and her responsibility as an educator is to contribute to improving educational contexts that inform the aspirations of all children and young people, as they learn what it is to live a satisfying and productive life that enhances their well being and well becoming. She is working to develop her inclusive and inclusional practice through living theory research to reflect her growing understanding of what she means by extraordinary achievement and the educational environment in which it can flourish.

Dr Barry Hymer is a graduate of the Universities of Cape Town, Port Elizabeth, Cambridge and Southampton, and he obtained his doctorate from Newcastle University. From 1991 to 2001, he was employed as an educational psychologist in Cumbria where he coordinated the county's Able Pupil Project, and with a working group of teachers and consultants he coordinated the preparation of a resource pack of strategies for combating boys' underachievement.

Barry is a national trainer for NACE, and he has authored a number of books and articles on learning, teaching and gifted education. He is currently an education consultant and Visiting Fellow at Newcastle University's Centre for Learning and Teaching. He has a special interest in Philosophy for Children for which he runs training sessions for schools.

Dr Tara Jeffs, associate professor, is the director of the Irene Howell Assistive Technology Center at East Carolina University, Greenville, NC. Her primary research areas include implementing assistive and emerging technologies in general and special education classrooms, integrating technology into teacher preparation and universal design for learning.

Professor Diane Montgomery, PhD, is emeritus professor in Education at Middlesex University, London. She is a qualified and experienced teacher and teacher educator. Her doctorate is in improving teaching and learning, and she is a chartered psychologist specializing in research on giftedness and learning difficulties. She authored and ran three distance education MA programmes for Middlesex where she was formerly Dean of Faculty of Education and Performing Arts and Head of the School of Education. She writes MA Gifted Education, MA SEN, and MA SpLD (Dyslexia) programmes and runs the Learning Difficulties Research Project from her home in Essex. She has written more than 20 books and many articles on a range of education topics – gifted education, able underachievers, double exceptionality, dyslexia, spelling, handwriting, behaviour problems, appraisal, learning difficulties, and classroom observation. She lectures widely nationally and internationally.
DMont507@aol.com

Dr William F. Morrison is an associate professor in the School of Intervention Services at Bowling Green State University, Ohio. He is a former special educator who taught children with severe emotional and behavioural problems. Currently, he teaches graduate and undergraduate courses in special and gifted education. He serves as a consultant to schools in Ohio on the identification and programming for the twice exceptional. Dr Morrison's research interests include the issues related to the identification and programming for the twice exceptional, use of literature-based instruction and assistive technology in classrooms.

Dr John Munro (B Sc, Dip.Ed, B Ed, BA Hons, MA, PhD) is senior lecturer in Educational Psychology and Giftedness in the Faculty of Education, University of Melbourne. He lectures and researches in areas of effective learning and teaching, learning difficulties in numeracy and literacy, educational psychology and giftedness.

Originally, he was a secondary maths and science teacher and retrained as a psychologist because of an interest in maths and literacy learning problems. He works in schools with parents on strategies for enhancing opportunity for effective learning.

He has written articles and books in the area of effective learning and teaching, cognitive style, individual differences and giftedness.

Dr Mary G. Rizza is an educational consultant for Gifted Services in the Office of Exceptional Children at the Ohio Department of Education. Her primary responsibility is to inform gifted identification practices, particularly related to under-represented populations. She also provides technical assistance to parents and schools on issues related to twice-exceptional students, program quality and compliance with state regulations. Dr Rizza's research interests include issues related to the identification and programming for the twice exceptional, the use of technology in classrooms and program evaluation.

Belle Wallace initially worked in an advisory capacity (United Kingdom) with the brief for developing Curriculum Enrichment and Extension for pupils across all phases of education; she was co-director of the Curriculum Development Unit (University of Natal, SA) developing Assessment Strategies and Curriculum Enrichment and Extension for very able, disadvantaged learners and training curriculum planners; she designed and was the senior author of a school series of 48 language and thinking skills texts to enhance cognitive development in pupils from 6 to 17+ years. She now works as a national and international consultant on Problem-solving and Thinking Skills Curricula, and is director of TASC International.

Belle has served on the executive committee of the World Council for Gifted and Talented Children; she has been editor of *Gifted Education International* (AB Academic Publishers) since 1981 and is immediate past president of NACE, United Kingdom.

Her publications are many: most recently, she has published a series of 5 problem-solving and thinking skills books extending topics taken from the National Curriculum Framework, United Kingdom, and *Diversity in Gifted Education: International Perspectives on Global.*

Recently, Belle has been made a Fellow of the Royal Society of Arts, in recognition of her service to education.

belle.wallace@btinternet.com

Ian Warwick, after 20 years teaching in inner city comprehensives, Ian wrote the vision document and assembled the consortium, which became London Gifted & Talented. Ian's chief areas of interest are urban education, disadvantaged and underachieving students, teacher training and e-learning. Ian has published extensively in the field of education, and has spoken at many regional, national and international conferences. He is a consultant editor for Gifted Education International, and has written e-learning and face-to-face modules for LGT and the National Strategies Training and Guidance materials.

Jack Whitehead began his research programme into the nature of educational theory in the Department of Education at the University of Bath in 1973. His original contributions to educational knowledge include the idea that each individual can generate their own living educational theory as an explanation of their educational influence in their own learning, in the learning of others and in the learning of the social formations in which we live and work. He is a former president of the British Educational Research Association, and is now a visiting professor at Ningxia Teachers University in China.

Lee Wills (B Ed, TPTC, ITC, MACE) has been a teacher and administrator in state primary and secondary, independent schools and tertiary institutions in Australia since 1960. From 1986 to 1995, she worked as an education consultant privately and in industry.

In July 1993, she was invited to Ruyton Girls' school to develop an enrichment programme for boys and girls aged 5–12, and so the Victorian Enrichment Centre at Ruyton was born.

In 1994, she attended the European Council for High Ability Conference in Nijmegen in the Netherlands, and has since then presented papers annually on her work at ECHA and World Council conferences. From 1997 to 2007, she was Assistant Principal and Head of the junior school at Ruyton Girls' School, Kew Victoria. Since 2007, she has been director of the Victorian Enrichment Centre.

Dr Carrie Winstanley's interests lie in inclusive and special education, with an emphasis on the needs of able children with difficulties, and on broadening diversity in all phases of education, with reference to social justice. Carrie is a principal lecturer at Roehampton University, London, and has taught in schools and higher education for 20 years. She continues to run regular holiday and weekend workshops with able children from disadvantaged backgrounds in museums, galleries, schools and science centres. With higher degrees in psychology, philosophy and history of education, Carrie's practical work is strongly grounded in theory (both conceptual and empirical). She has served on various advisory groups, acting as a consultant across the United Kingdom, sharing ideas on how best to support able children.

I

The Nature and Identification of Underachievement and the General Principles and Practices in Raising Achievement

1

Why Do the Gifted and Talented Underachieve? How Can Masked and Hidden Talents Be Revealed?

Diane Montgomery

Introduction

Underachievement is the term used when the estimated potential of individuals is not realized in their achievements. This may be in the preschool period, in school or in later life. Although it seems to be a widespread phenomenon even so research suggests that much of it appears to go undetected.

It has come to be of particular concern during the school years especially lately since Standard Attainment Tests (SATs) and other national statistics show differences in achievements of boys and girls and minority groups. Since intelligence and ability should be equally distributed across the groups it is surprising to find that it is not matched by attainment.

Teachers know that there are always pupils who are capable of more could achieve more or are hard to reach, and research backs up these observations. In the past such pupils might have been dismissed as unmotivated or lazy. Some might have considered them beyond help because of their disadvantaged backgrounds or lack of culture. Now we know better. We also know that good schools and expert teachers can and do make a difference.

Studies show that underachievement (UAch) affects pupils across the ability range but is more common and more damaging in some groups than others. In order to understand this and counteract the effects it is necessary to try to understand the origins and causes of UAch as well as how it may be identified. But it is a complex phenomenon and will take some unravelling.

In general terms underachievers show an inability to sit still, pay attention and stay on task. Deeper investigation shows that they have a very poor

Able, Gifted and Talented Underachievers, Second Edition   Edited by Diane Montgomery
© 2009 John Wiley & Sons, Ltd

self-image. What they typically say of themselves is, 'I'm useless at this or that . . . I hate school . . . school hates me . . . it's boring.'

Baum, Cooper and Neu (2001) found that underachievers felt:

> Everyone in the school knows what I can't do, absolutely no one knows what I can do.

This is not untypical for we can tend to focus on the overt and negative aspects and try to deal with these when research shows that when we concentrate on the positives and celebrate what pupils achieve we help them do better (Montgomery, 1989, 2002).

Concentrating on the negatives can cause pupils to become demotivated and to feel failures. It can also lead in some to even more undesirable depressive and behavioural side effects.

It would be a mistake however to locate UAch only as a problem intrinsic to the pupil. There is a range of external factors that can also cause UAch that the pupil can do little about.

Such factors are underachieving schools whose aspirations for pupils are too low; underachieving departments and teachers whose teaching and learning strategies need to be improved; and underachieving environments where children cannot be given quality nurturance that enables them to take advantage of schooling.

Finally, the ethos and the models of schools, families, popular culture and modern ways of life may not encourage pupils to value the schooling or education in the wider sense that is on offer.

Nor is UAch only a modern preoccupation. The Board of Education for England and Wales in 1923 stated in *Differentiation of the Curriculum between the Sexes in Secondary Schools*:

> It is well known that most boys, especially at the period of adolescence, have a habit of healthy idleness (Board of Education, 1923, p. 20). Nearly 70 years later Brereton felt able to write:
>
> Many girls would work at a subject they dislike. No healthy boy ever does (Brereton 1990, pp. 34–35).

These are however not sentiments we would want to accept today but there are still countries, cultures and homes in which women and girls predominantly do all the work and boys and men have all the disposable time.

In fact our own history of education shows that it is only since the middle of the nineteenth century that girls could expect an education and might have aspirations beyond marriage and the running of a home. It took a further 100 years for the Raising of the School Leaving Age (ROSLA 1970–71) to 16 to ensure that girls might have equal opportunities to stay on at school to gain the qualifications necessary for different careers. Employers still complain that the standard of school leavers is not as high as it once was not recognizing that they are fishing in a different pool.

Finally, the pressures of global economics demand that modern technological societies create a workforce with ever-increasing levels of skill and this places stress upon schools and learners to improve the qualifications of all the pupils. What still perhaps needs to be addressed is the perceived mismatch between school inputs and career and economic outcomes for the learners, the issue of 'relevance'.

Once upon a time the 'grammar' schools defined their role as only teaching Latin and Greek. Headmasters had to be paid extra for offering arithmetic and other subjects. Pupils (boys) were herded into classes of 100 or more and were 'taught' by rote and made compliant by force of the cane. Relevance was not considered and school riots at three major public schools had to be put down by soldiers. After the day spent in rote learning the pupils in public schools were left for hours to their own devices with no organized games or activities.

In 1978, the Scottish HMI surveyed all their primary and secondary schools and compiled a report (SED, 1978) that found that the curriculum and pedagogy were the *main causes* of learning difficulties in the schools and pupils were unable to see the relevance of much they were required to learn. Today, despite the introduction of the National Curriculum (NC, 1989) and now its many revisions and updates to 'the New Curriculum' our pupils are still complaining of the lack of relevance of much of what they do in school. This was evidenced in the 1000 and more composition scripts I analyzed (Montgomery, 2008). They go home to a dwelling set in an environment where they feel there is little for them to do and nowhere for them to go. Teachers report an increasing tide of disaffection. Everything has changed and everything stays the same.

However, as will be seen as the various chapters unfold lack of relevance, disaffection and UAch are not a necessary consequence of compulsory education although they are the result of inept policies and practices delivered from above.

This chapter will discuss the complex nature of UAch and then outline ways in which it may be identified. A key feature will be 'identification through appropriate provision (ITAP)'.

Common Indicators of Underachievement

The profile of more able underachievers in school has been well researched and a common list of characteristics is shown below based on Kellmer-Pringle (1970), Whitmore (1982), Butler-Por (1987), Silverman (1989), Wallace (2000) and Montgomery (2000).

A checklist to aid identification of more able underachievers

- Large gap between oral and written work.
- Poor literacy skills.
- Failure to complete schoolwork and homework.
- Poor execution of work.
- Refuses to do work.
- Dissatisfaction with own achievements.
- Avoidance of trying new activities.
- Perfectionism and extreme self-criticism.
- Sets unrealistic goals and aspirations.
- Does not function well in groups or subverts group work.
- Lacks concentration.
- Poor attitudes to school.
- May have difficulties with peers.
- Low self-image.
- Performs satisfactorily in all areas at a level with peers.

Able underachievers do not show all these characteristics, they tend to form in clusters but the overriding feature seems to be the problem over written work. It is probably difficult to find a pupil who does not at times show at least one or two of the above characteristics but with UAch the pattern is persistent. The resultant problem behaviours can mask our ability to see the real potential underneath.

In cases of very high ability, giftedness, then the pupil may simply refuse to do any of the work because it is too low level or it has been covered before. The overt expression may just be, 'It's boring'.

In schools where a lot of written work is required the general profile is of an inability or a refusal to produce written work of a suitable quality and to sit still and pay attention in class, Lee-Corbin and Denicolo (1998) confirmed this in their detailed comparative study of 18 able achievers and 16 lower achievers in three primary schools in Key Stage 2. Teacher assessment and scores at and above the 90th percentile on the British Picture Vocabulary Test (Dunn, Whetton and Pintilie, 1982) and Raven's Standard Progressive Matrices (1991 version) were used to help select the groups.

Boy's achievement in general is seen to be lower than that of girls'. Government statistics show that this deficit in boys' achievement is in the order of 10% (DfES, 2006).

There may also be an uneven pattern of performance across subjects with higher performance in arts and sports or good behaviour and performance in just one subject with a favoured teacher. Out of school achievements may be significant in a number of spheres at home and in the neighbourhood yet school achievements are low. Some pupils will only attend on days when their favourite subject is on offer.

Whilst looking across the board at achievement and commitment there are also those individuals who make no impact and function at an average level consistent with that of peers. The 'rhinos' – 'Really Here in Name Only' who are serving time until they can escape from schooling and get into the real world. Some disappear from view and some become highly successful entrepreneurs. The Confederation of British Industry estimates on a regular basis that 30–40% of their most successful industry leaders were 'school averse' or school failures.

My observations in 1250 lessons over a period of years (Montgomery, 2002) suggested that some 80% of pupils underachieved a large part of the time even in the best of lessons in these particular classrooms. Whitmore (1982) found 70% of pupils identified by IQ were underachieving by at least one standard deviation, however, IQ tests do not necessarily identify many of the most able. Richert (1991) found at least 50% of the gifted identified by IQ underachieved academically.

If we think back to our own schooldays few of us can claim to have spent all day on task totally focused. It is too tiring. We need time for thinking, consolidation and mental relaxation within a lesson's time frame. Good lessons arrange for these to happen in legitimate ways without allowing 'dead time'. 'Covering' the syllabus in an overfilled curriculum allows little time for more effective or deep learning, nor thinking and consolidation as the learners construct their own knowledge. This is the constructivist theory and approach to learning (Desforges, 1998).

Persistent UAch is a great waste of potential. But it is a complex phenomenon and a careful analysis is needed to identify it and find ways of overcoming it. No single strategy for intervention is likely to work.

The diagram shows a summary of what seem to be the major contributory factors in UAch in the presence of an individual's particular potential and ability.

Internal factors are motivational ones or the drive to behave in particular ways, the personality factors or the type of people we are and the traits that we have that interact with the general and specific learning difficulties barriers we bring to learning. These can undermine progress in all school subjects. Intrinsic barriers are modifiable but will interact with extrinsic barriers set up for example by disadvantage and poor quality schooling that we have acquired in interaction with the environment.

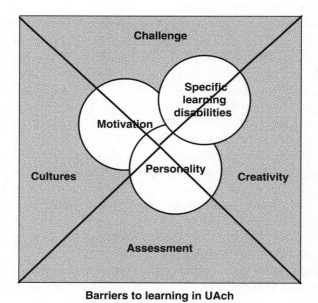

Barriers to learning in UAch

Figure 1   To show internal and external factors contributing to underachievement (UAch).

Internal Factors

Motivation

Intrinsic barriers are modifiable but will interact with others that we have acquired in interaction with the environment. For example Ryan and Deci (2000) found that extrinsic rewards such as gifts and prizes actually caused a decline in motivation to learn and study whereas a positive supportive learning environment raised intrinsic motivation. In addition, work that was self-directed and involved an element of creativity also increased intrinsic motivation. A punitive assessment system with multiple targets and objectives and an overloaded curriculum reduced intrinsic motivation (Feller, 1994).

Thus, whilst we aspire to encourage pupils to become lifelong learners our objectives-based assessment driven school system may militate against this. Pupils in early years education can quickly perceive themselves as system's failures when they do not achieve school targets or the highest levels. Their failures can be extended and reinforced at each subsequent assessment point, added to this is the misery when it is all made public knowledge.

As demotivated pupils move through school some will cease to try, others can become alienated, school averse and exhibit behaviour problems. A coercive system cannot gain the best from such pupils (Mongon and Hart, 1989a) unless the teachers unite under strong leadership to make a difference.

It is the teachers who are the prime source of motivation for pupils in classrooms, providing interest, enthusiasm, positive feedback and feed forward in assessment for learning and who 'catch them being good' rather than catch them being off task and a nuisance. A positive, supportive system can offer education as 'therapy' giving emotional support though learners' engagement with the task.

Personality

Some personalities are more vulnerable than others to lack of success and their self-esteem is more easily lowered. One of the personality dimensions that influences our view of the world and how the world perceives us is the tendency to be more introvert or more extravert. Although extraversion seems more common in younger pupils, as they grow older they become less overtly responsive.

The characteristic outgoing, responsive and more social extravert can be observed in classrooms as well as the more quiet and reflective introvert, preferring to work alone. The 'locus of control' in extraverts tends to be external and so they blame others, the teacher and peers for any shortcomings whereas introverts have an internal 'locus of control' and tend to blame themselves when things go wrong or they fail at something. They are thus more vulnerable to failure and fear of failure and even fear of success than other pupils. More boys than girls tend to have an external locus of control and will blame teachers if they do not understand or if they do not succeed in school. Recently schools have been expressing concerns about their highly able girls' perfectionist attitudes (Sisk, 2003) and their perceived inability to cope with perceived failure. In interviews (BBC Radio 4, 24 March 2008) with head teachers and gifted girls they discussed the problem of 'failure'. The girls were expected to gain A and A* in 10 subjects at General Certificate in Secondary Education (GCSE). The girls said they felt they would be failing if they did not get A* grades in all 10 subjects. They had always succeeded throughout school and the possibility of 'failure' however relative left them without the experience to cope. Some who had gained 9 A* and an A or a B wanted to retake the 'failed' subject. Those set on a particular high status university or career appeared to have no fall back position. School had not equipped them to deal with life in the real world.

The 'big five' personality traits are – neuroticism, extraversion, agreeableness, openness and conscientiousness. Underachievers will have a mix of positions along each of these dimensions like other people. Although some might argue they are not very conscientious where written work is concerned.

Special educational needs (SEN) and underachievement

Many SENs are the result of internal factors such as genetic, congenital, biological and psychological factors whose origins are still being unravelled. Some of them can have a strong impact on learning especially in school subjects and create barriers to progress and achievement unless they can be dismantled or counteracted at an early stage. The SENs that are the most common and contribute most to UAch in school are specific learning difficulties (learning disabilities) such as dyslexia and attention deficit hyperactivity disorder and social emotional and behavioural difficulties. In each category there is a continuum of difficulty from mild through moderate and severe to profound.

The chapter on Dual and Multiple Exceptionality explores these difficulties and their remediation in more detail.

English as an additional language and underachievement

These pupils do not form part of the SEN group because unless they have a learning difficulty or disability their language development will follow a rapid but normal developmental profile. The Ravens (2008) test can give an indication of their intellectual potential and then immersion in the second language in school will help their language abilities to develop. However, they will at first need some second language support and a buddy in class to help them ease into the new system. It is also helpful if an older pupil from the same language background can be identified to be a mentor. The chapter by Ian Warwick explores the needs of learners with English as Additional Language, the identification of their potential and their support. It gives examples of good practice from schools and Local Authorities.

External Factors

Challenge and creativity

Teachers are the prime resource for motivation of pupils in the classroom providing interest, enthusiasm and feedback. It is they who design and implement the lessons connecting the curriculum with the pupils.

Developing *intrinsic motivation* through the task is a guiding principle in teacher education courses. When pupils are off task and misbehaving student teachers are advised to develop more interesting and relevant activities. To a large extent this is good advice but it fails to work where pupils have a learning history that lacks such experiences or where they come from undisciplined settings. Teachers have to become experts in crowd control.

Managing individuals and small groups is quite unlike managing a class of 30. Herd rules have to be known and understood, rules have to be operated.

The problem is that many of these 'rules' or strategies are implicit. However, they can be taught (Montgomery, 2002) but are often only learned by hard experience.

Positive behaviour management needs to be accompanied by motivating work, curriculum tasks and teaching and learning methods that generate interest and maintain enthusiasm and keep the pupil involved. Tasks have to offer active participation and personal involvement in the outcomes, for these too are prime intrinsic motivators.

It is teachers who design tasks to offer cognitive challenge, creativity and undertake the assessment for learning. These represent the key extrinsic factors in Figure 1. The DfES (Higgins, 2002) initiative on teaching and learning in foundation subjects in primary schools and at Key Stage 3 (11–14 years) matches the provision needed for gifted and talented pupils where challenging questioning, problem-based learning (PBL) and thinking skills are promoted.

It has shown that a wider range of pupils can be engaged and motivated when these strategies are incorporated into the ordinary curriculum for all pupils. Greater pupil activity, and more open ended and individualized learning approaches have enabled disaffected pupils to stay on task and become involved in school learning. This in turn needs to be reinforced by positive and supportive use of formative assessment and behaviour management. The chapter by Belle Wallace illustrates how these principles have worked in practice using her TASC (Thinking Actively in a Social Context) wheel.

Cognitive challenge and creativity built into tasks represent key *extrinsic factors* that have been found necessary not only for highly able learners but for all learners (Montgomery, 1990, 1996). These too develop motivation. They operate on the principle of 'cognitive dissonance'. When we set a more open problem to which the learner does not know the answer then the inbuilt propensity to seek closure or resolution (consonance) drives them to find one. Kelly (1955) called this natural tendency found from birth as one of 'man the scientist'. If teachers can harness this natural tendency by appropriate task design then they can motivate pupils very strongly. Setting too challenging tasks would quickly bring about the opposite effect, but getting the right level of challenge for individual learners is a key role for the teacher and is part of 'personalizing' the learning.

Getting learners to reflect upon their thinking as they engage in the problem solving and investigative activities is also a part of bringing about more effective learning. This has been evidenced in TASC (Wallace, 2000);

also in Cognitive Acceleration through Science Education (Shayer and Adey, 2002) and related programmes. Thinking about our thinking whilst engaged on solving or working through an issue is also referred to as metacognition and the process as metalearning. Teaching Children Philosophy (Lipman, 1991; www.sapere.org) is strong in this respect and is very popular with pupils in the schools observed for the NACE/London G and T Research Project on Lifting UAch (Wallace *et al.*, 2008). The schools were selected for study because they were known to be very good at counteracting UAch. Key factors showing how case study schools were successful are discussed in the final chapter.

The role of creativity in teaching and learning is often ignored of late. However, it is when more creative options and open-ended opportunities are offered that pupils and students feel satisfaction and pleasure. Creative work does require more space and time than a heavily loaded curriculum may offer. Teachers become anxious that they are not 'covering' the syllabus. But the pupils will spend longer on the task and put more effort into it out of school time and learn much that is not irrelevant to the main curriculum theme as I learned when all my pupils designed and conducted their own investigative/PBL task alone or with a partner in the final month of term. In such a setting the teacher's role changes to make links, to observe, to facilitate and manage the resources.

The new curriculum has freed up more time so that teachers can be more flexible and creative in what they do. Once basic skills at level 4 had been achieved in Key Stage 2 some schools have set aside a day in a week for projects involving creativity and out of school activities.

Not every task can be set to be a problem or creative activity, a rich mixture is what is required. However, too often the pupils do only get one type of approach, the teacher-directed top-down model seen in typical lesson plans– the mini lecture – the question and answer check for understanding – the 'seat work' based upon questions on a work sheet – finish off for homework. In other words, there is little 'engage brain' involved in these activities and the pupils can maintain a constant level of chat with friends during the written work in particular.

Increasing the cognitive stretch and challenge of tasks in ordinary lessons has shown that a wider range of pupils can be engaged and motivated (Montgomery, 1996, 1998; Wallace, 2000, Wallace *et al.*, 2004). This is important for most of the gifted and talented are not going to gain access to special provision and enrichment nor will underachievers and therefore this has to begin at classroom and subject level.

Assessment

Creative activities, even of the desk-based kind benefit from an audience and an appraisal or evaluation. It is not enough for the teacher to collect all the assignments in and give the assessment. Teacher assessment is of course a valuable part of the learning and teaching process but peer evaluation needs to be encouraged and the processes actually taught.

Pupils need to learn how to develop evaluative criteria and use these in a positive way to help the recipients to develop the work and the understanding. Such activities and presentations are common in the performing arts and often in design but this strategic approach to assessment needs to be developed across the whole curriculum and find a place in all subjects and in all age groups. The gross comments and bald statements of like and dislike so common in classrooms can then be replaced by considered views and consideration and respect for others.

Assessment for learning has always been an important part of the teachers' job. However, as the pressure for more and more work to be assessed rises, the quality of that assessment can be diminished. For example the characteristic view of teacher assessment is the mark out of 10 at the end of an exercise with a comment such as 'Good' or 'Mind your spelling!' Pupils always of course look first for their mark or their grade. It tells them how successful they have been in meeting the teacher's criteria. But what these were they may not know so that they go on to the next exercise, essentially in the dark.

Even in subjects where there are some right and some wrong answers the *summative* mark alone however good, does not tell them how to put right what was wrong. This is in essence the role of *formative* assessment. It feeds forward and it feeds backward. It tells the pupil the criteria that have been met and how well and it tells them how the work could have been improved and if they do so next time how the grade will improve.

Establishing assessment criteria with the pupils at the outset of a task can help all to understand what is required of them. However, making the task criteria necessary and relevant also needs consideration. Writing answers to questions using full sentences when one word might suffice, certainly fills time but also wastes it and disadvantages the 30% of the class with handwriting difficulties in form, coordination or speed (Montgomery, 2007). Many highly able pupils simply refuse to do such tasks and are they wrong to assert themselves in this way?

When formative assessment activities and criterion referencing is shared with pupils it makes it easier for them to engage successfully in peer and self-assessment. It helps overcome the over elaborate self-assessments that they might make and helps gain control of perfectionist tendencies when they run to extremes (Sisk, 2003).

Formative assessment is in fact a powerful teaching device that backs up and personalizes the more overt teaching and learning that takes place in classrooms. Sometimes it is delivered verbally and at other times in writing. When pupils are working independently or in groups on tasks it is essential for the teacher to move round the class and listen, encourage where necessary, redefine and give formative feedback. I call this on-the-hoof input 'Developmental PCI' (positive cognitive intervention). It acts as positive feedback and feed forward and demonstrates the teacher's involvement with the pupils and the task, again it is a motivating force.

Cultures

The cultures and subcultures into which we are born and brought up determine many patterns of our behaviour. Some cultures provide models inconsistent with education and learning which become attractive to disaffected youngsters seeking emotional support of the peer group and gang. The effects of culture can also be counteracted but this is a lengthy process. Again, it is the positive and supportive experiences that can bring this about for we learn from these what to do and how to do it. From negative experiences we only learn what not to do, not how to do it differently.

The potent effects of gender, disadvantage and culture in UAch will be examined in three separate chapters in more detail to show how some of the problems arise and what can be done to overcome them.

By secondary stage hormonal and biological differences and levels between boys and girls figure more in their responses to education and each other. Some schools and teachers can reinforce boy and girl 'codes' or cultures and stereotypes. Boys' behaviour can become more challenging and difficult to manage but some girls can show even more problematic responses and refuse to participate in an education they see as childish and irrelevant (Montgomery, 2002).

Media models, football icons and older siblings may also offer models inappropriate to play out in schools. Maintaining 'cool' can be inimical to schoolwork and as a result of spending much time off task pupils begin to underachieve.

Any difference may be picked on by an 'in group' for no good reason but just to assert themselves. This can be very threatening and distressing for the victim. We are all different in many respects so can all become victims. Difference should be enriching yet is often seen as perverse in a traditional schooling culture modelled upon a nineteenth century education that pervades much popular and political debate. This is the model of Dicken's Mr Gradgrind – 'What we want is facts'.

Dynamic Interactions Between Intrinsic and Extrinsic Factors

Positive processes   For some pupils the intrinsic and extrinsic factors may be in advantageous forms that help them to progress in school and later life. In particular intrinsic motivation, an inner drive, to go on and pursue studies for their own sake, to be able to plan ahead and follow the plan without anyone encouraging them to do so, is very important for success in life. Schools that fail to motivate and interest pupils will fail to help them develop autonomy in learning and intrinsic motivation.

A family background that is supportive and educative and uses extended language is also well known to enhance a child's learning experiences and capabilities (Freeman, 1991, 2001). Rearing patterns that are positively reinforcing, consistent and clear help develop a strong sense of self, self-esteem and identity. All these prepare them to fit in well at school.

Equally rejection, inconsistent rearing, family discord and distress can diminish a child's potential to succeed (Rutter, 1985), as can a coercive, threatening and negative schooling ethos and experience (Mongon and Hart, 1989b).

Positive class control and management (Montgomery 1989, 2002) for misbehaving underachievers

Teachers are not only responsible for the task setting but also maintaining discipline and time on task. Sometimes even the most interesting tasks do not initially make the pupils work at them. Socializing and 'get the teacher' might be more fun. The social interactions between pupils and between pupils and the teacher as well as between the pupils, teacher and task create a set of dynamics that contribute to or can diminish UAch. For example when pupils are allowed to cooperate this can raise their achievement. However, keeping them sitting singly in rows can be a means of helping keep control of a difficult class. Class control procedures act between the extrinsic and intrinsic factors to provoke UAch signs or diminish them. Consistent, fair and positive class control acts to counteract previous negative experiences and provides models for appropriate behaviour and respect.

Secure knowledge of positive behaviour management routines and strategies by the teacher are important when dealing with underachievers for they are often in the habit of not getting on with the task. They chat continuously, do funny walks and make odd noises to attract attention and annoy. They are prime participants in the continuous low-level chatter that Elton (DES, 1989) found disturbed and stressed teachers so much, and it still does (NUT Survey, 2008).

There are five strategic principles that were evolved from the research on effective behaviour management in the 1250 classrooms. In the process it was found possible to convert unsuccessful teachers into successful ones and consolidate and even improve the skills of good teachers by sharing these strategic approaches with them. The learners settled and got on with their work.

The five strategic principles

1. *CBG:* '*Catch them being good*'. That is, both the pupils and the teachers, for people grow more from strengths and then learn to overcome weaknesses. The idea is to catch the pupils when they are on task and praise and support these behaviours rather than continually catching them off task and being a nuisance.

   A positive supportive attitude and classroom ethos set by the teacher contribute to feelings of worth and well-being and enables pupils to respect others as they enjoy respect. Too often underachieving pupils arrive at school from a home in which no one has thought to say a kind word to them. The CBG is directed equally to the social as well as the task behaviours. It consists of smiles, 'goods', giving attention to and nodding in support.

2. *PCI.*
   (a) *Cognitive stretch and challenge.* Whatever is being learnt should be presented so as to appeal to the intellect, or 'engage brain' and should provide opportunities for problem-solving type learning and the learning and exercise of higher order study skills so that

pupils learn how to learn. The lesson plan and the tasks must be designed for this by the teacher and there is discussion and examples in Chapter 5.

(b) *Developmental PCI*. Pupils must not only know that a piece of work is good through CBG; they must have explained what makes it good and what can be the next stage of development – the formative approach that is given in developmental PCI. The detailed interest taken in the work makes it significant in pupil's eyes. If every pupil in every lesson receives some positive, constructive comment upon work, the off task attention-seeking behaviours diminish. PCI in this form need only take 10 seconds but ways must be found for all to receive it.

3. *Management, monitoring and maintenance (3Ms)*. In any lesson there are basic ground level *tactics* that teachers use in order to gain and maintain pupils' attention whatever teaching method they subsequently use. The 3M's strategy represents a set of related tactics which the effective teacher uses time and again to get and keep classroom control.

Management phase

(a) The teacher makes an *attention gaining noise* or *signal* that the class learns to recognize and respond to. The signal varies from sharp closing of a door; a sharp noise of ruler on the table; handclap; a speech noise such as 'Uhmm!', 'Now then!', 'Right!', 'Year 7', 'Good morning everybody', and so on. Some teachers stand quietly and wait.

(b) The teacher gives a *short verbal instruction* (Short Verbal) such as 'Everybody sit down', 'Sit down and get out your books'. 'I want you to listen carefully.' A lively class of pupils will respond to this instruction to the extent of about 70%. Five pupils will continue talking and doing their own thing. The mistakes usually made are either the teacher repeats the instruction louder, and again louder still, so that pupils are either startled and resentful only waiting until later to get their own back; or the teacher anxiously begins the lesson over the talkers who will now continue with others perhaps joining in. Some very difficult classes who have experienced a number of teachers with control problems like this will continue talking whilst the teacher shouts, 'Be quiet!' or some other instruction louder and louder. The pupils thus demonstrate *they* are in control and drive the teacher to threaten and bully and perhaps get him or herself into an irretrievable position.

(c) It is important not to get into this inescapable route to disaster and after the short instruction follow it by *individual instruction*. This simply means following up the 'Everybody sit down!' instruction with a pause, looking carefully round and then asking an individual still standing or talking, 'Richard turn round please!' The effect of this quietly done is to cause the group around the individual also to fall silent or get out their books. It creates a *Ripple Effect* (Kounin, 1970). This indicates the importance of learning some names or having a classroom plan as soon as possible.

(d) When there is quiet, introduce the *main theme* of the lesson immediately. The longer the teacher spends on activities other than this, for example dealing with latecomers, minor administrative matters involving individuals, keeping the rest waiting, the more likelihood there is that other pupils will start to behave in challenging or undesirable ways.

The introductory sequence should have a good pace and soon a habit of getting on with the work will be set up so that all the teacher has to do is enter the room or call for attention and the children will respond appropriately. Student teachers may try to model themselves on the teacher without the same success, because they have not observed the training stage when the teacher has set the ground rules and taught them to respond to the cues.

Monitoring phase   Once the individual or group work has been set then the crucial phase of monitoring begins for not all children will settle immediately. The usual response is for the teacher to deal with individual requests and then go out amongst the class to help some get started or iron out difficulties, really the maintenancing function. Some few teachers remain at their desks withdrawn from the class issuing occasional instructions or giving information sometimes engaged in other work. This can create an attitude in the pupils of 'them and us' or represent to them an authoritarian style of teaching that is not interested in them or what they produce only concerned that they should do as they are told.

Pupils who feel even mildly anti-authority in this depersonalized setting may be prompted to undermine the teacher, that representative of authority. Thus, whilst the teacher is *in* legal authority and must be *an* authority in terms of subject content, this is to be distinguished from displays of overt authoritarianism for the cues are very easily picked up by older pupils who particularly resent this style (Galloway and Goodwin, 1987).

Monitoring involves standing back, casting one's eye round the class over the whole group and observing individuals who are the focus of disturbance or those who have not yet settled. The teacher then needs either to mention the individual name, for example 'John hurry up and get started please', 'Susan, if you have a problem I will come and deal with it in a moment, just settle down now', or quickly move round the work groups quietening the loudest member. It is important to settle the whole class down to work *before* giving detailed help otherwise some may never start at all.

Once the pupils know the teacher is engaging in this monitoring activity eye contact with ring leaders or a hand gesture to settle or move them is all that is needed. The whole session can be controlled by *non-verbal cueing*, 'conducting' the class by eye contact and gesture. It is much more restful to achieve control by non-verbal methods for any noise the teacher makes can contribute to the pupils modelling and using their voices even louder. I observed a noisy and disorganized teacher convert a class of well-behaved individuals into a herd of ill-behaved out of order children. The noisier the teacher the noisier the children.

The monitoring phase should be short but can be repeated as required throughout the next phase when noise level *seems about to rise* or one or two pupils suddenly can be heard above the general work murmur. Pupils continually test even the experienced teacher's level of observance only resuming work if eye contact is made.

Maintenance phase   Once the pupil's part of the work has been set and they have begun to work it is advisable that the teacher moves round the class to find out how well the task is going, to help those with difficulties, to involve those whose motivation is hard to encourage. The pupils should know that *each one* of them can expect to receive some positive comment – PCI, from the teacher about their work or some help during the lesson not just those who are having difficulty or are being a nuisance.

It is this individualized attention to the task that encourages interest and effort. The pupils come to want to work for the teacher because s/he treats the work as important by taking a personal interest in it. Each pupil comes to feel significant and that his or her effort is an important and relevant contribution to their own development. It enhances self-esteem and generates an active interest in schoolwork. The teacher meanwhile through close observation of performance on task can obtain feedback on the effectiveness of the teaching content and method, and so is able to modify further work or personalize the process.

4. *Tactical lesson planning (TLP).* Many teachers have been trained to plan their lessons under the following general headings: Objective, Introduction, Method, Contents, Materials and Evaluation. The rejection of this teacher-centred approach in favour of one that mirrors the changes in the learners' activities required at different phases of the lesson, the Tactical Lesson Plan, helped failing teachers become successful (Montgomery, 2002).

   The TLP may well begin with the short verbal introduction supported by PowerPoint or pictures, what needs to follow is an activity change on the part of the pupils, that is not more listening by them but perhaps some quick note taking; then some sharing/talking about notes to a peer; followed by some listening again and then some active practical work, next recording what was done and found out ending up with a plenary. The options are listening, thinking, talking, writing, drawing, acting/role-play, practical/making work.

5. *Learning conversations.* In order for teachers to be able to improve their own performance they needed to be helped to reflect on their teaching and hold 'learning conversations' in their heads about it, another way of describing this is that they were able to label and tap into their metacognitions and metalearning. This short form language CBG, 3Ms, PCI and TLP enabled them to monitor their work in lessons by focusing on the key variables. It appeared to facilitate the processes of tapping into these metacognitive processes and reflections even after the mediator had left.

   Teaching is also about helping pupils engage in their own reflective learning conversations. This theme will be developed in several chapters throughout the book.

As can be seen already it is not only intrinsic and extrinsic factors that cause pupils to underachieve, it is also their dynamic interaction with each other and processes between that contribute to a particular pattern of UAch.

In the next section of this chapter a range of identification procedures will be explored.

Instruments for Identifying Underachievement

Ability tests in common use in schools

The IQ tests that most secondary schools use for initial screening for potential are the Cognitive Abilities Tests (Thorndike, Hagen and France, 1986). These are group tests of verbal and numerical abilities and some aspects of spatial performance. Schools may also use MidYIS in year 7 and YELLIS in year 10 to compare performance with potential.

Most primary schools tend not to use formal ability tests to identify potential or separate out groups of pupils. Instead they tend to identify those for special provision by SATs levels and teacher observation. If tests are used then the NFER group tests for non-verbal and verbal reasoning, or Young's tests are common as well as the British Picture Vocabulary Scale (Dunn, Whetton and Pintilie, 1982). There is a range of similar tests available from the testing agencies.

Individually administered tests used in primary schools are the English Picture Vocabulary Scale and Raven's (2008) Coloured and Progressive Matrices. At this stage, the literacy and maths levels are generally the key to access to more advanced provision outside the classroom and differentiation is the strategy within the classroom.

For pupils whose culture and first language are different, deaf pupils and traveller children it may be helpful to give them the Raven's Progressive Matrices test (Raven, 2008). This is a non-verbal and nearly culture-free test. It is also a very useful indicator of higher ability in pupils with learning disabilities such as dyslexia.

IQ tests model used

Discrepancy model – an uneven pattern of abilities   The simplest strategy is to give pupils an IQ test and then see if their attainments in school match up. We would look for

- discrepancies between a higher IQ and lower school performance or SATs;
- discrepant scores on IQ tests between verbal and performance items or within scales on subtests when performance in class is average;

- uneven patterns of high and low achievements across school subjects with only average ability test scores;
- high achievements only in out-of-school or non-school activities;
  Cut-off points become an issue here, should the gap be 8, 10 or 12 points and more? It of course depends on the standard error of the test and significance of differences. As a rule of thumb, 8–10 points difference should be regarded as significant.

The discrepancy technique will not however find all the underachievers, many will be missed and so broader strategies are needed. Some of the reasons for this follow.

Test construction and the issue of validity   Tests must be well standardized and applicable to the samples they are going to test. Thus, most major instruments undergo regular restandardization using stratified random sampling procedures. The crucial and concerning factors are their Reliability and Validity. Reliability is usually well established by retesting the sample or a parallel one within a few days and checking that the results are the same to within a few points. It is the issue of Validity, which is most concerning even in the IQ test, used worldwide by researchers such as the Wechsler Intelligence Scale for Children (WISC-IV, 2008). What does this test really measure? Certainly only a small sample of something that can be captured in an hour with an individual child in an interview setting. The test can only be given and interpreted by a trained administrator, usually an educational psychologist. Thus, schools only have this data when a pupil has been referred because of special problems.

One validity issue arises because the subtests were given labels that have changed little since the test's first edition emerged as the Bellevue Intelligence Test in the 1940s. For example one subtest is called Perceptual Organization but is this a valid construct and is there evidence to support the nomenclature other than at face value – it looks apt? What aspects of perception? What is organized? How does it relate to intelligent behaviour?

Another test is called coding. A set of symbols is given to another set of signs and these have to be transcribed. The test involves near point copying, a slow strategy or paired associate learning of the symbols and then handwriting skills for the transcription. Speed of response in number of items transcribed is recorded. Between inspection and recording it is also possible to encode the symbols verbally – subvocally or internally. We have to ask does IQ then depend on speed of handwriting abilities, on verbal coding or strategic overview? A handwriting problem will result in lower scores as does a dyslexic verbal processing problem.

It is perhaps digit span, an additional test item, used to check the dyslexic profile that is most concerning. Ostensibly digit lists forward and backward have to be recalled and dyslexics tend to have problems with this. The test is even included in a new WISC Subscale for Working Memory. But what does it really show?

If the pupil scores below average the teacher concludes that the pupil has a poor short-term auditory memory and so gives training on Working Memory and auditory training. However, other research shows that poor digit span does not show a poor auditory memory but a verbal coding problem, that it is in saying or subvocalizing the digits the dyslexic has the problems that starts to wipe the memory trace or hampers the encoding (Vellutino, 1979, 1987) not in memory per se.

In addition, Koppitz (1977) and Montgomery (1997) found that digit span increased in direct proportion to literacy skills. Thus, it is dependent on phonological coding that underlies most literacy problems and at which most dyslexics are now known to be poor. This was not known when the WISC was first designed. In fact the same issue arises in relation to phonological skills themselves today. Are they a function of poor literacy skills or do they in fact cause it? (Bishop, 2002). It looks as though both may be the result of a third, more hidden factor (Montgomery, 2007) and this is outlined in the chapter on dual exceptionality. It is the age-old issue of correlation or causation.

Even the mental arithmetic subtest is not a pure test of number skills it is dependent upon the same phonological coding skills as digit span. Dyslexics are frequently poor at reciting tables although they know the pattern of the correct answers (Miles, 1993). It is the verbalizing that seems to confuse them.

Some problems with IQ-based models

- Group IQ tests are not as reliable as individual IQ tests and also miss those of the highest ability because there is a ceiling effect, for example an IQ of 130 may be the top score available and half the class of bright individuals may score this.
- Most dyslexics do not show discrepant scores on IQ verbal and performance scales unless they have additional difficulties (Al-Hroub, 2007; Montgomery, 2007).

- Some dyslexics may show an uneven pattern of subscale scores on individual IQ tests – the 'ACID' profile (deficits on Arithmetic, Coding, Information and Digit Span), but it is more usually seen across groups so is not a reliable indicator (Alm and Kaufman, 2002).
- Selection of only 5–10% of pupils to put on the 'G and T' register can discriminate against significant numbers of the more and most able. Tannenbaum (1993) showed that in order to identify most of the highly able, it is necessary to select the top 15–20% by *both* ability *and* attainment and even then some of the most able or gifted will be missed.
- In the Welsh proposals for the highly able (Raffan, 2003), the selection of a top 20% is based upon comparisons with the size of the Warnock (1978) special needs group among other considerations. However, this SEN figure may also need to be updated and extended.
- Borderlines are used for setting and selection, but every test has a Standard Error of measurement of plus or minus at least 3 points, for example at an IQ of 130 we should be including those between 127 and 133. Is that child's IQ of 123 really borderline 130? If s/he is test anxiety prone we might then add a further 5–10 points.
- Most of those with the highest of IQ do not *achieve* at the highest level or gain eminence (Terman, 1954).
- Research of Torrance (1963) established that an IQ of only about 120 was required to gain the highest achievements. Crocker (1987) found that an IQ score of 125 could be used as a cut-off score that would identify the most able. Even so this did not necessarily predict high achievement, other factors such as interest, creativity, environment and motivation come in to play.
- IQ tests show what pupils have had the opportunity to learn in the form of intellectual skills, they do not really test cognitive abilities such as executive functions, planning and evaluation or wisdom. Boring (1963) an expert on testing said that IQ tests test what IQ tests measure.

Intellectual or cognitive skills?　Intellectual skills are about knowing 'that' and knowing 'how'. They include converting printed words into meaning, fractions into decimals, knowing about classes, groups and categories, laws of mechanics and genetics, forming sentences and pictures. They enable us to deal with the world 'out there'. Mostly, these are taught in schools within subjects and also make up most of the items on IQ tests.

Cognitive skills are internally organized capabilities that we make use of in guiding our attention, learning, thinking and remembering. They are executive control processes, which activate and direct other learning processes. We use them when we think about our learning, plan a course of action and evaluate learning outcomes. These were seldom taught in schools or given value there until recently. They form the basis of wisdom and are seldom tested except in real-life situations.

The reason for using these distinctions, first suggested by Gagne (1973), is to indicate that IQ is not only about capacity but also the extent to which skills and knowledge have been taught or absorbed from the contact with the environment, products of memory. Cognitive skills are different from this and calling IQ and phonological tests 'cognitive' could be a misinterpretation.

Attainment Testing

SATs and subject attainments in selecting the most able

English school children are currently tested for their attainments on entry to school at 4–5 years, then at 7, 11 and 14, before they sit GCSE exams at 16 and A levels or the Baccalaureate at 18. They often also have other tests in between:

- Levels achieved can be compared with results on ability tests.
- If teachers rely only on the results of SATs they would miss out on identifying many gifted and talented children and all the underachievers.
- False positives occur in that some do remarkably well by effort and organization in SATs.
- Those with poor literacy skills do worse than predicted by IQ.
- Subject knowledge and skills wider than SATs need to be taken into account.

Attainment tests – reading and spelling

It is very important for pupils entering secondary school to be given screening tests for reading *and* spelling or for these details to be taken from their recent records. They show if literacy skills are at a level needed to meet the demands of the curriculum. They can then be compared to the ability test results to check for any discrepancy between ability and literacy skills and between chronological age and these attainments. Attainment scores should be somewhat above those of the ability level if all is going well.

Typical tests used by schools for screening that are cheap, quick and easy to administer are Salford Sentence (Bookbinder, 1979) Reading test; NFER and Young's (1983) group reading tests, and maths tests; the Schonell and Schonell (1970) group Spelling tests A and B, or Daniels and Diack (1958) Spelling test among others. Speed of handwriting also needs to be assessed (Ch 10).

Diagnostic tests

When difficulties are observed then individual diagnostic tests are available that the SENCo usually administers. Some pupils will need referral for further investigation to an educational psychologist who will generally use WISC-IV. WISC is an individual test giving verbal and performance scales and subscales for working memory plus new reading and spelling assessments with Wechsler Oral Reading Dimension.

Other skills tests include NARA, the Neale Analysis of Reading Ability 2nd edition, the Macmillan Reading Tests (1989) and Detailed Assessment of Speed of Handwriting (Barnett *et al.*, 2007).

More able pupils show a profile of higher comprehension scores than reading speed and accuracy on NARA for example and this is an indication of UAch. They are able to make better predictions about story content than average readers from the partial cues they pick up during fractured reading.

One final note of caution on tests; in test conditions some highly able children work very slowly, others see uniquely different answers to items and problems and so their scores may appear artificially low until their performance and rationales are explored. A few children will deliberately exploit the tests and give wrong answers so as to remain with their friends or not appear to be noticeably different. If schools obtain high test scores and then pupils fail to shine in school subjects there is a tendency to perceive this as laziness and failure to pursue school goals. Pupils' reports read 'could do better', 'has good ability but. . ..', 'must work harder' and so on. This negative stance adopted by the school can be very frustrating for the pupil may not know why nothing seems to satisfy them – a scene set up to create an alienated able misfit.

Other measures to identify underachievement

Checklists   Teachers will have been trained by their coordinators and lead teachers to develop and use checklists and one has already been given to show the characteristics of underachievers. Each department needs to have its own agreed subject checklist based on the school's general one.

Checklists focus teacher attention on factors wider than IQ, SATs and attainment test scores. They offer a more rounded view of the learner's task behaviour as well as success in school subjects.

Traits   These are characteristic patterns of behaviour dependent on experience and the individual's personality. Underachievers may show a range of traits that give a clue to higher potential. Some of the positive ones are

- inventive and original when motivated;
- quick to learn new concepts;
- very good at posing and solving problems ingeniously;
- asks awkward and penetrating questions about everything;
- persevering only when motivated;
- streetwise and full of commonsense wisdom;
- perceptive about people and motives.

The negative ones appear in the earlier checklist.

Another set of traits is those related to personality. From birth we are known to exhibit characteristic patterns (Thomas, Chess and Birch, 1970). They found three that play out in classrooms. In behavioural terms as infants we are

- difficult to pacify and rear;
- slow to 'warm up', or;
- easy to rear.

In classrooms these characteristics are maintained. Some pupils who are difficult to get on with or get to do things may meet a teacher with similar traits and difficulties ensue. The teacher needs help in managing such pupils and motivating them to work and learning to be more flexible. The pupil needs help to learn adaptive strategies and conflict management. All these can be built into Continuing Professional Development by curriculum leaders through PBL and reflective teaching initiatives. These are discussed in the later chapters.

Typologies　Less frequently encountered are typologies. They appear mainly in the literature on personality. Richert (1991) suggests four types of underachievers and others such as Belle Wallace and I have added to the broad categories:

- Coasters the 'invisible underachievers'.
- Overactive inattentives.
- Class clown.
- Dreamers.
- Anxious conformist.
- Disruptive, behaviour problem.
- Absentee, truant.
- Doubly exceptional – masked gifted.

However, the research in 12 schools that were successful in overcoming UAch for the NACE/London G and T project (Wallace *et al.*, 2008) showed that effective schools intervened before these behaviour types evolved into problems. The schools were still however concerned that some pupils were coasting.

Informal Identification Procedures

Curriculum-based identification or identification through Performance

This form is also termed as Performance-Based Assessment or Authentic Assessment. Teachers will set more challenging curriculum tasks and observe the responses to them.

- This can be formalized so that responses to more challenging and open types of task are recorded.
- Some schools use the TASC criteria for this – Teaching Thinking in a Social Context (Wallace, 2000).
- All pupils, including slower learners with the right sort of support (Montgomery, 1990; Watson, 1996), can become more motivated and

develop their abilities when they are given tasks that require them to think or that involve personal and more creative responses.
- Paired and group problem-solving activities (problem-based learning– PBL) are particularly useful for these sorts of assessment. They frequently reveal some unsuspected results such as reversibility and flexibility in thinking.

An informal writing test

Because many underachievers have writing problems this informal assessment is very valuable and can reveal a number of previously hidden difficulties so that immediate interventions can be put in place.

Allcock's (2001) 20 minute writing test can be set up by the English department and all the pupils have to do after 2 minutes to make a plan is write on any subject of their choice for 20 minutes. The test was originally devised just to find pupils' speed of writing. The average speed was found to be 13.9 words per minute in Year 7 and went up about a word in each following year. This can be compared with the research of Roaf (1998) who found that pupils' writing slower than a speed of 25 words per minute on a 10 minute test were *failing* in all lessons.

The details of the spelling and writing results using the 20 minute test are discussed in the chapter on Double Exceptionality. Significant numbers of pupils across the ability range appeared to have problems with lower order writing skills after they were expected to have become fluent. It meant that they quickly became vulnerable to UAch in a curriculum that made heavy demands upon their writing abilities.

Strategic Approaches to the Identification of Underachievement

Grids

Schools now have registers for the gifted and talented and for pupils with SEN. Compiling a grid integrating this information is thus not a difficult task for year groups and tutor groups. The grid should be extensive, capturing as much information as possible and contributed to by the pupils, for example on out of school achievements and interests.

A typical grid/spread sheet has the pupils' names across the top and all the subject and test information available plus the outside school achievements and so on down the side.

	S1	S2	S3	S4	S5	S6	S7	S8	S9	S10	etc.
CA											
VQ											
PQ											
Full Q											
RA											
SA											
HW speed											
SAT Eng											
SAT Ma											
SAT sci											
School subjects											
Hobbies etc.											

In the first set of six or so columns the exact chronological age should be recorded followed by the test scores on verbal quotient, performance quotient, maths Q/score, reading age, spelling age, reading comprehension, and so on.

This can be followed by a general assessment by each of the 12 or more subject tutors. So as not to create a burden for staff the assessment should be a simple impression mark, for example A, B or C, with A representing more able/good and B average and C poor performance. An additional star can identify any especially good performers*.

After the subject columns there should be columns for behaviour (again denoted by A, B or C), this can be followed by SEN using an agreed code, then out of school columns/hobbies and so on.

Just scanning these completed grids can reveal many different and interesting patterns and they can also indicate need for interventions and support, praise and acclaim or mentoring.

Checklist grids

The checklist for identification of UAch can be converted into a grid if the problem items are listed along the top and the pupil names down the side. Each teacher can have a copy of the grid for each class and simply ticks any item that applies.

The teaching aide can then collate the responses for each pupil from the grids and put a score number in each square. This again will reveal patterns of persistent responses and show how strong they are.

Classroom observation

Good teachers use a wide range of verbal and non-verbal positive supportive behaviours towards behaviour and task behaviour of pupils (Montgomery, 2002; Scott MacDonald, 1971). This was in comparison with poorer teachers who used many negative interventions and desist responses.

When the desists and negatives were more frequent than the positives the lessons deteriorated and the learning declined, a whole class became underachievers. A positive school and classroom ethos can have a constructive impact on behaviour, learning and UAch.

Strategies for monitoring one's own and peers' interactions in classrooms can provide valuable data for identifying UAch. Audiotape recording (avoid video for legal reasons) of first 20 minutes of own lessons enables

- analysis using tallies for positive and negative statements;
- comparison of amount of teacher talk with pupil talk (Flanders, 1970);
- counting the number of open questions;
- counting the number of cognitively challenging questions.

Negotiation to observe a peer teaching a different subject can help develop a wider range of skills and techniques, as well as observing pupils in a different setting.

Shadowing

Pupils identified in the grids as being of concern can be followed for a day through all their lessons to see what is happening to them and their responses to it. Observing the daily diet of school to which pupils are subject can prove very revealing and enable plans to be developed for both teacher development and learner individual education plans.

Mentoring – an informal pupil voice

Many schools have adopted mentoring schemes for all pupils but it is difficult in a large school to find enough adult mentors to train and take on the role. There is thus room for schemes involving pupil mentoring, peer tutoring and 'buddies'; these can prove particularly beneficial for under-achievers.

All 'looked after' children need a mentor to identify their needs and help them through school. Similarly pupil counsellor schemes for identifying and dealing with bullying have an important place. Buddies are really helpful for pupils with language difficulties and English as an additional language

Schools councils – a formal pupil voice

Schools that have been most successful in helping underachievers were also found to have very active and live school councils that met regularly. They are usually based on a tutor group or classroom system. It is here that pupil voice can officially be heard and can provide a model for pupil–staff involvement at all levels. Often post boxes for suggestions are used. Despite the worries about abuses of such a system they can yield very useful information and feedback.

Nurture groups – linking identification and intervention

Pupils with low learning resources often express constant boredom. It may result from their low ability or a disadvantage and poor learning history. Both can be addressed by more personal involvement by the teacher in the task and the learning process with that particular pupil. This of course means that a smaller class size is essential to nurture these learners whether in primary or secondary school. Nurture groups can give these pupils a second chance and enable them to integrate well into mainstream classrooms (Bennathan and Boxall, 1996).

Nurture groups have been used both to identify and intervene in UAch. They consist of smaller class groups set up with specialist teachers who are skilled in working with, for example disadvantaged groups, behaviourally challenging pupils or pupils with additional language learning needs. They usually operate for one or two terms when most pupils can then be mainstreamed.

Some schools should consider making the transition year, Year 7, a year beginning with nurture groups since this is a key time in the lives of pupils when many fail to integrate into their new large schools, are already underachieving and become disaffected and alienated by the end of that year, 'nobody knows who I am'. Too often they can gravitate towards the gang for emotional support especially as they sink deeper into failure.

The parent voice

In a family one child may be of average ability and attainment, another may be of high ability doing very well in school and the third may be of even higher ability but functioning in school at a level lower than the average one. Parents very often know that such a child is underfunctioning but the school sees only the poor attainment and can conclude the pupil is of low ability or lazy and may refuse to investigate further.

It can be difficult for parents to secure an assessment through the school as there are often many other children whose special needs seem more severe. Even if an independent psychological assessment is obtained there is no guarantee that it will show the high ability or that if it does that any provision will be made.

Parents are on hand to observe the challenging questions raised and the ingenious ways their children may solve problems and how quickly they 'catch on' when being given an explanation or demonstration. They can note the different profiles of development. Teachers with large classes do not always have the time to observe these nuances. Parents have an important contribution to make to assessment of high ability especially when they can compare the different levels and profiles of several of their children. Parents of lone children can be helped by briefing meetings, examples and interviews.

Ian Warwick's chapter shows how the involvement of parents in the teaching and learning of pupils in and out of school can be a powerful motivational force for both and raises learners' achievement.

Links also need to be made with parents and the National Association for Gifted Children, UK, who also offer a network of support and understanding as well as special workshops and events for both pupils and parents.

Multidimensional assessment

The DCFS (2007) published a report into the nature of the problems of children who were losing momentum in English and mathematics in Key Stage 2 (www.teachernet.gov.uk/publications). The researchers used a range of assessment techniques including SATs, the G and T register, teacher assessments, interviews and classroom observation. The number of schools involved was limited but deemed to be representative. What the report shows is that more able underachievers who were making less than expected progress shared many of the following characteristics in response to English. They were

- generally well behaved;
- highly articulate and perceptive in small group discussions;
- could be quiet in whole class situations;
- confident, motivated and enthusiastic;
- overwhelmingly positive about reading;
- picked up on ideas quickly, constantly trying to improve and were eager to please;
- displayed a positive approach to learning;
- were however 'easy to miss';
- unwilling to take risks and did not like to make mistakes;
- did not ask for help and found difficulty in identifying their own success;
- usually persevered with the task set, especially where the task was routine and of limited challenge;
- when stuck they relied on a friend or were happy to leave a task incomplete.

In addition

- they often worked exclusively in mixed ability groups and rarely worked with children of similar ability;

- they often perceived themselves as additional support to less able children, especially those not regularly receiving class teacher or teacher
  assistant support;
- the majority of pupils said they would have liked more opportunities
  to work in ability groups or independently (DCFS, 2007, p. 6).

In mathematics, the results were similar but girls more often were the invisible children, quiet and undemanding, tentative and cautious, they had few self-help strategies.

There was also a smaller group of children who were overconfident and rushed their work often making mistakes. They were competitive and would try to finish first, they were demanding and misbehaved. They often wasted time if they finished early (DCFS, 2007, p. 31).

The report goes on to offer a number of practical suggestions to help overcome some of the difficulties observed. As can be inferred from these characteristics they arise in some measure from the type of curriculum and pedagogy on offer. Some of the questions to the children may also be considered to be leading questions, often a problem in interviews.

Conclusions

UAch is a complex phenomenon made up of a range of internal and external factors. These can interact to form different patterns of individual UAch or achievement. They are also mediated by the dynamic interaction of social communications in and out of school and the classroom management procedures that teachers use. These latter create a classroom climate and school ethos that promote achievement or hamper it.

There is a wide range of ability and attainment tests that can be used to assess potential and attainment. However, these have their limitations and it is found that schools that are successful in identifying UAch and then intervening use a wider range of techniques than tests. A range of these techniques are discussed and recommended especially the method of ITAP. The experienced practitioners who write in this volume go on to show how this method in particular is the method of choice, it identifies the hard to reach and teach, the hidden gifted and talented. It can then be backed up with other evidence.

In order to open up identification all the principles of open access and self-referral need to be applied. This does not prevent tutors and mentors suggesting to pupils they should try a programme nor does it prevent them from recommending them, for example masterclasses and special enrichment but it also means that every pupil needs a mentor, someone who will promote their best interests. Freeman's (2001) 'sports approach' is also relevant.

References

Al-Hroub, A. (2007) An analysis of WISC-1V factors for British and Lebanese intellectually gifted children with learning difficulties: a comparative study. American University of Beirut, pp. 1–15.

Allcock, P. (2001) Update. The testing of handwriting speed. *PATOSS Bulletin*, November.

Alm, J. and Kaufman, A.S. (2002) The Swedish WAIS-R factor structure and cognitive profiles f for adults with dyslexia. *Journal of Learning Disabilities*, **35** (4), 321–33.

Barnett, A., Henderson, S.E., Scheib, B. and Schulz, J. (2007) *Detailed Assessment of Speed of Handwriting*, Harcourt Assessment, London.

Baum, S., Cooper, C. and Neu, T. (2001) Dual differentiation: an approach for meeting curriculum needs of gifted students with learning disabilities. *Psychology of the Schools*, **38** (5), 477–90.

Bennathan, M. and Boxall, M. (1996) *Effective Intervention in Primary Schools: 'Nurture Groups'*, David Fulton, London.

Bishop, D.V.M. (2002) ' Cerebellar abnormalities in developmental dyslexia: cause, correlation or consequence?' *Cortex*, **38**, 481–8.

Board of Education (1923) *Differentiation of the Curriculum between the Sexes in Secondary Schools*, Board of Education, London.

Bookbinder, G.E. (1979) *Salford Sentence Reading Test*, Hodder and Stoughton, Sevenoaks.

Boring, E.G. (1963) Eponym as placebo, in *History, Psychology and Science; Selected Papers by E.G. Boring* (eds R.L. Watson and D.T. Campbell), John Wiley & Sons, Inc., New York.

Brereton, C. (1990) *Modern Language Teaching in Day and Evening Schools*, University of London, London.

Butler-Por, N. (1987) *Underachievers in Schools: Issues and Interventions*, John Wiley & Sons, Ltd, Chichester.

Crocker, A.C. (1987) Underachieving working class boys, are they wrongly labelled as underachieving? *Educational Studies*, **13** (2), 169–76.

Daniels, J.C. and Diack, H. (1958) *The Standard Reading and Spelling Tests*, Chatto and Windus, London. Reprinted by Hart Davis Educational 1979.

DCFS (2007) *Getting There: Able Pupils Who Lose Momentum in English and Maths in Key Stage 2; Making Good Progress Series*. DfES Publication, London.

Desforges, C. (1998) Learning and teaching: current views and perspectives, in *Directions in Educational Pasychology* (ed. D. Shorrocks-Taylor), Whurr, London, pp. 5–18.

DES (1989) *Discipline in Schools: The Elton Report*, HMSO, London.

DfES (2006) *Statistics of Education*, The Stationery Office, London.

Dunn, L.M., Whetton, C. and Pintilie, D. (1982) *The British Picture Vocabulary Scale*, NFER/Nelson, London.

Feller, M. (1994) Open book testing and education for the future. *Studies in Educational Evaluation*, **20** (2), 225–38.

Flanders, N.A. (1970) *Analysing Teaching Behaviour*, Reading, Mass: Addison-Wesley.

Freeman, J. (1991) *Gifted Growing Up*, Cassell, London.

Freeman, J. (2001) *Gifted Children Grown Up*, Fulton, London.

Gagne, R. (1973) *The Essentials of Learning*, Holt, Rinehart and Winston, London.

Galloway, D. and Goodwin, C. (1987) *The Education of Disturbing Children*, Longman, London.

Higgins, P. (2002) Teaching and learning in the foundation subjects: overview of the strand. *Curriculum Briefing*, **1** (1), 3–6.

Kellmer-Pringle, M. (1970) *Able Misfits*, Longman, London.

Kelly, G. (1955) *Personal Construct Theory Vols 1 and 2*, Norton, New York.

Koppitz, E. (1977) *The Visual Oral Digit Span Test*, Grune and Stratton, New York.

Kounin, J.S. (1970) *Discipline and Group Management in Classrooms*, Holt Rinehart and Winston, New York.

Lee-Corbin, H. and Denicolo, P. (1998) *Recognising and Supporting Able Children in Primary Schools*, David Fulton, London.

Lipman, M. (1991) *Thinking in Education*, Cambridge University Press, Cambridge.

Miles, T.R. (1993) *Dyslexia: The Pattern of Difficulties*, Whurr, London.

Mongon, D. and Hart, S. (1989a) *Making a Difference*, Cassell, London.

Mongon, D. and Hart, S. (1989b) *Improving Classroom Behaviour: New Directions for Teachers and Pupils*, Cassell, London.

Montgomery, D. (1989) *Managing Behaviour Problems*, Hodder and Stoughton, Sevenoaks.

Montgomery, D. (1990) *Children with Learning Difficulties*, Cassell, London.

Montgomery, D. (1996) *Educating the Able*, Cassell, London.

Montgomery, D. (1997) *Spelling: Remedial Strategies*, Cassell, London.

Montgomery, D. (1998) *Reversing Lower Attainment*, David Fulton, London.

Montgomery, D. (ed.) (2000) *Able Underachievers*, Whurr, London.

Montgomery, D. (2002) *Helping Teachers Develop Through Classroom Observation*, David Fulton, London.

Montgomery, D. (2007) *Spelling, Handwriting and Dyslexia*, Routledge, London.

Montgomery, D. (2008) Cohort analysis of writing in Year 7 following 2, 4 and 7 years of the National Literacy Strategy. *Support for Learning*, **23** (1), 3–14.

NARA (1989) *The Neale Analysis of Reading Attainment*, MacMillan, London.

NC (1989) *The National Curriculum*, National Curriculum Council, York.

NUT (2008) *National Union of Teachers Survey*, Hamilton House, London.

Raffan, J. (2003) *The Welsh National Proposals for Highly Able*. Conference Presentation: 9th ECHA Biennial Conference, Rhodes.

Raven, J. (2008) *Raven's Progressive Matrices and Vocabulary Scales*, Harcourt Assessment, London, www.pearson-uk.com (accessed 10 September 2008).

Richert, E.S. (1991) Patterns of underachievement among gifted students, in *Understanding the Gifted Adolescent: Educational, Developmental and Multicultural Issues* (eds M. Birely and J. Genshaft), Teachers College Press, New York, pp. 139–62.

Roaf, C. (1998) Slow hand. A secondary school survey of handwriting speed and legibility. *Support for Learning*, **13** (1) 39–42.

ROSLA 1970–71, *Central Advisory Council (England) 1863 Half Our Future: The Newsom Report*, DHMSO, London.

Rutter, M. (1985) *Helping Troubled Children*, Penguin, Harmondsworth.

Ryan, R.M. and Deci, E.I. (2000) Intrinsic and extrinsic motivation: classic definitions and new directions. *Contemporary Educational Psychology*, **25**, 54–67.

Schonell, F. and Schonell, E. (1970) *Attainment Testing*, Oliver and Boyd, Edinburgh.

SED (1978) *The Education of Pupils with Learning Difficulties in Primary and Secondary Schools: A Progress Report*, Edinburgh: HMSO.

Scott MacDonald, W. (1971) *Battle in the Classroom*, Intext, Brighton.

Shayer, M. and Adey, P. (eds) (2002) *Learning Intelligence. Cognitive Acceleration Across the Curriculum from 3 to 25 Years*, Open University Press, Milton Keynes.

Silverman, L.K. (1989) Invisible gifts, invisible handicaps. *Roeper Review*, **12** (1), 37–42.

Sisk, D. (2003) Gifted with behaviour disorders: marching to a different drummer, in *Gifted and Talented Children with SEN* (ed. D. Montgomery), David Fulton, London, pp. 131–54.

Tannenbaum, A.J. (1993) A history of giftedness and 'gifted education' in world perspectives, in *International Handbook of Research and Development of Giftedness and Talent* (eds K.A. Heller, F.J. Monks and A.H. Passow), Pergamon, Oxford, pp. 3–27.

Terman, L. (1954) The discovery and encouragement of exceptional talent. *American Psychologist*, **9**, 221–30.

Thomas, A., Chess, S. and Birch, H.G. (1970) The origin of personality, in *Readings in Scientific American*, W.H. Freeman and Co., San Francisco, CA, pp. 220–7.

Thorndike, R.L., Hagen, E. and France, N. (1986) *The Cognitive Abilities Tests (Revised Edition)*, NFER, Windsor.

Torrance, E.P. (1963) *Education and the Creative Potential*, University of Minnesota, Minneapolis.

Vellutino, F. (1979) *Dyslexia: Theory and Research*, MIT, London.

Vellutino, F. (1987) Dyslexia. *Scientific American*, **256** (3) 20–7.

Wallace, B. (2000) *Teaching the Very Able Child*, David Fulton, London.

Wallace, B., Maker, C.J., Cave, D. and Candler, S. (2004) *Teaching Problem-solving and Thinking Skills: An Inclusive Approach*, David Fulton, London.

Wallace, B., Fitton, S., Leyden, S. *et al.* (2008) *Raising the Achievement of Able, Gifted and Talented Pupils within an Inclusive School Framework*, NACE/London Gifted and Talented, Oxford.

Warnock, M. (1978) *Special Educational Needs: The Warnock Report*, HMSO, London.

Watson, J. (1996) *Reflection Through Interaction: The Classroom Experiences of Pupils with Learning Difficulties*, Falmer Press, London.

Whitmore, J.R. (1982) *Giftedness, Conflict and Underachievement*, John Wiley & Sons, Inc., New York.

Young, D. (1983) *Group Reading Test*, NFER, Windsor.

WISC-IV (2008) *Wechsler Intelligence Scale for Children*, www.pearson-uk.com (accessed 10 September 2008).

2

Literacy, Flexible Thinking and Underachievement

Joan Freeman

Introduction to Literacy

My concern here is the strong relationship between literacy and quality of thinking; particularly the flexible and creative kind of thinking that enables children of high potential to demonstrate excellence in a variety of situations. Using developmental evidence, I argue that without literacy even the brightest children must underachieve. Yet the very concept of literacy is rapidly changing as the new means of electronic communication, which I have called 'electronic literacy', affect the way youngsters think and express themselves.

Literacy is a relatively new skill for us (human beings) in our many millennia of existence: the earliest (Egyptian) script dates from only 6000 years ago and the move from handwriting to print by Gutenberg happened only in 1439. The church saw this as threatening to its absolute authority, but none of its draconian methods could stop the spread of universal literacy and independent thinking in Europe. Our learning curve has been steep, though only in a minority of languages. Of the 3000 languages spoken today, probably only about 80 have a written literature. The written word added vastly to the understanding of verbal concepts which include history, novel ideas, the reformation of existing ideas – and vitally, the ability to study. Oral expression, though, does become more complex in print-orientated societies, such as Shakespeare's solo invention of about 1700 words in the sixteenth century when most of the population of England could not read.

My term, 'electronic literacy', describes competence in electronic communication. Its explosion since the late twentieth century is bringing immeasurable changes in communication and style of thinking to those who are

Able, Gifted and Talented Underachievers, Second Edition   Edited by Diane Montgomery
© 2009 John Wiley & Sons, Ltd

electronically literate, greatly increasing new vistas of the world which are closed to those who are not (Kress, 2003; Ong, 2002). As the dominance of reading and writing shifts swiftly from page to screen, concern with literacy must include the electronic multimedia.

The electronic mode changes thinking because it reorders the conception and presentation of ideas. It cuts out the obligation to present an orderly progression of ideas in immoveable print, and by using words and display together, has massively increased the ease, cheapness, speed and multidirectionality of even complex communications. Nor are ideas confined to one or a few thinkers; they can be exchanged between many as they are being formed. To paraphrase Marshall McLuhan, the medium is ever more the message. But unfortunately, electronic-type thinking also increases the gap between the haves and have-nots, bringing greater social, financial and cultural power to the already haves. The extent to which such media are available differs widely. In some countries where the daily circulation of newspapers may be less than 1 per 1000 inhabitants, people may also lack a national broadcasting network or even a reliable telephone system. Electronic communication now helps illiterate people to bypass the printed word. They can now be reached in ways, such as radio and notably the mobile telephone.

The usefulness of basic literacy depends on how much people are obliged to read and write in their daily lives. In general, the more complex a society's economic and social structures, the more an individual must be literate to a higher and even a technical level. Basic literacy is considered as the ability to read and write to some extent, and numeracy is sometimes included in this. Most definitions place literacy firmly in the context of a particular society. In some areas of deprivation, it may simply mean being able to read written letters or make a mark to sign one's name. This is how it was for many in the developed world until the late nineteenth century, when education was expanded. Just as it was for the church four centuries earlier, spreading literacy seemed to some to be a dangerous idea because lower class people might read seditious pamphlets and aim to improve their lot in life.

The definition of literacy therefore varies with context: while some may be deemed illiterate in one context, in another time and place they may have been adequately literate (Street, 1990). In the context of the technically developed society of the United States, for example, a government report classed up to 44% of the population as having very low literacy; 25% of those were immigrants, 62% did not complete high school, and 19% had visual difficulties (Kirsch, 1993). Yet in pre-literate societies, such as tribal

Indians deep in the rain forests of Brazil, the same people would probably have been considered adequately literate.

The Council of European Communities (1988) states that the term, illiteracy, does not apply to people incapable of reading or writing because of physical or mental handicap. Rather it is people who 'experience difficulties in, or are totally incapable of, for example, filling in official forms, reading public transport time-tables, understanding bills; all of which obviously restricts their access to information, excludes them from rewarding social function and confines them to the role of socially assisted persons' (p. 5).

Being literate not only implies the mechanics of reading, but it also means being able to present ideas by using the written word, as well as understanding, storing and analyzing words to react appropriately. The chances of becoming literate are affected at different levels of a society (Dubbeldam, 1991). At the family level, for example, a literate family encourages familiarity with the written word and improves a child's chances of going to school. However, compulsory schooling is not in itself sufficient to eliminate the problem of illiteracy. Disadvantaged or differently cultured children may come under the care of teachers who are not able to cater for their needs and who may mistakenly accept that some reading failure is inevitable.

For an infant, after the development of language, literacy is probably the most important foundation stone of lifelong learning. Yet millions of people all over the world are illiterate – a social and intellectual disablement which is unlikely to be due to any deficiency in themselves. Given enough time and suitable help, most normal children should be able to read. But before any individual can reach the stage of reading and numeracy, he or she must first be acquainted with adequate language and numbers.

The Development of Language

Babies have to learn to make sense of what adults say, not only to understand intended direct meanings but also the implications of their gestures and body movements (Freeman, 1996). Learning to speak correctly requires yet further effort. This begins with pronouncing individual sounds, then comprehending words (8–10 months of age) ordering them into grammatical sentences (20–36 months), and then sentences into groups of ideas. The aim is to manipulate language correctly for both understanding and production. Only then can children control and reflect upon their language exchanges. Conversation involves getting one's own meanings across, as well as interpreting what other people are saying, which means sharing some assumptions about the way in which language is used in the society. Sentences that do not express intended meanings will not be socially adaptive, even if their grammar and pronunciation are perfect. Part of the reason why children acquire language so quickly and with such apparent ease appears to be their inbuilt desire to communicate.

There is wide variation in language development – females, firstborns and high socio-economic infants are quicker and usually stay in advance of others. Babies cry first, then they coo, then they babble, and then they produce words. All languages reflect those first sounds by making them the names of caretakers – mama, papa, abba, ima and so on. – so that the first words and word meanings of children throughout the world are similar. The first words refer to people, animals, toys and other tangible objects that attract and interest children. By the end of the first year, language and thought become bound up together, each affecting the other's development (Mehler and Dupoux, 1994).

Research at California University at Fullerton has found that even by the age of 1 year, future intellectually gifted children were more advanced in their language development on both receptive and expressive language skills (Gottfried, Gottfried and Guerin, 2008). They describe this as 'early cognitive acceleration' – a head start in thinking skills. The parents of these children rated them as more advanced on intellectual and language skills compared with the ratings of comparison childrens' parents. Freeman used a similar longitudinal comparison model in the United Kingdom and found similar results (Freeman, 2001, 2006).

In the Fullerton study, independently from each other, hundreds of teachers in different schools provided assessments of the sample children. Analysis of their reports showed that when the early speakers reached school, they were advanced in many subject areas, in classroom competence and in different types of achievements that lasted across time. They were less likely to have their kindergarten entry delayed and were never held back in a grade. As gifted children, they were significantly more likely than their cohort comparison to obtain at least one extremely superior test score in the opening years of their education. The early lives of children who grew up to be of world status have also been found to be highly verbal and interactive (Radford, 1990).

The highly intelligent child aged under 5 often demands and so receives more verbal interaction from the family, and in this sense, alters his or her

own learning environment (Freeman, 2000). Competent language development is helped considerably by this – not just what is exchanged in daily
chatter – but when adults make a systematic effort to converse (Fowler,
1990). Language is developed with feedback – being heard, corrected, using
words to demand – the rate and breadth of this process being clearly related
to that of the adults who look after them. Underprivileged children can
miss this necessary feedback from parents, and the gap in communication
ability between them and better-off children widens inexorably over the
years. Developing spontaneous complex speech in older children who are
not used to conversing in this way is not easy, because as children they are
often also impoverished in the exercise of their intellectual abilities.

In most homes, conversation between adults and children is more evenly
balanced than at school. Even in nursery schools, teachers tend to dominate
children's thinking by constantly asking questions, with an answer already
in mind, which can actually inhibit the child from thinking up questions
(Tizard and Hughes, 1984). The teacher's well-educated style of speech
can also be confusing to young children from less favoured backgrounds.
It is important for teachers to encourage children's questioning and to
listen to them, allowing them to think out loud and use all their powers of
imagination.

Learning to read

The interactive model of children's reading holds that it is a deliberate
cognitive process pulling meaning from previous knowledge and ideas in
the text. The reader controls and regulates comprehension, the actions of
metacognitive processes. It is a high-level thinking skill which demands
flexibility. In trying to understand what an author had in mind, the reader
has to check the new ideas, and then organize and compare them with what
she or he already knows. Even the newest of readers selects from the text,
leaving out details that do not seem central to the message, while adding
extra information from memory (and from the wider culture) that is needed
to make it intelligible.

To develop a lively mind, the more one reads the better. A difference in the
sheer *amount* of reading can show measurable differences in thinking. This
includes vocabulary size, verbal fluency, general knowledge and a variety of
other verbal skills. It happens because reading increases knowledge which
is the basis of thinking.

Strangely, children may have an advanced ability to pronounce the written words yet lag behind understanding the meaning of the text. Guided wordplay, a form of cognitive practice, can help to close this gap. Young children who get practice in wordplay jokes such as 'How do you make an apple puff?' – chase it round the garden! – can develop better reading comprehension than children who can only remember jokes with little linguistic ambiguity such as 'How do you get six elephants in a car' – three in the front and three in the back! By the time children can make up their own jokes they are already fluent concept manipulators (Yuill and Easton 1993).

Looking at 5600 Australian children, Rowe (1991) and his team found that their age, gender and socio-economic levels had no effects on their reading levels: the significant differences were due to reading at home, which also had a positive effect on their general attentiveness and achievement. Indeed, parental involvement is consistently found to increase reading skills, as shown in the study of London primary schoolchildren. Those whose parents listened to them learning to read were more advanced than others who only learned at school. Not only do little ones need to be taught specific reading skills, but they also have to be given the chance and encouragement to practice them. This is considerably helped by the involvement of parents in their play and conversation, and the same appears to be true for learning to write (Blatchford, 1991).

Very highly intelligent children are sometimes said to teach themselves to read, but this depends on the materials they have to learn with and their language experience. Early apparently insatiable reading is one sign by which intellectually gifted children can be identified. Clearly though, however high a child's natural potential, without access to literature and permission to learn the child will not read.

Learning numbers

What is true for words is also true for numbers. Babies start to learn numbers by listening to parents counting things, such as fingers or steps, over and over again. Many children's rhymes have counting in them, and the language of mathematics can emerge quite naturally in a lively home. Seymour Papert (1980), the influential American mathematician, proposed that a home should be 'mathematically literate', so that in the same way that children are expected to learn their letters, they should learn to use numbers. Papert views the child as a builder who needs materials to build with. Children who fail at mathematics usually come from environments that are poor in 'maths-speaking' adults, meaning that they arrive at school lacking the basic learning essential for school mathematics.

Papert also refers to 'cultural toxins'. These are negative ideas that contaminate children's images of themselves as learners, so that they think of themselves as incompetent in any subject area. Their imagined deficiency becomes part of their identity – 'I can't do maths.' Learning ability then deteriorates from the young child's open exploration of the world to become a chore, limited by insecurities and self-imposed restrictions. Many children who grow up with a love and aptitude for mathematics owe this positive feeling, at least in part, to picking up to what he calls the 'germs' of their 'maths culture' from adults who know how to 'speak' mathematics. For such fortunate children, their preferred play is often puzzles, puns and paradoxes, and they may be seen at school as mathematically advanced.

Maths phobia is a block that is endemic in Western culture, especially affecting girls. It prevents people from learning anything which they perceive as numerical, although if they do not recognize it as such they may not have any trouble with it. In school, such children can be placed into learning situations that generate powerful negative feelings about numbers, which can generalize to all school learning. This sets up a downward self-perpetuating cycle. When they become parents themselves, they will not only fail to pass on mathematical 'germs', but will certainly 'infect' their children with the intellectually destructive germs of 'mathmatophobia'. Breaking this self-perpetuating cycle should be started at the earliest possible stage in a child's life, although it could also be done by a good teacher in the child's first school.

The verbal context within which school mathematical questions are presented has a big influence on children's ability to answer them. The tangled wording of many arithmetic problems is a burden on a child's memory, simply increasing the difficulty of the problems in a way that has nothing to do with the arithmetic. Even when the wording is not overcomplex, unfamiliar contexts often strain children's competence and prevent them from applying procedures that they use successfully in other contexts.

This is illustrated in a study of 9- to 15-year-old Brazilian street children, the sons and daughters of poor migrant workers who had moved to a large city (Nunes, Schliemann and Carraher, 1993). The children contributed to the family financially by working as street vendors, selling coconuts, popcorn, corn on the cob and other foods. Their work required them to add, subtract, multiply and, occasionally, to divide in their heads. (One coconut costs $\times$ cruzeiros; five coconuts will cost. . .?) Despite little formal education, the children could tell customers how much purchases cost and how much change they should get. They were quick witted and articulate in their own environment, with excellent fluidity in 'street' language.

In an experiment, the children were asked to solve three types of problems. Some were typical of buying and selling transactions, while others involved similar problem-solving situations, but without the goods the child was used to. Another type was arithmetically identical problems presented without a problem-solving context, such as how much is $85 + 63$. The children were able to solve 98% of questions that could arise at their food stall, and 74% of the items that involved selling unfamiliar goods, but only 37% of those outside a problem-solving context. The children clearly knew how to add, but were not flexible enough in their thinking to transfer it to other situations.

These children did not, in fact, understand the fundamental laws of mathematics, but just a very limited selection of techniques. There was almost no insight or reflection involved in what they were doing, so that it was difficult, if not impossible, for them to transfer their techniques to other mathematical situations or subjects. What they were using were basic coping skills that made use of numbers, rather than any genuine competence in numeracy. Though, it was possible to get by with enough superficial information to live, without tuition and practice in cognitive skills no child can reach the numerical ability and accordingly flexibility of thinking of which they are capable.

Flexible thinking

Flexible thinking can be seen in the ability to deal competently both with information and with other people. But no matter how high a child's potential, thinking does not develop to a high level without emotional support and a foundation of knowledge. It remains at the minimum needed for short-term everyday problem solving. The human potential for learning and flexible thinking has been seriously underestimated, since the decoding and learning of the spoken language is, of itself, a brilliant feat that is accomplished by just about everyone, including slow learners.

But even with good education, it cannot be assumed that bright children are also capable of thinking flexibly and creatively. This was seen in the results of my British 33-year comparative study of 210 gifted and non-gifted children (Freeman, 2001, 2006). Some of the academic high-flyers, the ones who were keen to learn, left school flushed with examination successes, but with their curiosity dimmed and their outlooks narrowed. Successful academic achievement, which demands considerable learning and its reproduction, appeared in my study to be related to fear of experimenting with new ideas. Those who were able to show flexible creative thinking had been brought up to think for themselves and had greater emotional security. This appeared to have provided them with the courage to explore intellectually and artistically, and it showed in the creativity of their thinking (Freeman, 2001).

Thinking is social. From birth, individuals adjust their behaviour according to the people they live amongst. Assessing the capacities and predicting the behaviour of other people are an important part of intellectual growth. The ways in which we behave can be seen as ongoing 'experiments', their results providing feedback from the environment which helps to determine future behaviour. One can see the effects of the social context in the ways an individual deals with any problem, which may change radically in different situations. For example, a child may think more creatively at home, but conform at school; or may fail examinations at school, but pass all tests with honours in the challenges of the street gang.

Indeed, good performance in one place may be inappropriate in another. Flexible thinkers should be able to operate in a great variety of situations, especially when these are complex, to exploit their opportunities and adjust their own behaviour to others. As research findings from psychology, the social sciences, neurobiology and medicine show, the way people think and behave is directly related both to their experiences and to the way they have learned to interpret them. Therefore, it would be a good idea to look at these origins.

The roots of thinking skills

Once a baby is in the world, every sense is active, though usually with a bias towards vision and hearing. From the first days of life, infants are curious and look around for what interests them, staring at some objects and events more than others. The refinement of their earliest perceptions is very rapid, and what they are learning then provides a very important foundation for their future mental life.

Even in babies, intellectual development can be thought of in terms of problem-solving skills (Mayer, 1992). By a few weeks old, they begin to use their own experiences for simple problem solving, and so have begun to store them in memory – however fragile and unreliable. But the human brain is never passive; we always try to make sense of our experiences by transforming them into simplified, coded versions that become models to work from. Adults have thousands of codes and models in memory. The earliest coding starts with coordinating sensory impressions, such as feeling the way a ball is round and then watching it roll.

Culturally disadvantaged children find it difficult to practice and increase the complexity of their early perceptual learning. This lack can be seen in little children who are below average in recognizing objects and situations and also less able to describe them. It is well recognized today that children's learning includes active as well as passive mechanisms, and qualitative as well as quantitative changes (Siegler, 2005). For flexible thinking, the underlying learning must itself be flexible, allowing for changing strategies and timing.

Obedience is an emotional model, which may be useful in some childhood situations. But if it becomes fixed, because children are not allowed to practice making decisions for themselves, they are more likely to continue to accept others deciding for them. Independent questioning, thinking and stepping out of line can then be difficult for the individual.

The strongest early indicator of a future lively mind is the ability to communicate, which is traceable from the age of 3 months (Lewis and Michalson, 1985). Vygotsky (1978), in his 'socio-historical' approach, described how while children are learning their language they are also taking in 'ready-made' parcels of culture to use in communicating and thinking. The system works, he wrote, because adults have learned it and share these cultural assumptions. Language thus mediates our perceptions, resulting in extremely complex mental operations – the analysis and synthesis of incoming information, the perceptual ordering of the world, and the encoding of impressions into systems and models. In this way, it serves as a basis for highly complex creative processes.

The Effects of Context

Language and culture

Learning to speak, read and write is affected by a number of factors, such as the infant's emotional security and the need to communicate with words.

Mothers normally provide a baby's introduction to the prevailing culture by mediating or filtering experiences of the world. The mother's own emotions play a role in this, which can significantly affect the intellectual life of the baby. Even infants of 10 weeks can recognize the difference between happiness, sadness or anger in their mothers (Collins and Gunnar, 1990). Her happiness encourages the infant to explore, her unhappiness produces sadness or anger, and her distress causes the infant to withdraw.

Any condition that causes stress to infants increases their need for their mothers, and decreases their urge to explore. What is more, the ill effects of anxiety-arousing experiences (such as poverty) are cumulative. As a result, children raised in a stable, happy family are more likely to be curious and to persist with their own explorations, especially when the tasks become more complex. In a comparison study, 3 $^1/_2$-year-olds, who had been classified as securely attached when they were babies, thought of new ideas and participated more in nursery activities, and they also attracted more friends than the less secure children. Their teachers rated them as more curious, eager to learn, self-directed and effective (Waters, Wippman and Stroufe, 1979).

Human beings are social by nature. They come together in groups which have their own particular cultural identity, made up of what their members have learned and how they behave. Cultural influences – for example historical interpretations and religions – legitimize this behaviour, seen in the division of labour or status. Culture filters downwards through generations, but it also spreads horizontally. In this way it affects other cultures; the most notable example being worldwide American influence. It can also move upwards, as when new expressions in language, coined by the young, are absorbed into general speech. Changes also come from creative endeavour, for example the psychological ideas of Sigmund Freud or Pablo Picasso's concepts of art, which become absorbed by the cultural network. With any change in culture, the language changes accordingly: new words are introduced, and others become obsolete or disappear altogether. With all these currents and cross-currents, the culture that is inherited by a particular generation can never be the same as one that comes later.

To understand each other, people have to learn the specific codes, signs and language of their culture. In almost all countries, people are marked as belonging to different subcultures by using different words and dialects within the common language. Their ideas about social values are equally varied. Non-verbal, physical expressions, such as the way people compliment or insult each other, are just as culture based.

Deprived children

For millions of the world's children, schooling is almost an irrelevance in the daily battle for survival (Freeman, 1990, 1992). Voluntary truanting happens when children find non-school activities more attractive than school activities. Working children lack choice, career goals and hence any incentive to persevere with formal learning. Indeed, absenteeism from school, whether voluntary or not, has a poor prognosis in many respects. For example, longitudinal British research has found that truants are significantly more prone to breakdowns in marriage, health and achievement (Hibbett and Fogelman, 1990). This individual human loss is enormously significant in world terms.

When children are obliged to earn money, it interferes both with the time they can spend at school and also with their inclination to acquire school-type knowledge. Non-school work is not necessarily bad. It can be a source of personal fulfilment at any age, and can provide a positive stimulus that enhances the quality of life. But it can also be mind numbing for small reward – no more than a destructive drudgery.

At the beginning of the twenty-first century, a conservative estimate of the number of children worldwide under the age of 15 in full-time work is 52 million. For most, there is no alternative, because they are contributing to essential life support, and may even be the family breadwinner. Child soldiers are recruited in countries such as Sri Lanka, Nicaragua and Peru; in Bangkok, girls and boys as young as 6 swell the ranks of prostitutes, of whom about 30 000 are under the age of 16. By the end of the century, half the world's population will be under 25. Their chances of receiving the education they need in order to achieve their potential are minuscule.

Children who work from an early age can bypass some stages of development, resulting in stunted psychological maturation. This may affect the development of their intelligence for which a minimum input of mental stimulation is needed at any age. Although they may learn to cope with everyday obligations, they may have difficulty in thinking and planning beyond the present – the younger they are when they start work, the worse the problem is likely to be. Child workers are often given the most menial and boring tasks, during which they survive by 'switching off' mentally, so damaging their developing ability to think and to acquire a feeling of control over their lives.

Deprived children's development is also dependent on the less tangible nourishment of the social environment. For example, in most parts of the world, the least attractive work is done by immigrants and their children. In addition, they usually suffer from the major handicap of not speaking the host language as their native tongue. Consequently, when they do go to school, the childrens' lack of verbal fluency may appear as stupidity. Underachievement by immigrant children, such as Gypsies in Hungary or Turks in Germany, has been found in many schools. The majority language and literature of a country carries much of the outlook on which its culture is based, so that when children are brought up without that language basis they are somewhat barred from those ways of thought. Effectively, they remain 'foreigners' in the country of their birth.

This is not to say that all immigrant children succumb to such problems, as evidenced by the current brilliant performances of Vietnamese and Korean children in California, or of Jews in Western Europe and America and the Chinese in the United Kingdom. The essential difference seems to be in parental attitudes to education. Even in poor families where children do have to work and miss school, they may continue to develop intellectually if there is provision at home.

Literacy and Women

In poor countries, education, especially basic literacy, is identified with status, self-esteem and empowerment. This can be tragic for some, because not all members of the family may be seen as having the same rights to education (see Freeman, 2005). Women's lives are often restricted to the home and they may be denied literacy. Communication with the wider society is selected for them by their male relatives. In some countries, such as Pakistan, Nepal, Afghanistan and Yemen, more than three-quarters of young women have no education at all and cannot read, with negative implications for their thinking and sense of self.

In truth, though, reading for women has proven value of better family health and nutrition, lower maternal and child death rates and lower birth rates. Important research in areas of high illiteracy, where one group of mothers were taught to read and a control group was not, found that women with even a little education produced healthier and intellectually brighter children (Hundeide, 1991). Such evidence suggests that where education is in short supply, that of females should take precedence over that of males, rather than the other way round, as it is at present.

New-Style Thinking

A strange new phenomenon has been growing since about 1950, now called the 'Flynn effect', describing an increasing gain in measured intelligence, the average rise in a population being about three IQ points per decade (Flynn, 2007). Rates are very varied, though, and while advanced countries are possibly reaching a plateau, developing countries have yet to see this rise at all. James Flynn's explanation is that environmental changes arising from modernization – such as more intellectually demanding work, greater use of technology and smaller families – have meant that young people are far more used to manipulating abstract concepts such as hypotheses and categories than a century ago. So, it is not so much native intelligence that is rising, but the way it is used.

Indeed, the increase can be seen most strikingly in tests measuring the ability to recognize abstract, non-verbal patterns, notably the Raven's Progressive Matrices. This implies that something is happening inside youngsters' heads that is more profound than the old-style reproduction of data, still largely the kind of material taught for examinations. Thus, it is not an all-round general intelligence that is burgeoning but a more specific increasingly well-practiced abstract problem-solving ability. Flynn gives an example of the change in intellectual dynamics in answers to the question 'What do a dog and a rabbit have in common?' Whereas a bright modern child would say they are both mammals – an abstract answer – a century ago they might say that you catch rabbits with dogs – a concrete answer. This new mode of more abstract thinking is important because it offers a greatly enhanced ability to see and think through problems than simpler adaptive behaviour used to deal with more concrete situations.

The generally accepted explanation is that bright children are able to function at an increasingly higher intellectual and abstract level because of improved education and a more interesting environment. The growing use of computers for education and even games at an early age may boost the curious child's knowledge, abstract reasoning and intellectual agility. Just using everyday appliances, such as VCRs, ipods and mobile communications equipment, demands a more abstract type of perception and reasoning, which the older generations can find extremely difficult.

Conclusions

The major goals of good education have long been recognized as reaching beyond the accumulation of knowledge and basic literacy, the three Rs – reading, 'riting and 'rithmetic. They also encourage children to develop curiosity, problem-solving attitudes and a love of learning that will last for the rest of their lives. In addition, people act most positively and creatively when they have enough self-confidence and courage to use experience in new ways. Although the promotion of versatile thinking must have a basis of acquired knowledge, this must be learned in a manner which is meaningful to the learner and the learner's wider world, and which can be used in many situations.

Ideas of what literacy is and its wider effects are in a state of rapid and measurable change. A hundred years ago, one was highly literate if one read great literature and could compose a rounded essay in response to it. Today, children's fresh, agile minds are grasping new approaches to knowledge and modes of action. They find old-style school exercises relatively meaningless in terms of the promise of their own lives. The new style of thinking is a richer and more complex dynamic mix, producing a higher level of abstract thinking along with a level of digital dexterity never before demanded of the literate. These recent changes in ideas of literacy and the means of exercising them have gone hand in hand. Those who have a natural ability to think in the new way and also have access to the means of practising it tend to want even more of it. Those with the same potential ability, but with little or no access to practice, are effectively handicapped and underachieving in terms of current sophisticated thinking skills.

The bad news is that millions of underprivileged children are likely to become even more left behind as technology becomes increasingly more central in young people's lives. The good news is that intelligence and ways of thinking can change; genes are not in absolute control and there is hope for greater liberation from rigid to more creative thinking for everyone.

Perhaps this is real democracy in action, when literacy and flexible thinking are no longer the domain of just a privileged few.

References

Blatchford, P. (1991) Children's writing at 7 years: associations with handwriting on school entry and pre-school factors. *British Journal of Educational Psychology*, **61**, 73–84.

Collins, W.A. and Gunnar, M.R. (1990) Social and personality development. *Annual Review of Psychology*, **41**, 387–419.

Council of European Communities (CEC) (1988) Social Europe: Report on the Fight Against Literacy, Supplement 2/88.

Dubbeldam, L.F.B. (1991) *Literacy and Socio-Cultural Development*. Paper presented at the International Conference Attaining Functional Literacy: A Cross Cultural Perspective, Tilburg, The Netherlands.

Flynn, J.R. (2007) *What Is Intelligence? Beyond the Flynn Effect*, Cambridge University Press, Cambridge.

Fowler, W.F. (1990) *Talking from Infancy: How to Nurture and Cultivate Early Language Development*, Brookline Books, Cambridge, MA.

Freeman, J. (1990) Working children. *Education Today*, **40**, 46–50, www.Joan Freeman.com (accessed June 2008).

Freeman, J. (1992) *Quality Education: The Development of Competence*, UNESCO, Geneva.

Freeman, J. (1996) *How to Raise a Bright Child: Practical Ways to Encourage Your Child's Talents from 0–5 Years*, Vermilion, London.

Freeman, J. (2000) Families, the essential context for gifts and talents, in *International Handbook of Research and Development of Giftedness and Talent* (eds K.A. Heller, F.J. Monks, R. Sternberg and R. Subotnik). Pergamon, Oxford, pp. 669–83, www.JoanFreeman.com (accessed June 2008).

Freeman, J. (2001) *Gifted Children Grown Up*, David Fulton, London.

Freeman, J. (2005) Permission to be gifted: how conceptions of giftedness can change lives, in *Conceptions of Giftedness* (eds R. Sternberg and J. Davidson), Cambridge University Press, Cambridge, pp. 80–97, www.JoanFreeman.com (accessed June 2008).

Freeman, J. (2006) Giftedness in the long term. *Journal for the Education of the Gifted*, **29**, 394–403, www.joanfreeman.com (accessed June 2008).

Gottfried, A.W., Gottfried, A.E. and Guerin, D.W. (2008) The Fullerton Longitudinal Study: a long-term investigation of intellectual and motivational giftedness, in *The Development of Giftedness and Talent across the Lifespan* (eds F. Horowitz, R. Subotnik and D. Matthews), American Psychological Association, Washington, DC, in press.

Hibbett, A. and Fogelman, K. (1990) Future lives of truants; family formation and health related behaviour. *British Journal of Educational Psychology*, **60**, 171–9.

Hundeide, K. (1991) *Helping Disadvantaged Children*, Jessica Kingsley, London.

Kirsch, I.S., Jungeblut, A., Jenkins, L. and Kolstad, A. (1993) *Adult Literacy in America: A First Look at the Results of the National Literacy Survey*, US Government Printing Office, Washington, DC.

Kress, G. (2003) *Literacy in the New Media Age*, Routledge, London.

Lewis, M. and Michalson, L. (1985) The gifted infant, in *The Psychology of Gifted Children* (ed. J. Freeman), John Wiley & Sons, Ltd, Chichester.

Mayer, R.E. (1992) *Thinking, Problem Solving, Cognition*, Freeman, Oxford.

Mehler, J. and Dupoux, E. (1994) *What Infants Know: The New Cognitive Science of Early Development*, Blackwell, Oxford.

Nunes, T., Schliemann, A.D. and Carraher, D.W. (1993) *Street Mathematics and School Mathematics*, Cambridge University Press, Cambridge.

Ong, W.J. (2002) *Orality and Literacy: The Technologizing of the Word*, Routledge, New York.

Papert, S. (1980) *Mindstorms*, Harvester, Brighton.

Radford, J. (1990) *Child Prodigies and Exceptional Early Achievers*, Harvester Wheatsheaf, London.

Rowe, K.J. (1991) The influence of reading activity at home on students, attitudes towards reading, classroom attentiveness and reading achievement: an application of structural equation modelling. *British Journal of Educational Psychology*, **61**, 19–35.

Siegler, R.S. (2005) Children's learning. *American Psychologist*, **60**, 769–78.

Street, B.V. (1990) *Cultural Meanings of Literacy*, UNESCO, IBE, Paris.

Tizard, B. and Hughes, M. (1984) *Young Children Learning: Talking and Thinking at Home and School*, Fontana, London.

Vygotsky, L.S. (1978) *Mind in Society. The Development of Higher Psychological Processes*, MIT Press, Cambridge, MA.

Waters, E., Wippman, J. and Stroufe, L.A. (1979) Attachment, positive effect and competence in the peer group: two studies in construct validation. *Child Development*, **50**, 821–9.

Yuill, N. and Easton, K. (1993) Joke comprehension. *The Lancet*, **342**, 858.

Further Reading

Freeman, J. (1994) Gifted school performance and creativity. *Roeper Review*, **17**, 15–19, www.JoanFreeman.com (accessed June 2008).

UNESCO (1988) *Compendium of Statistics on Literacy*, UNESCO Office of Statistics, Paris.

3

What Do We Mean by an 'Enabling Curriculum' That Raises Achievement for All Learners?

An Examination of the TASC Problem-Solving Framework: Thinking Actively in a Social Context

Belle Wallace

Introduction

This chapter will initially trace the early development of the TASC (Thinking Actively in a Social Context) Framework in KwaZulu/Natal, South Africa from 1984 to 1998. This discussion is essential since it lays the foundation for the latest stages of TASC development that have taken place mainly in the United Kingdom and the United States from 1998 to 2008. In addition, an evaluation of the success of TASC across 4000 UK classrooms will be reported, together with summaries of in-depth case studies of two schools that are successfully using the TASC Framework to raise standards. The essential tenets of the TASC Problem-Solving Framework are:

- When learners have ownership of their learning and are part of the decision-making process about what is learned and how it is learned, then their motivation and self-esteem soars.
- When the brain is actively engaged in problem solving, then learners are engaged in 'living learning', and are consequently alive and committed to the project in hand.

Able, Gifted and Talented Underachievers, Second Edition   Edited by Diane Montgomery
© 2009 John Wiley & Sons, Ltd

- When teachers work as facilitators of thinking rather than as dispensers of knowledge, then learners' emotional, social, cognitive and creative abilities are greatly enhanced.
- When all learners celebrate their diverse 'gifts', then we truly have inclusion with differentiation.

This chapter summarizes and collates key points from recently published papers and chapters written about the TASC Framework.

My education fell neatly and very aptly within the framework of the Freire's 'banking' concept, it was a series of acts of depositing

> . . . in which the students are the depositories and the teacher is the deposi-tor. Instead of communicating, the teacher issues communiqués and makes deposits which the students patiently receive, memorise and repeat (Freire, 1998b, p. 72).

I was a disengaged observer of happenings and incidents that had no relation to my own life; I was not a participant in an interactive learning–teaching process, I was an object to be processed in the ritual-istic practice of listening and memorizing to increase my level of 'academic' achievement. I was denied access to any form of enquiring, questioning or real-life experiential learning, and was 'disabled' from learning rather than enabled to learn (Wallace, 2008a, 2008b).

Although my personal life path has led me to work in many countries for short periods of time, I spent an intensive and extensive period in KwaZulu/Natal (South Africa), and this first section of the chapter will trace this particular journey. I hope that I can provide a rich case study based on real-life experiences milled and refined both cognitively and emotionally through many processes of analysis and reflection, as an in-dividual engaged in quiet contemplation: and also as an interactive mem-ber of the communities I have worked with in partnership, joy and love. Walking in Paolo Freire's shoes, and seeing with his understanding, I have tried

- to share in the humanity and reality of the community as an equal member of the group, sometimes a mentor, always a learner, but never, I hope, the benevolent imposer of 'liberation' on the 'oppressed';

- to allow the students the ownership of the creation of their own thinking especially around the concepts of freedom, autonomy and possible life journeys;
- to develop students' awareness of their own powers for reflective participation in their affairs

(Freire, 1998a, 1998b; Ramos, 1974).

Learning and Teaching through the Lens of South Africa (KwaZulu, Later Called KwaZulu/Natal)

Background

The impact of South Africa on my life and educational vision has been paramount in formulating and refining my personal life path, my aims for education and my practice. Finding myself in a totally different cultural context from that of the United Kingdom, the impact of KwaZulu/Natal (SA) was raw, stark and overwhelming: brilliantly vibrant and colourful, socially, emotionally and politically complex and convoluted; a mixture of resilience and submission; a kaleidoscope of despair and hope and profoundly challenging in its need for change. The nation of Zulu people was excluded within their own country, then under apartheid rule, and forcibly segregated in an impoverished, infertile mountainous area euphemistically then called their 'homeland'. So an intended stay of 1 year's sabbatical leave became 15 years of personal commitment from 1984 to 1998: these 15 years witnessing the crumbling of the apartheid regime. The beginning of this period was characterized by an intense civil war in KwaZulu/Natal, the contest involving members within the system of government of the traditional Zulu king and tribal chiefs; the rising African National Congress, and the South African National Government. This conflict coincided with the release of Nelson Mandela in 1990. The latter part of my time in South Africa was characterized by a turmoil of instability and change brought about by the new fledgling government, the Government of National Unity, as it endeavoured to establish a new social system: the struggle fraught with considerable contention for political and financial power, and a populace desperate for rapid change and anticipated benefit.

The following perspectives need to be seen in the light of the volatile situation briefly summarized in the preceding paragraph.

Causes of underachievement in KwaZulu students

The 'banking' system of education   Kwazulu then consisted of (and is largely still) mainly rural settlements of subsistence farming and low socio-economic urban settlements located outside the main 'White' towns. In 1984, the school enrolment was estimated at 1.5 million with only 67% of that population attending school. Another estimation was that 53% of the entire population was under the age of 15. The high levels of school dropout, 'failed' students being retained to repeat the same year several times, and failure in the Senior School Certificate at 17+ years indicated severe 'underachievement' amongst Black students. Only 1% of the initial year group gained a level of matriculation which could possibly allow them entry to university: even for these students there was no financial support (Dostal and Vergani, 1984; Vos, 1986).

I use the terms around the notions of 'underachievement' and 'failure' in quotes because they were used on the basis of judgements formed on a narrow definition of school and examination success.

The concept of SA education lay firmly within Freire's 'banking' paradigm. Rote learning and repetition characterized overcrowded, ill-equipped, mainly tin-roofed and mud-walled classrooms, and many teachers were grossly underprepared both with regard to pedagogy and subject knowledge. Moreover, because the traditional Zulu culture promoted a deep and compliant respect by the young for the elders, it was considered culturally inappropriate for students to question their teachers, or even to make direct eye contact.

The school syllabus had fixed and immutable content firmly rooted in a Western paradigm that had little reality for Zulu learners – comprehension topics such as 'defrosting a refrigerator', the geography of Japan, the history of the castles of Europe, had no relevance or reality for learners living in simple brick or mud huts without electricity and running water. Regular tests (control tests) were compulsory every few weeks with learners being required to answer questions soliciting facts reproduced in the exact words of the teacher who read from the prescribed textbook. Students seldom had a textbook of their own.

Even at university, the curriculum was Western oriented and there was little attempt to analyze the causes of the gross underachievement of the few Black scholars who gained entry in case 'standards' would fall.

The deprivation of language for learning

Freire's thinking on the power of literacy to enable or to deny access to formal learning and life opportunities is well known as one of his most fundamental premises.

In KwaZulu, the language of learning and teaching was conducted in English, while the home language of the students was Zulu. The majority of students lived in homes with parents who were working away from home in the White towns, and they were cared for by older Aunts and Grandmothers who had received no formal schooling and whose English was sparse and colloquial. A great number of students were themselves carers of their younger brothers and sisters, and after school, had the responsibilities of fetching water and wood and cooking the evening meal.

Although positive self-concept is an essential component of learner motivation and self-empowerment, the fundamental processes of learning interactions depend on how learners receive, understand and communicate through language – both verbal and non-verbal. Although there is growing acceptance of pupils' differentiated personal profiles of strengths across the full range of human abilities (Wallace *et al.*, 2004), essentially language is the dominant mode of communication between people. Not only is language central to both informal and formal learning, it is essential to the processes of thinking. We rationalize and make sense of the world through language which establishes our cognitive map of processes and meanings. But our language and cognitive development is inextricably bound up with our emotional development: from the earliest exchanges of language, our sense of self, our feelings of worth, our emerging identities are reinforced.

When language is developed through interactive dialogue in the active process of problem solving, then the more capable learner leads the less capable learner through the stages of the uncertainty of not knowing and not understanding, to the full realization of knowing and the crystallization of meaning and understanding. The adult learner reaches out to identify the level of understanding of the child, and constructs and builds understanding within the child's 'zone of proximal development' (Vygotsky, 1978). We can see immediately what this means for the teaching–learning interaction: through active, relevant problem solving, mediated by appropriate language, the child understands and gains mastery and is ready for further learning.

The acceptance and practice of *additive bilingual* language acquisition as the means of negotiating and making meaning, allows learners to understand and to think in their home language and then to translate into the language of formal learning. Given the space and time to think, learners can switch between the informal language of home and the formal language used in school, negotiating the meaning from one to the other (Wallace *et al.*, 1996). Additive bilingual learning, however, is still dependent on the learning being related to the social context of the learners: their culture, home background, sense of values and so on. The heavy cognitive load of negotiating meaning by straddling two languages is lessened when learners can identify with the content and find relevance within their own lives (ibid). The teacher input *has to be comprehensible and relevant* to learners (Freire, 1998a, 1998b). Moreover, the processes of teaching and learning using an additive bilingual approach are necessarily interactive, with learners having the time and opportunity to think, negotiate meaning and communicate.

Dromi (1993) and Krashen (1981) identify three variables that relate to learners' ability to access the meaning of teacher/pupil exchange:

- When learners' motivation is high, they can take risks with expressing ideas, however tentative that expression may be.
- When learners have high self-confidence and good self-image, they tend to be more open to accepting adaptations to their everyday language and to accommodating the new school-based language.
- Low levels of personal and classroom anxieties are indispensable for the acquisition of both informal home language and formal school language.

I maintain that successful teaching and acquisition of language, and the teaching of problem solving and thinking skills, are inseparably fused together and, consequently, share the same common aims and purposes:

- Both should seek to develop language and cognitive skills through purposeful real-life situations that provide learners with authentic and meaningful contexts for learning.
- Both should view the acquisition of language and learning to think effectively as active processes. It is not sufficient for learners to learn

about them; they need to *do* something constructive *with* the acquired skills.

- Both should see language and thinking skills as vehicles for self-expression, personalization and ownership of the learning processes.
- Both should see the development of language and thinking as skills to be used and transferred across the curriculum.
- Both should have an underlying philosophy of curriculum development in which a range of appropriate teaching/learning processes that develop learners' positive self-image, internal locus of control and the belief in lifelong learning (Wallace and Adams, 1993).

The TASC Project: Thinking Actively in a Social Context

To begin to address some of the issues embedded in the school learning of Zulu learners which are outlined above, in 1985, I, together with Harvey Adams, established the Curriculum Development Unit attached to the Faculty of Education, University of Natal, South Africa. We began a Project which was to last for 14 years. The overall aims were to research the needs of the disadvantaged Zulu population in the then apartheid homeland of KwaZulu; to develop teachers' and learners' home language and school language skills; to develop a range of appropriate thinking skills to promote self-esteem, independence and empowerment and to design curricula which were relevant to, and contextualized in, Zulu culture. We worked within a repeating spiral framework of collaborative, reflective action research (Kemmis, 1983, in Carr and Kemmis, p. 11), using a constructivist approach (Desforges, 1998) involving pupils, teachers, educational psychologists and parents or carers. Vitally we did not work from a deficit framework of the skills the learners apparently 'lacked', but from a framework of skills the learners already had: namely strong powers of memory due to their rich oral culture, well-developed group listening and leadership skills; democratic ways of working through discussion and sharing of ideas; ease of, and enjoyment in, cooperative learning; a tremendous motivation to learn as a means of self-development and a deep and incisive awareness of the political, economic, social and emotional dimensions within a country wracked by division and inequality.

The Project began with an initial group of 28 mid-secondary school students identified by their teachers as amongst the 'most able'; this rather crude assessment being based on the fact that these students were achieving relative success in the school when compared with other students. From a purely pragmatic standpoint, we also needed to begin by working with students who had a reasonable command of English, since our command of Zulu was very elementary and we wanted to work in an additive bilingual way, mediating purpose and meaning. We wanted to work in Freire's mode of interactive teaching and learning, with Vygotsky's notion of 'zone of proximal development', Sternberg's (1985) concept of 'intelligence' as problem solving and Maslow's (1970) taxonomy of self-actualization. We wanted learners and teachers as equal partners; although in practical reality we were learning extensively from the students. As we gained confidence and greater fluency in Zulu, the Project was extended to involve groups of students perceived as 'mixed-ability' in both primary and secondary schools.

The following detailed case study will focus on the intensive work carried out with the first pilot group of 28 mid-secondary students, although the Project rapidly widened its target group as we gained understanding and greater confidence. The Project came to be known as 'TASC: Thinking Actively in a Social Context'; its name evolving from a series of workshops where the students and their teachers identified the needs and problems they faced in both home and school. It is important to stress at this point that the learners very perceptively expressed their need to work in ways already discussed earlier in this paper: they cemented through their personal experience and insight, the interpretation and practical application of the theories of learning and teaching summarized above. The development of language and thinking through practical problem solving was symbiotic – the one refining the other through reflective discussion. The students also identified their need to be able to think and learn in ways that made the imposed Western curriculum manageable, but they could not yet identify or formulate the particular thinking and learning skills they needed. They strongly articulated their need for a more relevant curriculum, but expressed their immediate, practical need to manage their current studies. Generalizing from these vivid and often emotional discussions, and clarified by the current theory and research, the following tenets of TASC emerged:

- *Thinking.* Although all learners can, and do, think, there is a vast range of 'formal' thinking tools and strategies that learners need to develop, so that the capacity of every learner increases. All learners can cope with complexity if they understand the task and can communicate effectively. The power and confidence to engage in effective thinking stems from the individual's self-efficacy and self-regulation. Although language is a major tool for thinking, people can think using the full range of human abilities, for example through dance, art, music, architecture and so on.

- *Actively.* Learners need ownership of their learning; they need to play active roles in decision making about how and what they learn; and they need to be involved in discussion of both immediate and long-term goals.
- *Social.* Cooperative learning is powerful in its mediatory function; learners need to learn with and from each other. But there is also a need for learners to know how to work independently; and additionally, there is a need for learners to realize that they are globally responsible and environment dependent.
- *Context.* Learners need to start learning in a context that is practical, related to real life and concrete. The context needs to be relevant and meaningful so that they can relate to it and bring their own knowledge into the learning situation. As learners develop mastery, they move into deeper, more abstract contexts, but these contexts are still related to their own world and level of understanding.

Theoretical underpinning of TASC

The theoretical underpinning of TASC evolved directly from the philosophy of Paolo Freire, but we adjusted our pragmatic application of Freire's ideas to meet the needs of the learners within their particular and immediate contexts. In addition, other theorists' ideas played both supportive and formative roles. The work of Vygotsky supported and extended that of Freire: namely that the importance of social and cultural transmission and construction of knowledge as the fundamental vehicle of education, runs parallel with the vital role of mediation for understanding and mastery. Through cooperative, interactive learning, pupils negotiate language and meaning, internalizing concepts and gaining conscious control over their thoughts and actions. As they develop these understandings, they form language and thinking tools for further learning: the role of the teacher is to scaffold the task until learners become independent. Modelling thinking behaviour and thinking language is another key strand in TASC: the senior learner demonstrates, verbalizes and facilitates the active learning situation. A further element underpinning TASC is the essential requirement to develop self-esteem, self-efficacy and self-regulated learners through relevant context, constant success even in small stages and positive assessment that feeds forward to further learning (Eggen and Kauchak, 1997).

Since the early development of the TASC Project, the 'Western' curriculum is currently going through major revision to produce a curriculum more relevant to learners in a multi-racial, multi-cultural context.

When we consider the range of thinking skills and strategies encompassed within TASC, then the work of Sternberg (1985, 1997; Sternberg *et al.*, 2001) has had a dominant influence. Sternberg proposes that 'intelligence' consists of three inter-related aspects:

- The contextual sub-theory in which intelligence is viewed as mental activity directed towards the purposeful adaptation to, selection of and shaping of real world environments relevant to life. There are clear indications in this for the recognition of cross-cultural differences in cognition.
- The experiential sub-theory which proposes that intelligent performance on any task requires the ability to deal with novel tasks; and the ability to automatize the processing of information.
- The componential sub-theory that specifies the strategy for information processing, i.e.
  - the executive (meta) processes that are used to plan, monitor and evaluate strategies used in problem solving;
  - the performance components used to carry out the task; and
  - the knowledge acquisition components that are used to learn how to solve problems in the first place.

    All three components outlined above, are interactive and need to be trained in parallel.

Many theorists stress the importance of metacognition, which Freire refers to as reflection, but the particular influence of the seminal work of Campione *et al.* (1984), Borkowski (1985) and Sternberg (1985) is particularly evident in the development of the TASC Framework. Metacognition is viewed as an essential component of intelligent behaviour used throughout life; as a process of generalizing effective thinking strategies; and, as a key link between intelligence, self-knowledge and self-regulation. Through the process of metacognition, learners reflect upon their learning, crystallizing and automatizing thinking skills and processes. Problem solving is the key to effective learning and involves reflective processes of creative, analytical and practical action and thought.

Teaching and learning principles of TASC

The teaching and learning principles of TASC evolved dynamically as we engaged with students and teachers in real, practical problem-solving challenges, whilst constantly reflecting on the kinds of thinking we needed to use and develop in order to solve the problem successfully. Gradually, the following principles emerged:

- Derive, trial, refine and adopt a generalized working framework of universal problem solving, through processes of collaborative action research and evaluation, solving problems relevant to learners. Learners and teachers need ownership and understanding of both the problems and the problem-solving process.
- Negotiate and use relevant language for thinking and problem solving: naming strategies and skills appropriately to enable students to label and later recall these strategies in further problem solving.
- Model relevant thinking strategies then provide real experiences for learners so that they use the strategies and perceive themselves as successful problem solvers.
- Give attention to motivational aspects through praise and positive reinforcement of thinking and problem-solving behaviour. Celebrate the criteria for success, the criteria having been negotiated with the learners.
- Use cooperative, interactive teaching and learning methods with learners working in small groups.
- Encourage self- and group-monitoring, evaluation and reflection on success, ways of improving and opportunities for transferring skills and strategies to other contexts.

Outline of the TASC Problem-Solving processes of teaching and learning

The processes of the TASC Problem-Solving Framework can best be described as a flexible spiral of sub-processes that are simultaneously cognitive, emotional and metacognitive. The stages are sometimes cyclical, sometimes sequential and sometimes recursively flexible as the situation demands. Learners evolved the nature of the TASC Framework through active and practical, hands-on, everyday problem-solving activities which they identified as problematic to themselves. Examples of these everyday problems included the following:

- How they could locate sources of electricity in order to do their school homework at night. This was negotiated with the local community by offering to give Zulu and English lessons to younger students in the church hall in exchange for the use of the church building, which had electricity.
- How they could get schoolbooks for further study. This was resolved when students organized themselves into choirs and gave concerts at local celebrations in return for small donations. In addition, the students negotiated with the 'White' librarian in the nearby town that the library would be available for them on a Saturday morning.
- How they could present their grievances to their teachers about the poorly prepared lunch that was provided free. This was resolved by setting up discussion groups, recording and prioritizing the most important grievances and appointing leaders to represent them in a meeting with the staff. On a previous occasion, the students had 'rioted' by locking their teachers into the staffroom and noisily demonstrating outside.

There were many practical problems solved by the students themselves that gradually eroded their common feelings of 'learned helplessness'. During and after each completed action, they reflected on and extrapolated the successful thinking and action strategies they had used, and discussed how they could transfer and regularly use the same strategies both in their lives and also in their formal school learning.

The following Figure 1 shows the essential stages of the TASC Problem-Solving Process; Figure 2 extends those stages and provides the rationale underpinning each stage.

Gradually, the Framework for TASC evolved in line with 'living theory' (see Jack Whitehead and Marie Huxtable in Chapter 4) and encapsulated a wide range of teaching and learning principles for developing thinking and

Figure 1   The TASC framework.

problem-solving skills. The early formative and simplified outline of these principles is given below:

- First *gather and organize* what you already know about the subject, topic, problem, situation. Then decide how and where you can find out more information. All learners have a store of previous knowledge and learning: they need to fully recognize this and actively draw on and use prior learning. This stage brings into the working memory a range of ideas and knowledge ready for action.
- Clearly *identify* what the problem actually is by stating it simply as 'What am I trying to do?' (Goal[s]) and 'What is preventing me from doing it?'(Obstacle[s]). Then decide on the criteria for success and work towards that (Possible Solution[s]). Many learners in situations of disadvantage and frustration are overwhelmed by the emotions of

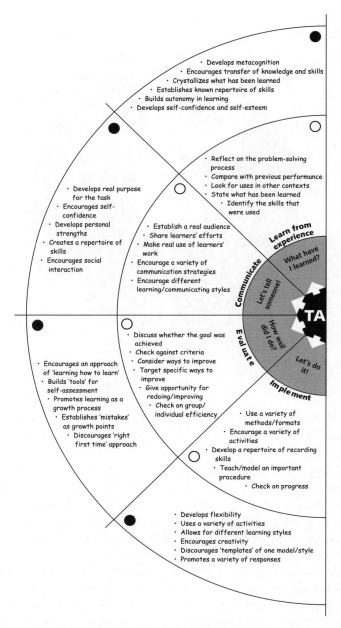

Figure 2   The extended TASC framework.

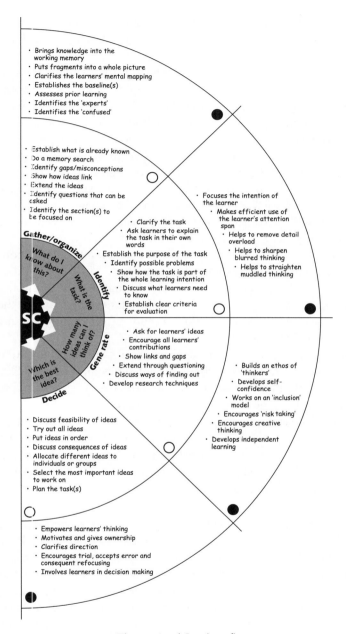

Figure 2   (*Continued*)

anger and injustice which are all-consuming and debilitating: taking control over the situation needs thoughtful, planned and sustained action.

- *Generate ideas* – together with others, think of many possible ways of solving the problem without stopping any flow of thoughts by prejudging the value of them. Hitchhike on to other people's ideas, think laterally and allow all ideas without contradiction. All learners are creative, but many have been conditioned into being spoon-fed by the teacher because they think they have no ideas of their own.
- *Decide* on the best ideas and outline a possible course(s) of action: plan the stages systematically: outline stages of the task clearly and discuss who is responsible for the carrying out of each stage of planning. Taking responsibility for personal decision making and consequent action is fundamental to self-actualization and self-efficacy.
- *Implement* the ideas by putting the decision(s) into action, monitoring progress and adjusting plans as is necessary.
- *Evaluate* the progress and success throughout the project, judged against the agreed goals, obstacles and solutions discussed at the Identify stage. If necessary, backtrack and reformulate ideas and plans previously agreed upon.
- *Communicate* and share ideas throughout the whole project, but also take time to share and celebrate the outcomes and successes. Share successes with the wider community and discuss the stages and processes of overcoming obstacles and achieving goals.
- *Reflect and learn from experience* – discuss the success of strategies that were used, evaluate the quality of the group interaction, reflect on how the successful strategies can be transferred to other situations including school. Discuss changes that need to be made in any future project to make the whole action more effective and sustainable.

There was unanimous agreement by students and teachers that the Euro-centred curriculum needed to be completely rewritten to make it Afro-centred: however, students realized that this needed a long process of change. Importantly, teachers and students would need to be involved in any discussions about a new curriculum with the resultant writing of new school texts; and also closely involved in discussions of appropriate pedagogy. Meanwhile, there was an urgent and pragmatic need to embed the problem solving and thinking skills into the current curriculum so that learners and teachers could not only survive within the Euro-centred curriculum, but also use appropriate thinking strategies to surmount the obstacles presented by turgid and lifeless content. Students wanted to break through the barriers of segregation caused by 'failing' the matriculation examination and wanted to obtain higher levels of learning so that they could access opportunities that would enable them to become leaders of change.

The 28 students in the first pilot TASC Project all gained the highest matriculation results ever achieved amongst Black students in KwaZulu/Natal in their Senior School Certificate. All students entered universities with scholarships to pay their fees and support their studies. In a follow-up meeting, all 28 students said that the first thing they had done on arriving at university was to set up a TASC club so that they could teach fellow students the problem solving and thinking strategies they had used to master their studies. Very poignantly, one student said, 'I now believe that I belong in my own country, and that I can lead change'. At that, the group of now young adults burst into the wonderful close harmony of Zulus singing a round of 'Communication! Oh yes, Communication!' All of these particular 28 pilot students, now adults, are in positions of leadership in education, commerce, business and industry.

See the series of language and thinking texts written within the TASC Framework for pupils from 6 to 18 years of age: *Language in My World* and *Reading in My World*, Nasou Via Africa Publishers, Cape Town, SA. The TASC Framework of skills and processes is still being refined and extended (see Wallace, Cave and Berry, 2008).

Developing the TASC Problem-Solving Process in the United Kingdom

The 15 years I lived and worked in KwaZulu/Natal taught me a great deal about joy and laughter despite crippling disadvantage; about love, friendship and sharing, although there were few resources to share; about resilience and determination to succeed, surmounting all obstacles; about the rich quality of communication and striving towards a common goal.

When I returned permanently to the United Kingdom to work as a consultant in schools nationally from 1999, I became aware of the mechanization of the teaching and learning processes in schools, and also in other areas of public life, that had been brought about by the insistence of the government on 'measurable' achievement targets and 'universal' standards. I am certainly not against learners and teachers striving to reach goals; but not every learning goal can be quantified and measured, organized statistically and then compared and contrasted in what came to be labelled 'the shame and blame culture.' Teachers were reporting that they were treated as mechanical technicians delivering set content, rather than as educators interacting with learners. They reported that increasing numbers of pupils were demotivated and disaffected with school; increasing numbers of pupils were manifesting disruptive and anti-social behaviour. However, it is fair to say that increasingly from 1999, the published education documents have sought to reduce the rigidity of the prescribed national curriculum and to encourage creativity and problem solving. One of the problems with these new, more flexible education guidelines is that many teachers have lost their confidence to interpret the national curriculum creatively and flexibly.

As a result of extensive Continuing Professional Development introducing and developing the TASC Framework, many schools in the United Kingdom are now adopting the TASC Framework to guide their planning, and learners are using the TASC Framework as a flexible structure to guide their own problem solving both in real-life situations and also in topics across the national curriculum. Figure 3 shows the range of planning for TASC learning activities.

During the academic year from September 2005 to July 2006, several follow-up studies were carried out in a wide range of UK primary schools in the local education regions of Barnsley, Berkshire, Hampshire, Kent, Lincolnshire and Nottinghamshire. The primary schools included Nursery pupils (3–5 years), Reception and Key Stage 1 pupils (5–7 years) and Key Stage 2 pupils (8–11 years). In all, 350 schools supplied their evaluations of the impact of their TASC work: this number of schools contained more than 4000 teachers with some of the evaluations reflecting on the whole school development, and some of the evaluations reflecting on the work of individual teachers in single classrooms. The evaluations were based on qualitative teacher and pupil responses to TASC projects carried out by the pupils using broad topics linked with, or taken from, the UK national curriculum. In addition, a range of quantitative evaluations were carried out based on the assessment levels outlined by the UK national curriculum guidelines (Wallace, Cave and Berry, 2008).

TASC	Gather and Organize	Identify	Generate	Decide	Implement	Evaluate	Communicate	Learn from Experience
Key questions	*What do I already know about this? Make links and group ideas together. Maybe organize information as a mind map.*	*What are we trying to do? What are our success criteria? How will we know if we have done a good job? What do we need to do this?*	*How many ways can we do this? Who can we ask to help us? Where can we find out? Let's all think about this.*	*Which is the best way? What should we do first? Why should we do it this way? What will happen if we do this?*	*Is our plan working? Should we change anything? What do we do next?*	*Are we pleased with this? Have we done it well? Have we achieved our success criteria? How could we do it better?*	*Who can we tell about this? How can we show other people? How can we explain? How can we make it interesting?*	*What have we learned to do? How else can we use this? How do we feel now? What are we proud of?*
Advanced thinking skills	Searching memory Recalling from past experiences Recalling from recent stimuli Hitch-hiking onto others' ideas Organizing links	Clarifying goals Considering success criteria Consulting others	Creating a 'think-tank' Considering end product and research possibilities Consulting others	Looking at both sides of an idea Exploring the consequences Considering all factors Prioritizing Hypothesizing Predicting Consulting others	Interpreting Applying Creating Designing Investigating Composing Consulting others	Observing, interacting and responding to others Appraising process and product Consulting others	Presenting Demonstrating Explaining Clarifying Justifying Consulting others	Reflecting Making connections Transferring across the curriculum Crystallizing Consolidating Extending

Figure 3 Leasson planning incorporating TASC thinking processes, skills and strategies.   *(Continued)*

TASC	Gather and Organize	Identify	Generate	Decide	Implement	Evaluate	Communicate	Learn from Experience
Useful strategies (tools)	Ordering pictures Branch diagrams Mind Mapping Bubble maps Deliberate mistakes KWHL grids Follow-me cards True or False cards Concept Cartoons	Think–Pair–Share Flowcharts Forcefield Analysis 'What? When? Where? Why? How?'	Thought showers Hitch-hiking Concept maps Creative connections Graphical metaphors Forced metaphors	Think–Pair–Share Ranking charts Flowcharts Practical, not Practical SWOT analysis	Think–Pair–Share Planning grids Flowcharts Sketches	Think–Pair–Share Extend mindmaps 3 stars and a wish Next steps	Recording across the multiple abilities: displays, performances, visuals, structures, role plays, recordings, video clips, games	Think–Pair–Share Extend mindmaps 3 stars and a wish Consequences
Higher order thinking skills	Organizing Linking knowledge, senses and feelings	Questioning Rephrasing suggestions Initiating ideas	Generating ideas Questioning Comparing and contrasting	Reasoning Questioning Clarifying Disagreeing Justifying Revising ideas Decision making Planning	Organizing Reviewing Monitoring Questioning Rethinking developing ideas Adapting	Evaluating Questioning Assessing Judging	Summarizing Sharing Expressing ideas and opinions	Reflecting Generalizing Summarizing
Repertoire of basic thinking skills	*These basic thinking skills need to be taught, practised and developed and form the basic building blocks for thinking and problem solving.* *Appropriate, fluent use of prepositions, conjunctions, verbs, adverbs, nouns, adjectives in different contexts across the curriculum* *Appropriate use of basic concepts in number, measures, shape, space* *Appropriate use of basic communication and recording skills* *Rich repertoire of varied sensory experiential learning*							

Figure 3   (*Continued*)

Evaluation of TASC Problem-Solving Framework in Schools

The following characteristics were common throughout the teacher assessments:

1. *Motivation, independence and engagement.* All teachers reported that pupils' motivation and engagement with the learning tasks were increased to the point where they hardly needed to intervene in the learning activity. The TASC Framework supplied the structure which all children were keen to engage with, and the teacher's role became that of a facilitator rather than an instructor. Obviously, teaching assistants were present to help children with special learning needs:
   - 'I have never experienced pupils so intent on their chosen project. They were totally engaged and I did not have to keep them on task.'
   - 'I found I was almost redundant! I had time to observe the children and saw a number of children in a new light.'
   - 'Children who are never engaged with learning and who generally need constant supervision just got on with the task they had decided on. They were making their own decisions, I realised it was because they had ownership.'
   - 'I have several children who are Statemented (requiring intense, usually individual, support) and several children on the Special Needs Register (requiring general learning support), but you really couldn't pick them out from the rest. They were engaged and contributing to the group.'
   - 'The more able children took to the TASC Framework straight away and needed no extra support, but when I provided the minimum support for lower ability children, they could refer to the TASC Framework for further support. Even for these children I was just a "gofer!" '
   - 'Disaffected boys are hard to motivate! But I couldn't stop them! They talked all day about their *project* – not about soccer – their usual conversation!'
2. *Self-esteem, enjoyment and success.* All teachers reflected that the children enjoyed their work, and entered fully into the celebration of their success:
   - 'Some children who always struggle were so happy that they could just do "re-thinks"! They realised that TASC is error free because

they can go backwards and forwards in the TASC Wheel and put their thinking right!'

- 'There is always a happy buzz when the children are working on their TASC project. They constantly ask if today is a TASC project day!'
- 'The celebration of their TASC work sent all children and parents home with smiling faces. We didn't rehearse their feedback to parents – the children explained the kinds of thinking they had been doing quite easily.'
- 'Although a lot of the discussions are class or group work based, every child created their own mini-beast. They took pride in their own creation.'
- 'A child who is normally the 'outsider' was an accepted member of the group. I realised that he is an excellent practical problem-solver and when the group praised his work, he just beamed!'

3. *Diminished anti-social behaviour, and increased socially acceptable behaviour*. All the teachers commented on the positive change in pupils' emotional and social behaviour.
   - 'On TASC days – the Incident Book (a record of anti-social behaviour) is empty! Children choose to stay in and continue at play-times, eating their snacks and lunch while carrying on with their project.'
   - 'My class is a very challenging class and I was sceptical that working in the TASC way would make any difference. But I was amazed at what the children already knew and how excited they were because they could choose which questions they wanted to explore. I really was surprised that they could work without arguing and shouting!'
   - 'Some children who are the lowest in ability (language and mathematics) and who are usually very disruptive, really shone when they realized that they could solve the problem in any way they chose. The most disruptive child has shown himself to be a very able leader and he revelled in the fact that the group appointed him the leader. He worked very fairly and gently when he was monitoring the group's progress. When things went wrong, it was he who helped to sort them out.'
   - 'We realised that the whole school attendance picked up! One parent asked what we had done to X because she got up early for school – usually she has to be nagged and dragged up!'

- 'A very quiet group of girls have blossomed. They are speaking up and taking the lead, whereas previously, they just got on with their work and said very little.'

General comments from the teachers

- 'The atmosphere in the school is very different now. We are looking at all the pupils with new eyes. The National Standard Attainment Tests (SATs) only looks at Literacy and Numeracy, so we drill that in the Spring Term before SATs week. But we have discovered those children who are very able in other ways. We are now looking at children across the full spectrum of human abilities.'
- 'Our very able children on the "gifted" Register (for language and mathematics) have exceeded all our expectations. We realised that they were just coasting. We have been amazed at what they have been able to do! But we have extended our concept of "more able" and now we celebrate every child.'
- 'It is so much more exciting to work in the TASC way because the children respond better. You still have to do the background planning to assemble possible resources and you still have to guide what it is possible to do in the time and space; but we share the planning with the children now, and they can understand what is possible and what is not feasible. Their questioning skills have leapt in depth and breadth!'
- 'Our Standards in SATs have been the highest ever, and we think it is because the children are so motivated and on task. We still have to be concerned about our SATs results but we are going for the thinking first!'

General comments from the children reported by the teachers

- 'TASC Projects give us a chance to show what we can do. They are a break from school work.'
- 'TASC days are a chance to be creative and not have the teachers telling you all the time what to do.'
- 'I realised that TASC is already in my head but I didn't know it! I use the TASC Wheel to guide my thinking.'
- 'TASC days "confidences us up" so we are not afraid to speak out in front of other people.'

- 'TASC gives us a full packed education! We didn't realise until afterwards that we had done research, history, ICT (Information and Communication Technology), art, craft, DT (Design Technology), drama, speaking and listening. We even did some Literacy and we enjoyed it!'
- 'TASC days are exciting because "you can open up your creative side". Teachers don't say that's wrong and it takes a lot of pressure off you.'
- 'My mind is usually disorganised and whizzing around! The TASC Wheel helps me to organise my thinking better.'

Conclusions

The initial step in teacher development has to be the practical, hands-on experience of trialling the TASC Process which leads to the realization that the TASC Problem-Solving Approach actually does lift motivation and self-esteem, and also promotes independent learning. The next stage is for teachers to discuss how they and the children will monitor and assess the improvement of their problem-solving skills: they also need to learn how to analyze the types of problem-solving activities they and the children are negotiating. This development links directly into the DISCOVER work developed by June Maker and her associates (Maker, 2006).

The TASC processes are in line with the recent government initiative to Personalize Learning through providing learners with Ownership and the Development of Independence. TASC is an Inclusive Framework, and this correlates with the government initiative 'Every Child Matters' (DfES, 2004). The TASC approach maintains that the role of the teacher is to encourage learners to think and solve problems, to help all learners to discover and celebrate their gifts and to equip all learners with the skills of 'learning how to learn'.

Perhaps, the highest role of the teacher is to develop learners' self-confidence and self-esteem so that they feel able to function effectively in a very complex and fast changing world.

References

Borkowski, J.E. (1985) Signs of Intelligence: strategy generalisation and metacognition, in *The Growth of Reflective Thought in Children* (ed. R.S. Yussen), Academic Publications, New York.

Campione, J.C., Brown, A.L., Ferrara, R.A. and Bryant, N.R. (1984) The zone of proximal development: implications for individual differences and learning, in *Children's Learning in the "Zone of Proximal Development". New Directions for Child Development, no. 23* (eds B. Rogoff and J. Wertsch), Jossey-Bass, San Francisco.

Department of Education and Skills (DfES) (2004) *Every Child Matters: Change for Children*, DfES, UK.

Desforges, C. (1998) Learning and teaching: current views and perspectives, in *Directions in Educational Psychology* (ed. D. Shorrcoks-Taylor), Whurr, London, pp. 5–18.

Dromi, E. (1993) Language and cognition: a developmental perspective, in *Language and Cognition: A Developmental Perspective*, Vol. **5** (ed. E. Dromi), Ablex, Norwood, NJ.

Dostal, E. and Vergani, V. (1984) *Future Perspectives on South African Education. Occasional Paper No 4*. Institute for Future Research, University of Stellenbosch.

Eggen, P. and Kauchak, D. (1997) *Educational Psychology: Windows on Classrooms*, 2nd edn, Merrill, New Jersey.

Freire, P. (1998a) *Pedagogy of Hope*, Continuum, New York.

Freire, P. (1998b) *Pedagogy of the Oppressed* (New Revised 20th-Anniversary edn), Continuum Publishing Co., New York.

Maker, J.C. (2006) Creativity, intelligence, problem-solving and diversity, in *Diversity in Gifted Education: International Perspectives on Global Issues* (eds B. Wallace and G. Erikson), Routledge, London.

Kemmis, S. (1983) The action research planner, in *Becoming Critical: Knowing through Action Research* (eds W.C. Carr and S. Kemmis), Deakin University Press, Geelong, Victoria, p. 11.

Krashen, S.D. (1981) *Second Language Acquisition and Second Language Learning*, Pergamon Press, New York.

Maslow, A. (1970) *Motivation and Personality*, 2nd edn, Harper and Row, New York.

Ramos, M.B. (1974) *Paulo Freire's Pedagogy of the Oppressed*, Seabury, New York.

Sternberg, R.J. (1985) *Beyond IQ: A Triarchic Theory of Human Intelligence*, Cambridge University Press, NY.

Sternberg, R.J. (1997) *Successful Intelligence*, Plume, New York.

Sternberg, R.J., Nokes, K., Geissler, P.W. *et al.* (eds) (2001) The relationship between academic and practical intelligence: a case study in Kenya. *Intelligence*, **29**, 401–18.

Wallace, B. (2008a) Evaluation of TASC in schools in the UK, in *Gifted Education International*, Vol. **24**, Nos. (2 and 3), AB Academic Publishers, Oxford (in press).

Wallace, B. (2008b) Using the lens of life experiences to understand the essential dynamism of learning and teaching, in *Pioneers in Education: Essays in Honor of Paulo Freire* (eds M. Shaughnessy, E. Galligan and R.H. de Vivas), Nova Sciences, Hauppauge, New York, in press.

Wallace, B. and Adams, H.B. (1993) *Thinking Actively in a Social Context: TASC*, AB Academic Publishers, Oxford, UK.

Wallace, B., Cave, D. and Berry, A. (2008) *Teaching Problem-Solving and Thinking Skills through Science*, Routledge, London, in press.

Wallace, B., Maker, C.J., Cave, D. and Candler, S. (2004) *Teaching Problem-Solving and Thinking Skills: An Inclusive Approach*, David Fulton Publishers, London.

Wallace, B., Thomson, C. and Mattson, E. *et al.* (1996) *Language in My World*, Nasou Via Africa Educational Publishers, Cape Town, South Africa.

Vos, A.J. (1986) Aspects of education in KwaZulu. *Paedomenia*, **13** (2)

Vygotsky, L. (1978) *Mind in Society: Development of Higher Psychological Processes*, 14th edn (eds M. Cole, V. John-Steiner, S. Scribner and E. Souberman), Harvard University Press, Cambridge, MA.

4

How Can Inclusive and Inclusional Understandings of Gifts/Talents Be Developed Educationally?

Jack Whitehead and Marie Huxtable

Introduction

The major cultural dichotomy affecting educational provision for the gifted and talented is between the largely Eastern perception – 'all children have gifted potential' – and the largely Western one – 'only some children have gifted potential' (Freeman, 2002, p. 9).

This chapter explores how the gifts and talents of all pupils can be engaged and enhanced in improving the quality of learning by moving beyond attempts to define and categorize people in terms of an objective measure or judgement of gift and talent. A living educational theory approach is used to show how, inclusive and inclusional practices can develop gifts and talents that contribute to a world of educational quality as described in the values, aims and purposes of national strategies and agendas including those underpinning the national curriculum (http://www.nc.uk.net/nc_resources/html/values.shtml).

'Gifted and talented' as defining categories used to classify children, dictate their attainment targets and prescribe their education programme is an emotive and controversial issue. A very different educational concept is communicated if we talk of developing theory and practice to improve contexts within which children are supported to recognize their aptitudes, interests and passions, develop talents and create, value and offer gifts over time.

Able, Gifted and Talented Underachievers, Second Edition Edited by Diane Montgomery
© 2009 John Wiley & Sons, Ltd

White (2006) asserts that the beliefs about intelligence and a subject-based curriculum, which underpin many of the English national strategies and implementation plans, and so much of the practice in schools, are rooted in the values of bygone eras. White says

> ...if you look for sound supporting arguments behind them, you will be disappointed. There are no solid grounds for innate differences in IQ; and there are none for the traditional subject-based curriculum (p. 1).

He concludes by seeking to refocus on the aims and purposes that drive our practice when he writes:

> The school curriculum is not a thing in itself. It is a vehicle to realise larger aims.
>   The school curriculum is – or should be – a vehicle to enable young people not only to lead a fulfilled personal life, but also to help other people, as friends, parents, workers and as citizens, to lead as fulfilled a life as their own (p. 151).

We believe that to articulate and understand why we do what we do is part of our professional responsibility as educators. This is expressed in the Children's Workforce Development Council Induction Training Programme: for Level 3/4 children's workforce practitioners – Learning Mentor Role Specific Modules: Handbook

> What we value and believe has an impact on how we behave and the choices that we make. It is therefore very important that practitioners examine their values, beliefs, attitudes and opinions and consider how these may affect their practice (p. 8). http://www.standards.dfes.gov.uk/learningmentors/downloads/ModAHB.pdf

The handbook explains the following:

> Beliefs are what we hold to be true. Values are what we hold to be important (p. 10).

When we test our beliefs as offering valid explanations of the educational influence we are seeking to have through researching our practice, mindful that we are researching to improve what we are doing, we begin to create our own living educational theories. Eisner (1993) put this very well

. . .we do research to understand. We try to understand in order to make our schools better places for both the children and the adults who share their lives there (p. 5).

Eisner connects educational research clearly with values and it is beholden to us to say what we mean by making schools better places. As educational research is values based we understand our progress with reference to our living values as standards of judgement.

The titles of the units written on the master's programme give an indication of what we are meaning by educators connecting with their values as they research to improve their practice.

How does the Writing of a new Gifted and Talented Policy enable me to reflect upon and evaluate my Personal values about Gifts and Talents? In what ways am I living my values in this area? Hurford (2007).

How can I carry out Masters level educational research without abandoning my own educational values? Harker (2006).

In 2006 Mary Hartog won a National Teaching Award. Mary gained her doctorate for a self-study of her educational practices. In her doctorate, Mary sets out the values based standards to which she holds herself accountable and she asks that her readers use the following values to judge her writings from her educational research:

If this Ph.D. is differentiated or distinguished as a research process, it is because its methodology is underpinned by the values I as a researcher bring to my practice. It is with this in mind that I ask you to bring your eye as examiners to bear on the following questions, asking yourself as you read this thesis whether these questions are addressed sufficiently for you to say 'yes, these standards of judgment have been met':

- Are the values of my practice clearly articulated and is there evidence of a commitment toward living them in my practice?
- Does my inquiry account lead you to recognise how my understanding and practice has changed over time?
- Is the evidence provided of life-affirming action in my teaching and learning relationships?
- Does this thesis evidence an ethic of care in the teaching and learning relationship?
- Are you satisfied that I as researcher have shown commitment to a continuous process of practice improvement?

- Does this thesis show originality of mind and critical thinking?

(Hartog, 2004, p. 3)

We are not saying that *research in education* is not important. We learn a lot from investigations into different instructional and training techniques and from ideas from the philosophy, psychology, sociology, history and other disciplines of education, but that is not sufficient. We make educational decisions that are influenced not only by the efficiency with which we can 'deliver' curriculum content or skills and by ideas from disciplines of education but also by considerations for the child and young person's well-being and well-becoming as described in the Economic and Social Research Council paper:

> Wellbeing is a state of being with others, where human needs are met, where one can act meaningfully to pursue one's goals, and where one enjoys a satisfactory quality of life (ESRC, p. 1).

We have a responsibility to theorize our practice, in other words not to simply describe but to *explain* our practice and to make explicit the values we are using as standards of judgement. It is fundamental to appraising what constitutes good practice, how we evaluate our work, and what constitutes evidence of improving educational practice. As Deborah Eyre (2002) said when she led the National Academy of Gifted and Talented Youth.

> Change is, in itself, not difficult to achieve but judgements also need to be made regarding whether such change has actually been beneficial (p. 7).

'Evidence-based practice' is a phrase increasingly heard yet the question, 'evidence of what' is not being asked with sufficient rigour, vigour or educational authenticity. Here, we are encouraging educators to attend to this question for themselves as White has done and Ginott (1972) expressed in the 1970s

> 'What is the goal of education?' he would ask, 'When all is said and done, we want children to grow up to be decent human beings . . . By recognising that the process is the method, that the ends do not justify the means, and that in our attempt to get children to behave in a way that is conducive to learning, we do not damage them psychologically. Also, that we do not talk to children in a way that will enrage them, diminish their self-confidence, inflict hurt, or cause them to lose faith in their competence and ability' (p. 10).

We are asking this of ourselves as we seek to develop inclusive and inclusional gifted and talented educational theory and practice. Our research rests on the bedrock of our values of an inclusive, egalitarian, loving society. A society where people are supported to become emancipatory influences in their own learning and their own lives able to make valued and valuable contributions to a world worth living in. Formby (2007) shows how influential this perspective can be as a teacher in an infant classroom in her enquiry:

> How do I sustain a loving, receptively responsive educational relationship with my pupils that will motivate them in their learning and encourage me in my teaching? *What has love got to do with receptive responsiveness?* Earlier I wrote about the mutual affection that I enjoy with the children in my class, described by Lewis as . . . warm comfortableness (p. 34). I wrote that I don't think those words adequately express what I feel for the children or what I mean by receptive responsiveness.
>
> One consideration for me could be Lohr's (2006) understanding of an aspect of Ruddick's Maternal Thinking:
>
> She (Ruddick) defines preservative love as seeking to work with the child's personality, with the way the child sees the world. It is a way of thinking through feeling, which is focused on giving the child what it needs in terms of education, training and security. Thinking through feeling then develops in the process of carrying out, and then reflecting on, her mothering acts (Lohr, 2006, p. 5).
>
> However for me a more relevant consideration is Divine Gift-love, which Lewis says can also inspire us to love not just that which is lovable but also that which is not. He relates Divine Gift-love to our Need-love of God in the following rather beautiful simile. He says it is: . . .like a magic wine which in being poured out should simultaneously create the glass that was to hold it (Formby, 2007; p. 118).

We recognize that we have to work with the policies and strategies emanating from central and local government and our institutions but we also believe we have a responsibility to develop educational practice that is consistent with our educational values. We see ourselves having a professional responsibility to improve by researching and theorizing our practice; to examine and explain what we do, to understand what we and others believe to be true about the educational processes we are engaged in and to constructively and creatively challenge those beliefs, which are inevitably communicated through everything we do.

We are seeking to respond to the 'given' demands made of us by national strategies and the prevailing wisdoms, by engaging constructively and creatively with these 'givens', by explicating our 'living' embodied knowledge, theories and values, recognizing and acknowledging where these are contradicted, offering possibilities for movement and describing our living standards of judgement by which we judge our progress. Skuse offers us an example of what this looks like as she deals with her concerns about Standard Attainment Tests.

> This essay is based upon my personal experiences as a teacher within Year 2 and the subsequent research undertook as a result of this experience. I found the year very stressful in terms of the underlying pressure that existed from the knowledge of the judgment my pupils would receive at the end of the year in terms of teaching and learning. I was also conscious that the children felt some anxiety and this therefore sparked an enquiry into assessment in school, reasons for national testing in the UK and the affect that this has upon children and teachers in the primary classroom. This essay will define assessment and outline its purpose within school. It will then examine how assessment has evolved in the UK and explore why current changes and debates maybe happening. I have drawn on both my personal perceptions and pupils' experiences as well as further research and I will conclude with my opinion on how we can move forward in the area of assessment within schools (Skuse, 2007, p. 1).

'Gifted and Talented Education' is a national initiative in England but the implementation is not rooted in a universal truth; there is heated debate at conceptual and practical levels by educators and academics in the Western traditions. An example of this can be seen in the paper by Howe, Davidson and Sloboda (1998) where their research examines findings from a number of sources that appear to either support or contradict that viewpoint, and considers alternative causes of exceptional abilities. It is noteworthy that the protagonists in this particular publication are all highly respected academics who have worked in the field of gifted and talented education for years. What is missing in the interchanges are clear descriptions of the beliefs and values of the researchers. Despite their shared recourse to statistics and accepted logics and research methodologies, it is uncommon for any of the arguments mustered to lead anyone to change their mind and the same arguments continue to be rehearsed today.

In this chapter, we shall introduce another form of logic and research methodology that has allowed us to move from the debate as to who is gifted or talented, to exploring how gifts and talents can be developed educationally.

The prevailing wisdom in England, as demonstrated in the national strategies, is rooted in a

> . . . largely Western one – 'only some children have gifted potential' (Freeman, 2002, p. 9).

This expectation leads to a preoccupation with definitions, categories and the development of associated tools. Hymer (2007) asserted, 'Children don't get gifts, or have them – they *make* them'.

This invites us to shift our focus to the educational processes that support gift creation and devote our energies to exploring what we can do that makes a difference to the educational experiences of children and young people to open the doors of their futures to the possibilities that life offers.

In this account, we will focus on the work of researchers such as Hymer, Wallace, Dweck and Mounter because we can see them recognizing, and seeking to resolve, the problem of resisting the damaging prolonged imposition of technical skills on their imaginations in their own practice and theorizing. They offer, as we do, narratives of how they have done this as educational gifts. Their gifts are offered not as recipes, as packages with the manuals to ingest and replicate. Rather they open a space for the imagining of possibilities for other researchers exploring the implications as they seem to improve their practice. The individual accounts offer understandings for others to relate to their own circumstances rather than claiming theories as explanations of the learning of all people as do the traditional forms of research.

Evaluation drives practice and they are intimately intertwined. A great deal has been written about the affect of 'high-stakes' tests (Gipps, 1994). However, there is as yet little offered by researchers by way of living educational standards that are values based by which we can judge improvement in our practice or that we can be held to account to with respect to inclusive and inclusional gifted and talented educational practice.

In this chapter, we will seek to show our living values, educational theories and standards of judgement as we research answers to our question 'How can inclusive and inclusional understandings of gifts/talents be developed educationally?'

Starting with Educational Relationships

In the masters degree programme at the University of Bath, Jack has been tutoring educators for their units on 'educational enquiry', 'understanding learners and learning', 'research methods' and most lately 'gifts, talents and education'. His purpose is to enable the educators to bring their embodied knowledge into the Academy for legitimation as they develop their educational understandings. You can access the master educator accounts at http://www.actionresearch.net/mastermod.shtml.

At various points in this text we shall be stressing the importance of Joy Mounter's masters enquiry

> Can children carry out action research about learning, creating their own learning theory?

We think it is important for a number of reasons. As Joy explained to her 6- and 7-year-old pupils that she was studying a unit on understanding learners and learning, the pupils expressed some indignation that she thought she could do this without sharing the enquiry with them, the learners. Joy agreed and together with her pupils explored the above question. So, we think the enquiry is important because it shows how teacher and pupils' voices can be combined in an educational enquiry into understanding learners and learning. The account includes video clips of the pupils describing their work with Wallace *et al.*'s (2004) TASC (Thinking Actively in a Social Context) Wheel and explaining how they would modify it to make a more appropriate model to explain their learning. The video clips show the expressions of a life-affirming energy, a relationally dynamic awareness and a gaze of recognition between teacher and pupils that can be so easily missed from accounts that consist solely of words on printed pages of text. Here is an extract from the account that focuses on the children's creativity in forming a representation of their approach to learning they called QUIFF:

> Perhaps learning is a journey we undertake our whole lives, by realising the quality of the experiences on the journey and not the results, we learn more about ourselves and our values grow and change (Wallace *et al.*, 2004).

The children thought about this quote for a long time, trying to understand the message she was sharing. They felt strongly that achieving the end result you want is important as well as the journey to sustain you to want to go on. But felt definitely that through the process of research and the reflecting necessary they had learned a lot about themselves and how they had changed even in the last year, as learners and their self-belief.

Our discussions often tend to wander from the path that we set out on. What follows is one such occasion. The talk about theories had awakened a keen need to begin planning and articulating their ideas to form a learning theory of our own. Following the idea that TASC meant something when you looked at each letter, the children talked in pairs for a special word of their own to summarize the learning theory. I was amazed as 'A' suggested the word 'Quiff', quite quickly. The children liked the sound of the word and began thinking what the individual letters could stand for, just like in TASC. They did not have to argue or even debate ideas, they quickly agreed and all ideas seemed to come from the group almost as a collective mind.

Q 'questions we all have to ask to learn';
U 'understand – making sense of things around us and ourselves which is harder;
I 'I am important';
F 'feelings' so important as a learner;
F 'focus' to be able to concentrate and persevere.

QUIFF, 'I' as in I am important is in the centre, just as we are the centre of our learning and self. 'I' is surrounded by our understanding of 'things' and ourselves, feelings which often control our learning. Focus applying ourselves as a learner.

The class then decided that as TASC is represented by a circle, they needed a visual image for *QUIFF*. Paper to draw out ideas was quickly given out, and thoughts turned to the shape *QUIFF* would be. The pictures are all so different and thoughtful. Below is 'A's' picture. She has used a triangle with I at the point, represented by an eye, the most important point. An eye to the world and into ourselves. Questions are at the bottom, the start and widest part of the shape. Focus is almost like an egg floating in between our questions and feelings that control us, our thoughts and learning. Kellett (2005) highlights the opportunities for pupils to engage with a subject in great depth and work with primary, self-generated data. The depth of the children's thinking shocks anyone we share our journey with. Age, knowledge and skills have often been quoted as barriers to children taking part in action research successfully, but this study will challenge these preconceptions, encouraging the children to critically challenge each other's thinking and funnel down their research question and test their hypotheses.

Shock, surprise and pleasure at what the young people are capable of are characteristic responses to the account and the video clips. The young people are expressing their creative talents in the generation of shareable understandings of their learning. They are describing and explaining their learning and showing, in action, their educational influences in their own learning. We refer to such explanations from young people and adults as their living educational theories. We are advocating a living educational theory approach to answering questions of the kind, how can inclusive and inclusional understandings of gifts/talents be developed educationally?

A Living Educational Theory Approach

The argument is based on assumptions concerning the meanings of a living educational theory approach to the educational development of inclusive and inclusional understandings of gifts and talents and is concerned with showing how the generation of living theories with educational action research can contribute to the creation of a world of educational quality which contributes to the realization of the values expressed in national strategies and agendas.

Whitehead (1989) originated the idea that individuals can generate their living educational theories as explanations of their educational influence in their own learning, in the learning of others and in the learning of social formations. Like Biesta (2006), Whitehead believes that educational researchers must go beyond learning in establishing what counts as educational knowledge and theory through the exercise of educational responsibility. In Whitehead's view, this educational responsibility is expressed and developed in relation to one's own form of life in learning to live more fully the values and understandings that contribute to loving and productive lives (Fromm, 1949). It is expressed in educational relationships as a responsibility towards the other to assist in developing the values and understandings that contribute to their loving and productive lives. It is expressed as an educational influence in the learning of social formations in contributing to the social, material and cultural conditions that support the development of loving and productive lives.

Living educational theories are distinguished as the explanations that individuals produce for their educational influences in learning. The explanations often emerge from educational enquiries of the kind, 'How do I improve what I am doing?' in personal and professional contexts where the 'I' is experienced as a living contradiction. In experiencing ourselves as living contradictions, we are aware of holding opposites together. It was the use of video in his classroom with his pupils in 1971–1972 that revealed to Whitehead such a living contradiction. He believed that he has established enquiry learning with his pupils. The video showed that he was giving his pupils the questions and organizing the learning resources in a way that was not conducive to enabling the pupils to ask their own questions and work on appropriate answers. In responding to his experience of himself as a living contradiction Whitehead moved through action reflection cycles of experiencing concern because his values were not being lived as fully as they could be; imagining possible ways forward and choosing one in an action plan; acting and gathering data with which to make a judgement about the effectiveness of the actions; evaluating the effectiveness of the actions in terms of the values and understandings; modifying the concerns, imagined possibilities and actions in the light of the evaluations.

An assumption in a living theory approach to improving practice, in the sense of improving educational influences in learning is that the validity of the explanations one gives to oneself for what one is doing are significant in improving practice. Another assumption is that whatever is educational flows with a life-affirming energy. In a living theory approach, the explanatory principles of educational influences in learning include a flow of life-affirming energy with values and understandings. We cannot do anything without energy and the representations of flows of energy, in explanatory principles for what we do, contribute to the explanations of educational influences in learning.

A further assumption is that whatever is educational is values laden and involves learning. So, in a living theory the explanatory principles individuals use in explanations of their educational influences in learning, involve flows of life-affirming energy with values. The importance of recognizing the importance of enquiry in explaining what an individual does has been stressed by Vasilyuk (1991):

> Conceptions involving energy are very current in psychology, but they have been very poorly worked out from the methodological standpoint. It is not clear to what extent these conceptions are merely models of our understanding

and to what extent they can be given ontological status. Equally problematic are the conceptual links between energy and motivation, energy and meaning, energy and value, although it is obvious that in fact there are certain links: we know how 'energetically' a person can act when positively motivated, we know that the meaningfulness of a project lends additional strength to the people engaged in it, but we have very little idea of how to link up into one whole the physiological theory of activation, the psychology of motivation, and the ideas of energy which have been elaborated mainly in the field of physics (Vasilyuk, 1991, pp. 63–64).

At least three forms of educational influence in learning can be distinguished in the generation of living educational theories. There are explanations that individuals generate for their educational influences in their own learning, in the learning of others and in the learning of the social formations in which they live and work.

The increase in accessibility of multimedia technology with video and web space is enabling many more practitioners to use video to see themselves as others see them in educational relationships. The use of visual media in the production of visual narratives is also enabling individuals to see themselves in relationally dynamic educational contexts and to appreciate the multiple influences in the educational development of individuals and their social formations. Some of the latest living educational theories to be legitimated in the Academy are flowing through web space and can be accessed from http://www.actionresearch.net/living.shtml.

Developing inclusive and inclusional gifted and talented educational practices

The assumptions about an inclusive and inclusional approach to gifts and talents are taken from Hymer's (2007) enquiry, *How do I understand and communicate my values and beliefs in my work as an educator in the field of giftedness?* In his doctoral research that answers this question, Hymer describes and explains the source of his dissatisfaction with traditional Western, rationalist approaches to the field of gifted and talented education, with their instrumentalist, dualistic, individualistic, pragmatic, tool-for-result knowing-centred associations. He suggests an inclusional, non-dualistic alternative to the identification or discovery of an individual's gifts and talents by arguing in favour of educational environments that lead to the creation of gifts and talents.

In developing a living theory approach to the creation of gifts through the development of our talents we are working with a commitment to inclusive education; to support all children and young people to create, value and offer their gifts. We are making a distinction between 'inclusive' and 'inclusional(ity)' as we draw on Rayner's (2004) idea of inclusionality as a relationally dynamic awareness of space and boundaries as connective, reflective and co-creative. This recognition of inclusionality as a relationally dynamic awareness carries implications for the generation of new living standards of judgement in the Academy as an answer to Schon's (1995) call for a new epistemology for the new scholarship.

We will now explain how a living theory approach to the creation of gifts through the development of talents has generated a new epistemology for educational knowledge with living standards of judgement that are consistent with some of the values in the national curriculum and in Office for Standards in Education inspections. We are using Whitehead's (1989) view of living theory:

> In saying that the theory should be in a living form, I recognise that this creates a fundamental problem. The way academics think about theory is constrained by propositional logic. All academics working in the field of educational theory present the theory in terms of propositional relationships. However, the purpose of my own text is to direct your attention to the living individuals and the contexts within which a living theory is being produced. Again I wish to stress that this is not to deny the importance of propositional forms of understanding. In a living educational theory the logic of the propositional forms, whilst existing within the explanations given by practitioners in making sense of their practice, does not characterise the explanation. Rather the explanation is characterised by the logic of question and answer used in the exploration of questions of the form, 'How do I improve my practice?' (Whitehead, 1989).

We draw on Wallace *et al.*'s (2004) action research approach in the TASC Wheel, in which teacher and pupil researchers ask, research and answer questions and issues of the kind:

What do I know about this?
What is the task?
How many ideas can I think of?

Which is the best idea?
Let's do it?
How well did I do?
Let's tell someone!
What have I learned?

Wallace's TASC Wheel enables us to describe our learning in a way that communicates to others and is so elegantly simple that a 6-year-old can follow. We have pointed to the evidence for this in the account by Joy Mounter described above and you can hear and see the sophistication of thinking of her pupils as they critique TASC with her to develop their own learning theories to account for their own learning:

> What use is the TASC Wheel? (http://www.youtube.com/watch?v=hH2-5xexbAQ)
> What do you think of the TASC Wheel? (http://www.youtube.com/watch?v=ti4syOrIDdY and at http://www.youtube.com/watch?v=LSqg1phEEaM)

TASC offers a framework for communicating, not a constraint to our thinking. What the children show us is that their learning is multidimensional, flowing and relational and they understand and can communicate the complexity of their thinking as they strive to go beyond TASC while constructing their own living theories as explanations of their learning.

Bringing the work of Whitehead and Wallace together enables us to see how the given curriculum (that provided by the Department for Children, Schools and Families) and the living curriculum (that which comes from the person) can be worked with as distinct but not discrete demands. As we live we go through a process of reflecting on what we have learnt and as we communicate that, to and with ourselves and others, we create new knowledge, embellishing or rejecting our embodied knowledge and create new explanations as our living educational theories. We learn more about the disciplines and our world, and about ourselves as learners with aptitudes, passions, interests and developing skills and understandings in various domains, which include the cognitive, the intra and interpersonal, the physical and the emotional. We learn more about ourselves as the person we are; the values we hold, what is important to us, what makes us uniquely ourselves, our dreams and aspirations, how individually we want to be in the world and how we want to earn a living. As we enquire, whether within the terrain described by the curriculum, living and/or given, or our practices as adults

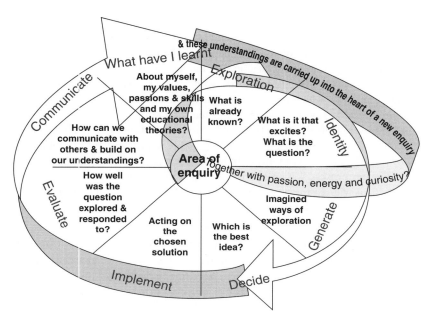

Figure 1 The TASC knot.

trying to do the best job we can, we gather and organize what is known, focus on questions, imagine possible ways forward . . . in other words engage in the processes described in the multidimensional TASC knot (see Figure 1).

We do not learn systematically, in the sense of a linear process with each in a discrete place, in a predefined order with what is to be learnt already known. Our learning is better described as systemic, flowing and relationally dynamic, and arises as we construct knowledge of our worlds and ourselves. But to have an educational influence in our own learning, the learning of others and the education system we need to communicate our stories to and with each other in a form which is comprehensible. Our research is at times systemic, organic and flowing with many different processes happening at the same time, at other times systematic with our learning brought together into an order that creates new understandings. As Murray (2007) writes

> One of the consequences of my epistemological nomadism for producing a clearly communicable text that I have come to understand through my inquiry is that I have this creative, excessive, or 'leaky' tendency where my imagination is still working out the possibilities that have moved further

on than I have been able to communicate in my text. This produces a 'gap' because I have not stabilised either my meanings of writings before I have moved on again in the direction of new, insightful 'oases'.

The flow of my liquid imagination requires a solution, or moment of stability, perhaps a stabilising process, in which the runaway liquidity of my meanings are staunched *just long enough* for me to translocate them in communicable ways into my text. This tension of exposing and opening up new ideas set against the practical need to hold them steady and stabilise them so that I can communicate their meanings has remained with me throughout my research inquiry as a journey of liquid discovery, and ever-present in my writing-up process. I have not resolved this issue. The tension remains: I imagine it will require a very conscious effort of self-discipline on my part whenever I write (Murray, 2007, p. 208).

We therefore need to tell stories that are systematic without too much distortion of the non-linear processes that characterize our lives in education. TASC offers us a way of linearizing a non-linear dialectical and inclusional process. Generating our stories as our living educational theories (McNiff, 2007) offers us a way of acknowledging the non-linear processes that characterize our lives in education.

The creative and improvisatory, non-linear processes in our educational development is reflected in McBeath's (2006) important introduction to the personalization of learning and the study support framework:

Personalised learning is not something that can be 'done' by teachers to pupils. Rather it arises when pupils themselves take charge of their own goals and progress, together with a heightened awareness of their own learning styles and preferences. When young people enjoy a range of opportunities to test themselves, to explore their talents and cultivate new interests, they come to a deeper appreciation of how learning works, what can inhibit it and in what ways it can nourish self belief. When there are rich extended sites for learning, young people grasp that the purpose of school is not to provide an education but to stimulate a thirst for learning, and to give it life beyond the school gate (p. 12).

Dweck (2006) also shows clearly the power that self-theory holds over the destinies that we create. My educational theory is an explanation I give to myself not as a disembodied theory of learning but an explanation of how I learn and what I am capable of learning. Dweck calls these growth or fixed mindsets.

Being human we can hold both theories to account for ourselves at the same time. In recognizing the disease that creates in us we experience ourselves as living contradictions (Whitehead, 1989) and we seek to resolve this internal conflict. Our way of seeking resolutions to experiencing our values negated in our practice has been through evolving research processes such as the TASC knot and action reflection cycles, which we engage with systemically through our living practice and systematically when we seek to communicate a comprehensible story of our living practices.

Dweck's (2006) personal story illustrates the power of that self-fulfilling prophecy and the transformational power of working with educational theory. We make a distinction between educational theories and theories of education; it is what people believe about themselves and the values they seek to live, and how those beliefs and values are influenced that has educational significance and it is the messages we convey through our practice as educators or our own educational theories that should concern us. We draw on theories of education in the creation of our living educational theories.

In answering our question, *How Can Inclusive and Inclusional Understandings Of Gifts/Talents Be Developed Educationally?* we return to Mounter's (2006) account of her pupils' educational influence in her own learning and her influence in her pupils' learning as she answers her question, *Can Children Carry Out Action Research About Learning, Creating Their Own Learning Theory?* You can access this account at http://www.jackwhitehead.com/tuesdayma/joymounterull.htm together with three video clips of the 6-year-old pupils expressing their talents in the gift of their understandings of their theories of learning. In the clips the pupils are explaining to their teacher how the two-dimensional model of learning of TASC Wheel (Wallace *et al.*, 2004) should be modified into a three dimensional and dynamic understanding in order to adequately represent their learning. The three 6-year-olds are exercising their creative talents in the generation of their gifts of new understandings. The educational relationship we see in the video clips is consistent with Biesta's (2006) ideas about the qualities of uniqueness and responsibility that distinguish educational relationships:

> One of the central ideas of the book is that we come into the world as unique individuals through the ways in which we respond responsibly to what and who is other. I argue that the responsibility of the educator not only lies in the cultivation of 'worldly spaces' in which the encounter with

otherness and difference is a real possibility, but that it extends to asking 'difficult questions': questions that summon us to respond responsively and responsibly to otherness and difference in our own, unique ways (p. ix).

Biesta asks, What is learning? He responds that learning theorists of both an individualistic and a socio-cultural bent have developed a range of accounts of how learning – or more precisely, how the *process* of learning – takes place. He claims that many accounts assume that learning has to do with the acquisition of something 'external', something that existed before the act of learning and that, as a result of learning, becomes the possession of the learner (p. 26). Biesta offers a different view of learning in seeing it as a *response.* He says that

> instead of seeing learning as an attempt to acquire, to master, to internalize, or any other possessive metaphors we can think of, we might see learning as a reaction to a disturbance, as an attempt to recognize and reintegrate as a result of disintegration (p. 27).

Biesta believes that learning as response is educationally the more significant

> if it is conceded that education is not just about the transmission of knowledge, skills and values, but is concerned with the individuality, subjectivity, or personhood of the student, with their 'coming into the world' as unique, singular beings (p. 27).

We also see educational relationships as involving the quality of responsibility that Biesta describes in a section called 'The Space of Responsibility: Ethical Space' in which he draws on Levinas' notion of responsibility for the other. Biesta argues that the educational responsibility is not only a responsibility for the coming into the world of unique and singular beings; it is also a responsibility for the world as a world of plurality (Biesta, 2006, p. 117) and difference. Like Biesta, we are committed to the use and development of a language of education in the age of learning (p. 118). However, where Biesta appears to accept Levinas' notion of responsibility for the other, we prefer to exercise our responsibility towards the other. The distinction is important to us because of a feeling of oppression we both feel if someone assumes a responsibility for ourselves.

Values Based Living Standards of Judgement

Amrein and Berliner (2002a) illustrate a problem that educators have in trying to evaluate their work.

> A distinction is made between education and training—a difference of degree, but an important distinction, nevertheless. While training can provide some useful skills, including cognitive skills, we think of education as signifying thinking, that is, engagement in cognitive activity that is more demanding than the ability to employ skills. This report is an inquiry into the effects of high-stakes testing on learning, asking whether the imposition of high-stakes testing results in a more narrow form of training or a broader form of education for our students. The evidence reviewed here suggests that high-stakes testing creates a 'training effect' only (Amrein and Berliner, 2002a, p. 4).

Methods and means of evaluating the 'impact' of 'training' abound but as Amrein and Berliner (2002b) point out the unintended consequence of using such tools to evaluate efforts to improve educational contexts can be detrimental rather than simply irrelevant. Simply using the same logic and related research methodologies does not provide a way forward. James (2005) shows how the mistake is easy to replicate.

> One of the defining features of the Teaching and Learning Research Programme is that it, . . . aims to improve outcomes for learners of all ages in teaching and learning contexts across the UK. This paper argues that although it is possible to use the terms outcomes for learners and learning outcomes interchangeably, they have an important difference in connotation (James, 2005, abstract).

If we focus on 'learning outcomes' we are focusing on a 'given' curriculum where learning is construed as a deliverable product not as a dynamic, organic, creative process with the learners literally changing their minds as they create something new or are coming into presence (Biesta, 2006, p. 53). If we were to focus on outcomes for learners our gaze shifts to what changes have been brought about in the learner, the person not just as an absorber and regurgitater of received wisdoms but as a complex individual with intrinsic drives in a relational dynamic with others and as a co-creator of valued and valuable knowledge.

In his conclusion Sternberg (1999) wrote:

Intelligence tests measure developing expertise. Tests can be created that favor the kinds of developing expertise formed in any kind of cultural or subcultural milieu. Those who have created conventional tests of abilities have tended to value the kinds of skills most valued by Western schools. This system of valuing is understandable, given that Binet and Simon (1905) first developed intelligence tests for the purpose of predicting school performance.

Moreover, these skills are important in school and in life. But in the modern world, the conception of abilities as fixed or even as predetermined is an anachronism. Moreover, our research and that of others (reviewed more extensively in Sternberg, 1997a) show that the set of abilities assessed by conventional tests measures only a small portion of the kinds of developing expertise relevant for life success (p. 373).

The inclination is to develop new tests resting in the same logics and research methodologies to 'tap' other sets of abilities which, like the ant in the amber, lose contact with the living reality. Dweck (2000) expresses our concerns.

When I think of a person's life ruled by an entity theory and performance goals, I think of a life in which there is proof after proof of one's ability. What does it add up to? Thousands of proofs of ability, but, of course, never enough . . .

Or I think of a life in which time upon time there is a flight from risk, so as to protect an image of oneself. This adds up to an armed fortress containing all the things one could have been or done (p. 154).

Our concern is not with what the various types of assessment and evaluation tools purport to measure but the use that is made of them that has no connection with the values or living standards of judgement of the learner. Our intention is to develop living approaches to evaluating our educational influences in learning which are dynamically interrelated with the standards by which we make those judgements and have the possibility of contributing to our educational endeavours. To do this we need to develop new forms of logics, research methodologies and evidence which keep connection with the values we are seeking to live.

For example, the majority of theory in the Western Academy, uses a propositional logic with a 2500 year history going back to Aristotle, with the law of contradiction stating that two mutually exclusive opposite statements cannot be true simultaneously. Dialecticians however, hold that human beings hold living contradictions together in their practice. For example, in questions of the kind, 'How do I improve what I am doing?' individuals can experience themselves as a living contradiction in recognizing that they hold together certain values with their negation at the same time. Dialecticians and formal logicians tend to deny the rationality of the other's position. We believe a third logic, a living logic of inclusionality can include insights from both propositional and dialectical theories without denying the rationality of either logic. We accept Marcuse's (1964, p. 105) idea of logic as a mode of thought that is appropriate for comprehending the real as rational.

Mounter (2006) shows this living logic of inclusionality in her master's enquiry

> . . .the awareness that we don't know exactly where the path will lead us or who will inspire us, but the openness to recognise it and explore it when it comes. . . .
>
> I have learnt to never underestimate my skills of craft and learning, because nothing is impossible to a child with imagination (Learning evaluation by R. aged 10).
>
> I read this and felt very touched and tearful. I wanted to show everyone how far we have travelled as learners, how exciting the journey is and the self-realisation that comes with it. The process of this action research has been an enlightening and thought provoking process for myself, the learners in my class and staff in my school.

The more we understand ourselves the more we can understand the standards by which we judge our lives to be satisfying and productive and it is that which we are researching to bring to children and young people; enhancing the possibility of them understanding themselves and improving the chances they have of being the person they want to be, valued and valuable, contributing to a humane world, when they earn a living. We hold this possibility to be at the heart of education.

This is reflected in the values statements in the English national curriculum document.

> Foremost is a belief in education, at home and at school, as a route to the spiritual, moral, social, cultural, physical and mental development, and thus the well-being, of the individual. Education is also a route to equality of opportunity for all, a healthy and just democracy, a productive economy, and sustainable development. Education should reflect the enduring values that contribute to these ends. These include valuing ourselves, our families and

other relationships, the wider groups to which we belong, the diversity in our society and the environment in which we live. Education should also reaffirm our commitment to the virtues of truth, justice, honesty, trust and a sense of duty.

An extract reads:

Education influences and reflects the values of society, and the kind of society we want to be. It is important, therefore, to recognise a broad set of common values and purposes that underpin the school curriculum and the work of schools. In planning their curriculum, schools may wish to take account of the statement of values finalised after widespread consultation by the National Forum for Values in Education and the Community (May 1997).

The statement of values, the self we value, ourselves as unique human beings capable of spiritual, moral, intellectual and physical growth and development.

On the basis of these values, we should (http://www.jackwhitehead.com/tuesdayma/joymounteree.htm (accessed 8 December 2006))

- develop an understanding of our own characters, strengths and weaknesses;
- develop self-respect and self-discipline;
- clarify the meaning and purpose in our lives and decide, on the basis of this, how we believe that our lives should be lived;
- make responsible use of our talents, rights and opportunities;
- strive, throughout life, for knowledge, wisdom and understanding;
- take responsibility, within our capabilities, for our own lives.

Relationships
    We value others for themselves, not only for what they have or what they can do for us. We value relationships as fundamental to the development and fulfilment of ourselves and others, and to the good of the community.
    ... the full document is accessible from http://www.nc.uk.net/nc_resources/html/values.shtml.

And the document concludes:
Schools and teachers can have confidence that there is general agreement in society upon these values. They can therefore expect the support and encouragement of society if they base their teaching and the school ethos on these values.

The *Every Child Matters* (DfES, 2003) green paper identified the five outcomes that are most important to children and young people:

- Be healthy.
- Stay safe.
- Enjoy and achieve.
- Make a positive contribution.
- Achieve economic well-being.

The five outcomes are universal ambitions for every child and young person, whatever their background or circumstances. Improving outcomes for all children and young people underpins all of the development and work within children's trusts.

In working with a living theory approach to the development of inclusive and inclusional gifted educational practice we see the possibility for keeping a connection between the demand to hold ourselves to account given standards by our government and institutions and our desire as educators to hold ourselves to account to educational standards that embrace the living and embodied knowledge, values, theories and living standards of judgement of the children and young people who are the future of our world.

Conclusion

We see 'gifts' and 'talents' as values laden terms and we are working with an educational intent. We recognize personal volition in deciding where an individual decides to devote time and to developing their talents and creating their gifts which is influenced from various quarters. We are working with a living theory approach where the educational intent is to support the skills, understandings and sophistication not only in 'gift creation' but also in the emerging understandings of the child's own living values and theories by the child as they grow to live the life they judge as a life worth living. Through this approach we are working for the individual to learn about, and to develop, their own living standards. These contribute to their decisions as to how they will develop their talents and what gifts they value and will work to create and offer, to whom and in what manner which will enable them to contribute to their own and other's well-being.

References

Amrein, A.L. and Berliner, D.C. (2002a) The Impact of High-Stakes Tests on Student Academic Performance: An Analysis of NAEP Results in States with High-Stakes Tests and ACT, SAT, and AP Test Results in States with High School Graduation Exams, http://epsl.asu.edu/epru/epru_2002_Research_Writing.htm (accessed 1 August 2007).

Amrein, A.L. and Berliner, D.C. (2002b) An Analysis of Some Unintended and Negative Consequences of High-Stakes Testing, http://epsl.asu.edu/epru/epru_2002_Research_Writing.htm (accessed 1 August 2007).

Biesta, G.J.J. (2006) *Beyond Learning; Democratic Education for a Human Future*, Paradigm Publishers, Boulder.

DfES (2003) *Every Child Matters. The Green Paper*, London Stationery Office.

Dweck, C.S. (2000) *Self-Theories: Their Role in Motivation, Personality, and Development*, Psychology Press, Florence.

Dweck, C.S. (2006) *Mindset: The New Psychology of Success*, Random House, New York.

Eisner, E. (1993) Forms of understanding and the future of educational research. *Educational Researcher*, **22** (7), 5–11.

Eyre, D. (2002) Structured tinkering: improving provision for the gifted In ordinary schools. Unpublished paper.

Formby, C. (2007) How Do I Sustain a Loving, Receptively Responsive Educational Relationship with my Pupils Which Will Motivate Them in Their Learning and Encourage me in my Teaching?Masters Educational Enquiry Unit, University of Bath, http://www.jackwhitehead.com/tuesdayma/formbyEE300907.htm (12 March 2008).

Freeman, J. (2002) Out-of-school Educational Provision for the Gifted and Talented Around the World: A Report to the DfES, http://www.joanfreeman.com/mainpages/freepapers.htm (18 January 2008).

Fromm, E. (1949) *The Fear of Freedom*, Routledge, London.

Ginott, H. (1972) *Teacher and Child*, Colliers Books, New York.

Gipps, C. (1994) *Beyond Testing: Towards a Theory of Educational Assessment*, Routledge, Abingdon.

Harker, E. (2006) http://www.jackwhitehead.com/tuesdayma/ehee06.htm (December 2006).

Hartog, M. (2004) A Self Study Of A Higher Education Tutor: How Can I Improve My Practice? Ph.D. Thesis, University of Bath, http://www.actionresearch.net/hartog.shtml (8 September 2008).

Howe, M.J.A., Davidson, J.W. and Sloboda, J.A. (1998) Innate talents: reality or myth? *Behavioral and Brain Sciences*, **21**, 399–442.

Hurford, R. (2007) http://www.jackwhitehead.com/tuesdayma/roshurfordee2. htm (8 September 2008).

Hymer, B. (2007) How do I understand and communicate my values and beliefs in my work as an educator in the field of giftedness? D. Ed. Psy. Thesis, University of Newcastle, http://www.actionresearch.net/hymer.shtml (accessed 17 July 2007).

James, D. (2005) Importance and impotence? Learning outcomes and research in Further Education. *Curriculum Journal,* **16** (1), abstracts, http://www.tlrp.org/dspace/handle/123456789/251 (accessed 1 August 2007).

Kellett, M. (2005) *How to Develop Children as Researchers: A Step-by-Step Guide to Teaching The Research Process,* P.C.P Publishing, London.

Lohr, E. (2006) Love at Work: What is my Lived Experience of Love, and How May I Become an Instrument of Love's Purpose? Ph.D. Thesis, University of Bath, http://www.actionresearch.net/lohr.shtml (Retrieved 8 September 2008).

McNiff, J. (2007) My story is my living educational theory, in *Handbook of Narrative Inquiry: Mapping a Methodology* (ed. Clandinin, J), Thousand Oaks, London.

Marcuse, H. (1964) *One Dimensional Man,* Routledge, London.

McBeath, J. (2006) Study Support Makes a Difference in Study Support – A National Framework for Extending Learning Opportunities, www.standards.gov.uk (accessed 11 June 2007).

Mounter, J. (2006) Can children carry out action research about learning, creating their own learning theory? MA unit on Understanding Learners and Learning, University of Bath, http://www.jackwhitehead.com/tuesdayma/joymounterull.htm (accessed 17 July 2007) (http://www.jackwhitehead.com/tuesdayma/joymounteree.htm, accessed 8 December 2006).

Murray, Y.P. (2007) How I develop a cosmopolitan academic practice in moving through narcissistic injury with educational responsibility: a contribution to an epistemology and methodology of educational knowledge. Ph.D. submission to the University of Bath, August, 2007.

Rayner, A. (2004) INCLUSIONALITY: The Science, Art and Spirituality of Place, Space and Evolution, http://people.bath.ac.uk/bssadmr/inclusionality/placespaceevolution.html (accessed 17 July 2007).

Schon, D. (1995) The new scholarship requires a new epistemology. *Change,* **27** (6), 27–34.

Skuse, A. (2007) How Have my Experiences of Year 2 SAT's Influenced my Perceptions of Assessment in Teaching and Learning? MA Unit on Educational Enquiry, University of Bath, http://www.jackwhitehead.com/tuesdayma/amyskuseeeoct07.htm (4 March 2008).

Sternberg, R. (1999) 'Intelligence as developing expertise'. *Contemporary Educational Psychology,* **24**, 359–75.

Vasilyuk, F. (1991) *The Psychology of Experiencing: The Resolution of Life's Critical Situations*, Harvester Wheatsheaf, Hemel Hempstead.

Wallace, B., Maker, C.J., Cave, D. and Candler, S. (2004) *Teaching Problem-Solving and Thinking Skills: An Inclusive Approach*, David Fulton Publishers, London.

White, J. (2006) *Intelligence, Destiny and Education: The Ideological Roots of Intelligence Testing*, Routledge, London.

Whitehead, J. (1989) Creating a living educational theory from questions of the kind, 'how do I improve my practice?' *Cambridge Journal of Education*, **19** (1), 41–52.

5

Effective Teaching and Learning to Combat Underachievement

Diane Montgomery

Introduction

After nearly a decade in teaching I took a degree in psychology with subsidiary social anthropology and entered teacher education in the 1970s. To my alarm I found that I was to teach the theory and practice of education for three full days a week to Years One, Two and Three teacher education students, and follow them with others assigned to me out on teaching practice for the rest of the time. On Thursday mornings with a group of four colleagues I was set to teach the Psychology of Education to rotating groups. The educational psychology programme was well planned by a senior colleague and up to date for that time. My alarm was caused by the education groups – there was no programme and no syllabus, just a room and a group of 36 eager male and female students.

I spent the summer vacation vigorously planning and researching my programmes and designing timetables of lectures, seminars and workshops. Suffice to say there was little relevant theory and practice to find especially of UK origin at that time. My psychological training had offered details of the learning of rats, cats and pigeons but not much on humans except some developmental psychology of Piaget and Bruner. None of which helped me to teach my students to deal with problems in primary and secondary classrooms in difficult London schools. I had to rely on my own teaching experiences and what I observed on teaching supervision in these settings then bending and extending the grand theories to fit the practices that I knew had worked. Early on, I found that telling the students my 10 quick tips to teaching did not work. Whatever 'good practice' they heard and said

Able, Gifted and Talented Underachievers, Second Edition   Edited by Diane Montgomery
© 2009 John Wiley & Sons, Ltd

they understood, in practice they seemed to forget and try to teach in the 'talk and chalk' way in which they had been taught as bright students. They ignored the tips and wondered why their classes frequently disintegrated into chaos. I quickly learned that imparting knowledge, telling, was not teaching. In teaching the implicit assumption is that the learner has learned at least some of the essence of what was 'taught'. I had to change my strategies to focus on students learning to teach learners to learn (Montgomery, 1993), this was much more complex set of processes in theory and practice.

Now, I see that I was in the same position as Jack Whitehead in constructing a living theory about my and my students' teaching. In that process, I became transformed from a dedicated subject teacher to a dedication to pupils learning subjects through the support and expertise of their teachers. I found that the majority of the undergraduate teachers also needed to learn through the same processes that I can now label as 'constructivist theory' and practice of learning (Desforges, 1998). For secure and stable deep learning to take place learners need to play a role in constructing their own knowledge and skills. It is especially important in professional training for our implicit theories direct our actions and sometimes they need to be changed. Words alone do not do it.

The most powerful methods involved being with the student in the classroom and coaching them on the teaching–learning task (Montgomery, 2002) and then setting up simulation activities and reflective feedback sessions to accompany the talk about teaching.

In 1981, I had set up the Learning Difficulties Research Project with a small grant from The Schools Council to write up inservice projects on Study Skills, Managing Behaviour Problems and Teaching Gifted Pupils that I was working on in a range of schools and across six Local Authorities. The handbooks about these projects became used as the course texts by the undergraduates. Writing up this work made me make explicit the theories to account for what I was doing. Annual conferences followed to disseminate the findings and gather new research from experts. By 1985 there were six action research projects running in effective teaching and learning/ study skills; teaching reading through spelling – a dyslexia remediation programme; Managing Behaviour Problems; Appraisal – evaluating and improving teaching performance; Teaching the More Able and Gifted Pupil in the ordinary classroom; Teaching Pupils with Learning Difficulties. These projects all became the subject of books that publishers commissioned. Since then the topics covered have moved in and off the national agenda.

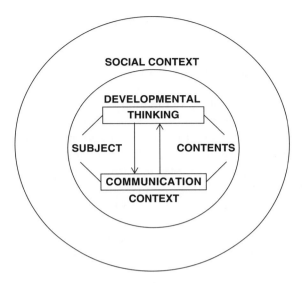

Figure 1   A 'model of modern teaching' (Montgomery, 1981).

The chapter that follows represents summation of the journey I have made in theory and practice in teaching and learning for the more able and gifted underachiever.

Teaching the Teachers of the Gifted

Belle Wallace invited me to write an article about my work for the journal she edits *Gifted Education International* and in the article 'Teaching the teachers of gifted children' (Montgomery, 1983) I set out the main principles. It was summarized in Figure 1.

The model illustrated the central objectives that I had developed in teaching the more able to rekindle their interest and motivation in learning. What I had discovered was that when these strategies were used with the more able groups, all the children wanted to join in and even the slower learners could do so and gain benefit with a little extra support and training in the new ways of working (Montgomery, 1985). The central objectives in the model were to

(a) enable the pupils to think efficiently;
(b) then express those thoughts succinctly.

In a climate where the object was to teach as much subject content as possible the emphasis on process methods was not then popular. However, it seemed essential to me that we should proceed in this direction incorporating the process methods into all the subjects of the curriculum including in teacher education. It was also necessary to do this to meet the needs of the new industrial revolution, the technological age when knowledge would be widely accessible and we needed to learn to manage it. The process approach was concerned with methods by which the teacher teaches the usual subject content to best enable the learner to learn. The focus was thus more upon learning to learn than teacher directed learning. Motivation was a key concept in the learning to learn process and I had found that the thinking and study skills approaches (Montgomery, 1982) were very powerful motivators.

Another aspect of the approach was to recognize the different brain hemispheres' contribution to different learning styles and how these should be incorporated into lesson planning encouraging more flexible and creative responses encompassing both sequential logical and holistic learning. It was emphasized that teachers also needed to be flexible and creative and that their roles would change during lessons from teacher, to facilitator, supporter, follower and so on.

However, the government began to take control of teacher education (CATE, 1983) and then education in schools. This culminated in the National Curriculum (1989) and centralized control over the curriculum and training of teachers (TTA, 1991) and with it the endorsement of the product-based approaches in teaching. Process methods were condemned and thus many of us in gifted education in the United Kingdom became the subversives, the underground movement banished to the margins. We continued to work on and develop our methods and ideas.

Our work with gifted learners in mixed ability settings needed a theoretical base or definition. The model of differentiation from special educational need (SEN) was becoming popular, especially the model of 'differentiation by inputs'. The teacher would teach to the middle ability group and then offer extension work for the more able and simpler work for the least able. The problem was that the extension work was too often more of the same and lacked the intellectual challenge needed. This input differentiation was a model of differentiation that I had already found did not work well because

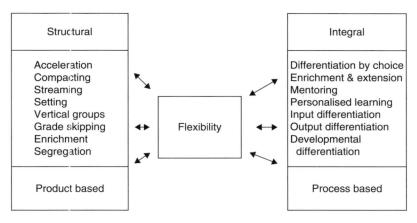

Figure 2   The two main models of curriculum differentiation provision.

the less able felt that they were being given inferior work. Importing exciting enrichment and extension activities into this setting was socially divisive. It was merely recreating a selective education system within a classroom. Instead the term 'developmental differentiation' was coined for the chosen methods.

In essence developmental differentiation involves

'the setting of common tasks to which all students could contribute their own inputs and so progress from surface to deep learning and thus be enabled to achieve more advanced learning outcomes (Montgomery, 1996, p. 97).

The method of developmental differentiation has now been renamed '*inclusive teaching*' as this places it in its modern context.

Achieving this form of differentiation resulted not from changing the curriculum itself but by making modest changes in the methods by which it was taught across all subjects. It needed to become the basis of all class teaching by every teacher. This does not mean that no other provision for the gifted is needed (see Figure 2) or that all lessons need to be inclusive in design.

Inclusive teaching raised old issues about the problems of mixed ability teaching. In product-based lessons (didactics) mixed ability teaching does not work so well (Rogers and Span, 1993). However, if the teaching methods are process based the results are different. On mixed ability grouping in schools, Hallam (2002) found the following:

Successful mixed ability teaching can

- provide a means of offering equal opportunities;
- address the negative social consequences of structured ability grouping by encouraging cooperative behaviour and social integration;
- provide role models for less able pupils;
- promote good relations between pupils;
- enhance pupil/teacher interactions;
- reduce some of the competition engendered by structured grouping;
- allow pupils to work at their own pace;
- provide a sense of continuity for primary pupils when they transfer to secondary school;
- force teachers to acknowledge that the pupils in their class are not a homogeneous group;
- encourage teachers to identify pupil needs and match learning tasks to them (p. 89).

Hallam also warned that to engage in successful mixed ability teaching the teachers needed to be highly skilled and appropriately trained and have at their disposal a wide range of differentiated resources to match to their pupils' needs.

Inclusion does however raise major questions for the education of the gifted and talented and the highly able underachiever. If inclusive education is the most appropriate form of education for all our children we have to think about how this can be compatible with any form of acceleration, enrichment, extension, selection, ability grouping or special provision for a more able group however they are defined.

If we are to operate on the basis of inclusion how can those at the extremes be catered for? How can teachers possibly cope, especially in secondary schools as the ability and achievement gaps widen? Would inclusion only increase the disaffection and disadvantage of the most able and lower their achievements? Does it decrease the motivation of other learners as they compare themselves and their achievements with the most able of their peers?

In Figure 2, a model of the main differentiation options is set out.

The structural methods consist in organizing the school's response to identified groups then accelerating/fast tracking them. Occasionally individuals may be accelerated by grade skipping. Some pupils respond well to this and others do not so the pupil needs to be at the centre of the advice taken. Product enrichment creates more problems than it resolves for the teachers teach topics that will be covered in the later stages of a pupil's career in school or college. This means that later on the material has been covered at least in part and it can be tedious to go over the ground again. Process extension and enrichment are frequently part of gifted education provision and for recapturing the interest of underachievers. If it is selective, pupils are chosen to participate, rather than can elect to join in, then underachievers will frequently be left out. In addition the potential of many other pupils can be overlooked. This was why I have advocated Identification through Appropriate Provision.

Schools frequently become attached to one form of provision when all should be available to suit different circumstances, the emphasis should be on flexibility. Figure 3 illustrates the seven types of curriculum differentiation that should be on offer in every school.

Schools have in the past adopted, for example setting, acceleration or enrichment models and thought they had coped with the needs of their most able pupils. What the research has shown is that this is not so and that schools must develop flexible and multiple approaches to provide for these

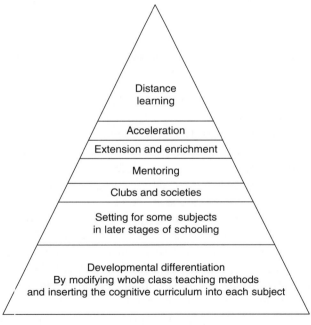

Figure 3   The 'pyramid for potential.

needs especially if they are to capture the interest and motivation of their underachievers. The case studies of schools that are effective in their work with underachievers show that they use all of these options to construct their provision (Wallace *et al.*, 2008) and raise the achievements of all the learners.

The essential condition is that the *effective provision* should begin at classroom level and in every subject area. The nature of effective provision in the ordinary classroom is described in the following sections. The principles and practices discussed then need to be applied up through the pyramid in each of the different formats. Thus clubs and societies, enrichment and extension and mentoring for example must all help develop the pupils' cognitive capabilities and offer more cognitive stretch through challenging learning experiences.

As the centrally directed curriculum and methods began to show their results it was becoming clear that a curriculum designed for the average learner, in rigid age cohorts, was causing many of the more able to underachieve and become disaffected. Standards were not rising sufficiently and a wide range of pupils were becoming depressed and obsessed by Standard Attainment Tests and exam results (Visser and Rayner, 1999).

Government Initiatives in England in Gifted Education

Early researchers such as Hollingworth (1942) and Pickard (1976) showed that with good quality teaching most highly able children could be well catered for up to IQ levels of 150. This is a level of IQ above three standard deviations and has an incidence of 1 in 1000. The problem thus is to define 'good quality' provision and wonder if today with web based and other resources it might not offer self-regulated learning opportunities and distance learning so that all can be included.

In 1999, the UK government (DfEE, 1999) introduced a 'Gifted and Talented' strand in their *Excellence in Cities* programme for England. It was argued by Dracup (2003) that it would bring the middle classes back to inner cities. The social engineering argument was used because there was a fear that inner city education was in steep decline and that pupils were becoming unmanageable in cultural ghettoes.

The DfEE adopted the structural model and thus encouraged master classes, summer schools and the selection of the 'top 5–10%' of a school's intake for some form of '*special*' provision. The other three countries in the Union began to develop their own different policies. Wales for example selected the top 20% (Raffan, 2003).

What the special provision should be was not initially specified nor how the pupils should be selected. Changing the intakes, instituting a national curriculum, upgrading the facilities and renaming schools as 'academies' and specialist schools had already been trialled without sufficient success. Success was measured in comparison with achievements of other countries with advanced economies. Frequently, however what was measured was not comparable (TIMSS, 1997, 2000) but this did not seem to matter in the drive for change.

Attitudes in schools to the 'G and T' policy were divided. There were considerable numbers against what they saw as a return to the elitist grammar school type tradition. In this, the top 20% had been selected on the basis of an 11 plus IQ test for a grammar school education (the gymnasium type) with all the divisiveness that such selection had engendered in social and political terms.

After the experimental stage a G and T policy was formulated and both primary and secondary schools were included. The first phase saw a focus on differentiation, based on the inputs model pursued in Special Education. The most able on the G and T register would be expected to receive some exposure to differentiated specialist provision. The model from the 1970s was reinvented and teachers were expected to make different levels of provision within lessons so that the most able went faster or deeper, or had more challenging work to do. At about the same time another branch of the DfES (Higgins, 2002) had developed a new strategy for improving teaching in the foundation subjects in Key Stage 3 in secondary schools. This had as its core the teaching of thinking skills, challenging questioning and formative assessment to enhance learning, all of which had been the thrust of the NACE policies and the 'underground movement'. The learning curve at the DfEE/DfES had followed that made by many of us two decades earlier.

As the results from international surveys, Office for Standards in Education reports and Chief Her Majesty's Inspectorate's reports on schools in England were published it was evident that the challenge of raising standards had not been met and a new 5-year plan was developed by the DfES named personalized learning (PL). This was to be a conversation about learning and schools could interpret it to suit their needs. It was not this time to be a policy imposed from above but to be developed by the teaching profession itself.

Personalized Learning – DfES, 2004–2009

This is the latest initiative in which the needs of the gifted and talented and improving teaching and learning for all pupils have been brought together. PL means 'a tailor-made education for your child' (DfES, 2004), it is an extension of the government's initiative on improving teaching and learning. The DfES briefing states that it can be compared with the trend towards customization in business where goods and services are tailor-made but at the cost of mass production. In education it means meeting the needs of learners more fully than we have done before but at the same cost. In other words another new initiative and no money to drive it. State education teachers are expected to get the same results as the private sector with double the size of classes and half the resources.

International comparisons of education had shown that the system in England and Wales did well on excellence but did not achieve equity in achievement. For example only 58% of 11 year olds who had free school meals reached the expected level in English whereas 81% of the rest did. It was hoped that PL would break the link between disadvantage and attainment. At the same time PL was designed to stretch and challenge the more able thus bringing together the best features from several initiatives.

The Minister for School Standards in 2004, then David Milliband, defined PL as 'high expectations of every child, given practical form by high-quality teaching based on a sound knowledge and understanding of each child's needs. It is not individualized learning where pupils sit alone at a computer. Nor is it that pupils left to their own devices which too often reinforces low aspirations. It can only be developed school by school. It cannot be imposed from above.'

There are five interlinked aspects for development and which form the Institutional Quality Standards

The inner ring. Assessment for Learning (AfL); effective teaching and learning; a flexible curriculum – extension and enrichment.

The outer ring. Organizing the school for a pupil focus; beyond the classroom – community involvement, partnerships 'We must – create an education system that focuses on the needs of the individual child. This means – extra stretch for the gifted and talented. It means every pupil being able to extend their learning and develop their interests and aptitudes through extra support and tuition beyond the school day. And, most important of all, it means excellent, tailored whole-class teaching with all the resources available – from extra support staff to improved ICT (Information and Communication Technology) – being used to ensure that every pupil gets the education they need.'

(Source: 'Higher Standards, Better Schools for All', DfES, 2005)

A Summary of Personalized Learning Approaches

AfL. Using evidence and dialogue to identify where pupils are in their learning, where they need to go and how best to get there. For example work which is both formatively and summatively assessed.

Effective learning and teaching. These are strategies that develop the competence and confidence of every learner by actively engaging and stretching them; changing teacher roles and activities; extending professional expertise; researching teaching and pupil experience, pupil-regulated learning and learning to learn at teacher and pupil level.

Flexible curriculum. The learning journey involves a combination of entitlement and choice that delivers a breadth of study and personal relevance with increasing choice for learners 14 years and over. The flexible curriculum includes – a guaranteed core curriculum – the national curriculum, religious education (RE), collective worship, sex education, careers education, citizenship and so on; enrichment and enquiry – high-quality opportunities to extend the learning experiences in and out of school; increasing choice over the school career; flexibility leading to relevant qualifications for all.

Organization of the school for a pupil focus. A more creative and flexible team approach to learning is required. It may involve – increasing planning, preparation and assessment time for teachers; using ICT effectively and creating a 'behaviour for learning' environment and policy.

Beyond the classroom. Building partnerships with the community beyond the school, giving guidance and universal support for every pupil with pastoral care, catch up help and integrated multi-agency support.

Of increasing importance in these developments is the attempt to free the lockstep of age cohorts to the movement through the school, the curriculum and the assessments when the child is ready.

PL is the first government policy since the 1980s that I feel I can really work with. It demonstrates a good understanding of learners' needs. I feel optimistic that it will help many underachievers and others to fulfil their potential. There is one caveat, greater autonomy for schools under pressure of decreasing resources can lead to taking the least expensive options such as setting and acceleration and losing the balancing effect of appropriate and effective teaching and learning methodologies. My suggestions on these follow.

Effective Teaching and Learning

The populist approach to education still dominates some sectors of the press and political influence. In summary, the position is – since everyone has been to school they assume they therefore know all about teaching and learning and teacher education. Even the pupils hold the Gradgrind view that 'what they want is facts'. Highly able 8 year olds may learn all the names of the seas of the world and the rivers of their own country to fill up their want of knowledge and will enjoy doing so. But this does not mean that rote learning all aspects of the curriculum is a valid exercise in education although in the nineteenth century it was a common method. Delaying gratification by suggesting that the 10 years of learning grind in schools is all contributing to some superior abstract master plan to make them educated persons and fit them for adult life and the world of work can no longer be believed. Paul (1990) distinguished this didactic method of teaching and learning from what was needed in the new millennium that he defined as critical thinking theory. In critical theory contexts we learn to analyze and criticize and construct our knowledge whereas in didactics a body of knowledge is handed down that we uncritically commit to memory and do not challenge. When vast stores of knowledge are available at the click of a 'mouse' or fingertip touch we need an education that helps us garner and manage the knowledge. The public needs to be educated about teaching and learning but there is no critique in the media that will help to do this. No programmes discuss current education theories and practices, no experts critique government policies or review education books despite the banner 'Education, Education, Education'.

There was also a distinct mismatch between what employers and governments have said was required of workers in this new millennium and what was intrinsic to school learning. The people and workers in this new age need to have the necessary skills and abilities for their countries to compete in world markets. Such as:

- Good communication skills, problem-solving skills, creative thinking abilities, flexibility, good listening skills, ability to learn from experience, ability to learn from others, cooperative abilities.
- Now we can see that PL and the new initiatives will move some way towards this in a critical theory context.

Experts in gifted education such as Passow (1992), former president of the World Council for Gifted and Talented Children, concluded in his review that the gifted needed a curriculum that provided additional depth and breadth of coverage, a speeded-up coverage tailored to individual needs, modification of the material to take account of needs and interests and the development of critical and creative thinking, heuristics and problem solving, and effective interpersonal communication and social skills. I think we are now back on target!

Learning

Teaching and learning as already noted are intimately related. If we teach then the assumption must be that the pupils are learning or have learned most of what we sought to impart. Thus lecturing, or telling information, is not teaching although listeners may learn some of it. Learning in lectures takes place when much of the content and the concepts are already known and the lecturer seeks to restructure this to illustrate new models, principles, analogies and ideas. If the information and concepts are not known then the students have to work autonomously to acquire this information as they grapple with the new ideas – *concept attainment*.

In school much of the learning is related to *developing and forming concepts and scripts* (procedures) and acquiring knowledge. The learning processes appropriate to concept development are more suitably developed through teaching processes using strategies different from the lecture. Because secondary education was originally based upon the nineteenth century university model many teachers over the decades have used the mini lecture method or didactics to impart knowledge. Gifted pupils are renowned for their excellent memories and some have photographic memories but this does not ensure that they can apply what they have learnt to new problems or deal with problems at all.

In any consideration of effective teaching there needs to be a study of what makes for effective learning. De Corte (1995) in an extensive review of the literature summarized the nature of effective learning. His main points were that:

Effective learning is to be found where the following conditions apply:

- Learning is constructive.
- Learning is cumulative.
- Learning is best when self-organized.
- Learning is generally goal oriented.
- Learning is situated.
- Learning is individually different.
- Learning is usually best when collaborative.

Learning in classrooms seldom complies with these conditions. It is often cumulative in the teaching sequence but not in the learning. Individuals are seldom given opportunities to construct their own learning or organize it themselves. They rarely have opportunities to set their own goals or make learning individually different and situated. Classroom learning is situated in the same place, only at times the emotional climate varies and embeds the learning to make it more memorable. Learning may take place in groups but it is most often the case that students are seated together but doing individual work not collaborating (Bennett, 1986).

It can be seen that there is overlap between the conditions for effective learning and the curriculum needs of the gifted. In addition, there is overlap between both of these and what Gibbs (1990) has identified as key elements of 'good teaching', these were

- intrinsic motivation, a need to know and have ownership of knowing;
- learner activity rather than passivity although doing is not enough, we need to reflect and connect present to past learning;
- interaction with others so that ideas can be discussed and negotiated or 'taught' by students for the best way of learning is to teach it to someone else;
- a well-structured knowledge base where knowledge is displayed and integrated into meaningful wholes not disparate units. This is best seen in interdisciplinary studies.

It is notable that Gibbs actually avoids defining effective teaching methods that bring about these conditions.

One final distinction needs to be made before looking at methods and models of effective teaching and that is to clarify the meaning of intellectual versus cognitive skills that sometimes seem to be used interchangeably. The definitions are based upon Gagne (1973).

Intellectual skills. These are about knowing 'that' and knowing 'how'. They include converting printed words into meaning, fractions into decimals, knowing about classes, groups and categories, laws of mechanics and genetics, forming sentences and pictures. They enable us to deal with the world 'out there'.

Cognitive skills. These are internally organized capabilities that we make use of in guiding our attention, learning, thinking and remembering. They are executive control processes that activate and direct other learning processes. We use them when we think about our learning.

It is clear from this that tests which purport to assess cognitive abilities, most frequently do not, they are testing what has been learned in the form of intellectual skills. Sometimes there is a close link between the two as when we might argue that sequencing and ordering text is a cognitive skill but when we are sequencing letters in words and numbers in an IQ test we are using an intellectual skill.

In this context 'cognitive process teaching methods' were developed.

Reframing Teaching for Lifting Underachievement

There are four elements that have been found necessary to develop teaching theory and practice to overcome underachievement (Montgomery, 2003, 2004). These elements are

1. *The cognitive curriculum.* This is expanded upon in a later section.
2. *The talking curriculum.* This is intimately related to the cognitive curriculum. It consists of the following techniques:
   - TPS (Think – Pair – Share).
   - Circle time.
   - Small group work.
   - Group problem solving.
   - Collaborative learning.

- Reciprocal teaching.
- Peer tutoring.
- Thinkback (Lockhead, 2001).
- Roleplay, games and drama.
- Debates and 'book clubs' (Godinho and Clements, 2002).
- Presentations and 'teach – ins'.
- Poster presentations.
- Exhibitions and demonstrations.
- Organized meetings.

Underachievers in particular need to talk things through before they are set to writing them down. In fact, all young learners need such opportunities for often we do not know what we think until we try to explain it to someone else. Where such children come from disadvantaged cultural and linguistic environments the talking approaches are essential. This helps not only vocabulary learning and comprehension but develops organizational skills in composition. To support the organizational abilities direct teaching of 'scaffolds' can be especially helpful and is the logical extension of the developmental writing curriculum. The talking curriculum can be built into the approaches to the cognitive curriculum.

3. *The developmental writing curriculum* (Montgomery, 2000, 2007). This will be outlined in Chapter 10 as a whole school policy on Cognitive Process Strategies for Teaching Spelling plus a school policy on an agreed format for teaching fluent joined handwriting in both primary and secondary schools.

4. *A positive approach to behaviour management* (Montgomery, 1989, 1998, 2002). Positive behaviour management and classroom control has been extensively researched in the observation and feedback to teachers in over 1250 lessons and the five main strategies were outlined towards the end of Chapter 1.

What is clear from my studies is that intrinsic motivation is developed by the methods to be described and children's time on task extends in their enjoyment long after the lessons end. Disaffected children remained at school for these lessons and gifted students recorded such things as 'This is much better than the usual boring stuff we get'. They all began to spend extended periods of time on, instead of off task. The quality of their work frequently exceeded all expectations as did that of the most modest of learners and there were sometimes the most surprisingly interesting and creative responses from unsuspected sources. The collaborative nature of many of the tasks meant that mixed ability groups could easily access the work and all could be included in the same tasks with no diminution of achievements of the highly able.

The Cognitive Curriculum

This consists of

- developmental positive cognitive intervention (PCI);
- cognitively challenging questioning – open and problem posing;
- deliberate teaching of thinking skills and protocols;
- reflective teaching and learning;
- creativity training;
- cognitive process teaching methods.

Each is discussed in more detail below.

Another aspect of this type of provision is that it allows students to be more participative and allows them to choose from a range of response modes to cater for their different talents (Gardner, 1993; see the next chapter by Lee Wills and John Munro). In the following sections, some examples of each approach are outlined to clarify the cognitive challenge offered. The topics are ordinary curriculum activities.

1. Developmental positive cognitive intervention

PCI is highly effective in classroom control (Montgomery, 1984, 2002). The teacher who systematically visits every pupil during a lesson to see what progress is being made and to offer a constructive suggestion about how the work might be developed, will calm the pupils and motivate them to work. This reduces the off-task behavioural difficulties and random noise. Thus, PCI has a strong effect on personal development and self-esteem and is an essential aid to the development of intrinsic motivation. It is information contained in verbal or written feedback on tasks. As such it is crucial for transformational learning and conceptual development and thus it plays a vital role in the constructivist approach (Desforges, 1998). It is also a means for providing formative verbal assessment in PL.

2. Cognitively challenging questioning

Closed questions still make up the most frequently asked questions in classrooms. They consist of asking 'How many' – 'What is' – 'Where was' – and so on. These types of questions elicit one word answers based on the recall of factual information. They are the lowest level responses in Bloom's (1956) taxonomy of educational objectives, the recall and comprehension modes.

To challenge pupils to think, open questions are required that begin with, for example 'Why'. Such questions may require the student to give a personal response or to engage in causal reasoning. However, there is one factor that is not given enough consideration and that is how can the teacher manage an extended response from each of 30 pupils, for when one is talking the others must in a traditional classroom, be quiet and listen. A 'progressive' response to this would be to use the routine TPS (Swartz and Parks, 1994). For example:

Q. Study the text and with your partner decide who if anyone was responsible for the death of Romeo and Juliet?

T. Consider each of the following:

(a) The feuding parents?
(b) The Prince?
(c) Friar Lawrence?
(d) The lovers?

Now make a case for each one in turn being responsible. Make some notes on each.

Now select the 'best' argument and each draw the causal chain you have described.

Q. Are there any analogies between the play and life today? Discuss this with your partner then we'll share it with the class (e.g. TPS).

The teacher then discusses with the pupils the relevance of the task to any current issue. Causal reasoning is important to almost every job and profession where well-founded judgements are needed about causes. In daily life we use it to decide on what to buy to eat and which car to buy.

3. Deliberate teaching of thinking skills

There is range of strategies used to teach thinking skills but for them to be effective what is taught needs to be transferable to everyday life. Some techniques are better for this than others in this list.

(a) *Teaching of thinking*. This refers to 'bolt on' provision and examples are Cognitive Research Trust (CoRT) Thinking Skills Programme (de Bono, 1983); Instrumental Enrichment (Feuerstein *et al.*, 1980). These are taught as regular special thinking skills lessons not integrated into the curriculum. Transfer is a problem. However, the ideas and materials can easily be incorporated into subject plans in the Humanities.

(b) *Teaching for thinking*. Examples are the Cognitive Acceleration in Learning projects in science, geography, mathematics and technology. CASE CAGE CAME CATE (Adey and Shayer, 1994; Shayer and Adey, 2002). A significant element is the special follow-up discussion lesson in which learners discuss and reflect upon not only what they have learned but also how they learnt it. Philosophy for children (Lipman, 1991) fits into this group with children's story books used to raise wider philosophical issues.

The principles underlying accelerated learning (AL) are that the methods develop the thinking ability of the pupils. This includes knowledge acquisition, concept change and the development of processing power. AL encourages the concept of lifelong learners.

There are three main principles in developing AL, these are:

- Cognitive conflict.
- Social construction.
- Bridging.

Cognitive conflict involves stimulating thinking and motivation to learn by offering cognitive or intellectual challenges of moderate difficulty. This is accompanied by support in the form of leading questions, invitations to discuss problems and ideas, looking at them from different angles and so on. This work could be in the form of class discussion, group or pairs work.

In order to promote discussion the learning environment should be supportive so that pupils are not discouraged from putting forward their ideas. They are not 'put down'. The teachers model fairness, consistency and a problem-solving approach.

In relation to social construction of knowledge and understanding the work is based on Vygotsky (1978) principles – understanding develops during social communication and then becomes internalized by individuals – this is promoted by the discussion and 'group think'.

Bridging involves developing new thought processes where a range of associated ideas are taught and solutions generated that apply to new contexts.

AL in general use is structured on learning cycles.

- At the beginning of the task the pupils are introduced to the 'big picture'.
- The outcomes are then described, sometimes these are written on cards – the learning outcomes.
- The learning input follows and may involve visual, auditory and kinaesthetic activities. The student is then asked, 'What are the most important things for you?'
- 'Take five key words and sing them to a tune.'
- Next the pupils demonstrate what they have learned to the rest of the class.
- They review together what they have done and learnt and finally it is all linked back to the 'big picture'.

As can be seen many influences such as Brain Gym, collaborative learning, reflection, active learning and cognitive challenge have all been bound into AL. The research on its more general effectiveness is still awaited but pupils and staff enjoy the collaborative enterprise and it should have long-term gains in promotion of language skills. This is particularly important when many children arrive at school unable to speak in sentences and the billion pound project 'SureStart' to promote the development of pre-schoolers has not yet been shown to deliver improved literacy and numeracy in later years.

For gifted learners the AL process may be too slow but the overall strategy can be used in outline. My concern is what takes place in the learning input and the method by which it takes place. This is where the old didactics can creep in rather than the cognitive process methods to be described.

(c) *Infusion methods* (Swartz and Parks, 1994). Activating Children's Thinking Skills – ACTS (McGuinness, 1999) and TASC – Thinking Actively in a Social Context (Wallace, 2000). TASC and its outcomes have already been described in Chapters 3 and 4 and further examples can be found in Chapter 9 by Ian Warwick.

ACTS is based upon the Swartz and Parks methods and materials. All can be used in mixed ability settings and emphasize the visual organizers that can be used. Each teaches the particular thinking skill strategy and then uses it in application to a curriculum area.

4. Creativity training

There is no true giftedness without creativity according to Cropley (1994). What is overlooked in many schools is that it is not just the arts subjects that are the substance for creative activities, science and maths, and in fact all subjects can be areas of opportunity for creative activities and creativity training. Time to explore and play with ideas and materials are essential elements in the development of creativity and there has often not been enough time in schools for these until now with the New National Curriculum and PL.

Pupils can be trained to develop their creativity and some teachers are better at fostering creativity than others. Teachers who fostered creativity helped pupils to

- be independent learners;
- formulate their own ideas;
- be motivated to think and reason;
- cultivate their interests in new knowledge;
- ask challenging questions.

The teachers gave the students challenging tasks, stimulated different analyses, respected pupils' ideas, were enthusiastic and accepted students as equals (De Alencar, 1999).

Creativity is destroyed by a stress on standards and an emphasis on extrinsic motivators such as bribes, prizes and awards (Deci, 1988). Creativity needs opportunity, time, flexibility and intrinsic motivation.

5. Reflective teaching and learning

Reflection upon learning has been found to be a powerful tool in the consolidation and development of constructs. It is assisted when teachers themselves modelled reflective processing and encouraged reflection amongst learners. They always reserved time for reflection upon what had been done and learned even with the youngest pupils. This has been found to improve the learning outcomes of the learners and raise the achievements of schools adopting the strategies (Pollard, 1997).

The reflective teacher is one who is able to develop teaching and learning for critical thinking. Developing reflective thinking and metacognition of learners is a key objective.

The aim of reflective teaching as a move from routine action to reflective action. While routine action is the type of practice that is relatively static, reflective action embraces a notion that teacher competence and professional development is a career long process guided by self-appraisal and empirical evidence. Through making the unconscious explicit the teacher is in a better position to decide whether what is believed in fits the purpose of what s/he is trying to achieve.

Reflective teaching has six key characteristics.

Reflective teaching implies an active concern with aims and consequences, as well as a means of technical efficiency (p. 11). This means that teachers are not only concerned with what goes on in their classrooms, but with the whole school and with national policy. There is a commitment to be actively involved in all aspects of school development and to be constructively critical in order to be able to justify effective practices.

Reflective teaching is applied in a cyclical or spiralling process, in which teachers monitor, evaluate and revise their own practice (p. 13). This process involves teachers reflecting, planning, making provision, acting, collecting data, analyzing the data and evaluating the data. While this process is similar to action research the fundamental difference is that reflective teaching involves examining all practices from national policy to curriculum planning and the hidden curriculum. It is in this way that reflective teaching leads to professional competence and development.

Reflective teaching requires competence in methods of classroom enquiry, to support the development of teacher competence (p. 14). In order to be able to complete the reflective process described above it is necessary for teachers to develop competences in collecting data in many different ways, to be able to make sense of the evidence and to be able to see how the results from the evidence can be applied to future decision making about policy and practice.

Reflective teaching requires attitudes of open-mindedness, responsibility and wholeheartedness (p. 15). Open mindedness is necessary to make the step from routine action to reflective action. A certain degree of responsibility to students and to their professionalism is necessary for teachers to embark on reflective teaching and an enthusiasm or wholeheartedness allows the process to continue.

Reflective teaching is based on teacher judgement, which is informed partly by self-reflection and partly by insights from educational disciplines (p. 16). This involves a recognition that while reflective action involves constant self-appraisal, which helps teacher judgement; all answers cannot and should not be expected to be found by teachers alone. Educational research is a valuable resource.

Reflective teaching, professional learning and personal fulfilment are enhanced through collaboration and dialogue with colleagues (p. 18). Lastly, reflective action should be shared action. Firstly, in order to share, clarify and hone ideas and secondly for change to come about.

Reflective teaching can take place on many different levels. The first is looking at ourselves as teachers, at the students and their relationships. By examining these aspects, teachers can be enabled to identify their own strengths and weaknesses. They will also be in a better position to make the environment more conducive to learning and to plan for all the needs of the pupils.

Other levels are to examine pedagogy and the curriculum, the learning environment, classroom management, communication and issues of equality, assessment and the benefits of formative assessment to inform their planning and teaching, the hidden curriculum, which can influence both the way children learn and how they view themselves within society, this process of reflection should be collaborative to ensure that each child is treated equally and it is central to the ethos of the school; examining school policy and finally national policy. This responsibility to provide the best education can then be taken further by looking critically at national policies and again collaborating with others to put forward points.

In summary, through reflective teaching, teachers are being asked to examine their personal values and aims. Reflective teaching is flexible and learner orientated so that learners also can become reflective and learn in ways best for them. Their contribution and collaboration is important in the intimate relationship between teaching and learning.

As can be seen there are close links between reflective teaching and learning and PL. It is probably safe to say that we cannot achieve the goals of PL if we are not reflective teachers and learners.

6. Cognitive process teaching methods

These are the core of inclusive teaching (developmental differentiation) and PCI and enable them to be achieved. Cognitive process teaching methods are based in Critical Thinking Theory and are the means by which higher order thinking and metacognitive skills can be developed through the ordinary curriculum. They are also powerfully inclusive. The whole class can be introduced to the basic idea and then mixed groups or pairs work on the main ideas or subthemes and then pool their knowledge and experience with the teacher's support. These strategies can be widely used to promote inclusion at primary and secondary level.

There are six main types of cognitive process strategies or pedagogies so far identified:

- Developmental PCI, this has already been outlined.
- Cognitive study and research skills.
- Problem solving and investigative learning.
- Experiential learning.
- Games and simulations.
- Language experience methods.
- Collaborative learning and team building.

Some examples follow.

Cognitive study and research skills   Study skills are a set of strategies that students must learn to use in order to

(a) acquire more information independently of the teacher;
(b) rehearse, transform and memorize relevant aspects of what they have been taught; and
(c) demonstrate what has been learnt in examinations both theoretical and practical, and also perhaps in real-world situations.

These purposes can be achieved in two different ways traditional or progressive (this latter was the term that came to be used to denigrate methods other than traditional in the 1970s). In traditional methods, the student seeks to memorize the contents and reproduces them as well as possible to fit the questions asked or problems to be solved. The traditional strategies recommended are frequently devoted to the aftermath of teaching in revision sessions and focus upon the following:

(a) Memorizing – mnemonics are made to remember key points from the lesson notes; acronyms are devised and lists made; diagrams practised, notes reread and rehearsed.
(b) Organizing – organizing self and setting; planning the revision study sessions and areas to cover; selecting topics in order of importance.
(c) Note taking – students write down the main points; headings; cram all of a topic onto a single revision card or computer file page, make flow charts and diagram summaries, use highlighters on texts during reading to link together later in writing.
(d) Revision strategies – rereading lesson notes; rehearse the points on the revision cards; Survey, Question, Read, Rehearse, Review (SQ3R).
(e) Exam techniques – studying past exam questions and making answer plans, learning how to structure answers, underlining key concepts in the questions and ensuring they are answered.

The main support to study skills in traditional lessons is seen in the concept completion exercises (cloze procedures) and comprehension questions. Both are related to recall of information and comprehension checking. These may include inferential questions and a few which require abstract reasoning.

Often, even with the best intentions, after an hour or two of such study the students will become bored and distracted. Revision is a tedious process. The most able have good memories so that the very act of making revision notes can cement the topics in the memory so that SQ3R is unnecessary. The more creative of students find revision excessively boring and do 10 other 'essential' things leaving no time for the revision grind. They need to be strongly extrinsically motivated to pursue their revision on a regular and consistent basis. The 'prize' has to have a high value to keep them on task. The most able in this traditional setting are found to be able to reproduce the factual content of what they have learned very well but are less good at transforming it and summarizing it for different purposes (Thomas, Harri-Augstein and Smith, 1984).

If we turn now to 'progressive methods' of teaching we see a very different position. The system is 'frontloaded', that is the study strategies are part of the system of teaching and train the learner during the process of learning. The purpose is to enable the learners to construct their own concepts and thus arrive at a state of deep learning. This then needs a much lighter touch on the revision accelerator. The cognitive process pedagogies have been shown to achieve this at school and degree levels (Montgomery, 1993, 1996, 2000).

What has been argued is that 'progressive' methods of teaching can enable the students to accommodate (Piaget, 1952) or construct their own learning (Desforges, 2000) during the learning process and so become more effective learners at all levels. This fits with the principles of effective learning established by De Corte. In the first set of examples which follow I have called the strategies 'cognitive' to indicate the essential element of 'engage brain' that they demand.

Typical cognitive study and research skills
- Concept mapping, 'brain maps' 'mind maps'.
- Locating main points or ideas.
- Locating main and subordinate points and structures.
- Flow charting using main and subordinate points.
- Completion and prediction exercises.
- Sequencing.
- Comparing and contrasting.
- Drafting and editing.
- Summarizing, précis, bullet points, poster methods, book/chapter critical reviews, flow charting, minisagas, timelines, critical incident analysis, chronologies.
- organizing – tabulating, classifying, ordering, diagramming, categorizing.
- Drawing inferences and abstractions.
- Identifying causes – causal reasoning.
- Recognizing intent and propaganda.
- Identifying text structure or schema.
- Assessing performance.
- Teaching subject material.

As can be seen this list includes a range of research strategies that a student writing a thesis, dissertation or a project might be expected to undertake. It helps if they have already mastered these skills before they arrive at the degree level. Regrettably this is seldom the case. The skill most students will have acquired is the précis during their Baccalaureate and Bachelor degree programmes.

Concept mapping – the student tries to represent what he or she knows about a subject by drawing a 'mind map' of it rather than writing about it. If we use the example RUN as the concept we wish to map then all that we do is write around the key word other words (concepts) which we think of that are related to it or suggested by it. Each of us will produce somewhat similar and somewhat different maps when we draw lines to show relationships between our concepts. Students can inspect their maps and discuss similarities and differences between them. Some will be simple and others complex depending on our experiences and reflective processing.

A useful strategy is then to give the students something new about the key concept to read or experience and then after a short time ask them to draw another map. They can then be asked to write 5 or even 10 differences between map one and map two. This demonstrates their own learning process and encourages them to be aware of their metacognitive processes. Older pupils can then try to assess the complexity of their learning outcomes using the Structure of Observed Learning Outcomes (SOLO) taxonomy (Biggs, 1991). I use this in the Masters (MA) programmes to help students to begin to analyze their critical levels of thinking on, for example G. Ed, SEN, SpLD (specific learning difficulties) from simple relational structures to advanced multistructural abstract and relational complexes.

Classification – It is traditional in maths lessons to teach about triangles. Students are introduced to the types of triangles by name such as isosceles, scalene and right angle. They are told the different properties of the angles and sides of the different types of triangle. They might then be given examples to measure and confirm as a practical exercise. In conclusion, they may be given drawings of a set of triangles to measure the angles and sides so as to identify which type of triangle each is.

The 'progressive', problem-solving approach would be to start the other way round and give them the set of triangles to explore and discuss with a partner. Their tools are a ruler, a pencil and a protractor. They can be told that there are three main types of triangle and their job is to find out how the three types can be distinguished. When they have done this and all have been discussed then the names can be hypothesized, Latin words looked up and correct name assigned to the appropriate examples.

Concept completion – 'Ultima Ratio Regum' is the title of a poem by Stephen Spender and the first verse is given here to illustrate the strategy:

The guns spell money's ultimate reason
In letters of ———— on the Spring hillside,

But the boy lying ————- under the olive trees
Was too young and too —————
To have been notable to their important eye.
He was a better target for —————.

As pairs study the verses it causes their brains to engage at a deeper level with the meaning of the poem as they try to supply the missing word. It is not as easy as it seems and the answer by Spender is surprising yet very satisfying once you know what it is.

Summarizing – this is most often seen as the précis of a passage or a chapter. The student learns to do such summaries for course work or tests but is seldom introduced to the vast range of summarizing techniques available or indeed how to tackle the précis. For them it boils down to reproducing the text in a shortened form with as little brain effort as possible. Often they splice lumps of text from web sites or books into what appears to them to be a coherent account. They do not notice that it is in a different register from their own words or that it reads as a set of elaborated notes drawn straight from other sources.

To equip them for reading and writing in different registers and for different audiences practice on a range of summarizing techniques is needed such as:

Main points – Pairs of pupils can be set to find the key or main point of a section of text. Most simple texts have the main point in the first sentence, for example the food surplus.

> With a food surplus, the Pueblos were able to turn their attention to other activities besides locating or growing food. In one particular area – pottery making – the Pueblos developed a high degree of artistry. Potters became artists and developed individualised techniques, painting fine-lined geometric designs as well as reproductions or life forms on their vessels. Paints were improved and pottery has been found that contains three or four different colours.
>
> (Royce-Adams, 1977 taken from *Columbus to Aquarius*,
> Dryden Press, 1973)

Subordinate points in the paragraph can be identified such as the pottery making, artistry, colours and designs.

Flow charts can then be made of the meaning of the text. This set of strategies can be used independently or together on all kinds of textual, performance and visual material such as paintings, advertisements and film or plays.

Lists of main points – bullet points – if students are set to find the 5 or 10 main points of a chapter or article and compare their points in pairs then this is a much more challenging task than just listing what they think is important. They work hard to find all the points. The mental work and the negotiation between partners will fix the ideas in their long-term memories making them easier to recall later.

Schemas – There are different writing patterns to be found in texts, just as plays, paintings and music have particular organizing structures. In the Pueblos passage, we can ask the students to decide which type of schema is used in the text construction, for example is it

(a) illustration – example?
(b) definition?
(c) comparison – contrast?
(d) sequence of events?
(e) cause and effect?
(f) description?
(g) a mixture? State which.

Typical structures students learn to use but often without being aware of them are:

- Explain a process or how it works.
- Describe the way things are.
- Instruct how to make or do.
- Recount or retell events.
- Persuade and argue a point of view.
- Discuss by presenting an argument or an essay.

Book or chapter reviews – Students can be asked to write a critical review of a text in say 500 words. They can be given the basic structure – one-third factual summary – one-third critical points – one-third personal opinion. Other structures will be appropriate for different types of text.

Minisagas – Students can be asked to write the story of a book they have just read in 50 words.

Timelines, chronologies and critical incident analyses and pathways are all also forms of summarizing techniques.

Problem solving and investigative learning   Human nature is such that if you present a person with an open ended situation in which the answer is not given the mind automatically tries to resolve it. Humans are born scientific investigators (Kelly, 1955). Although not everything can be converted into a problem there is considerable scope for doing so across the curriculum. This means that we can use this natural form of intrinsic motivation to our advantage in helping students learn.

Characteristic of the approach is that there needs to be plenty of content material around to research to help develop ideas and strategies or verify solutions. Because the activities start from the pupil's own ideas and knowledge each is building up their own cognitive structures and the learning is individualized. The teacher is not only a resource but also a manager and facilitator of learning and thus has many roles including teacher.

Real problems are essentially 'fuzzy' and time has to be spent in finding the issues. To begin with students may need help to learn how to approach such problems but with practice can take over all of this themselves.

According to Gallagher (1997) there are four elements to 'fuzzy' problems, there is an ill-structured problem; substantial content, student apprenticeship, self-directed learning. He found that Real Problem Solving (RPS) and PBL are better than traditional teaching methods for long-term retention; conceptual understanding, self-directed learning and intrinsic motivation. Deci and Ryan (1983), Ryan and Deci (2000) and Gibbs (1990) both showed that intrinsic motivation is essential to effective learning and good teaching.

The essence of problem-based learning (PBL) is to promote and develop thinking skills and abilities both intellectual and cognitive (Gagne, 1973). We can identify both lower and higher order thinking skills as follows:

Some 'lower' order thinking skills:
- Sequencing and ordering.
- Sorting, classifying and grouping.
- Analyzing, identifying parts/wholes.
- Comparing and contrasting.
- Distinguishing fact from opinion.
- Identifying bias and checking evidence.
- Drawing conclusions and giving reasons.
- Making predictions, hypothesizing.
- Relating cause and effect.
- Designing a fair test.
- Weighing up pros and cons.

Some higher order thinking skills:
- Defining and clarifying problems.
- Thinking up different solutions.
- Setting priorities, goals and targets.
- Testing solutions and evaluating outcomes.
- Planning and monitoring progress towards goals.
- Revising plans and managing progress.
- Making decisions.
- Real problem solving.
- Generating new ideas and solutions.
- Team building (using emotional and social intelligence).
- Creative problem solving.

It is in fact difficult to assign some of these so easily to separate categories but a general principle might be that lower order thinking is more closely associated with curriculum content typical of intellectual processing. Higher order skills – cognitive skills are much more to do with running the executive control processes.

An example of the approach is as follows: 'It is 1280. You are King Edward 1's master mason. You have been told to design and organize the building of a new castle at David in North Wales. Draw up a castle design and cost it within budget for King Edward' (Essex Curriculum Enrichment Materials, 1985).

It is suggested that the pupils work in pairs or threes.

Information given:

- Labour force details and costs.
- Materials and equipment.
- Purposes of the build – defence.
- Site of the Gatehouse.
- Bursary for reconnaissance visit.
- Budget for the whole project.

Additional costs to be built in

round versus square towers;
price per crenellation;
windows and doors versus slits;
overhangs;
accommodation, storage and armoury.

The resources available could include the ground plans of parts of actual castles, pictures of a range of castles, web clips of castles in lieu of site visits, maps to illustrate the terrain. Alternatively the teacher may decide to work in a more open way in approaching the subject and start first with a different strategy, a simulation or game such as the following.

Games and simulations   The class is shown an outline map with six proposed castle sites, a plateau, hills, a lake island, a village, land surrounded by marsh and land on a low peninsula between rivers. The class is divided into six groups with about five students in each. Each group is randomly assigned one of the sites. They are then given the following brief:

> You are agents for your site and your task is to prepare a marketing brief to sell your plot to the Lord/Lady potential purchaser. The year is 1250.

The groups are then given about 5–10 minutes to discuss their site and come up with selling ideas. Each group then gives a mini presentation to the rest of the class and the teacher (potential purchaser). Much fun is had by all but a wide range of cognitive, social and linguistic skills are exercised in the process. In the plenary session, the teacher can then help them draw up a complete set of criteria for deciding where a castle should be built taking into account the needs and potential costs. The second lesson in the series can then address the analysis of the site and construction of an actual castle of their choice and so on.

Characteristic of all games is that they must be followed by a discussion–debriefing session to analyze what transpired so that emotional, educational and metacognitive objectives can be achieved.

Experiential learning   Briefly the essence of experiential learning is any occasion when we learn by doing or action learning. The learning is not circular returning the learner to the same point each time. Instead, at each turn, the experience, the talking about the experience and the reflecting upon the learning and doing add to the sum of knowledge and change the processes and the understanding in an additive way.

The result is a learning spiral (Montgomery, 1994), progressing from surface to deep learning (Marton and Saljo, 1984) often with the mediation of the teacher (Feuerstein, 1995; see Figure 4).

The cognitive learning spiral illustrates the sort of processing that is necessary to move learning to the deep levels. In the first spiral there is

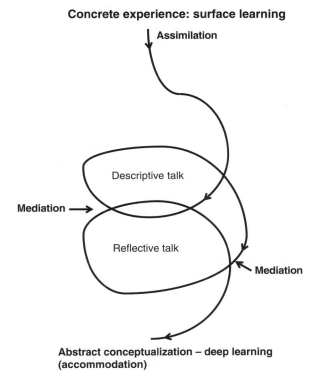

Figure 4   Cognitive learning spiral.

discussion about the concrete events in which pupils explain and expand on what they have just experienced, this may take place with or without help from the teacher – mediation. In the next cycle, they may receive further related input or experience and then go on to reflect and discuss how they learnt and what was their thinking during this activity. This process of thinking about one's thinking is known as metacognition and is a major contributor to increasing a persons' intelligence (Flavell, 1979).

According to Gibbs (1990), the characteristics of surface or superficial learning are a heavy workload; relatively high class contact hours; an excessive amount of course material; a lack of opportunity to pursue subjects in depth; a lack of choice of subjects; a lack of choice over study methods; a threatening and anxiety-provoking assessment system. Deep learning consists in the reverse of these conditions. Surface learning does not easily enable the material to be built into the students' internal schemas or constructs and scripts and so it remains inert and inaccessible. It is often capable of being repeated 'parrot fashion' but without significant understanding.

Teachers in their instruction mode give mini lectures on topics to pupils and when this is well structured this gives rise to the condition known as reception learning (Ausubel, 1968) similar to surface learning. It is repeatable in an examination after revision but it does not become incorporated into the student's conceptual understanding. It does not become part of them constructing their concepts and scripts but was still the basis of the competency approach underpinning the centralized system of teacher education stemming from the 1990s.

Language experience methods   These methods began at first as strategies in developing the motivation and reading skills of poor readers. The pupil would tell an aide a story or news from the weekend and it would be word processed and printed off in book form and pictures added to make a personal book of stories which the author would then read to the aide or the teacher. The vocabulary was thus set at an appropriate level and interest.

More able pupils might also author stories for younger pupils or peers and produce them as projects in good book form. Developing from this they might also design and make study skill games based on the books or produce travel guides for places and projects they are studying. Writing in different registers for different audiences can be built into these projects.

Now pairs of pupils can compose narrative and other materials on the word processor and gain the same benefits. They can also design PowerPoint presentations to show to other audiences.

The teacher or the pupils might take a chapter or a whole book and base a game board upon it. When the players land on particular squares they have to answer a study skills card question. The questions should reflect both comprehension and problem-solving items. Dyslexics and second language learners have found these games most powerfully motivating. Highly able underachievers can also design games and try them out with younger children. It increases their interest and skill with text and presentation.

These are just a few outline examples of the cognitive process approaches that have been tried out on a wide scale with slow learners, remedial, gifted and mixed ability groups.

Collaborative learning and team building   Collaboration means that students work with each other towards the framing and design of problems and strategies as well as in their resolution or solution. Each contributes some part to the whole. Quite often the process is called 'cooperative learning'. When pupils sit in groups they may be doing individual not collaborative work (Bennett, 1986).

Collaborative learning facilitates extended language use and thinking as well as assisting in team-building skills. It can be used in both content free (Rawlings, 1996) and content dense situations. The 'maligned wolf' is a reconstruction of the story of Little Red Riding Hood from the wolf's point of view (Bowers and Wells, 1988; Rawlings, 1996).

Circle time is a term used to describe a setting when all the pupils sit round in a circle or a horseshoe and share in an activity such as saying something positive about the person sitting to the left or right of them in turn round the circle. They may do a few such icebreakers or positive supportive warm-up activities and then focus on problems such as 'What are our rights?' or a bullying incident and then share experiences and decide what should and could be done about it. 'Brainstorming' and problem solving and resolving sessions on human issues are a common feature.

These sessions are widely used in schools and have helped in the management of pupils with behavioural problems and learning needs. They contribute to the language and emotional development of children as well as to problem solving and creativity development. Conflict management and mediation strategies are also often developments of this type of work.

For underachieving pupils they offer opportunities for affirmation and expression of concerns and needs, as well as guiding them in ways of expressing themselves in reasonable terms. These techniques derived from the crowd control techniques that were developed in America after the student and race riots in order to keep people safe and focused on their legitimate objectives rather than to be swayed by crowd emotion to riot and loot. The beneficial effects of the techniques were recognized by the Quaker movement and introduced by them through such groups as the Kingston Workshop Group led by Bowers, Wells and Rawlings during the 1970s and 1980s.

What is clear from past and current MA students researches on Cognitive Process Strategies for Teaching is that intrinsic motivation is developed by these methods and pupils' time on task extends in their enjoyment long after the lessons end. Disaffected children remained at school for these lessons and gifted students recorded such things as 'This is much better than the usual boring stuff we get'. They all began to spend extended periods of time on, instead of off task. The quality of their work frequently exceeded all expectation as did that of the most modest of learners. There were sometimes the most surprisingly interesting and creative responses from unsuspected sources. The collaborative nature of the tasks means that mixed ability groups can easily access the work and all can be included in the same tasks.

In these inclusive settings, Hallam (2002) found that mixed ability groups do not diminish the achievements of the highly able. All are enabled to achieve higher learning outcomes. Thus, it is that in secondary schools I have worked with we can see one science or maths department insisting that all classes must be mixed ability groups whilst another insists it cannot operate thus and must have classes set by ability. It would seem that it is those with the higher teaching skills who can work with mixed ability groups.

Enjoyment and legitimized social interaction were not often connected in some underachiever's minds at first with school learning and so at each stage they had to be shown in explicit ways how much they had learned and how their work was improving. This was done by giving detailed comments on their work and their learning processes both verbally and in writing couched in constructive terms (AfL using PCI). At intervals they were helped to reflect upon the products and the processes of their learning. Once they began to make these connections they became avid learners and other teachers began to notice a transformation and comment upon complete positive changes in the behaviour and attitude. It is in these ways that effective teaching methods can also be seen to be making a major contribution to classroom management and behaviour control. This is in addition to the general benefits created by a positive and supportive classroom climate and school ethos using positive behaviour management.

Assessment for Learning

Assessment can be summative, formative or diagnostic. AfL can be made up of all three. The most common form is summative when at the end of an assignment a grade or mark is given indicating the quality of the piece such as 9 out of 10 or A – in a similar scale of grades. This might be accompanied by a comment about the quality, for example 'this is very pleasing work', 'a high standard of work'. In AfL, we would expect to see some cognitive component to the remark such as – 'If you had added a section on xxx this would have gained the highest mark'. Or, 'You needed to explore the reaction to xxx in more detail, to justify your conclusion.' The learner needs to learn what to do to achieve the standard and the teacher thereby has to have a set of previously established criteria by which to judge the work. This type of marking is called constructive feedback and needs to be couched in positive or neutral terms so as not to discourage the learner especially when a number of shortcomings are to be found. Negative feedback only tells the learner what not to do, not how to improve. It can also engender negative emotional side effects. AfL also has the property of feed forward, it can be used to develop future plans and lessons.

AfL has also been extensively used in performance appraisal of teachers (Montgomery, 1984, 1999, 2002) and had a powerfully good effect. It was given as a running written record on classroom observation sessions using the framework CBG, 3Ms, PCI and tactical lesson planning outlined in Chapter 1. The feedback was read to the teacher and discussed in a post-observation interview and was able to improve the performance of teachers in just two sessions. It affirmed the skills and performance of very good teachers. Most often they did not know how their good teaching and learning success of the pupils was constructed. After the inputs they had a theory of teaching and teaching tactics to draw on to reflect upon their practice and continue their professional development. They also had a method they found they could easily share with others.

The technique has also been extended to the three MA distance learning programmes feedback (MA Gifted Education; MA SEN; MA SpLD – Dyslexia). A running commentary is written on the task responses pointing out the good features and any omissions and improvements. The purpose as with the interview feedback is to set up a 'learning conversation' or metacognition in the student's head. It is the detail and the quality of this interaction that gradually improves the student performance. It does of course take much longer than a rapid read through and a grading.

AfL requires additional planning, preparation and marking time. It is also why what is to be marked should be distinguished from mere 'copy book' writing.

Pupils even of a young age can be good evaluators of other's work. They need first to learn how to evaluate and give feedback that is encouraging and not insulting. This can be learned in collaborative workshops practising on written, performance and artistic work of unnamed previous writers and artists. Evaluating and marking have been found to be the best way of learning, even better than teaching things to other people (Race, 1992). They can be taught as cognitive study skills.

AfL is more than a means of evaluating performance it is a powerful and individualized teaching method in its own right. It deserves more attention and could be promoted by reducing class sizes so that teachers not only have the opportunity to give formative AfL on task during lessons as part of PCI but also formative written comments. Post hoc AfL has less power in schools as there is seldom the opportunity to sit down with the pupil and personalize them. Often they only will only read the grade.

Evaluation of Methods and Materials

It is usual now for teachers preparing curriculum enrichment and extension materials and developmental differentiation to use Bloom's (1956) taxonomy of educational objectives as a guideline. This means they try to produce materials and methods even for 5 year olds that tap into Bloom's higher levels of analysis, synthesis and evaluation. I have examples of mixed ability groups of 5 year olds all working at these higher levels. Higher levels of cognitive operation thus need not be reserved until the teenage years when vast bodies of content have been learned as was once thought. Thinking and study skills by then may have been dimmed. All learners need the opportunity for cognitive stretch and challenge.

Care has to be taken when using Bloom's taxonomy that the use of words such as analysis and evaluation do really have the meaning intended. For example in a Dinosaur project analyzing the meaning of the parts of the words such as -saurus, mega- and ichthio- and putting them together in new combinations as titles for illustrations is not really analysis and synthesis but applications level putting together known parts in a different context. Evaluation is not evaluation because the word itself is used, it needs to involve the consideration or the development and use of external or internal criteria. Sometimes a task is considered challenging or complex when it is not, for example finding or recalling the names of all the major rivers in a named country is still a recall task, it is difficult not cognitively complex.

In addition to using Bloom's taxonomy as a guideline we can add a composite checklist or seven point plan for evaluation of materials for the gifted and if we are to offer challenge for all children.

- Are they beneficial to the development and use of higher order thinking abilities?

- Do they enable the exploration of new knowledge and important ideas in breadth and in depth?
- Can they teach and encourage study and research skills in the selection and use of sources?
- Do they offer opportunities to engage in increasingly autonomous learning and induce intrinsic motivation?
- Do the processes help integrate knowledge between and within subjects?
- Are some problems 'fuzzy' or open ended and so promote multilogical, innovative and creative responses?
- Do the activities promote real collaborative learning and abilities to work in teams?

If the answers to these questions are in the affirmative by all teachers in a school then we can begin to be assured that we are beginning to work out the 'applications programmes' for the curriculum that will prepare pupils to achieve and nations to succeed in the twenty-first century for they are teaching the gifted and all students more effectively.

Conclusions

For many teachers, teaching the gifted and talented underachievers effectively, means change. This is because the principles of effective learning need to be incorporated into our thinking about teaching when they may have been inert knowledge before. It has been argued that general teaching methods also need to be adapted to make education in subject contents more intellectually challenging for all learners and this can be achieved by making methods more inclusive at the classroom level. Tackling this at the subject and class teaching level enables the widest range of learners particularly underachievers to receive an education suited to their needs.

When these methods target thinking and communication skills they are particularly suited for the gifted and talented. However, they also need to be incorporated in all the levels of provisions made for the gifted and talented. Thus, enrichment and extension should focus on these skills rather than teaching content from older year's curricula. Likewise clubs and societies can also concentrate on intellectual challenges. Pupils also need more quality time on task and time to think.

They need to be helped to learn autonomously and in teams and through these may establish the habit of lifelong learning. Developing pupils' skills as evaluators of their own and other's learning and improving AfL in schools will act as an important teaching method for lifting achievement.

Worldwide there are a number of models for teaching the gifted, most of them promote segregated provision and Olympiads and so on. However there are others, often 'pull out' programmes that can also be used in inclusive situations across the subject, age and ability ranges. They have common features although they were developed in isolation from each other and from the foregoing. The best known are the Multiple Intelligences approach (Gardner, 1993); Renzulli's Schoolwide Enrichment Triad Model (Renzulli, 1977, 1995, 2006) and Clark's Integrative Education Model (Clark, 1986) all adopt a problem solving and holistic approach with teachers taking on a variety of different roles such as manager and facilitator.

In this chapter, it has been suggested that lack of cognitive challenge in the curriculum is a major cause of underachievement. Stereotypic views of the 'good' pupil, gender, ethnicity, culture and the 'able child' can also cause pupil's abilities to be overlooked and lead to underfunctioning as expectations are lowered.

It was proposed that every elementary, secondary and high school should make available seven levels of gifted and talented provision in the 'pyramid for potential' to meet the needs of all the learners and access to that provision should be open and self-selecting.

The key to intrinsic motivation to learn in schools is that pupils should want to do what they do rather than what they wish. Intrinsic motivation is developed when pupils enjoy what they are doing, have ownership of their learning, can see its purpose and relevance to their lives and gain in self-esteem from the process and the appreciation of the products of what they do.

When learning is constructive, contextualized, cumulative and at relevant times collaborative it meets the conditions for effective learning. Effective teaching is the process by which intrinsic motivation and effective learning are brought about within a curriculum context for the learners.

A range of strategies were identified under the umbrella of 'effective teaching' and these were – developmental PCI, challenging questioning, teaching of thinking skills, creativity training, reflective teaching and learning and cognitive process teaching methods.

These methods and strategies were found to be particularly necessary for the remotivating and enabling the underachieving able learners to achieve at a level more fitting their potential. In the process identification through appropriate provision was also possible. In these processes of implementing the methods in inclusive settings it was found that the achievements of all learners could be promoted.

References

Adey, P. and Shayer, M. (1994) *Really Raising Standards: Cognitive Intervention and Academic Achievement*, Routledge, London.

Ausubel, D.P. (1968) *Educational Psychology. A Cognitive View*, Holt, Rinehart and Winston, New York.

Bennett, N. (1986) 'Cooperative Learning. *Children Do it in groups, or Do They?*' Paper presented at the Division of Education and Child Psychology Conference; British Psychological Society, London, April.

Biggs, J.E. (ed.) (1991) *Teaching for Learning. The Viewpoint from Cognitive Psychology*, Australian Council for Educational Research, Hawthorne.

Bloom, B.S. (ed.) (1956) *Taxonomy of Educational Objectives*, Vol. 1, Longman, London.

Bowers, S. and Wells, L. (1988) *Ways and Means: A Problem Solving Approach*, LDRP, Kingston.

CATE (1983) CATENOTE 1, DES, London.

Clark, B. (1986) *Optimising Learning: The Integrative Education Model in the Classroom*, Merrill, Columbus, OH.

Cropley, A. (1994) Creative intelligence: a concept of true giftedness. *European Journal of High Ability*, **5** (1), 16–23.

De Alencar, E.M.L.S. (1999) 'Training Teachers to Teach for Creativity'. WCGTC Biennial Conference Keynote Paper, Istanbul, 2–6 August.

de Bono, E. (1983) *CoRT Thinking*, Pergamon, Oxford.

De Corte, E. (1995) Learning and high ability: a perspective from instructional psychology, in *Nurturing Talent* (eds M.W. Katzko and R.F. Monks), Van Gorcum, Assen, The Netherlands, pp. 148–61.

Deci, E.L. (1988) *Motivating the Highly Able to Learn. Some Controlled Research Studies*. Lecture to the 10th International Symposium on Education Plovdiv, Bulgaria, October.

Deci, E.L. and Ryan, R.M. (1983) *Intrinsic Motivation and a Human Behaviour*, Plenum Press, New York.

Desforges, C. (1998) Learning and teaching: current views and perspectives, in *Directions in Educational Psychology* (ed. D. Shorrocks-Taylor), Whurr, London, pp. 5–18.

Desforges, C. (2000) '*Teaching for Thinking*'. Keynote Paper 10th Annual Conference on Thinking, Harrogate.

DfEE (1999) *Excellence in Cities*, The Stationery Office, London.

DfES (2002) *Teaching and Learning in Foundation Subjects at Key Stage 3*, The Stationery Office, London.

DfES (2004) *A National Conversation about Personalising Learning*, London: DfES.

DfES (2005) *Higher Standards: Better Schools for All*, DfES, London.

Dracup, T. (2003) Understanding the national approach to gifted and talented students. *Curriculum Briefing*, **1** (2), 7–10.

Essex County Council (1985) *Essex Curriculum Materials: Dinosaurs*, ECC, Chelmsford.

Feuerstein, R. (1995) *Mediated Learning Experience*. Keynote Paper Mediated Learning Conference, London, Regents College, February.

Feuerstein, R., Rand, Y., Hoffman, M.B. and Mitter, R. (1980) *Instrumental Enrichment*, University Park Press, Baltimore, MD.

Flavell, J.H. (1979) Metacognition and cognitive monitoring. *American Psychologist*, **34**, 906–11.

Gagne, R. (1973) *The Essentials of Learning*, Holt, Rinehart and Winston, London.

Gallagher, J. (1997) Preparing the gifted student as independent learner, in *Connecting the Gifted Worldwide* (ed. J.A. Leroux), WCGTC, Seattle, pp. 37–50.

Gardner, H. (1993) *Frames of Mind: The Theory of Multiple Intelligences*, Basic Books, New York.

Gibbs, G. (1990) *Learning Through Action*. Further Education Unit, London.

Godinho, S. and Clements, D. (2002) Literature discussion with gifted and talented students. *Educating Able Children*, **6** (2), 12–8.

Hallam, S. (2002) *Ability Grouping in Schools*, Institute of Education Publications, London.

Higgins, P. (2002) Teaching and Learning in Foundation Subjects, *Curriculum Briefing*, Optimus Press, London.

Hollingworth, L. (1942) *Children Above 180 IQ Stanford-Binet: Origin and Development*, World Books, New York.

Kelly, G. (1955) *Personal Construct Theory*, Vols **1** and **2**, Norton, New York.

Lipman, M. (1991) *Thinking in Education*, Cambridge University Press, Cambridge.

Lockhead, J. (2001) *THINKBACK: A User's Guide to Minding the Mind*, Lawrence Erlbaum, London.

Marton, F. and Saljo, R. (1984) Approaches to learning, in *The Experience of Learning* (eds F. Marton, J. Hownesell and N.J. Entwistle), Scottish Academic Press, Edinburgh.

McGuinness, C. (1999) From Thinking Skills to Thinking Classrooms Report RR115, Norwich DES.

Montgomery, D. (1981) Education comes of age. *School Psychology International*, **1**, 1–3.

Montgomery, D. (1982) Teaching thinking skills in the school curriculum. *School Psychology International*, **3** (4), 105–12.

Montgomery, D. (1983) Teaching the teachers of the gifted. *Gifted Education International*, **2** (1), 32–4.

Montgomery, D. (1984) *Evaluation and Enhancement of Teaching Performance*, LDRP, Kingston.

Montgomery, D. (1985) *The Special Needs of Able Children in Ordinary Classrooms*, LDRP, Kingston.

Montgomery, D. (1989) *Managing Behaviour Problems*, Hodder and Stoughton, Sevenoaks.

Montgomery, D. (1993) Learner managed learning in teacher education, in *Learner Managed Learning: Policy, Theory and Practice* (ed. N. Graves), World Education Fellowship/Higher Education for Capability, Leeds, pp. 59–70.

Montgomery, D. (1994) The role of metacognition and metalearning in teacher education, in *Improving Student Learning* (ed. G. Gibbs), Oxford Brookes Centre for Staff Development, Oxford, pp. 227–53.

Montgomery, D. (1996) *Educating the Able*, Cassell, London.

Montgomery, D. (1998) *Reversing Lower Attainment*, David Fulton, London.

Montgomery, D. (1999) *Positive Appraisal Through Classroom Observation*, David Fulton, London.

Montgomery, D. (ed.) (2000) *Able Underachievers*, Whurr, London.

Montgomery, D. (2002) *Helping Teachers Develop Through Classroom Observation*, David Fulton, London.

Montgomery, D. (ed.) (2003) *Gifted and Talented with SEN: Double Exceptionality*, NACE/David Fulton, London.

Montgomery, D. (2004) Double exceptionality: gifted children with SEN and what ordinary schools can do. *Gifted and Talented International*, **19** (1) 29–35.

Montgomery, D. (2007) *Spelling, Handwriting and Dyslexia*, Routledge, London.

NC (1989) *The National Curriculum*, National Curriculum Council, York.

Passow, A.H. (1992/1990) Needed research and development in teaching highly able children. *European Journal of High Ability*, **1**, 15–24.

Paul, R.W. (1990) Critical thinking in North America, in *Critical Thinking: What Every Person Needs to Know to Survive in a Rapidly Changing World* (ed. A.J.A. Binker), Sonoma State University, Sonoma, pp. 18–42.

Piaget, J. (1952) *Origins of Intelligence in Children*, 2nd edn, International Universities Press, New York.

Pickard, P.M. (1976) *If You Think Your Child Is Gifted?* Allen and Unwin, London.

Pollard, A. (1997) *Reflective Teaching in the Primary School*, 3rd edn, Cassell, London.

Race, P. (1992) *'Developing Competence'*. Professorial Inaugural Lecture Series Glamorgan, University of Glamorgan.

Raffan, J. (2003) *The Welsh National Proposals for Highly Able*. Conference Presentation, 9th ECHA Biennial Conference, Rhodes.

Rawlings, A. (ed.) (1996) *Ways and Means Today*, Kingston Friends Publication, Kingston-upon-Thames.

Renzulli, J.S. (1977) *The Enrichment Triad: A Model for Developing Defensible Programs for the Gifted and Talented*, Creative Learning Press, Mansfield Center, CN.

Renzulli, J.S. (1995) New directions for the schoolwide enrichment model, in *Nurturing Talent: Individual Needs and Social Ability* (eds M.W. Katzko and F.J. Monks), Van Gorcum, Assen, The Netherlands, pp. 162–7.

Renzulli, J.S. (2006) *The Schoolwide Enrichment Model*. European Council for High Ability Conference presentation Lahti, Finland, September.

Rogers, K.B. and Span, P. (1993) Ability grouping with gifted students: research and guidelines, in *International Handbook of Research and Development in Gifted Education* (eds K.A. Heller, F.J. Monks and A.H. Passow), Pergamon, Oxford, pp. 585–92.

Royce-Adams, R. (1977) *Developing Reading Versatility*, Rinehart and Winston, New York.

Ryan, R.M. and Deci, E.I. (2000) Intrinsic and extrinsic motivation: classic definitions and new directions. *Contemporary Educational Psychology*, **25**, 54–67.

Shayer, M. and Adey, P. (eds) (2002) *Learning Intelligence. Cognitive Acceleration Across the Curriculum from 3 to 25 Years*, Open University Press, Milton Keynes.

Swartz, R.J. and Parks, S. (1994) *Infusing the Teaching of Critical and Creative Thinking into Elementary Instruction*, Critical Thinking Press and Software, Pacific Grove, CA.

Thomas, L., Harri-Augstein, S. and Smith, M. (1984) *Reading to Learn*, Methuen, London.

TIMSS (1997) *Third International Mathematics and Science Survey*, Boston College, School of Education, Boston, MA.

TIMSS (2000) *Sixth International Mathematics and Science Survey*, Boston College, School of Education, Boston, MA.

TTA (1991) *Teacher Training Agency*, TTA, London.

Visser, J. and Rayner, S. (1999) *Emotional and Behavioural Difficulties; A Reader*, Q Ed, Birmingham.

Vygotsky, L.S. (1978) *Mind in Society*, MIT, Cambridge, MA.

Wallace, B. (2000) *Teaching the Very Able Child*, David Fulton, London.

Wallace, B., Fritton, S., Leydon, S. *et al.* (2008) *Raising the Achievement of Able, Gifted and Talented Pupils within and Inclusive School Framework*, NACE, Oxford.

6

Changing the Teaching for the Underachieving Able Child: The Ruyton School Experience

Lee Wills and John Munro

Introduction

This chapter reports an ongoing study examining the learning characteristics of underachieving, able children, together with their monitoring and suggestions for appropriate teaching and learning procedures. These children need teachers who understand the reasons why some children underachieve, so that they can encourage the children to share their feelings and to look on achievement in the most positive manner.

The sobering thought is that most observers believe that this group comprises at least 10–15% of the intellectually able:

> ... one would think that there would be a major focus upon this by professionals in the field. Nothing could be further from the truth. Instead the gifted underachievers largely have been ignored since 1965 or thereabouts (Gallagher, 1995: 414–415).

Changes in classroom practices are at the hub of reform for these children; however, changes that are made can be achieved only when the child understands the need for such change, and indeed wishes to support these changes.

A major issue for schools in this time of rapid change in education is how to

(a) help teachers keep up to date with changes in thinking;
(b) develop an understanding of how children best learn; and

Able, Gifted and Talented Underachievers, Second Edition   Edited by Diane Montgomery
© 2009 John Wiley & Sons, Ltd

(c) recognize methods of teaching in order to accommodate these changes.

Theories relating to 'how children learn most effectively' are changing. Teachers need to be aware of changes, and how to develop the ideas in their teaching. In 2000, the Curriculum and Standards Framework (CSF) was introduced to schools in Victoria, Australia, in order to accommodate new thinking in relation to the curriculum. In 2006, the CSF was replaced by the Victorian Essential Learning Standards. These teaching strategies and standards are designed to support purposeful teaching of individuals and small groups of students who have similar learning profiles, for example gifted learning disabled students. How schools approach these tasks has been supported by the Australian Government Quality Teacher Programme (AGQTP). The objectives of the AGQTP are to

- equip teachers with the skills and knowledge needed for teaching in the twenty-first century;
- provide national leadership in high priority areas of teacher professional need; and
- improve the professional standing of school teachers and leaders.

One area that is central to good teaching is how best to enrich the learning of all students. Recent newspaper and journal articles describe how some schools accelerate their most able students. An alternative perspective is to believe that all students have talents in some areas, and that the learning of all of them can be enriched. Schools that accept this second perspective will put in place a broadly based approach to teaching that takes account of individual ways of learning and that encourages the acceleration of all students. There will be a number of 'spin-offs', particularly for the group of 'underachieving able' children.

Ruyton Girls' School accepted this second perspective and was involved in an ongoing professional development activity that familiarized all of its junior school staff with recent developments in learning and how these developments could be put into practice in their teaching.

The approach, based on 'facilitating effective learning and teaching', was a programme developed by Dr John Munro at the University of Melbourne. The programme began with four sessions each of 2 hours facilitated by Dr Munro. Prior to the first session in Term 2, 1997, teachers selected a CSF topic that they intended to teach during Term 3. Throughout the course of the activity, teachers applied the ideas discussed to the development of their chosen topic. In this way, they were able to implement the ideas in their teaching immediately and could see how they needed to fine-tune them. This was important for teacher change, because research shows that the longer teachers delay before using new ideas in their teaching, the less likely they are ever to use them.

Retraining the Teachers

During the first session the teachers examined

1. what they do when they themselves learn;
2. the structure of an ideal lesson;
3. recent research on how students can be motivated or challenged to learn; and
4. the different ways in which students store and use knowledge.

The second session examined

- how students use their thinking spaces while learning;
- the different ways of learning; and
- a structure for assisting students to learn by reading.

The teachers worked on developing an understanding of the different ways in which students learn, and how they could design activities that matched these different ways of learning.

The third session had the teachers examine how students could work on and update what they had learnt by questioning what had been learnt in different ways and by applying and transferring the knowledge. They worked on activities in which students

- would use the ideas in new situations;
- take the ideas apart;
- use the ideas to help them think ahead;
- forecast and infer;

- synthesize the ideas with other ideas in different ways;
- evaluate the ideas;
- organize the ideas to achieve a specific outcome or solution; and
- use the ideas in creative ways.

Important considerations were for teachers to use open-ended tasks that encouraged further learning, and explicitly to teach students to ask various types of questions that would extend their knowledge.

The teachers also examined the different ways in which students could show what they knew and how they could communicate ideas both verbally and nonverbally. Students who preferred to learn in different ways worked on their knowledge differently, by being able to describe in words, pictures or actions how their knowledge was changing. This had strong motivational value for the students.

During the fourth session, the teachers worked on ways of helping students

- to remember ideas;
- with how they could store what they had learnt in memory;
- learn in different formats, for example cooperatively; and
- learn how to organize themselves as learners.

Finally, the teachers described the teaching units they had developed with colleagues.

This particular format for the professional development had been chosen to overcome many of the limitations of the more traditional 'one off' activity. First, it is firmly based on what was known about the most effective ways in which adults can be helped to learn to change their practice. Second, it encouraged ownership of ideas and, third, it provided teachers with time for linking their existing knowledge with contemporary theories of learning. Before each session, the teachers worked through guided reading that gave them a background to the ideas to be discussed and how they could be applied to their teaching.

The teachers then applied the ideas practically in their teaching and shared the outcomes with the group at the next meeting. Ongoing contact with Dr Munro enabled Ruyton staff to discuss ways in which the learning programme could be continued for the children. This also helped give support to new members of staff; the objective was to link the most effective combinations of learning and teaching procedures. We believe that this must benefit all children.

The teachers continued to work in collegiate groups, and these provided the forum for discussing and sharing ideas and also provided mutual support. This has also been shown to be important if teachers are to be up to date in their teaching.

Characteristics of Underachieving Students

In order to direct the teachers' attention to the needs of the able underachievers, first the characteristics of 'gifted children' needed to be identified:

> ... these students usually learn quickly and readily and see connections between existing and new ideas faster than their peers (Munro, 1996a, p. 3).

These characteristics are examined under six major headings. The list (Munro, 1996c) provided us with an insight as to the reasons why many of our able children became underachievers.

It is of major significance that gifted children prefer to work alone. They may avoid group learning situations and develop behavioural problems if directed towards closed learning situations or repetitive tasks.

Superior learning processes

Gifted children's superior learning processes enable them to

- make decisions quickly;
- keep track of several ideas at once;
- think in larger increments, skipping steps in their thinking;
- require fewer repetitions of, and less exposure to, an idea in order to learn it;
- use imagination, fantasy and humour at a high level; and
- have a well-developed memory, particularly for the areas of interest.

However, they

- may have difficulty learning in particular areas, for example rote learning, spelling, handwriting, rote recall of arithmetical information;
- may show carelessness in handwriting and other routine tasks;
- may ignore details in some areas.

Changing the Teaching for the Underachieving Able Child

Able underachievers

may become bored and frustrated if the learning pace is too slow; and they may have difficulty putting into words how they thought or solved problems because
(a) they are thinking faster than they can vocalize; or
(b) they do not believe they need to communicate to others how they think.

Learning outcomes

These students often

- have a wide general knowledge; and
- an extreme knowledge in areas of interest which is commensurate with that expected of older pupils;
- know about things of which other pupils seem unaware; and
- may demonstrate advanced vocabulary – particularly in areas of interest – and communicate ideas fluently.

Motivation to learn and learning style

These students

- are often 'self-driven' and motivated to want to know, learning spontaneously without direct teaching;

- frequently learn independently, preferring to direct their own learning, and may have difficulty in situations in which their learning is directed (authoritarian teaching contexts) and those in which their curiosity is not challenged;
- may question group learning situations and may even develop behaviour and discipline problems in more directed, closed learning contexts or in repetitive tasks;
- may rebel against conformity; and
- can concentrate for prolonged periods and show high levels of perseverance.

However, this high level of energy expenditure may lead to complications in other areas.

Interpersonal interactions

They may feel different from peers and alienated because they do not see themselves as getting the necessary positive affirmation from their peers and teachers, but do not understand why. They

- may not see their exceptional abilities as worth valuing, and may not get affirmation because they do not know how to show what they know so that it fits with the group expectations;
- may have difficulty identifying with a peer group, feeling that they have little in common with peers – that their peers may not comprehend their ideas and/or will feel that there is something wrong with them;
- have difficulty communicating with same-age peers because of interest difficulties, and with older children, who may find them emotionally immature. Often they seem 'the odd one out', and experience loneliness and isolation and do not feel part of any group;
- may not find suitable role models in the peer group;
- may 'overconform' in the peer group situation when they find social acceptance difficult. They are often sensitive to rejection by others and try to conform so that they do not seem different;
- may display heightened perceptions and sensitivities;
- may not be as carefree and easy-going as class peers, but instead are more serious;

- may be irritated by class peers who do not understand their ideas at the same depth;
- may seem to lack confidence in their interaction with their peers;
- may have difficulty understanding and valuing the learning of others;
- may have difficulty trusting others; and
- may feel for others and for events in the world, worry about children whom they see being unfairly treated, take on the problems of others and world problems as personally affecting them, and have a heightened awareness of moral values. They and their peer group need to learn to accept and value individual strengths and differences.

Self-perceptions and affective aspects of talented children learning

These children often

- have low self-esteem that restricts their preparedness to produce academically. Their self-talk is frequently more pessimistic than optimistic and they need to learn more optimistic scripts as options;
- set high (often unrealistically high) standards and goals for themselves and judge themselves harshly; and
- worry about expectations that they should be 'perfect' and yet know that they are not;
- If their giftedness or creativity is perceived to be threatened they withdraw – frequently they lack the analytic strategies necessary for dealing with the threat more constructively. They may also
  - have difficulty understanding the importance of 'risk-taking' in learning;
  - have a real sense of failure and may become school refusers;
  - be more anxious than other students, putting stress on themselves and feeling stress from others owing to unrealistic expectations;
  - be interested in consequences, the future, and so on, but may see consequences that peers do not; and
  - tend to worry, seem less self-confident, be unsure of themselves and may have difficulty resolving inner conflicts.

Uneven rates of development

These students often show uneven rates of development, with aspects of their overall functioning developing at different rates. They show 'asynchrony' in development so that they may

- present as emotionally or physically immature; and
- show specific learning disabilities in particular areas, for example rote learning, spelling, handwriting and rote recall of arithmetic information.

It is, therefore, essential to identify a model of learning that can explain these types of characteristics that will enable teachers to make decisions and develop strategies to deal with a broad range of issues related to the teaching of gifted students.

For example, contemporary teachers need to develop strategies that will equip them to implement effective teaching, assessment, management and discipline procedures that reflect the diversity of learning approaches in the class and that encompass the directions and constraints which society imposes on education.

Teaching strategies need to be student inclusive and provide students with the opportunity to see themselves making optimal progress. As discussed earlier, gifted and talented students display learning characteristics different from those of their peers and often do not match the 'gifted stereotype'. Their learning characteristics can be perplexing and frustrating to teachers. They frequently need assistance and counselling in forming functional peer interactions.

To do maximum justice to these students, teacher decisions need to be based on a sound model of learning. Helping students to acquire an understanding of learning and the ability to manage themselves as learners, which are usually seen as essential outcomes for schools as we move into the next century, can best be achieved when school staff have explicated their personal theory of learning.

Many of the problems that arise with gifted children in classes originate in teaching practices that do not take account of how these students learn. The unrealistic expectations that teachers frequently have of them, for example are reflected in the expectation that they will be 'good at academic learning across the board'.

In many school situations, it is easy to overlook the needs of some gifted and talented students and to make decisions that do not take account of how they learn. This is the perfect breeding ground to promote underachievement.

General underachievement traits

The parallels that can be drawn between this list and the earlier list for gifted and talented children must give rise to concern, if we are to prevent the number of underachieving children from growing. The traits identified are as follows:

- Low self-esteem.
- Poor performance in one or more basic skills areas: reading, writing, and mathematics.
- Daily work often incomplete or poorly done.
- Pursues projects or shows initiative in the non-school environment.
- Superior understanding and retention of concepts when interested.
- Dislikes drill work or practice exercises.
- Significant quality gap between oral and written work.
- Perfectionist, often unhappy with own work.
- Fear of failure, avoids trying new activities.
- Wide range of interests and possibly special expertise in an area of investigation and research.
- Tends to withdraw or be aggressive in the classroom.
- Exceptional memory for factual knowledge.
- Creative imagination.
- Does not work well in groups.
- Sensitive, both in perception and defensiveness.
- Tends to set unrealistic self-expectations.
- Daydreams, finds it hard to concentrate on tasks as directed by others.
- Negative school attitude.
- Resists teacher efforts to motivate or discipline behaviour in class.
- Difficulty in making or maintaining friendships.

Underachievers with spatial strengths

The following additional traits may indicate high spatial strengths:

- Early ability in puzzles and mazes.
- Sophisticated sense of humour.
- Elaborate doodler.
- Daydreamer – rich fantasy life.
- Creative thinker.
- High abstract reasoning ability.
- Keen visual memory.
- Avid TV fan.
- Loves computers – especially computer graphics.
- Highly capable in science.
- Excels in geometry.
- Grasps metaphors and analogies.
- Enjoys music.

As with all checklists, not every item applies to each individual.

Underachievers, like other children, will all have an individual profile of talents and difficulties. However, they will present a pattern that includes many of these key indicants. The above checklists were developed from various sources, mostly unnamed, which were collected and edited by Farmer (1993) for the New South Wales Association for Gifted and Talented Children.

Characteristics of a useful model of learning

Having shown the need for a foundation model of learning, what might be its characteristics? One aim of this chapter is to synthesize the learning needs of gifted and talented children with a useful model of learning.

Earlier theories of learning include:

Behaviourist theories, which see learners as passive organisms who during learning are programmed in different ways (Skinner, 1971);

Developmental theories, such as Piaget's (1952), which see learners as actively rearranging their knowledge in a predictable, predetermined way as they move along the same path;

Network-type schema models, which see learning in terms of how knowledge is organized (Norman, 1977);

Information processing models, which explain learning in terms of how information is processed (Newell and Simon, 1972);

Socio-cultural interaction models and transaction models, which explain learning in terms of the internalization of socio-cultural knowledge (Bandura, 1986);

Constructivist models, which explain learning in terms of the building of subjective models of the world (Desforges, 1998).

None of these has had a lasting effect either on general teaching and educational processes or, more particularly, on the education of the gifted and talented learners, for a number of reasons, not least because they were not classroom or teacher friendly.

A 'User-Friendly' Model of Learning

A 'user-friendly' model of learning explains gifted learning. It needs to do more than simply describe it; it needs to account for the types of learning behaviours that gifted and talented children exhibit. It explains as much as possible the 'whole-child' operation, explaining both positive and negative aspects of gifted students' learning. It should also predict particular areas of learning behaviours, and map into useful teaching strategies.

What do we mean by learning? (Munro, 1996c)

Learning involves a change or reorganization of an individual's knowledge base. It is more likely to happen when learners construct challenges or purposes for which they judge their existing knowledge to be insufficient in some way, and when they expect to achieve a level of success in the future. The goal of the learning is to deal more effectively with the challenge in the future. In other words, learning is purposeful or goal orientated; learners learn when they are motivated or have a goal for learning. The goal can range from satisfying curiosity and responding to one's own interests, to attaining a temporary goal (reaching an object in a novel way), or from solving a problem to being valued by others.

Learning can be individually or socially orientated. In looking at the learning of gifted and talented students in the present context, we are focusing more on school-based, institutional learning – that is, the learners internalizing socially or culturally determined ideas. The model of learning that we are using is developed more fully in Munro (1996a,b). It comprises two main dimensions: a socio-cultural dimension and an intra-learner dimension.

The social basis of learning

Learning is an interaction between the learner and the cultural-social groups in which it occurs. We are thus proposing a social-constructivist model; an individual's knowledge base changes within a socio-cultural context. Social processes influence people's learning in formal educational contexts in several ways. Students learn culturally determined and valued ideas, and often need to think in socially valued ways. Given the cultural origin of the ideas, the culture initiates the purpose for learning and needs to challenge the learner to 'know'. Gifted children, however, may prefer not to be 'programmed' by their culture.

In formal learning, learners need to align their experiences and interpretations with the culturally valued meanings. They need to engage in a meaning or understanding negotiation process (Voigt, 1994). They interpret ideas using their existing knowledge, try out their guesses and receive feedback for this trialling. The environment evaluates what learners display by discussing, challenging, validating or extending ideas. Learners learn to use how others respond to their displays.

The cultural-social dimension of the model of learning explains some of the difficulties many gifted students have in formal learning contexts. They construct impressions of an idea that are often qualitatively different from those of their peers. When they negotiate meaning, their peers frequently do not understand the ideas that they communicate. The feedback that gifted children receive may be distorted due to misunderstanding of the quality of the ideas by peers, who often communicate a lack of acceptance of them.

Communication, then, may lead to rejection by the group. This can lead in turn to a tension for them between how they think naturally and what they believe they are permitted to think and learn by the social group, if they are to receive positive group valuing.

Some gifted students prefer not to engage in meaning negotiation. They are less prepared to engage in group learning activities and show the outcomes of their guessing. Their earlier learning displays were not valued by the group, leading to their mistrusting it. They may see that the group does not value what they know; but they do not know how to go about getting more positive feedback. They frequently need to learn how to learn in groups and to understand how others learn.

A second aspect of the socio-cultural influence relates to the preparedness of these students to be programmed by their culture. Formal academic learning involves students learning culturally determined ideas. Students differ in their preparedness to be programmed in this way. Some expect to be programmed at school, whereas others seek to impose their own ideas on the culture. Gifted students are more likely to be in the latter group.

Students differ in their preparedness to be organized as learners. Gifted students are frequently less prepared to be organized. In addition, because their learning is more idiosyncratically orientated, they do not spontaneously encode in words what they do to learn, and often have difficulty describing how they went about learning an idea or solving a problem.

They often develop a greater susceptibility to group valuing than their peers. This is because they are more likely to receive negative feedback from peers, and they have a well-developed ability to perceive consequences a relatively long way down the line. Alternatively, they may simply withdraw from the social group and become, for a good deal of their time at school, a social isolate or 'oddity'.

These issues affect directly how we teach classes in which these students are members. It affects the opportunities we give them to negotiate meaning and their learning to give, receive and use feedback. It influences how different children perceive themselves as successful, and how learners frame up challenges for learning in different ways.

Our teaching needs to balance the learning of culturally valued ideas with individually valued ideas and more open-ended learning opportunities. Allowing some students to modify their ideas to match culturally defined ideas, as well as expecting others to internalize the culturally defined version, needs a broader range of teaching strategies. Providing greater opportunity for self-directed learning – in parallel with the opportunity to learn how to learn successfully in groups – is necessary. Helping these students create opportunities to show what they know – in ways that match their ways of learning and that increase the likelihood of group valuing – is also necessary.

Within-learner differences

In the social negotiation of meaning, different learners negotiate learning differently. Individual difference can arise in a range of ways. Students may represent their existing knowledge differently or engage in the reorganizing process in different ways. Some can communicate their ideas more easily than others. Learners may differ in their preparedness to construct challenges or to show that their existing knowledge is insufficient. In terms of a metaphor for learning at any time (see Figure 1 below), it may be proposed that:

- Learners have one or more sites for learning, in which the reorganization of existing knowledge occurs. Terms used to refer to these sites include 'thinking space' and 'short-term working memory' (Baddeley, 1990).
- The total amount of data that can be accommodated at any time in the learning sites is limited. This restriction can be interpreted in terms of thinking space and the allocation of attentional resources.
- New ideas are learnt in terms of the learners' existing knowledge.
- Learners interpret information during learning in idiosyncratic ways.
- The ideas the learner is thinking about can be coded or represented in these 'sites' in different ways; we can look at ideas in different ways.

Each code links the new ideas with what is already known in particular ways, is associated with thinking about the ideas in a particular way and delivers a different perspective on the same ideas. Ideas can be 'moved' between codes via a recoding process that brings the new code to bear on the ideas. The meanings they had in earlier codes can be retained.

Learners differ in how they act on the ideas during learning: some learners operate more analytically whereas others may operate synthetically. In any particular learning act, learners manage, control and direct their learning; they can, for example monitor progress being made during the learning, ask themselves questions about what they are learning, and so on. Our knowledge as learners affects how we learn. We tell ourselves early in learning

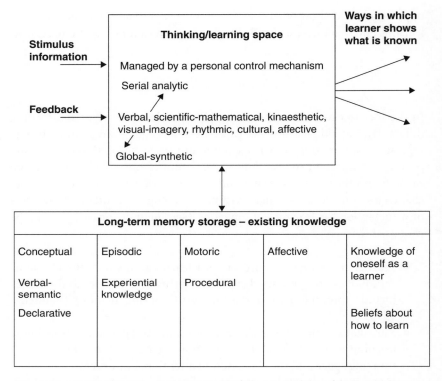

Figure 1 Diagrammatic representation of the metaphor of learning (Munro, 1996b).

how we will feel about learning the idea. The opportunity to display what has been learnt is necessary for a variety of reasons, as is the need to recognize that learners prefer to do this in different ways. We may ensure that the change in knowledge is retained, and we act on an idea in various ways to retain it.

Differences in how ideas are coded during learning

The ideas manipulated during learning need to be coded or represented in the 'sites', in forms that allow learners to think about them. Whenever we think about an idea we need to link it with other ideas, using what we already know. Our existing knowledge gives us these ways of thinking or 'thinking codes'. These codes represent what we already know about how ideas can be related or linked. Ideas can be coded or represented in different ways.

Each code involves organizing or relating the ideas in particular ways – that is, it draws attention to particular aspects of an idea. Contemporary models of cognitive processing propose two main encoding systems: verbal propositional and nonverbal imagery knowledge (Paivio, 1986). Preferences in how learners use particular thinking codes lead to cognitive styles that are dispositions in how we think.

The model presented above (Munro, 1996b) proposes that students have access to several alternative codes in which they can learn, as follows:

- *Verbal/linguistic* – knowing by using one's understanding of words and properties of language (thinking by using words, sentences and verbal propositions). This allows students to think at an advanced level using linguistic templates. They have a rich vocabulary, read and comprehend sophisticated text, engage in complex verbal discussions and debates, and reason about verbal concepts at an advanced level. They readily learn verbally referenced ideas in linguistic context, and think about ideas by discussing, arguing and debating. They may have difficulty using what they know to solve real-life problems and translating their ideas into action.
- *Scientific/mathematical code* – understanding by using abstract mathematical or scientific concepts, logic and symbols, to link ideas. This code allows students to build ideas by reasoning inductively and deductively; to look for organization and logic, analyze complex patterns and recognize order and consistency at a high level; and to make objective observations, draw conclusions and formulate sophisticated hypotheses, as well as applying general rules to particular situations.
- *Episodic/spatial or visual-imagery code* – understanding by making nonverbal images of ideas, either by processing earlier episodes or by constructing icons/templates that operate as prototypes for concepts that we have learnt. This code allows students to relate ideas using spatial or temporal properties. When used most efficiently, some students can manipulate a comparatively large number of spatial relationships – or images of episodes – at once, allowing them to synthesize high levels

of previously unrelated ideas. They 'slot' several specific pieces of information into a mental picture in unique ways. They can manipulate images by moving them around, imagining how they can change over time. This leads to high-level creative and lateral thinking.

- *Body/kinaesthetic code* – understanding by using actions to represent ideas. Learners using this code think in terms of action sequences or procedures. Some students think about action sequences in complex and sophisticated ways. They solve complex problems efficiently and elegantly using action-based comprehension.

- *Rhythmic code* – knowing by using rhythm, repetitive patterns and rhymes; learning ideas by rote or chanting. Some students develop an elaborate rhythmic knowledge that they use to identify and produce intricate and creative rhythmic pattern in music, movement and in other conceptual areas.

- *Affective/mood representation* – understanding in terms of affect, emotion, feeling or mood. Some students develop a highly differentiated and integrated mood representational system that they use to learn and understand ideas. They can recognize and respond to fine discriminations in affect or mood, can display differences in mood in a range of ways and can 'read' and respond effectively and rapidly to emotional characteristics of a context (a painting, a novel, a social interaction and so on). They can understand the factors that manage emotion (the attribution of success and failure, level of persistence, and so on).

- *Interpersonal representation* – understanding in terms of historical, social, cultural or religious knowledge. This involves ideas referenced against a network that is defined by historical, cultural or religious relationships. Cultural and religious 'logic' refers to the linking of ideas on the basis of cultural and religious belief systems. These beliefs achieve the status of propositions. These logics meet criteria that differ from those for mathematical-scientific logic, verbal-linguistic logic and episodic logic. Students from different cultures can interpret the same teaching differently. One cultural perspective may encourage unquestioning construction of the ideas as accurately as possible, whereas another may encourage questioning of the ideas as accurately as possible, and another may encourage questioning and successive approximations. Learning from a perspective that sees no gender differences in access to mathematics learning will be different from one that believes that males have a greater right to learn mathematics.

Moving Ideas between Codes

Learners need to learn how to move ideas between codes, to switch an idea from one code to another by a recoding process. This is important for gifted students. Learning situations usually provide a limited range of options for showing what one knows. Gifted students can learn how to show what they know, both in ways that fit within the constraints of the learning situation and in ways that their peers will be more likely to value.

This does not involve 'scaling down' the complexity of the idea, but rather recoding it to a form that takes account of the audience. Gradually, learners need to build an idea in one code (probably one of their preferred codes), and then switch it to another in order to show what they know in acceptable ways (Munro, 1996a,b).

Relating the ideas represented: analytic or holistic strategies

A second dimension is how the ideas are manipulated within each code, either

(a) analyzed into parts that are then linked up; or
(b) integrated with other ideas, with each idea being treated as a whole rather than being analyzed into parts.

The first type of strategy is described as 'analytic', and the second is 'synthetic' or 'holistic'. Although most learners use these strategies selectively, some use one excessively.

Gifted and talented students are more likely to use holistic than analytic-sequential strategies. They are more flexible in their thinking, and can often tolerate ambiguity and unanswered questions. Because they are often more likely to ignore or miss specific details unless these are integrated in a larger conceptual structure, they are more likely to have difficulty learning ideas taught in a sequential, rote way. They are often more able at reading comprehension than at reading words accurately, because they have the verbal reasoning knowledge necessary for high-level thinking but are less likely to engage in the analytic activities needed for learning to recognize written word patterns.

Formal teaching often assumes that students learn best by being presented with small parts of an idea at a time arranged sequentially. It supports learners using strategies that analyze ideas using criteria prescribed by the social group or culture.

Students can, of course, analyze ideas in idiosyncratic ways. When they do this, the criterion for the analysis is known only to them. Often when gifted students analyze an idea into parts subjectively, and manipulate it in a novel, creative way, they have difficulty describing what they did; they did not encode what they did in words.

When students analyze ideas into parts in the culturally recognized ways they also learn the ways of talking about the analysis, and can tell people more easily what they did. Those who prefer to use global-holistic strategies are less likely to do this, do not get positive regard for what they have learnt, and often become alienated from effective learning.

Just as each of the codes is linked with a set of thinking strategies, so the two types of manipulation or processing strategies are managed by self-instruction sequences. These are described more fully in Munro (1996a,b).

A 'management/control mechanism'

This is how learners manage or regulate their learning – that is, their metacognitive knowledge. They use this to plan how they will learn, to monitor their learning, to evaluate its effectiveness in terms of some goal or purpose, to take further strategic action if necessary, and to review their change in knowledge.

Gifted students use aspects of this control mechanism extremely effectively. Their ability to direct and regulate their learning, to plan and monitor their learning progress and to take further strategic action if necessary is obviously well developed. In fact, much of this activity by these students seems to be automatic.

Their knowledge as learners, on the other hand, and their lack of self-confidence in the group learning context can mean that on occasions they opt not to engage in learning. They perceive consequences but do not have the experience necessary to deal with this.

In summary, in this learning model, gifted learning is associated with the extremely efficient use of two or three of the codes, particularly in parallel with the use of global-synthetic strategies. Other codes may not be as well developed, and students may display gifted learning in some areas and immaturity in others. In the favoured codes, they can deal with several ideas at once because they have automatic response to these codes and give the impression of thinking synthetically or 'simultaneously' rather than sequentially.

Armed with the knowledge of the model of learning, the teachers at Ruyton Girls' School presented ideas in the range of codes discussed with Dr Munro. They designed activities that would develop an idea in each of the codes. They began with episodic knowledge of the idea, and then recoded it in a verbal-linguistic way and then in a decontextualized-action way. The example of evaporation that follows shows how it is possible to build ideas associated with evaporation in each of the codes.

Ways of Learning Using the Subject of Evaporation

Code ideas culturally, socially and historically. How has evaporation been used in history (to obtain drinking water, for refrigeration)? How is evaporation used in different communities? What are the problems? How can communities control it?

Code ideas logico-mathematically. Is there the same amount of water in a room when a dish of water evaporates? How has it changed? Same amount; change of state. What matches evaporation for solids? Why/when do things evaporate?

Code ideas verbal-linguistically. Brainstorm ideas, a conceptual map, a network map. Paraphrase, summarize text that explains evaporation. An evaporating liquid is interviewed. What would it say? Ask six hard questions about evaporation. Write a story/play about evaporation. 'Adventures of . . .' when else would you use the word evaporate? Discuss situations involving evaporation – what happens?

Code ideas affectively. What feelings would you have if you evaporated (light-headed, strung out)? How might liquids that are evaporating feel?

Code ideas visuo-spatially in episodes. Imagine, draw, collect situations in which evaporation occurs (water on a dish; clothes drying; petrol on the body of a car; vapour rising from the sea; dry ice foaming). Draw a comic strip of petrol evaporating from the body of a car. Invent useful icons for evaporation. Classify pictures of instances of evaporation.

Code ideas in actions. Make an action model of evaporation (e.g. corks flying out of a jar). Small groups of children act out gas evaporation (rising up, stretching, spreading out). Is there a reverse action to evaporation which can be enacted?

Teachers can use this type of structure

- For developing lesson plans that encourage students to encode ideas in different ways.
- To help students review the different types of activities and note how they can learn these different types of questions.

Presenting key ideas in this variety of ways allows students to learn in 'learner-friendly' contexts that take account of preferred ways of learning. Individual learning characteristics are acknowledged and accepted. It also encourages the valuing of others.

Cueing students to think about the idea in different ways

Teachers cannot control how students think about the ideas being learnt. Even if ideas are presented visually, this does not mean that the students will visualize them. Thus, one strategy is to cue them to think about an idea in particular ways.

Teaching the thinking or learning strategies associated with each code

Each code involves thinking about the ideas in particular ways, and teachers can make these explicit. Students can learn to ask the various types of question for the different codes.

Using codes selectively to achieve particular outcomes

Students can learn when it is useful to use each type of thinking, and how the different ways of thinking lead to different outcomes. They learn to match the desired outcomes of a context or task with the ways in which they need to think about it.

Switching ways of thinking about ideas

Learners need to learn how to move ideas between codes themselves, to switch an idea from one code to another. Gradually they need to learn

- to build an idea in one code (probably one of their preferred codes) and then switch it to another in order to show what they know in acceptable ways;
- to understand ideas better by building them in a preferred code and then converting them to the code in which they were presented.

Learning to look at an idea from different perspectives

Once learners have explored some core ideas in different codes, and have learnt some of the thinking strategies linked with each code and practised recoding ideas, they can practise looking at an idea from different angles. This will provide a richness and complexity to their understanding of an idea that it otherwise would not have. In the next example, the topic of 'flight' was undertaken by Year 4 at Ruyton Girls' School.

The class teachers worked in teams creating a learning environment that encouraged all the children to become involved. They were aware of the difficulty in learning caused by a mismatch between teaching and preferred ways of learning.

Example: flight – ways of learning

Culturally, socially, historically

- Key milestones in history.
- Timelines from Zeppelin balloons to Mir space station.
- Guest speaker aviators of importance.
- Excursion to the Royal Australian Air Force (RMF) museum.

Logico-mathematically

- Logo writer.
- Graphing Mach speed of various planes.
- Calculating differences in flight speeds over varying distances.
- Comparing speeds of various aircraft.

Verbally linguistically

- Brainstorm interest words to produce concept maps.
- Read and write related poems and stories.
- Examine journal records of the RMF museum and knowledge gained.
- Undertake 'jigsaw' activity (Lerner, 1971) on five pilots.
- Read stories about the Wright brothers and Amelia Ehrhart, for example.

Affectively

- Why has man always wanted to fly?
- How do you feel about flying?
- What have we learnt?

Visuo-spatially

- Imagine – draw situations of flight.
- Drama – flight machines; fighter planes.
- See video on flight.
- Make models of spacecraft, early aircraft.

Actions

- Design and make planes, gliders, whirligigs, aerofoils.
- Make balloons and test.
- Make and test planes and gliders using a variety of materials.

Mismatches   These can lead to

- difficulty in learning;
- high levels of frustration and anxiety;

- behavioural and discipline problems; and
- ultimately alienation from school.

Teachers too can explore the links between their learning styles and teaching styles and the learning styles of students who learn most or easily with them, and use this to broaden their teaching styles. Students can also be encouraged to recognize mismatches between teaching and learning styles, and explore ways of managing constructively.

Give a range of ways of showing what students know

Students who prefer to learn *visually* can record ideas in pictures and then convert them to symbols or words; those who prefer to learn *linguistically* can talk to themselves about ideas before they convert them to symbols; those who prefer to learn *kinaesthetically* can act out ideas before they write or speak about them. (They may try to avoid being seen to do the actions but they need to see that they are acceptable and will help learning.)

Help students monitor how they learn best and to understand and broaden their range of learning strategies

Key ways include:

- Encouraging them to focus on what they do when they are solving tasks and to talk about what they say to themselves, and so on.
- Students can be reminded to use their preferred strategy.
- Making them aware of additional strategies.
- Having them try out new strategies, observe their effectiveness and consciously add them to their set of learning strategies.
- Having them decide whether and when they might use the strategy in the future. They can keep a list of 'things to tell myself when I do . . .', writing down the strategies that have worked, and adding to it.

Verbalizing 'mental actions' makes them more 'concrete' and easier to recall, analyze and modify.

Storing information in long-term memory

Remembering ideas long term involves

- storing information in memory by linking it to knowledge already there; and
- retrieving it by gradually reconstructing information.

Types of long-term memory and different forms of storage involve storing ideas in terms of their meaningful relationships to other ideas, and storing ideas in nonverbal ways (episodic memory), in action sequences and in emotions.

A sequence of self-instructional strategies for storing an idea in long-term verbal-semantic memory

1. Describe the main ideas as concisely as possible.
2. Relate these ideas to the existing knowledge base. What do these ideas remind me of ? How are they like/different from things I have already learnt?
3. Draw a picture of the main ideas, or use a concrete model of them, showing how ideas are related.
4. Draw a semantic map of these ideas.
5. Describe when the ideas might be used in the future.

Summary and Conclusions

There are clear implications for learning in the content areas, and in displaying what one knows. In writing an essay, for example learners using analytic-sequential strategies are more likely to sequence the ideas in predictable, conventional ways that they have learnt. Those using global-holistic strategies are more likely to sequence the ideas in less predictable ways. An English teacher whose preference is for the analytic, is more likely to find sequential organization easier to read. However, a teacher whose preference is for the sequencing of ideas in ways that have not previously been taught is more likely to value the organization displayed by the students using global-holistic strategies. Generally, teachers and students operate from their perspective unconsciously.

The theme of this chapter is the need for the inclusion of learning criteria in the implementation of teaching activities for all students and a 'learning dimension' in the curriculum. This is not about adding to the curriculum, but rather is about examining ways of implementing it according to demonstrably sound learning principles.

Ten years on, since the implementation of the project, it is encouraging to report that teachers at Ruyton Girls' School continue to pursue the programme with their initial enthusiasm intact. Involvement of the students in their own and their groups' exploration across the core study areas, together with the way in which they have grown to value the participation and successes of their peers, has created an inspirational learning environment.

The areas of professional learning, AGQTP activities, mentioned earlier have focused on

- developing knowledge and skills in successful contemporary pedagogies to better meet the needs of students;
- developing knowledge and skills within and across subject-specific domains such as Information and Communication Technology and e-learning;
- supporting embedded professional learning as an integral aspect of daily work with the school;
- developing the knowledge and skills to design and implement data collection tools, and to analyze and evaluate the data to improve teacher practice and student outcomes;
- supporting teachers as members of learning teams with the school and as members of learning communities.

In summary, it is exciting to see our teachers at all levels and disciplines meeting periodically to discuss areas of pedagogy, and to participate in projects designed to examine their practice.

References

Baddeley, A.D. (1990) *Human Memory: Theory and Practice*, London Education Institute, London.

Bandura, A. (1986) *Social Foundations of Thought and Action: A Social and Cognitive Theory*, Prentice Hall, Englewood Cliffs.

Desforges, C. (1998) Learning and teaching: Current views and perspectives, in *Directions in Educational Pasychology* (ed. D. Shorrocks-Taylor), Whurr, London, pp. 5–18.

Farmer, D. (ed.) (1993) *Gifted Children Need Help? A Guide for Parents and Teachers*, Australian Association for Gifted Education, Strathfield.

Gallagher, J. J. (1995) *Teaching the Gifted Child*, 5th edn, Allyn and Bacon, Boston.

Lerner, J. (1971) *The Jigsaw Classroom*, Houghton Mifflin, Boston.

Munro, J. (1996a) *A Gifted Students' Learning: Basing the Teaching of Gifted Students on a Model of Learning*, Educational Assistance, Melbourne.

Munro, J. (1996b) *Social Constructivist and Information Processing: A Teacher Friendly Model of Learning*, Educational Assistance, Melbourne.

Munro, J. (1996c) *A Learning Base for Education of the Gifted and Talented Students, Seminar Series Paper No 56*, IARTV, Melbourne.

Newell, A. and Simon, H.A. (1972) *Human Problem Solving*, Prentice Hall, Englewood Cliffs.

Norman, D.A. (1977) Notes towards a complex theory of learning, in *Cognitive Psychology and Instruction* (eds A.M. Lesgold, J.W. Pellegrini, S.D. Fokkema and R. Glaser), Plenum, New York.

Piaget, J. (1952) *The Origins of Intelligence in Children*, International Universities Press, New York.

Paivio, A. (1986) *Mental Representations*, Oxford university Press, Oxford.

Skinner, B.F. (1971) *Beyond Freedom and Dignity*, Pelican Books, London.

Voigt, J. (1994) Negotiation of mathematical meaning and learning mathematics. *Educational Studies in Mathematics*, **26**, 275–98.

II

Identifying and Making Provision for Different Groups of Underachievers

Understanding and Overcoming Underachievement in Women and Girls – A Reprise

Carrie Winstanley

In the original edition of Able Underachievers, Lorraine Wilgosh's (2000) chapter on women and girls ended with the following paragraph:

> In conclusion, we must examine cautiously approaches which make the assumption that girls must be changed rather than recognising the need for educational and societal changes (Briskin and Coulter, 1992). Encouraging girls to succeed in mathematics is valuable, but not if it devalues other options. We must expand the options for individuals, supporting all individuals' learning preferences and styles. We must focus on changing and improving society, moving away from male-dominated structures, toward greater valuing of caring and connection over power and hierarchy (Kimball, 1994).

Almost a decade later, despite attempts to address these concerns, the need for change has not diminished. The focus of this chapter is predominantly on the Western context, where most girls are lucky enough to have the opportunity to attend school and live relatively free lives. The issues facing girls and women in other countries are very different, where daily life is dominated by poverty, war, cultural restrictions, religious dogma and political instability, more basic concerns need addressing before girls and women are able to express their true abilities.

The remit of this book is much narrower, however, and space and words are limited to a focus on the practical actions that can be taken by the intended audience. This chapter will initially consider the current facts about girls' achievement, and the extent to which the gender gap has or has not closed. Barriers to girls' achievement will then be considered, together

Able, Gifted and Talented Underachievers, Second Edition   Edited by Diane Montgomery
© 2009 John Wiley & Sons, Ltd

with suggestions for helping to lift these in the school context, allowing for more favourable conditions and outcomes.

The Nature of the Gender Gap and the Stereotype of the Gifted Girl

In recent years, there has been considerable concern about the plight of boys in our schools, and the role and development of men in wider society. From glancing at the popular press, it would appear that girls and women have caught up and even overtaken boys and men in terms of examination results and attainment in general. At times, the coverage of girls' improvements has been 'hysterical' (Francis, 2000: p. 8) and coverage has verged on apportioning girls with blaming for their success: 'girls' improvements are often presented in the media as having been at the expense of boys' (ibid: p. 10).

Even a cursory trawl through the headline opinion pieces in the popular and well-regarded educational press (Times Educational Supplement) reveals a certain stance. From a selection of more than 30 articles from 2005 to 2007, the following titles are listed as items about school and gender. The first five concern boys and the last two are about girls. The emotive language is typical of the media coverage of this topic; in fact this selection is relatively tame, but note how boys are presented in such a way as to elicit sympathy that contrasts with the focus on girls' bad behaviour.

1. 'Official: We fail white working class boys' (23 Nov '07, Mansell, W.).
2. 'New guidance seeks to boost boys' progress' (19 Oct '07, Stewart, W. and Ward, H.).
3. 'Rescuing the lost boys' (12 Jan '07, Abrams, F.).
4. 'Boys falter at English and fail to narrow gap' (15 Sep '06, Legg, J.).
5. 'Boys fail to talk way into top set' (07 Oct '05, Slater, J.).
6. 'In yer face and yer classroom!' (01 Dec '06, Passmore, B.).
7. 'There's a bad girl on the rise' (18 Aug '06, Doyle, J.) (www.tes.co.uk).

There have certainly been many improvements for girls in education, but the media's knee-jerk response is often overly simplistic; a look at the facts is revealing. In the United Kingdom, at the earlier stages of education, girls are performing better than boys and by the ages of 11–14 (Key Stage 3) the attainment differential is 13%. However by the time they reach higher education, this has almost halved, dropping to only 7%. The workplace is more starkly contrasted, with the following pay differentials:

> up to 39 years – women earn 6.6% less than men;
>   by their 40s, women earn 18.3% less than men (Office of National Statistics, 2006).

Freeman's (2003) research on gifted girls reinforces this, whilst contrasting this apparent UK shift in gender fortune with the situation in the United States, where girls have not been as successful. She notes that some of the targeted and specific strategies seem to have made a difference, citing changes in the curriculum combined with more focused inspections as key reasons for this improvement. Sustaining the success into womanhood is more problematic however:

> Although this managed change in gender equality of opportunity in schools is seen to be highly effective, female school advantage has yet to make a significant difference in the workplace (Freeman, 2003, p. 202).

This disquiet is echoed by Francis (2000):

> [Hence] it is important to point out that although media reports tend to present boys as being disadvantaged in terms of school achievement, there is no evidence to suggest that this has affected their future career prospects compared with women working in similar areas (Francis, 2000, p. 9).

In Germany, a review of pupils' achievement found that 'things actually have changed and a general convergence of boys and girls can be observed' (Schober, Reimann and Wagner, 2004). The paper set out to compare high school students (10th grade) and in the title they reflect current views on the issue: 'Is research on gender-specific underachievement in gifted girls an obsolete topic? New findings on an often discussed issue'. They found that in regular settings, differences are equally distributed but in specifically gifted programmes, girls do better than boys. Despite this, they note the following:

> Nevertheless, for both settings [gifted and non-gifted] lower self-confidence
> in the math self-concept can be observed among the girls. [. . .] it also became
> clear that some decisive differences – especially on behavioural levels – still
> exist (Schober, Reimann and Wagner, 2004, p. 43).

It seems that more able girls face the challenge of gradually diminishing
self-esteem as they grow from late childhood to early adolescence. In contrast to girls not identified as gifted, they demonstrate lower self-confidence
in a range of measures including their own abilities and their relationships at school (Gurian, 2001; Kerr, no date). Many of these issues reflect
the enduring stereotype of the gifted girl that still dominates many teachers' perceptions. Back in 1982, Gilligan identified that girls tend to find
a competitive structure intimidating and isolating and are inclined to assume a caring ethic, rather than adopting more masculinist competitive
and single-minded characteristics (Gilligan, 1982). Although, many have
argued against this depiction of females and things have moved on in some
ways, there is still a sense that the more 'male' traits are unsuitable when
expressed by girls. Of course, there is ample evidence that girls can be strong
competitors; their success in music and sports for example, attests to these
qualities. However, girls are still criticized for being too verbal, too intense
and too driven. Defying the accepted stereotype can lead to embarrassment,
shame and an attempt to mask their abilities, since revealing them brings
with it the risk of being perceived as deviant (Noble, 1994).

The UK government has attempted to crystallize its attempts to equal-
ize opportunities for girls, boys, women and men through introducing the
'gender equality duty' to be observed by all public authorities (Equal Opportunities Commission). This came into force in 2007 (7 April) and places a
requirement on English and Welsh schools to promote equality proactively
for all, and aims to eliminate sexual discrimination and harassment. The initiative relates to the Every Child Matters agenda (DfES, 2003), and should be
linked with general efforts to raise standards and meet key policy outcomes.

Just as this legislation is established, studies are starting to reveal that a
more nuanced approach is needed if real change is to be effected. One example of this is a project that revealed social class to be the major determinant
of success, more significant than either gender or ethnicity (Skelton, Francis
and Valkanova, 2007). Such findings reinforce the importance of avoiding
oversimplification and eschewing basic gender-based assumptions (such as
the notion that a particular pedagogy or subject will interest one gender
more than the other).

This research suggests the right way forward [. . .] is to challenge stereotypes about boys and girls, rather than taking the unshakable view that they have different learning styles (Skelton, Francis and Valkanova, 2007, reported at www.eoc.org.uk).

Because society gives out the message that being a girl means not behaving or liking the same subjects or having the same attitudes as boys (and vice versa), then gaps in achievement are inevitable (Skelton, Francis and Valkanova, 2007, p. 24, Para 3.7).These researchers analyzed England's 2006 Key Stage 2 results (11-year-olds) and found that whilst girls significantly outperform boys in English, disadvantaged girls trail behind their wealthier male peers, and that *social class is a bigger factor* in achievement than gender or ethnicity.

Overall, the performance of girls in schools has generally improved as a result of a heightened awareness of certain needs, but the reported sharp dichotomy between the genders is an outdated and clumsy reading of a complex situation. Whilst some of the strategies have met with success, they are insignificant in terms of general improvements for women within broader society and any school-based gains seem to be quickly negated once pupils are in the workplace. Kerr notes that despite improved academic performance from girls in some subjects, 'prescribed gender role behaviours continue to hold the power to bias education and research, and to restrict the psychological and life choices of gifted girls and boys, men and women' (2000: no page).

Asking if the gender gap has closed, is perhaps too simple a question. It is of more value to consider what is preventing success and how best to foster achievement.

Barriers to Achievement

A useful summary of the aspects that affect the development of gifted girls' abilities is Reis, 2005 model of 'talent realization in women'. She highlights three key initial factors:

- Abilities: such as cognitive abilities and above average potential;
- Personality: characteristics including determination, courage, intensity and so on;
- Environment: one's family support and personal relationships.

These aspects all feed into self-esteem, the development of the self-concept and the belief and the desire to develop one's talent with a sense of purpose. The last layer of the model is the realization of talent in women in a range of pursuits including the arts, research, social causes, maternal and family contexts, science, business, music and so on. This way of investigating the realization of talent can help teachers see where girls might be vulnerable, and fill in the gaps where a lack of resilience or support will negatively affect optimum development.

Similarly, although they are interrelated, it can be useful to distinguish between internal and external factors affecting development in order to tailor assistance more effectively. Most of the following discussion (internal and external barriers) is taken from general gifted education literature in which many writers make very similar points with only slight variations. For ease of reading, the ideas as text (and not punctuated throughout by lists of names), with the exception of a few specific concepts, the authors are listed here, rather than each point being multiply referenced: Eby and Smutny (1990), Freeman (2003), Jolly (2005), Kerr (2000), Noble, Subotnik and Arnold (1999), Reis (1995, 2005), Silverman (1993, 1998), Smutny (1998) and Subotnik and Arnold (1995).

Internal barriers – psychological factors

'Feminine modesty' often leads girls to attribute any success to luck rather than innate ability. Despite their excellent achievements, they can be blind to these accomplishments and if they exhibit habitual or occasional poor performance, they credit this to low intelligence, whereas boys explain their failure as bad luck or 'having an off day'.

Socially astute able girls often express ambivalence toward their abilities, recognizing that they may need to make a choice between being popular and being able. This can result in downplaying their ideas and abilities. They tend to avoid displays of outstanding intellectual prowess, preferring more acceptable ways to conform to their peer group. In these instances, abilities they could be using to develop talents are wasted on trying to modify the expectations of other people. It is also considered negative to be seen as too bookish or scholarly, for fear of social isolation.

Girls may actively avoid any kind of comparison with other people to avoid causing another person distress. They view any kind of comparison or competition as negative, since it must result in someone winning and someone losing. Neither option is easy; winners feel uncomfortable and like a fraud, while the loser is deficient and a failure. Where gifted girls deliberately suppress their talents in order to please others, the resulting fear of success is known as the 'Horner effect'.

Research consistently shows that gifted girls' confidence steadily decreases as they progress through school, and this is likely to be due to their acute sensitivity where even casual negative comments can have unforeseen devastating effects. Repeated negative reactions are internalized into feelings of inferiority. A sense of resignation can result, demonstrated through fear of engagement in tasks and in apathy. A different response, but just as negative, is a neurotic kind of perfectionism, rather than the normal level of perfectionism, which can be a typical approach to work for many gifted people. When it becomes a neurosis however, there is a fixation on making mistakes and the pupils become so anxious they are unable even to make a start on a task or a contribution to a group through debilitating fear and anxiety. Some gifted girls even worry about having made errors that they have identified and corrected before submitting work. The very fact that they made a mistake is enough for them to consider their work a failure, despite the pass grade. This rather unhealthy overemphasis on a flawless process seems to be confined to girls; boys tend to focus on the product and worry less about these passing issues.

Even when girls succeed, however, there are further potential internal pressures, such as the 'impostor phenomenon'. Here, the girl feels a need to justify any measure of achievement as it contradicts both personal and social expectations. Accomplishments are attributed to luck, or to some tendency to leniency or even error on behalf of their assessor.

Qualities such as caring and nurturing are traditionally ascribed to females, and this assignation can conflict with the kinds of personality traits that are more likely to assure success, such as personal drive and ambition. In these cases, where a girl expresses talents that could lead to social 'feminine' professions such as nursing or teaching, she builds a picture of herself in these caring roles. She is unable to project an idea of a more 'masculine' career, even if she has the requisite interests, propensities and abilities, with traits such as single-mindedness and intense focus.

Many girls face far-reaching dilemmas about how to prioritize their lives. The conflict between either developing a career or nurturing a family is a very real long-term practical problem. Numerous women do manage to juggle both successfully, but commonly express a sense of frustration that neither role can have their full attention. It can be that as girls grow, different circumstances provide solutions to these dilemmas, such as the end or start of a significant relationship, a change in management at work or the relief of financial pressures. Conditions may worsen or improve; either way, the complexity of these issues are likely to affect most women, young women in particular, sometimes rendering them unable to make decisions, leading them to defer their choices to the will of a partner or leave their life course entirely to fate. This may not be negative, but it is certainly a risky strategy.

Women often learn to take second place to their partners and their children, accepting this as inevitable. For example, in ex-patriot communities, women who move around the globe, with their main role as supporting a partner with an international career are known as 'trailer spouses'. Many a high profile divorce case reports the sacrifice of a woman's career in favour of caring for her children and husband. Colloquially, this is sometimes referred to as 'burnt toast syndrome'; a reference to the likelihood of the mother ending up with the one piece of toast that is burnt, not wanting to give it to their child or partner, preferring, instead, to settle for second best.

External barriers – society and the home

Society's role in the image of intelligent girls continues to be pervasive. Men dominate politics, the arts, science, business, sport, religion, and are the main figureheads of most public institutions even when the rest of the workforce is predominantly female, such as in schools and health provision. As a result, successful female role models who defy stereotype are still a minority. Despite a genuine increase in opportunities for girls, and the acceptance of many successful women, advertising, the print and visual media, even literature, and certainly general attitudes, doggedly defer to outdated, two-dimensional portraits of women. The overwhelming presentation of both girls and women conforms to one extreme of a spectrum of 'types', either careerist or maternal, earnest or frivolous, independent or delicate, cold or endearing, intelligent or sexually alluring, but rarely a complex melange of these qualities. This leaves girls with less than adequate visions for their developing identities.

Along with this is the persistent view that women are less able than men, and that their success comes from factors other than their own abilities. Sometimes, there are questions over whether they even merit their own accomplishments. This is also seen in school where the shift away from examinations and move toward coursework is often considered to favour the more plodding abilities of girls over the dynamic abilities of boys. Some critics have described schools (particularly primary and early years) as increasingly feminine environments, and they point to the dearth of male role models in education. This is also presumed to favour girls. Agendas such as personalized learning (introduced to UK schools by the DfES in 2004) emphasize collaborative group work and ongoing dialogic assessment, both viewed as beneficial to girls. As a result, increased success can be explained away by girls' apparent advantages in the school system and need not be anything to do with their own talents or efforts.

In the home, girls frequently have more domestic responsibilities than their male siblings, and sometimes more than any present male adults. This can interfere with schoolwork, and reinforce the conflict felt between the nurturing and studious aspects of the girl's persona. In many families, sometimes for reasons of necessity, sometimes out of unthinking habit or perhaps a narrow perspective, stereotyped gender functions are reinforced, making it difficult for girls to challenge traditional and potentially restrictive roles. As role models and guardians, parents' views on how girls are expected to behave are also vital and together with the extended family, they set standards for their daughters. Girls learn when to be restrained and when it is seemly to speak out, what clothes they should wear and how they should present themselves. They acquire manners and develop habits that are appropriate to their gender and build an identity as a daughter, granddaughter, niece, sister, aunt and so on. Gifted girls are likely to challenge more traditional roles, and this can result in family conflict.

The opinions and esteem of parents have a profound effect on children and this is amplified when they are gifted, particularly prone to sensitivity. It is not only verbal comments that pass on messages, but behaviours and non-verbal interactions, such as instances of perceived unfairness in how siblings are treated, inconsistent discipline and shifting boundaries of freedoms and responsibilities. Longitudinal studies show that memories of disapproving comments from parents can sometimes preoccupy gifted girls for the rest of their lives, stubbornly resurfacing as reinforcers of a brittle and negative self-image.

Ironically, harmful effects can arise from too much praise almost as easily as harsh criticism. Assuming that everything comes easily to a child who has exhibited a positive string of achievements can lead to increased anxiety at the possibility of disappointing their parents, through a drop in quality of performance. This is most likely to occur when girls who are already successful in one area, branch out to learn something new. They are accompanied by an expectation that they will be able to adapt their abilities with ease, and may find that despite being novices, they are instructed less rigorously than other pupils and they are somehow expected to bridge resulting knowledge gaps by themselves. Offhand comments like 'oh, this will be so easy for you, with your talent' can unwittingly create excessive pressure. It is difficult to strike the balance between offering encouragement and causing stress, but if this is misjudged too often, children can possibly be pushed into becoming timid and risk averse.

A further lifespan barrier to success that affects many women is the poor choice of partners. Although many gifted women have rich and fulfilling enduring relationships, longitudinal studies and interviews with accomplished women reveal that it can be difficult to find a partner who is willing to accept a relationship in which their own talents and gifts may well be overshadowed by a gifted woman's abilities. The habit of playing down achievements can result from wanting to avoid a sense of competition with a potential partner. Within the typical heterosexual model, society is more accepting than ever of scenarios where the woman is the main bread win-ner, but this remains an exception rather than the rule, and even where partnerships are largely between men and women of similar abilities and wage-earning potential, the default position is for household chores and childcare to be predominantly the woman's domain.

Career issues are also problematic for women in various fields of work. Many professions lack parity of pay, and the glass ceiling is very much in evidence. The main obstacle to career excellence for countless gifted women continues to be the unwillingness or inability of employers to provide family-friendly working practices. Flexible job options are ever-increasing, but the costs of childcare often make staying at home the only realistic option.

Improving Education for Girls

A subtle approach is needed in order to facilitate a better school experience for gifted girls. Those involved with supporting pupils need to move on from simple arguments about which gender is winning the race to be best at school and directly address girls' needs. Myriad studies have investigated the differences between how teachers interact with pupils, and it is repeatedly shown that girls receive far less reinforcement than boys, both in class and through written and oral feedback. Boys vocally dominate the classroom and highly verbal, curious able girls who enjoy debate are seen as aggressive or unfeminine by their teachers (e.g. Sadker and Sadker, 1994).

Girls are considered to be more competent in creative writing and less good at 'logical' subjects. Almost 25 years ago, Cooley, Chauvin and Karnes (1984) revealed that male teachers viewed female pupils as more emotional, more highly strung, more gullible, less imaginative, less curious, less inventive, less individualistic and less impulsive than males. This was reinforced by Arnold (1995) and Pajares (1996), who both found that teachers tend to ascribe high ability more often to boys than to girls. They also seem to cling to the common gender stereotypes that boys are innately more able than girls, and that when they match male success it must be the hard won result of blood, sweat and tears. Fennema *et al.* (1990) report that teachers attributed boys' success to ability for 58% of the time, but this was only cited for 33% of the girls' achievements.

The issue of teachers underlining these prejudices remains a concern, but increasing practical support is now available, partly as a result of the gender equality duty. There is still some way to go, as identified by Skelton, Francis and Valkanova (2007):

> The proposal set out here is that schools adopt a holistic framework to tackle gender stereotypes in achievement. [. . .] studies were undertaken with schools, teachers and pupils who were actively engaged in deconstructing gender stereotypes and raising achievement [. . .]. We have [. . .] given some examples of how and where teachers might pick up on events and use these with pupils in order to break down gender stereotypes. At the same time, we recognise that there is an evident lack of classroom resources and materials for teachers to draw on and recommend the development of such helpful materials (Skelton, Francis and Valkanova, 2007, p. 63).

Outdated opinions about subjects that are more appropriate for boys or girls persist in many schools, colleges and universities, and these views are bolstered by derisive comments from friends and family. Girls are often encouraged towards 'soft' subjects and although widespread strategies have been introduced to redress the balance, many careers remain steadfastly dominated by one of the genders. For example, in the United States, Kerr and Robinson (2004) noted that:

[. . .] males still outnumber female graduates in engineering and the physical sciences by two to one. Despite efforts to increase the number of women in these majors, women are still drastically underrepresented as compared to men (Kerr and Robinson, 2004, p. 86).

In the United Kingdom, there have been various schemes designed to meet the perceived differences in boys' and girls' needs. These have also met with mixed results. Skelton *et al.* find that:

[. . .] the strategies recommended have been divisive and often counterproductive in terms of their emphasis on gender *differences* and give the impression that all that was needed was to treat the two sexes as separate, homogenous groups (Skelton, Francis and Valkanova, 2007, p. 62).

Gavin and Reis (2003) have investigated some ideas that *do* work specifically to encourage gifted mathematicians, and these include a supportive learning environment with single-sex learning opportunities appealing to the strengths of females as motivators. They also recommend activities that are directly relevant to girls, creating a challenging curriculum and providing female mentors. Other recommendations include the clustering of girls with aptitudes for certain subjects within a mixed-ability class in order to boost their confidence, and provide a safety net for speaking out and admitting to interest and ability in the subject.

Career planning should be adjusted to dispel myths of having to make irreversible choices between profession or family. If gifted girls engage in useful career planning, they will be able to consider the possibilities of incorporating interruptions and delays for child rearing into their plans, or at least think about their potential options. Through thinking about the future, girls must be helped to build autonomy and resilience as well as accepting the likely ambiguity with which they will have to cope in the wider world.

Summary of Support Tactics

Key suggestions to help gifted girls become successful women can be summarized as listening to their views and thoughts, and dealing sensitively with their needs. Right through from early identification of girls' abilities, educational acceleration or the provision of stimulating and challenging tailored programmes will help encourage girls to take credit for their own successes and come to understand their gifts and talents. Improved resources and materials must be provided to recognize and reflect the valuable contribution of women across all aspects of society.

Like-minded peers should be sought out to foster friendships, and positive role models of successful women should be made available, including women whose key life role is as a mother (see Paule, 2007 for some media images). Every attempt should be made to avoid gender-role stereotyping and fathers, brothers, grandfathers and uncles are important for the redistribution of family responsibilities, as well as for encouraging high aspirations. Formal and informal mentoring opportunities should be provided, and when the family cannot or will not make efforts to help their girls, the school and wider community must rise to the challenge.

All girls need an ongoing support system and for gifted girls this must be very sensitive, especially where they are vulnerable, with an urgent need to build confidence and to develop independence and resilience through appropriate risk-taking. Although, there are still many aspects of school, home and society that act as barriers to girls and women, there have been significant improvements in opportunities for females to make their mark and live full and exciting lives. While there is no room for complacency in the battle to increase female life chances, prospects for gifted girls equipped with robust coping strategies, determination and an open mind, have never looked better.

References

Arnold, K.D. (1995) *Lives of Promise*, Jossey-Bass, San Francisco.

Briskin, L. and Coulter, R. (1992) Feminist pedagogy: Challenging the normative. *Canadian Journal of Education*, **17** (30), 247–63.

Cooley, D., Chauvin, J. and Karnes, F. (1984) Gifted females: A comparison of attitudes by male and female teachers. *Roeper Review*, **6**, 164–67.

DfES. (2003) *Every Child Matters*, HMSO, Norwich (available at:http://www.everychildmatters.gov.uk/publications).

DfES. (2004) *A National Conversation about Personalised Learning*, DfES, London.

Eby, J. and Smutny, J.F. (1990) *A Thoughtful Overview of Gifted Education*, Longman, New York.

Equal Opportunities Commission. http://www.eoc.org.uk/genderduty 11 April 2008.

Fennema, E., Peterson, P.L., Carpenter, T.P. and Lubinski, C.A. (1990) 'Teachers' attributions and beliefs about girls, boys and mathematics. *Educational Studies in Mathematics*, **21**, 55–69.

Francis, B. (2000) *Boys, Girls and Achievement*, RoutledgeFalmer, London.

Freeman, J. (2003) Gender differences in gifted achievement in Britain and the US. *Gifted Child Quarterly*, **47** (3), 202–11.

Gavin, M.K. and Reis, S.M. (2003) Helping teachers to encourage talented girls in mathematics. *Gifted Child Today*, **26** (1), 32–44.

Gilligan, C. (1982) *In a Different Voice: Psychological Theory and Women's Development*, Harvard University Press, Cambridge, MA.

Gurian, A. (2001) *Gifted Girls – Many Gifted Girls, Few Eminent Women: Why?* accessed via http://www.aboutourkids.org 11 April 2008.

Jolly, J. (2005) The woman question: An historical overview of the education of gifted girls, in *Teaching and Counselling Gifted Girls* (eds S.K. Johnsen and J. Kendrick), Prufrock Press Inc., Waco, pp. 3–8.

Kerr, B. and Robinson Kurpius, S.E. (2004) Encouraging talented girls in math and science: Effects of a guidance intervention. *Journal of High Ability Studies*, **15**, 85–102.

Kerr, B. (2000) *Gender and Genius* Keynote speech to the national curriculum networking conference, College of William and Mary, Arizona State University, March 7, accessed viahttp://www.davidsoninstitute.org 11 April 2008.

Kerr, B. (no date) *Gender and Giftedness*, accessed via http://www.courses .ed.asu.edu/gender April 2007.

Kimball, M. (1994) The worlds we live in: Gender similarities and differences. *Canadian Psychology*, **35**, 388–404.

Noble, K.D. (1994) *The Sound of a Silver Horn: Reclaiming the Heroism in Contemporary Women's Lives*, Fawcett Columbine, New York.

Noble, K.D., Subotnik, R.F. and Arnold, K.D. (1999) To thine own self be true, a new model of female talent development. *Gifted Child Quarterly*, **43** (4), 140–49.

Office of National Statistics (2006) http://www.statistics.gov.uk 4 April 2008.

Pajares, F. (1996)Self beliefs in academic settings. *Review of Educational Research*, **66**, 543–78.

Paule, M. (2007) http://www.smartgirls.tv/ 11 April 2008.

Reis, S.M. (1995) Talent ignored, talent diverted: The cultural context underlying giftedness in females. *Gifted Child Quarterly*, **39** (3), 162–70.

Reis, S.M. (2005) Feminist perspectives on talent development: A research-based conception of giftedness in women, in *Conceptions of Giftedness*, 2nd edn (eds R.J. Sternberg and J.E. Davidson), Cambridge University Press, Cambridge, pp. 217–45.

Sadker, M. and Sadker, D. (1994) *Failing at Fairness: How America's Schools Cheat Girls*, Charles Scribner's Sons, New York.

Schober, B., Reimann, R. and Wagner, P. (2004) Is research on gender-specific underachievement in gifted girls an obsolete topic? New findings on an often discussed issue.*High Ability Studies*, **15** (1), 43–62.

Silverman, L.K. (1993) *Counselling the Gifted and Talented*, Love, Denver.

Silverman, L.K. (1998) Personality and learning styles of gifted children, in *Excellence in Educating Gifted and Talented Learners* (ed. J. VanTassel-Baska), Love, Denver, pp. 29–65.

Skelton, C., Francis, B. and Valkanova, Y. (2007) *Breaking Down the Stereotypes: Gender and Achievement in Schools*, Equal Opportunities Commission, London, http://www.eoc.org.uk 5 March 2008.

Smutny, J.F. (1998) *Gifted Girls*, Phi Delta KappaEducational Foundation, Bloomington, IN.

Subotnik, R.F. and Arnold, K.D. (1995) Passing through the gates: Career establishment of talented women scientists. *Roeper Review*, **18** (1), 55–61.

Wilgosh, L. (2000) Understanding and overcoming underachievement in women and girls, in *Able Underachievers* (ed. D. Montgomery), Whurr, London, pp. 52–61.

8

Understanding and Overcoming Underachievement in Boys

Barry Hymer

Introduction

The intellectually gifted underachiever is a ubiquitous phenomenon, identifiable in all schools at all academic levels; but he appears a most significant
challenge at the secondary school level. He may appear in many guises –
lazy, disinterested in school, bored, rebellious, unable to relate to teachers, or
having difficulty with one or more subjects. Nonetheless, no matter what the
appearance, he is generally a youngster who is not using his intellectual potential in meeting the academic demands of the school. As generally defined,
the high ability underachiever not only fails to reach the academic excellence
that his outstanding ability suggests he is able to attain, but also is found
lagging behind the achievement level of students of average ability, or, at best,
only managing to hold his own with them. (Ralph, Goldberg and Passow,
1966, p. 1)

Why 'he'? Passow, in Supplee (1990), notes that in describing their
early study into high-ability underachievers, he and his colleagues followed
the writing convention of the time in using the masculine pronoun. At the
same time, however, it was acknowledged that underachievement is not the
domain of one sex alone, and Passow himself '. . . found EQUAL numbers of
boys and girls [able underachievers] – a first in the field, but a phenomenon
that has persisted over 5 years' (Supplee, 1990, p. xi).

In the United Kingdom, what has been generating the massive transfer of
focus in academic writing, the media and in applied fields (notably schools)
from female underachievement in the 1970s and 1980s to the 'discovery'
of male underachievement in the 1990s, has been the publication of data

Able, Gifted and Talented Underachievers, Second Edition   Edited by Diane Montgomery
© 2009 John Wiley & Sons, Ltd

accumulated since 1988 – when the General Certificate in Secondary Education (GCSE), the National Curriculum and new assessment procedures came into being in state schools. There had been early warning signs before then, but until the 1980s, 'the conventional wisdom was that girls had only an initial cognitive advantage, related to their reaching physical maturity at an earlier age, but that boys overtook girls in the teenage years' (Northern Ireland CCEA, 1999, p. 37).

The emerging data, however, were compelling and seemingly unidirectional in their conclusions, revealing, for instance, that girls develop a lead in reading at Key Stage 1 that is maintained at Key Stages 2 and 3. What is more, the gender gap in reading tended to widen between Key Stages 1 and 2. By 1995, boys were already lagging behind girls at GCSE in terms of the proportions obtaining five or more higher grade passes (grades C to A*), and this trend continued, with the gap between girls' and boys' GCSE performances widening to 10% by 1998: 51% of girls achieved five or more higher grade passes, compared with 41% of boys. By 2007, 59.1% of girls achieved five or more higher passes compared with 50.6% of boys. In other words, whilst national pass rates were improving generally, girls' improvements were outstripping boys'. Looking at the upper end of the performance spectrum, at the highest level of GCSE achievement (A and A* grades) in English, 13% of girls secured top grades in 2007, as opposed to 8% of boys. And at A-Level, having trailed behind boys since A-Levels began in 1951, girls have been achieving better average results than boys since the 1990s.

Closer reading of all the available data, however, suggested a far murkier picture: boys' and girls' performances in mathematics and science were more similar – from Key Stage 1 to GCSE – and at all levels of attainment. At A-Level, even in 1998, boys still had the edge over girls in traditionally 'masculine' subjects – physics, maths, computer studies and economics. As noted by Arnot *et al.*:

> Blanket statements about girls performing better than boys or vice versa are difficult to justify; reference should always be made to a *specific aspect* of the curriculum (Arnot *et al.*, 1998).

Janette Elwood of the Qualifications and Curriculum Authority observed that 'These huge benchmark figures make it seem that girls are surging ahead on every level. However, they mask areas where girls do not do as well at A-Level despite outperforming boys at GCSE. A-Level choices are still very gendered' (*Times Educational Supplement*, 6 August 1999). There have been other cautionary voices too: some have urged a more considered look at the possible impact of test construction, administration and marking on gender differences in attainment and on assessment data in general (Black and Wiliam, 1998; Davies and Brember, 1998). There have been careful critiques from the feminist perspective, noting for instance the historical antecedents of boys' underachievement and the attributions placed upon boys' scholastic successes and failures (Cohen in Epstein *et al.*, 1998), or more generally the risks of ignoring the knowledge and insights obtained through feminist research (Skelton, 1998). And there have been attempts to encourage schools and teachers to eschew stereotypical assumptions about boys' underachievement in favour of action-based research based on their own *unique* circumstances, and to intervene accordingly (Pickering, 1997). Moreover, addressing the subgroup of able underachievers, Joan Freeman had also advised caution in the wholesale transfer of attention from female to male underachievement (Freeman, 1996), noting that school achievement, however welcome, is imperfectly correlated with achievement in post-school life – especially for girls. The notorious 'glass ceiling', it seems, has not been shattered yet.

In the public domain, cautionary voices have had little effect: the over-whelming government and media interest since the mid-1990s has been in 'failing boys' and the search for solutions. A few examples of headlines from the UK national and educational press in the mid- to late-1990s: 'Girls doing well while boys feel neglected', 'Girls outclassing boys', 'Failing boys "public burden number one" ', 'Gender gap widens to a gulf ', 'Boys will still lag in literacy stakes', 'Anti-School bias "blights boys for life" ', 'Hard and macho – and their own worst enemies' and so on. Having been so vigorously fanned, the flames of public anxiety have risen high. A variety of possible explanations for boys' underachievement as revealed in national school-achievement statistics have been explored, each with its own implications for intervention. Those explanations that fall most readily within the reach of the school will be of greatest interest to educationists, but it may also be worth looking at others.

Some Explanations of the Gender Differences

Biological factors

There has been interest in *biological* differences between the sexes' per-formances in educational tasks for some time. In 1977, drawing on a range of extant genetic and neurobiological research, a vigorous argument for sex-differentiated teaching and learning was put forward by William Stewart, who spoke of the interplay of biological and cultural factors in contributing to sex differences and of 'conclusive research findings . . . that girls and boys experience more success and satisfaction with learning tasks which are selected with appropriate reference to sex differences' (Stewart, 1977).

More recently, the evidence has seemed less conclusive, at least in the area of cognitive styles and learning strategies, with Riding and Rayner, for instance, finding no significant differences between boys' and girls' performances on the Cognitive Styles Analysis (Riding and Rayner, 1998) – a heavily researched tool for exploring individuals' differing and habitual ways of organizing and responding to information. Cognitive style, it is argued, is independent of ability, personality and gender. Bray, Gardner and Parsons (1997) discuss genetic differences between the sexes from the prenatal stage – research suggesting, for example, that female babies in the womb respond better to sound and intonation patterns than do males, and related maturational effects have often been cited to account for girls' superiority over boys in early literacy skills.

Steve Biddulph, for instance, one of the leading exponents of the 'Men's Movement', makes much of the research suggesting that boys develop neuro-logically at a slower pace than girls, attributing this delay to boys' scholastic underachievement (relative to girls) in the United Kingdom, Australia and the USA (Biddulph, 1998a). Pickering explores the notion, founded in brain studies, of girls as analysts and reflectors, and boys as speculators and ex-perimenters, and notes that 'Given the current assessment system in the UK, which is based on a sequential and analytical approach to learning, girls are advantaged considerably' (Pickering, 1997, p. 48). Interestingly, the same arguments have been advanced for some time in the area of the learn-ing disabled, with many high-functioning dyslexic children, for instance, known to struggle in an educational system that exposes their weaknesses and cramps their strengths.

Where there has been reference specifically to gender differences and attainments at the extremes, it has often been in observation of boys scoring more at the extremes of the range in maths and English (Davies and Brember, 1998; OFSTED/EOC, 1996) – a phenomenon much noted in the literature: referring to a range of research studies conducted since Terman, McLeod and Cropley noted:

> Three facts have been established about able girls in comparison with boys: fewer girls than boys obtain extremely high IQ scores; there have been fewer girls than boys among prodigious achievers; girls as a group tend to achieve in different subjects from boys (McLeod and Cropley, 1989, p. 124).

Little reference is made in these sources to the tendencies of markers to assess boys' work more favourably especially in relation to giving the highest grades or to potential gender biases in IQ items and strategic differences in test taking.

Benbow and Stanley (1983) provided evidence that there is at least a contribution made by non-environmental factors to the skewed representation of males and females performing at the highest levels in maths, and more recently, VanTassell-Baska (1998), summarizes the results of further studies in the area of gender differences in mathematics, finding evidence of a range of differentials: in test performance and strategy use (Becker, 1990), tasks requiring high-level problem solving and untutored conceptual understanding (Mills, Ablard and Stumpf, 1993) and expectations of parents for student success (Dickens and Cornell, 1993), all favouring boys.

None of the above can, of course, lead one to a simplistic conclusion that in maths or in overall cognitive ability boys are abler than girls – or more precisely, that exceptionally able boys are abler than exceptionally able girls. The incomplete fit between ability and attainment, alongside concerns around ability test construction and other cautions exercised previously when describing boy–girl attainment differences, are likely to apply at the highest levels of attainment too. And coexistent with the observation that '. . . the incidence of some manifestations of giftedness might differ – at least actuarially – in males and females' (McLeod and Cropley, 1989, p. 126) could be the overall conclusion of Sutherland (1990) and Golombok and Fivush (1994) that the weight of evidence is that there is no sex difference in intelligence. The preponderance of boys performing at the extremes of attainment may well give substance to the impression of boys' underachievement (notably in literacy), as much as it might to the impression of boys' exceptional achievements (notably in maths), but the empirical data may be serving to mask the nuances.

Given the likelihood of some degree of gender difference in relation to specific subject areas, the most extreme formulation of the biological determinist's argument would suggest that there is little point in seeking actively to raise boys' (or for that matter girls') achievements, since boys (and girls) would simply be playing out their genetic life scripts during their school years – boys' underachievement in literacy as an educational construct would, by definition, not exist at all. The fact remains, however, that even if the evidence for inequalities in innate linguistic (or mathematical, or scientific) ability existed solidly at the level of *populations,* and OFSTED in 1993 failed to find firm evidence that the differences in boys' and girls' performances in English reflected differences in innate linguistic ability, at the level of the *individual,* there are known to be far greater differences in ability and attainment within each gender group than there are between them. In broad terms at least, underachievement remains a viable and gender neutral educational construct.

Social factors

In education, underachievement is more comfortably regarded as a behaviour than as a crystallized state. Behaviours are capable of change, as (at least in theory) are *social behaviours* – which it has been argued may also play a role in boys' underachievement in specific or more general areas of the school curriculum. Demographic factors, including the changes in employment patterns in society, leading in turn to altered perspectives on parenting roles – and particularly the role of fathers in boys' attainments, have been much discussed and researched: the *Tomorrow's Men* project (carried out by Oxford University researchers and reported in *The Independent* newspaper on 1 February 1999 and *The Times* newspaper on 17 March 1999) surveyed over 1400 boys aged 13–19, and found that over 90% of boys who felt that their fathers spent time with them and took an active interest in their progress emerged as confident, hopeful, 'can do' individuals. Seventy-two percent of boys with fathers perceived as having low levels of engagement fell into the group with the lowest levels of self-esteem and confidence, and with the greatest susceptibility to depression, poor attitude to school and delinquent behaviour. Exhortations to fathers to engage more actively with their sons, and to listen more to them, are a natural by-product of findings such as these. Steve Biddulph puts figures to the exhortations, saying that fathers who spend more than 55 hours a week at work are failing their children (Biddulph, 1998b).

Interventions

School-based interventions using the male-as-positive-role-model theme have included attempts to redress imbalances in the gender ratio of primary school teachers, encouraging fathers into the classroom and playgrounds, and the drafting in of high-status sports stars to combine football or rugby coaching with literacy-related activities – with considerable reported success in terms of enthusiasm and pupil attitudes in individual cases – but little by way of larger scale and longer term evaluation. Feminist critiques of this last-mentioned approach include the concern that by seeking to boost areas of low male achievement by linking these to stereotypical 'male' achievement, we may be narrowing the range of acceptable male behaviours – and entrenching the macho attitudes which may be contributing to underachievement in the first place (cf. Reed, in Epstein *et al.*, 1998).

Very little of the current flurry of activity in exploring boys' underachievement has focused specifically or even primarily on the area of the underachieving *able* boy, and it could be argued that much of the impetus for the 'failing boys' movement, in the United Kingdom at least, lies in the assumed link between underachievement and the social ramifications of disaffection – the traditional and stereotypical domain of the working class, low-attaining boy: 'Underperformance among working-class boys has become a particular concern for the government, because it is associated with high rates of vagrancy and crime' (*The Economist*, 29 May 1999, p. 36).

But the descriptions of the possible manifestations of the underachieving able boy as described by Ralph and his colleagues at the start of this chapter still resonate now, and the boundaries between ability, attainment and behaviour are blurred, if they exist at all.

Attitudinal factors

Related to social factors, another much-fingered factor in attempt to explain boys' scholastic underachievement is in the area of *attitudes* – including boys' and teachers'. Pickering, for instance, notes that

> There is a considerable amount of research evidence to support anecdotal suggestions that the attitudes of boys towards education in general and school in particular explain partly their recent poor examination achievement in comparison with girls (Pickering, 1997, p. 31).

He refers to the Keele University survey of around 30 000 pupils which suggests that boys' attitudes to school differ significantly from girls – by 4% – roughly the same difference as exists in GCSE and A-Level results! The image of the disaffected schoolboy, working hard to preserve his credibility with his peers at the expense of school achievement is widespread in the literature, and across many cultures. For example, Schneider and Coutts (1985) found that boys were particularly susceptible to anti-intellectual influences from peers, and a study by Warrington and Younger (1996), concluded that for many boys it was not acceptable to appear to conform to the school's expectations and values. A front of disengagement or, at best, reluctant involvement, seemed necessary.

Going beyond the external behaviours, a number of writers have commented on the attributions made by boys as opposed to girls about their academic successes and failures. Boys, it is thought, are more likely than girls to attribute their successes to ability, and their failures to lack of effort (Licht and Dweck, 1987). The same research suggests that boys are more likely than girls to overestimate their future performances – given their past and future achievements. Arnold (1997) details later research that seems to support the findings of Licht and Dweck, and which at first sight sits rather uneasily with the image of the reluctant schoolboy, wracked with insecurities arising from reduced employment prospects, evolving perspectives on masculinity and peer group expectations about classroom performance. The 'average' schoolboy it seems is rather more confident about his school performance and future prospects than he should be. He may be responding to a male-orientated classroom and society – to the reality of continuing hurdles to girls' achievements in society that is well summarized in Montgomery (1996) and Freeman (1996).

Interestingly, Downes (1994) gave higher ability boys a partial exemption from the observation that

> the prevailing 'macho' image, *to which middle and lower ability boys seem to be particularly vulnerable* [italics inserted], is that it is simply not expected that heroes do well in the classroom. The powerful role models from the world of sport, television, popular music, etc., are rarely projected as having academic gifts. If anything, they have got on in life in spite of 'being dim at school' (p. 8).

The extent to which more able boys are less susceptible to anti-school attitudes, is worth considering. It could be argued, for instance, that more able boys are less likely to take on their peers' definition of 'success', valuing more highly success in formal academic terms. Csikszentmihalyi, Rathunde and Whalen (1997), for instance, comment on '. . . the strong core of attributes that distinguishes the talented males and females from their average counterparts' (*ibid.*, p. 75), attributes that included achievement motivation and endurance. Certain attributes were more prominent amongst the boys – notably a degree of conservatism and reluctance to seek rapid change. The boys also possessed '. . . an unusual need for social recognition, a desire that . . . could also reflect concerns about social competence . . .' (*ibid.*, p. 78). In a small-scale study into the attributions of nine underachieving but able boys aged 6–12 years, Sadler found that whilst the major attributions for underachievement offered by the boys were curriculum factors, her boys

> . . . were far more concerned about their relationships with the peer group than either their teachers or their parents and saw this as influencing their performance (Sadler, 1998, p. 7).

Sue Leyden picks up on the dilemmas faced by highly able boys whose talents run counter to the peer group norms – talents in creative expression – in poetry or dance for instance:

> His talents can be crushed and driven out through mockery and insinuation. The desire to create an acceptable masculine image for himself can force a choice on a boy as unfortunate and as unnecessary as the one that can face the girls (Leyden, 1985, pp. 78–79).

The musical 'Billy Elliott' is currently having a significant counter effect to that witnessed by Leyden on some boys' attitudes to dance. Where schools have recruited male dancers to run dance clubs and put on excerpts from the show the attitudinal barriers are being broken down at least temporarily.

The tension between seeking social acceptance by his peer group and remaining true to his talents, interests and inclinations can be a source of great distress to an able boy – especially when the prevailing culture and attitudes in school encourage conformity: John, an exceptionally able and creatively gifted 9-year-old Cumbrian boy known to the present writer resisted huge pressures to conform in his primary school, but at appalling personal cost – only relieved by a change of school. At the height of his distress, he was asked to draw how he would be 'If things were better'. He drew four lines of primitive stick figures and said, 'I don't care which of these I am, as long as I know that there's someone else on my level.' For all his rejection of the attitudes of his peers and his fierce determination to maintain a sense of personal integrity, John, like all children, still needed a friend, a soulmate. Prof C.E.M. Joad expressed the tension well in 1948, 'My life is spent in a perpetual alternation between two rhythms, the rhythm of attracting people for fear I may be lonely and the rhythm of getting rid of them because I know that I am bored' (Gross, 1993, p. 233).

Intervention programmes

It is the uniqueness of John and of all children that confounds any routine prescription for the remediation of underachievement. Even in programmes focused specifically on the needs of underachieving able children, the uniqueness of the individuals needs acknowledging:

> The children identified for the special program to help them reverse their underachievement all displayed high potential and low achievement. But that is where their similarity to one another ended (Supplee, 1990, p. 5).

It is the reality of the *achieving* boy which gives the lie to stereotypical assumptions of underachievement, for perhaps every school, irrespective of its ethos, culture, organizational structures and curriculum, will have some boys who achieve – even against the odds. But this is not a call for complacency, or for minimizing the role of the *school*, its *structures* and *curriculum* (overt and hidden) in raising achievement – for all its pupils. There has, for instance, been a good deal of investigation into the merits of single-sex teaching as an antidote to underachievement. The evidence in support of this seems to be equivocal, with a recent review of research on single-sex education over the past 20 years suggesting that the strong performance of girls' schools in examination league tables owes more to social class, ability and school traditions than it does to gender (Elwood and Gipps, 1999). Individual schools, however, including mixed-sex schools operating single-sex classes in certain subjects, have reported evidence of improvements in behaviour and academic results – for boys and girls. And OFSTED/EOC in 1996 noted that even though the research in the area of single-sex schooling and teaching was inconclusive, boys' schools were well placed to address the issue of underachievement – being able to tailor strategies directly to the needs of boys.

The role of emotional literacy, and of creating emotionally literate schools and classrooms, has assumed prominence in the last decade. Pickering, in 1997, anticipated a possible connection with boys' underachievement in noting that

> Recent research suggests that pupils are more influenced by the human relationships aspects of teaching, and, for boys, this seems to be particularly marked (*ibid.*, p. 15).

He recommended that teachers take carefully the views of their own pupils, in responding to the question, 'What makes an effective teacher?' – comparing these results with the competencies-based approach of OFSTED (1995). It is possible that the 'woollier' virtues of fairness, being a good listener, friendliness, treating each pupil as an individual and so on. may be more significant virtues in the eyes of many pupils, despite their lack of prominence in the OFSTED list.

The salience of *language* and literacy skills in combating underachievement, and especially boys' underachievement, has been recognized at the level of Government (witness initiatives in literacy summer schools and pronouncements by ministers), at LA (local authority) level (cf. the summary of initiatives reported in a briefing paper from the National Literacy Trust, 1999), and by individual schools. As noted by Arnold (1997)

> Probably *the* most important ability that schooling demands is the ability to use language to acquire learning throughout the curriculum, and to express what one has learned (p. 23).

In the United Kingdom, National Curriculum Orders across all subjects are now prefaced with the requirement that pupils be taught to express themselves in both speech and writing, and to develop their reading skills. Arnold notes that many boys can be regarded as underachieving readers – adequately decoding print but failing flexibly to interrogate text, to infer and deduce, to attend to detail, to cross reference and to sustain their reading. Boys who do develop and implement these skills can reasonably be expected to achieve well not only in English, but also across the curriculum. Given the maturational sex differences referred to earlier, and the evidence of boys' delays in the development of early literacy skills, attention is being given to the ages at which children, especially boys, are expected to acquire formal literacy skills – with the suspicion in the United Kingdom that boys in particular need more time to develop their powers of expressive and receptive language – opportunities received more plentifully on the Continent. The primacy of oracy over literacy is being asserted, despite evidence of policy initiatives over the past decade being in quite the opposite direction – with many parents and teachers concerned that boys as young as four are being asked to grapple with fine motor and formal literacy skills beyond their levels of readiness.

Given the evidence of boys' underachievement in English detailed earlier, a report suggesting that boys are more sophisticated writers and better spellers, is worth noting (QCA, 1999). The study was based on an analysis of 300 A, C and F grade 1998 GCSE examination scripts, and the suggestion was that boys' tendency to write short, action-based stories with less detail or explanation than is provided by girls (Millard, 1997 and Hall and Coles, 1999, for detailed considerations of gender differences in literacy) is penalized in English examinations. Boys' strengths are thought to include a wider vocabulary than girls (pointed out in Freeman, 1996), and greater technical and punctuation skills. The mean sentence length was also greater. Again, as other researchers have pointed out, this study would seem to suggest that bald examination statistics may fail to reflect the gender implications of the forms of assessment used.

Many schools and LAs in the United Kingdom have introduced initiatives at combating boys' underachievement, especially in literacy (Arnold, 1997). One example at the junior-school level is quoted, in which the present writer was involved: in the knowledge that there is no clear evidence for gender differences in *innate* linguistic ability, but that Cumbrian boys are being heavily outperformed by girls at all levels of English attainment, including the highest levels at Key Stage 2 (National Curriculum Levels 5+) and at GCSE (A or A* grades), Cumbria Education Service has been preparing a resource pack of materials for use in primary schools (Cumbria Education Service, 2002) aimed at encouraging teachers to experiment with a range of strategies and techniques for boosting the achievements of junior-aged children in English. The strategies have been based around the knowledge and expertise of literacy consultants Paula Iley and Joan Stark, together with a group of class- and head teachers, but its effectiveness will be evaluated over time, as schools draw upon it.

Whether it is biological, social, attitudinal, pedagogic or linguistic factors that are most implicated in the underachievement of many boys in school, or whether the gender card has been much overplayed, it is the range of possible factors associated with boys' underachievement that makes the task of addressing the need so difficult for parents, teachers, education authorities and governments. What is known, is that more boys than girls are recognized by schools and LAs to have special educational needs, to be disaffected with school and to have poor attendance records (Grubb, 1999). What *can* be said with a good degree of certainty is that there is no *one* factor involved – certainly not at the level of populations, and possibly not even at the level of the individual. But the difficulties of teasing out the relative weightings of different factors in addressing boys' underachievement, where it is found, should not deter practitioners from setting out to make a difference, using the available evidence as a starting point, adapting this to their unique circumstances and monitoring the effects of any intervention.

Recommendations for consideration in a programme for combating underachievement

These recommendations for combating underachievement in boys are derived from the research and practices outlined in this chapter, and in particular from the following main sources: OFSTED (1993), Frater (1997), the Northern Ireland CCEA Report (1999), Freeman (1998) and Grubb (1999), DfES (2005).

At school level

- Recognize the significance of strong local effects underlying achievement and underachievement (there are wide attitudinal and achievement differences between schools, and statistical trends at the level of national populations may not be reflected in these smaller samples).
- Engage with parents, pupils, governors and teachers in opening discussion of the issues.
- Obtain a clearer insight into the issues affecting your own school by gathering a range of primary and secondary evidence, with as much detail as possible. Sample and survey, for instance, your attainment statistics, teacher and pupil attitudes, classroom practices, samples of work and policies.
- Use resultant local data to challenge stereotyped thinking about boys, girls and underachievement, being aware that positions which are hard to shift may reflect deeply held beliefs and/or anxieties.
- Look out for stereotypical or prejudicial beliefs and language in school policies and practices.

- Consider in whole school policies the value of baseline testing of all new pupils, provision for the targeting, monitoring and mentoring of individual pupils and explicit attention to staff development needs – for example for staff awareness of boys' needs.
- Develop a consistent approach to language across the curriculum.
- Accept and encourage differences in approaches to learning; consider staff training in cognitive styles and learning strategies.
- Develop a partnership with parents.
- Agree targets and a timetable for action, observable criteria against which to measure success, processes for monitoring and evaluation and key personnel to take the process on.

At classroom level

- Make lesson targets clear and explicit.
- Sequence tasks carefully and provide information in bite-size chunks.
- Provide for curriculum compacting – allowing pupils to undertake extension or enrichment work when mastery of a core area has been demonstrated.
- Value the role of challenge over completion – especially for the more able. Accept alternative product outcomes for some tasks – not confined to narrative writing alone.
- Vary the classroom groupings to suit the task: provide opportunities for group work, practical work, collaboration and active participation.
- Consider the merits of experimenting with single-sex or ability-setted teaching, but bear in mind the lack of definitive research evidence in these areas.
- Seat underachievers with high achievers for some tasks.
- Use homework for extension and enrichment of classwork.
- Take in and mark extended coursework in stages. Provide guiding comments and advice, rather than grades alone.
- Listen one-to-one, and provide time for self-evaluation.

In the area of language and literacy

- Survey boys' and girls' reading habits.
- Encourage discussion, role-play, oral contributions and structured story writing.

- Attend to the structure of English lessons and to the structuring of pupils' thinking–including 'thinking about thinking' (metacognition).
- Mark for content, use of vocabulary and technical accuracy, not just for quality of descriptions or dialogue.
- Provide writing frames as scaffolding for different kinds of writing.
- Provide a range of texts for reading which appeal to boys' and girls' interests – and not just narrative fiction.
- Encourage reading for pleasure, schemes for paired, silent and voluntary reading, and for boys sharing their ideas about 'favourite reads'.
- Use Information and Communication Technology to develop reading and writing skills.
- Teach the techniques and 'skills' of writing and reading. In writing, use examples from a range of authors, and in reading, teach the techniques of scanning, reading for meaning and so on.
- Consider the merits of using high-status male role models to promote reading and writing – for example sports stars.

Affective and motivational factors

- Use verbal encouragement to increase motivation and reduce the risk of public failure. Attribute success to the pupil's abilities or interests, and failure to lack of effort or external factors – for example level of task difficulty.
- Encourage attempts, not just successes.
- Offer praise and other reinforcement, but do this privately – not before peers.
- Keep homework tasks brief and focused; mark and return quickly.
- Encourage extra-curricular interests and achievements.
- Accept that some pupils value learning over the achievement of grades – there can be a difference!
- Be fair.
- Involve the pupil in setting his own learning goals.
- Seek, where possible, a close match between task and personal pupil interests.
- Encourage pupil to tutor younger/less able pupils in his area/s of strength.
- Consider the use of mentors.
- Communicate a genuine, unconditional concern for and interest in the individual pupil.

Conclusions

According to Caudill (2006), in gifted education we probably pay too much attention to gender differences when the abilities of gifted boys and girls are quite similar, if not identical. The problems arise because of the values and expectations taught to each gender by different societies and cultures.

In this chapter, it has been pointed out that the expectations of boys may be more subtly nuanced now than for girls and the standards of both are improving according to national criteria.

A range of biological, social and attitudinal factors were considered that may give rise to underachievement. It was stressed that the emphasis should be placed on the individual's pattern of abilities and needs if successful intervention is to be achieved. Such an individual may have to cope with many pressures from the denigration of high achievement from peers, having to play 'cool role' and perhaps having highly aspirational parents who are striving to promote his achievements. If he is twice exceptional, or from a minority or disadvantaged group then the pressures and expectations are increased.

References

Arnold, R. (1997) *Raising Levels of Achievement in Boys*, EMIE/National Foundation for Educational Research in England and Wales.

Arnot, M., Gray, J., James, M. *et al.* (1998) *Recent Research on Gender and Educational Performance*, OFSTED Reviews of Research. The Stationery Office, London.

Becker, B.J. (1990) Item characteristics and gender differences on the SAT-M for mathematically able youth. *American Educational Research Journal*, **27** (1), 65–87.

Benbow, C.P. and Stanley, J.R. (1983) Sex differences in mathematical reasoning ability: more facts. *Science*, **222**, 1029–31.

Biddulph, S. (1998a) *Manhood: An Action Plan for Changing Men's Lives*, Celestial Arts.

Biddulph, S. (1998b) *Raising Boys: Why Boys Are Different and How to Help Them Become Happy and Well-Balanced Men*, Celestial Arts.

Black, P. and Wiliam, D. (1998) *Inside the Black Box: Raising Standards Through Classroom Assessment*, School of Education, King's College, London.

Bray, R., Gardner, C. and Parsons, N. (1997) *Can Boys Do Better?* Secondary Heads Association, Leicester.

Caudill, G. (2006) Contemporary issues impacting gifted boys, in *Diversity in Gifted Education* (eds B. Wallace and G. Eriksson), Routledge, London, pp. 200–2.

Csikszentmihalyi, M., Rathunde, K. and Whalen, S. (1997) *Talented Teenagers – The Roots of Success and Failure*, Cambridge University Press.

Cumbria Education Service (2002) *Now, Bernard! Gender-Friendly Approaches to Raising Achievement in Key Stage 2 English*, Cumbria Education Service Able Pupil Project.

Davies, J. and Brember, I. (1998) *Boys Outperforming Girls: An Eight-Year Cross-Sectional Study of Attainment and Self-Esteem in Year 6*, University of Manchester School of Education.

DfES (2005) *Raising Boys' Achievement* HMSO: Norwich.

Dickens, M.N. and Cornell, D.G. (1993) Parent influences on the mathematics self-concept of high-ability adolescent girls. *Journal for the Education of the Gifted*, **17** (1), 53–73.

Downes, P. (1994) The gender effect. *Managing Schools Today*, **3** (5), 7–8.

Elwood, J. and Gipps, C. (1999) Boys, Girls and Literacy: Single Sex Pupils Get the Best Pupils. Reported by the National Literacy Trust.

Epstein, D., Elwood, J., Hey, V. and Maw, J. (1998) *Failing Boys? Issues in Gender and Achievement*, Open University Press, Buckingham.

Frater, G. (1997) *Improving Boys' Literacy: A Survey of Effective Practice in Secondary Schools*, The Basic Skills Agency.

Freeman, J. (1996) *Highly Able Girls and Boys*, Department for Education and Employment, London.

Freeman, J. (1998) *Educating the Very Able: Current International Research*, OFSTED Reviews of Research. The Stationery Office, London.

Golombok, S. and Fivush, R. (1994) *Gender Development*, Cambridge University Press, Cambridge.

Gross, M.U.M. (1993) *Exceptionally Gifted Children*, Routledge, London.

Grubb, J. (1999) Boys in Brief: Reduced Research on Gender and Underachievement. Report in Times Educational Supplement, 4 June 1999.

Hall, C. and Coles, M. (1999) *Children's Reading Choices*, Routledge, London.

Leyden, S. (1985) *Helping the Child of Exceptional Ability*, Routledge, London.

Licht, B.G. and Dweck, C. (1987) Sex differences in achievement orientations, in *Gender and the Politics of Schooling* (eds G. Arnot and G. Weiner), Hutchinson, London.

McLeod, J. and Cropley, A. (1989) *Fostering Academic Success*, Pergamon, Oxford.

Millard, E. (1997) *Differently Literate: Boys, Girls and the Schooling of Literacy*, Falmer, London.

Mills, C.J., Ablard, K.E. and Stumpf, H. (1993) Gender differences in academically talented young students' mathematical reasoning: patterns across age and subskills. *Journal of Educational Psychology*, **85** (2), 340–6.

Montgomery, D. (1996) *Educating the Able*, Cassell, London.

National Literacy Trust (1999) *Boys and Writing*, http://www.literacytrust.org.uk/ (accessed 19 April 1999).

Northern Ireland Council for the Curriculum, Examinations and Assessment (1999) *Focus on Boys: Guidance on Improving Attainment, Particularly in Literacy*, CCEA, Belfast.

Office for Standards in Education (OFSTED) (1993) *Boys and English: 1988–1991* (Report No.2/93), HMSO, London.

Office for Standards in Education (OFSTED) (1995) *Guidance on the Inspection of Secondary Schools*, HMSO, London.

Office for Standards in Education and Equal Opportunities Commission (1996) *The Gender Divide*, HMSO, London.

Pickering, J. (1997) *Raising Boys' Achievement*, Network Educational Press, Stafford.

Qualifications and Curriculum Authority (QCA) (1999) *Improving Writing at Key Stages 3 and 4*, QCA, Sudbury.

Ralph, J.B., Goldberg, M.L. and Passow, A.H. (1966) *Bright Underachievers*, Teachers College Press, New York.

Riding, R. and Rayner, S. (1998) *Cognitive Styles and Learning Strategies – Understanding Style Differences in Learning and Behaviour*, David Fulton, London.

Sadler, K. (1998) Attributions and solutions for the underachievement of able pupils, Unpublished paper.

Schneider, F.W. and Coutts, L.M. (1985) Person orientation of male and female high school students: to the educational disadvantage of males? *Sex Roles*, **13** (1–2), 47–63.

Skelton, C. (1998) Feminism and research into masculinities and schooling. *Gender and Education*, **10** (2), 217–27.

Stewart, W.J. (1977) *Sex Differences and the School*, ERIC Database.

Supplee, P.L. (1990) *Reaching the Gifted Underachiever: Program Strategy and Design*, Teachers College Press, New York.

Sutherland, M. (1990) Education and gender differences, in *Handbook of Educational Ideas and Practices* (ed. N. Entwistle), Routledge, London.

VanTassell-Baska, J. (1998) Girls of promise, in *Excellence in Educating Gifted and Talented Learners*, 3rd edn (ed. J. VanTassell-Baska), Love, Denver.

Warrington, M. and Younger, P. (1996) Gender and achievement: the debate at GCSE. *Education Review*, **10** (1), 22–7.

9

Improving the Quality of Identification, Provision and Support for Gifted and Talented Learners from Under-Represented Communities through Partnership Working

Ian Warwick

Introduction

Social justice and personalized education

Poverty of aspiration is as damaging as poverty of opportunity and it is time to replace a culture of low expectations for too many with a culture of high standards for all . . . The very idea of personalised learning is about helping children become more aspirational, that we identify talent, we shape education around the unique needs and aspirations of every child, we engage them in their own learning and we give them a thirst for education and knowledge that will stay with them long after they have left school . . . But we should also work on the principle of social justice for all, that no child should be left out or lose out, that as we raise standards we also narrow the social gap of attainment in education and that every child should be given the best chance to progress as far and as fast as they can . . . (Prime Minister: Gordon Brown, University of Greenwich, 31 October 2007).

The goals of excellence and equity are not necessarily conceptually incoherent. However, the current practices and processes of gifted education in a socio-economically unjust, multicultural society in which there are vast discrepancies of opportunity may well be currently serving to embed the

Able, Gifted and Talented Underachievers, Second Edition   Edited by Diane Montgomery
© 2009 John Wiley & Sons, Ltd

attainment gap between White and minority students. Children are particularly vulnerable to insidious disadvantaging forces and will, no matter how smart, enter school to face severe educational obstacles. Given such discrepancies within our educational system, perhaps there is a malign likelihood that this will continue to lead to the under-representation of certain groups of individuals on gifted programmes, which in turn obviates chances of equitable aspiration and provision.

All of the time that this injustice is allowed to continue, the credibility of gifted education is seriously undermined. It is simply a failure to respond to diversity and therefore the sceptics who continue to shout 'elitism' will win, and sadly, rightly so. Until the very clear message is defensibly put out there that outstanding talent is not only obviously present in all the diverse groups in society but is also being sensitively and appropriately identified and fostered, then we, as educators of the gifted, are guilty as charged.

As many of the gifted and talented student cohorts in the United Kingdom will be drawn from communities with distinct social, economic and cultural pressures, special attention must be paid to those from under-represented groups to ensure that they receive access to gifted programmes. This can be achieved in part by working through the school system to improve the general education offer. However, each school and local authority must use explicit strategies to identify individual gifted students from such groups and intervene to offer them targeted support and access to the highest quality opportunities that they require to realize their potential.

The Current Situation in the United Kingdom

The significant disparity of representation of culturally and linguistically diverse Black and Minority Ethnic (BME) and English as an Additional Language (EAL) students identified and provided for as gifted still concerns many researchers and educators. In the United Kingdom in 2005, Professor David Gilborn from the Institute of Education, drew attention to the fact that, according to the Department for Children, Schools and Families (DCSF) statistics, white pupils were at least twice as likely to be identified as gifted and talented as pupils from minority ethnic backgrounds in general. Gilborn commented:

> The government is committed to 'evidence-informed policy making'. The evidence on race and education is very clear: race inequality is sustained

and even worsened, where judgements are made about ability and academic potential but no safeguards are built-in to ensure that stereotypes and unintended consequences do not further institutionalise the disadvantage faced (First Report Proceedings of the Committee House of Common printed 25 January 2006, paragraph 20).

He continues, 'If the Government wishes to address educational disadvantage, it needs to take seriously the problem of the under-representation of minority ethnic groups in the gifted and talented programme.' In the submission, Gilborn further argued that 'the plans to extend the use of "setting by ability" and enhance "gifted and talented" provision threaten further to institutionalize the race inequalities that have scarred the system for decades.'

What Does the Most Recent Gifted and Talented National Data Suggest?

According to the School Census analysis of the number and percentage of gifted and talented students analyzed by ethnic group from January 2007 there is still a serious disparity in the incidence of certain groups as a percentage of the cohort. When this is then broken down further in terms of the representation of these groups the following shortfall is revealed, as shown in Table 1.

There appears to be a substantial 'missing cohort' of students being identified as gifted and talented which is most stark in terms of the number of Pakistani students. These students represent 2.1% of the identified gifted and talented cohort nationally but when this is expressed as a percentage of the total number of students of the same ethnic origin it reveals an under-representation of 3.6%.

They are not the most under-represented group (that dubious honour goes to travellers of Irish heritage). But when this is translated into real numbers it demonstrates that more than 7000 students who 'should' be on the gifted and talented register are missing (see Table 2).

The issues are expanded through the diagram below (Figure 1), which indicates the dimensions of the problem.

A strategy that seeks to identify and address the needs of gifted and talented BME/EAL learners should focus on the centres of these three rings.

Table 1 To show for maintained primary and secondary schools[a]: number and percentage of gifted and talented pupils by ethnic group[b] (January 2007).

		Maintained primary and secondary schools		
		Number of pupils	*Percentage of gifted and talented group[c]*	*Percentage of cohort (incidence)[d]*
White		568 700	83.6	10.5
	White British	548 810	80.7	10.6
	Irish	2740	0.4	11.5
	Traveller of Irish heritage	80	0.0	2.1
	Gypsy/Roma	220	0.0	2.7
	Any other White background	16 840	2.5	9.2
Mixed		24 700	3.6	11.6
	White and Black Caribbean	7890	1.2	10.8
	White and Black African	2460	0.4	11.2
	White and Asian	5720	0.8	13.0
	Any other mixed background	8640	1.3	11.7
Asian		44 730	6.6	8.9
	Indian	17 540	2.6	11.1
	Pakistani	14 010	2.1	7.0
	Bangladeshi	7080	1.0	8.7
	Any other Asian background	6110	0.9	9.4
Black		22 330	3.3	8.2
	Black Caribbean	8170	1.2	9.2
	Black African	11 500	1.7	7.5
	Any other Black background	2650	0.4	8.7
Chinese		4510	0.7	18.6
Any other ethnic group		6030	0.9	8.4

Table 1   (*Continued*)

	Maintained primary and secondary schools		
	Number of pupils	*Percentage of gifted and talented group*[c]	*Percentage of cohort (incidence)*[d]
Classified	670 990	98.7	10.4
Unclassified[e]	8880	1.3	
Minority Ethnic Pupils[f]	122 180	18.0	9.4
All pupils[g]	679 870	100.0	10.3

Source: School Census.
[a]Includes middle schools as deemed.
[b]Registered pupils.
[c]Number of gifted and talented pupils.
[d]Number of pupils of same ethnic origin.
[e]Information refused or not obtained.
[f]Includes all pupils classified as belonging to an ethnic group other than White British.
[g]Pupils of compulsory school age and above.

Table 2   The incidence of missing pupils.

	% incidence	*'Missing' pupils*
Any other white background	9.2	2600
Asian	8.9	8740
Of whom Pakistani	7.0	7200
Bangladeshi	8.7	1500
Black	7.5	6500
Of whom Caribbean	9.2	1200
African	7.5	4600
Minority ethnic pupils	9.4	16 000

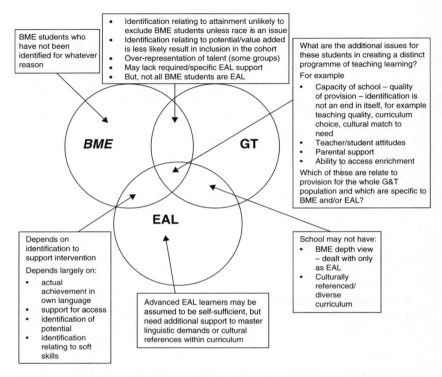

Figure 1   The figure shows where the focus for the BME/EAL learners should be.

In each other case, there is a risk that educational needs will not be identified, support will not be put in place and that underachievement will result.

How Can the Identification and Provision for BME/EAL Students Be Made More Equitable?

In order to address some of these core concerns London Gifted and Talented (LGT) began last year to improve the quality of identification, provision and support for gifted and talented learners from the BME and EAL through its Realizing Equality and Achievement for Learners Project (REAL).

The other partners involved were the DCSF, London Challenge, the London Local Authorities of Haringey, Hounslow and Islington and the Black Country Children's Services Improvement Partnership (BCCSIP), Local Authorities of Sandwell, Walsall and Wolverhampton. The REAL Project is the first national project specifically working to improve the overall quality of gifted and talented education for students from BME/EAL backgrounds.

To achieve this as a partnership we worked with a national network of schools and local authorities to develop a bank of web-based guidance, tools, resources and multimedia training materials. Our approach has been to develop positive models that are based on the premise that all learners are entitled to have their gifts and talents identified, recognized and met through challenging learning opportunities.

We began by asking what would improve the capacities of LAs (local authorities) and schools to address the distinct needs of BME and EAL students as actual or potential members of the gifted and talented population. Across the partnership we decided that any strategies we developed needed to demonstrate how to

- develop inclusive gifted and talented programmes, in line with the Every Child Matters agenda;
- develop existing data systems to target and track progress;
- enhance school self-evaluation, using GT quality standards so that it could become the core business for all teams;
- develop an understanding of identification and access issues and how to address them;
- support advanced learners once their learning needs have been identified and understood by the school;
- engage with the underachieving groups and those at risk of underachievement;
- engage with students, parents and communities to enrich the gifted and talented programme;
- clarify and strengthen the role of EAL and BME specialists and their contribution to gifted and talented strategies so that all staff can be alert to the needs;
- provide LAs with the means to support their schools and, where appropriate, to challenge them.

Partnerships and working practices

The foundations of The REAL Project have been the sharing of ideas, re-sources and expertise across schools and LAs to enable schools and LAs to provide stretch and challenge – not just support – for all gifted and talented learners. By generating scalable and transferable assets, our partner LAs across the country who are already 'ahead of the game' could develop their resources and practices to then support others in improving their provi-sion for this cohort of students and to add to their capacity to be able to specifically address the needs of their BME and EAL learners.

> One of the reasons The REAL Project has worked so well in Islington is that it has built upon what we are doing, not offer a one-size-fits-all solution for us to try out. We've always had a sense of there being a lot of respect from the REAL team for what we're doing in the first place, and without that respect we couldn't have moved on as we have through this project to the next level. One of the things we've really valued is the opportunity to talk to 'critical friends' who can say 'that's really good, do this' which takes our work to the next level. The other thing we have valued is being able to talk to colleagues doing the same things in other boroughs through the LGT network for this project (Graham Smith, Head of Achievement and Diversity, Cambridge Education @ Islington).

A key feature is that in all of the activities within The REAL Project, the majority of the work being undertaken is being done not by G&T specialists alone but in close working partnership with colleagues from other teams. The goal has not been simply to present a set of ideas or a statement of definitive guidance, but to derive interesting practices from real-life school and LA contexts and avoid top-down practices that are divorced from the social context of each of our partners.

> The REAL Project has required us to work more effectively across a wide range of LA and school teams to design specific interventions and pilot new practice: G&T Coordinators and teachers working with EAL specialists, data managers, learning mentors and parents. As a result we developed our practice and provision and have also added significant capacity to our work with gifted and talented students, their teachers and parents. One of the most valuable outcomes of The REAL Project has been the collaborative learning and sharing of work with partner local authorities in London and beyond (Stefani Shedden, Hounslow G&T Coordinator).

As a partnership we have all been looking at ways in which LAs have learned from each other and benefitted from the process of working together. Our central concern has been to think about how systems and strategies can be put in place to enable cross-LA communications and dialogues to take place. We have also endeavoured to chart how actions become refined across contexts. To do this, we have embraced multi-level, collaborative and cross-team working, encompassing relationships within schools, between different LA teams, between different government departments and with different external organizations.

> We have worked with The REAL Project to add a dimension of understanding in a non-London context to the tools and strategies being developed. Involvement in The REAL Project has provided a mechanism for bringing together different service groups within in the local authority, such as the national strategies and EAL unit. It has proved to be an effective means of raising the whole issue of underachievement in a very positive way, strengthening the partnership between the LA and schools. The work is already a fundamental success because its initiation has highlighted a need, especially in terms of making provision for international new arrivals that are potentially gifted and talented (Mark Story, Wolverhampton Primary Project Coordinator).

The REAL Project has been designed to enable LA and school leaders to provide the very best for their BME, EAL and G&T learners that their school can offer. Our approach has been that achievement of G&T students is the responsibility of all teachers and staff. We recognize that this requires effective and committed leadership at all levels of the system and as a partnership we are developing a transferable core of ideas, tools, resources and training materials to enable schools and LAs to adopt and adapt interesting practice for their own use to increase their delivery capacity (see Figure 2).

> The REAL Project has served to galvanise the BCCSIP local authorities involved into serious self-evaluation of their practice and that of their schools. Already, our involvement has resulted in much better representation of BME/EAL students in gifted and talented cohorts in the schools taking part. The productive partnerships that have been set up between EAL, gifted and talented and other professionals at both local authority and school level have radically increased our capacity. . . . With the momentum that has been generated, and the follow up work which will be carried out, the life chances of a large number of students will be greatly enhanced. The efforts of the different

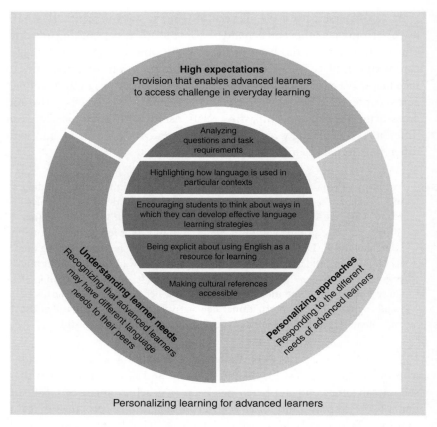

Figure 2 Factors in personalizing learning for advanced learners.

teams have created an impetus which has significant potential for realising the central focus of improving the quality of education for the thousands of gifted and talented students throughout the Black Country (Trevor Neat, REAL Coordinator, BCCSIP).

Development and quality assurance processes

Over the past 20 months, the development and production of each of the REAL projects have followed a broadly similar pattern. In the first place, schools and LAs were invited to come forward with their ideas and proposals, many of which were based on some of their existing practices. Project plans were scrutinized in terms of applicability and achievability. Three core LAs were selected by the LGT team. A key goal of the quality assurance (QA) process was then to ensure that sound educational principles were applied to the development of these individual LA-initiated REAL projects and resources. As the projects developed the QA process led by Kings College London and The Open University worked closely with the LGT team and with the LA coordinators and practitioners to ensure that the projects were developing in line with both the agreed project plans and the overall goals of The REAL Project.

All of the project ideas, materials and resources now made available through the REAL toolkit at www.londongt.org/real have grown out of actual school and LA-based initiatives. All the projects were conceived as responses to locally identified issues associated with the development of gifted and talented-oriented provision for BME and EAL students. Therefore the materials should not be seen as a solution for all challenges, nor should they be considered as 'quick fixes'.

Throughout this development period, the work on the individual projects was scrutinized regularly in steering group meetings (involving core LA practitioners, REAL and QA partners), working group sessions and partnership forums (involving colleagues from the DCSF and other public organizations). These constant interactions between the different groups have afforded opportunities to share ideas, to offer feedback and to review progress. The various bodies acted as 'critical friends' providing comments and observations drawing on bodies of knowledge and expertise from relevant fields of educational research.

This means that the individual projects have benefitted from a broad range of regular discussions and consultations that have provided constructive critique and helpful suggestions from a variety of perspectives. Furthermore, many of the materials and approaches developed have been trialled by teachers and LA teams working in contexts outside the immediate educational environments in which they were originally conceptualized. The materials and approaches have benefitted greatly from the feedback generated from these iterative processes.

> We have trialled tools from the London LAs which have led to valuable opportunities to share good practice, and reflect on our thinking with partners nationally. Done on our own, this work would have lacked the rigour of national scrutiny (Mark Story, Wolverhampton Primary Project Coordinator).

The QA process has sought to maintain two linked principles over the duration of the project. Firstly, we have endeavoured to preserve the distinctive characteristics of the different projects ensuring that the 'voices' of those involved and the contexts in which the work has taken place are not lost in the development and production process. Secondly, we have tried to make explicit the relevance and usefulness of specific projects for schools in different LAs serving potentially high achieving and gifted and talented BME and EAL students.

Our goal throughout this work has been to ensure that ideas and approaches put forward are not only 'sound' in relation to theory and research but also that they are workable in practice (see Figure 2). We believe that teachers and practitioners are more likely to use materials with clear principles and context offered, relating to the class and students as well as the processes that led to the production of the materials.

Identification and Assessment

The REAL Project has been grounded on the assumption that all students in the British education system should be considered as potentially gifted and talented, including those newly arrived in the country. This assumption consequently creates an imperative to effectively identify and support all gifted and talented students. This section explores how The REAL Project has engaged with the challenge for educators in assessing newly arrived students who may have little or no experience of schooling in English. If schools are to achieve exemplary level in the Institutional Quality Standards, then their gifted and talented cohorts need to be fully representative of the school population. The REAL Project offers practical strategies to assist schools in this process.

The REAL Project has produced the initial assessment process, a series of procedures and materials that can be used by schools to ensure appropriate assessment of potential and targeted support for newly arrived students. Through this assessment process, schools and educators can dramatically shorten the time in which potentially gifted and talented new arrivals can be identified and improve the quality of their assessment system for all newly arrived students.

We got involved with The REAL Project to look at the sorts of things we could include to pick out gifted and talented new arrivals quickly without making the whole assessment procedure very laborious and time

> consuming. Our experience has been that it is possible for students who may have been added to the gifted and talented register in a minimum of two years are, through this new route, likely to be on it after eight weeks (Manny Vazquez, Joint Head, Hounslow Language Service).

One of the things that we will not allow to happen is for people to equate low income, poverty and disadvantage with low educational achievement. The diversity in our schools means that there is a lot of cultural capital. Our very successful schools see the children and families who don't speak English not as a barrier to overcome, but as the strength on which they will build success (Graham Smith, Head of Achievement and Diversity, Cambridge Education @ Islington).

Representativeness of the gifted and talented cohort

The Institutional Quality Standards for Gifted and Talented Education (IQS) require that a school/college's definition and shared understanding of gifted and talented is sufficiently inclusive to ensure that the gifted and talented population is fully representative of the whole school/college's population. To do this, a rigorous identification process needs to be in place and with clear principles and the use of a wide range of data. The IQS, as a self-evaluation and improvement tool, should be used to support the process of monitoring the extent to which provision recognizes and meets the needs of our target groups.

> It is part of our usual school cycle to do a self-evaluation in every department annually, and what I have done with the IQS is pass it out to curriculum areas, asking them to highlight where their department stands in terms of each of the various criteria, whether they are entry level, developing or exemplary. This snapshot – the overall evaluation – which we get from the IQS provides us with an idea of where the school as a whole stands and feeds in very strongly to our school improvement plan (Margot Currie, Assistant Head, Heston Community School).

Nominating and identifying gifted and talented students invariably involves selection from factors such as performance in standard measures, high scores on tests, high scores in SATs (Standard Attainment Tests) and internal examinations and individual subject nominations. Some of these criteria cannot be easily applied to all students, particularly new arrivals with EAL. These students may have arrived in school midterm and without any record of this standard performance data or of gifted and talented potential. Given this scenario, there is a real danger that potentially gifted and talented new arrivals are not spotted in the short term due simply to their lack of proficiency in English.

> If one assumes that the normal percentages which apply in schools are correct – that 10% of a school population is potentially gifted and talented or is on a register – then one should also assume that 10% of all new arrivals could potentially also be gifted and talented. It is incumbent on us to try to put in some additional procedures or to sharpen up our own assessment procedures in order to pick up some of this potential (Manny Vazquez, Joint Head, Hounslow Language Service).

New arrivals initial assessment process (Hounslow)

In developing this assessment process, it was felt that the focus should be on arguably the most challenging group of EAL new arrivals – students with hardly any baseline data and with very limited fluency in English. The students chosen for this REAL project therefore all had to meet two criteria:

- they had to be newly arrived at the start of this project; and
- they had to be at an early stage in their knowledge of English (English NC levels 1 or 2 and below).

The process provides opportunities to collect information to justify inclusion within the school's gifted and talented cohort. It provides a balance of quantitative and qualitative data relating to a student's

- educational history and experience;
- speaking, reading and writing skills;
- current knowledge of the 1000 high frequency words of English;
- mathematical ability;
- higher order thinking;
- ability to think, reason and express themselves in complex language in the mother tongue.

The assessment process generally takes place over the course of 6–8 weeks following the student's arrival in the school.

The resources should meet all the school's requirements in assessing a new arrival, whether or not they are identified as gifted and talented, but can be tailored to suit the local context as appropriate. Two key elements of the process, the 1000 word level test and the mother tongue interview, are further described here.

The 1000 word level test

This online test, based on Paul Nation's vocabulary test, is a multiple-choice format where students are required to answer questions as 'true', 'false' or 'not sure'. The test provides a measurement of the student's active vocabulary size so that their development needs can be better understood.

If a student scores below 83% this suggests that the knowledge of the most frequent words is not secure – it is the equivalent to not recognizing some 200 out of every 1000 English words. To be able to access normal curriculum materials, language and learning situations, the learner may need targeted interventions for literacy development.

The 1000 word level test can also be used to look for early signs of progress. Students are given another test within 6 weeks. Rapid progress in the acquisition of language can itself be an indicator that a student may be potentially gifted and talented.

Mother tongue assessment

New arrivals may well not be able to talk freely and in full (in English) about themselves, their experiences, interests and achievements. Schools therefore risk missing out on important information about these students. With students who are beginners in English the mother tongue assessment may provide the main means to access a range of evidence of

- prior educational history and experience;
- the journey made by the new arrival from their home country to the United Kingdom;
- evidence of a range of interests;
- the difference between their prior experience of education and the United Kingdom;
- areas for further follow-up or investigation.

Hounslow schools have used the mother tongue assessment in two ways: to provide students with the opportunity to inform their new schools about their interests and abilities, and to give the interviewer an opportunity to assess or infer the student's language, cognitive and conversational ability. The mother tongue interview gives the learner the opportunity to talk for about 5 minutes. The contrast between this experience and the other elements of the initial assessment process can be remarkable, particularly for beginners in English.

In some cases schools have used two interviews, with the second being used to focus on a particular interest, which might relate to a specific subject where additional evidence would support the case for inclusion.

The interviewer could be a member of the Ethnic Minority Achievement team (EMA), another member of staff who shares the same mother tongue language, a community group contact or an older student. Schools have also developed ways to overcome the challenge of developing language capacity by using bilingual staff in supplementary schools, cultural or community groups, religious centres or even contact through embassies to access interviewers. If a language audit has been conducted in the LA or neighbouring schools, suitable interviewers may be found through the LA G&T or EMA coordinators.

At the end of the interview, the interviewer is asked to make summary conclusions in relation to the students' mother tongue competence, with particular reference to the length of answers, breadth of vocabulary, grammatical accuracy and their level of engagement revealed through conversation.

It is in the interest of both the student and the school for the assessment to be completed as quickly as is possible, as ability in mother tongue languages may start to deteriorate radically after even a few weeks.

The extent to which the interview is used may be limited by local circumstances, such as limited access to speakers of specific languages, or where the schools face a high volume of new arrivals. In these circumstances a checklist of early indicators of gifted and talented behaviours has been used to highlight those from whom the assessment would seem to be required.

The initial assessment process has been trialled in three Hounslow schools that are accustomed to receiving significant numbers of EAL midterm admissions (Hounslow Manor School reported that they had received over 80 new arrivals in the first term in 2007). The REAL Project has sought to provide a 'ladder up' that other schools can now take advantage of, not only in terms of recognizing their own position/progress in relation to these assessment practices but also providing the means by which interventions and progress can potentially be made.

> It improves the communication between EAL staff, students and the mainstream staff . . . it raises our profile and status. The children are happy that they get noticed; they get extended programs; they don't just get put at the back of the classroom or in the bottom set (Phyllis Bridge, EAL Coordinator, Feltham Community School).

Since trialling began, actual outcomes have been many and varied but mainly highly positive. These include much earlier nominations of EAL new arrivals to the gifted and talented register, placement of students in higher sets and an increased sense of expectation from both student and teacher perspectives. One of the Hounslow project schools reports a greater involvement of the EAL department throughout the school, which has raised awareness and contributed to a significant increase in the number of EAL students on the gifted and talented register. The effects are striking – the gifted and talented cohort is now significantly more representative of the whole school population (Table 3).

'Passport' project (Sandwell)

Sandwell LAs are working to improve their identification processes in a pilot project with two schools. LA EMA and gifted and talented staff have produced a 'passport' which is designed to give each newly arrived student an

Table 3   One Hounslow school's development of a more inclusive gifted and talented register.

	2006–2007: Pre-REAL		2007–2008: Post-REAL	
Year 7–11 school population	822		858	
Approximate G&T register (10% of school population)	82		86	
Number and percentage of EAL students on G&T register	1	1.2%	26	30.2%

entitlement to assessment and identification as being potentially gifted and talented. The process supporting the passport has been designed to build up the capacity to address both academic ability and to identify talents, including those that are culturally specific.

Taking the Hounslow initial assessment pack as a starting point, this project has incorporated parents into the mother-tongue assessment procedure. The parents are invited to be present at their child's mother-tongue interview, and this adds to the nature and scope of the information gained at this session. A teacher working with the target student is asked to monitor and record evidence of the student's progress over a 15-lesson period. The information gathered during this period is collated into a 'passport'. The students, parents and teachers add information about the child's prior school attainment and abilities as well as their achievements outside of their prior education system. This is intended to act as a means of alerting teachers to the gifts and talents the student has developed in their previous country or country of origin.

The acknowledgment of such gifts and talents can lead to recognition that the student's skills may be transferable and thus make them potentially gifted or talented in National Curriculum subject areas. It can also enable the school to seek extra curricular provision to further the student's development. The aim of this project is to identify students making exceptional progress, measured either through their rate of English acquisition or by their progress as evaluated by subject teachers.

Data delivered – aiding identification and intervention

Although there is a great wealth of data held in schools, it is not always accessible to G&T coordinators in a coherent and systematic way, with the result that it is more likely that cohorts are less effectively and accurately identified. The primary goal of this project was to develop a single user-friendly tool that would make a range of data streams available to school and LA colleagues. This includes the full range of 'hard' data such as attainment and attendance, but also gives parity to 'soft' data, such as the results of the Pupil Attitudes to Self and School survey, to give earlier and higher visibility to warning signs that students might be at risk of underachievement. The project was used as a tool to analyze the impact of other REAL interventions.

The data streams were collated and integrated into a spreadsheet format that enables G&T coordinators to identify and monitor potential underachievers as well as prior high achievers, and target interventions using a single data set. The tool can be used at an individual student, class or whole-school level, and may therefore be of use to lead LA/school officers, data managers as well as G&T coordinators. Combined with other regularly updated data this tool may provide a means by which a good sense of change and impact could be drawn.

Staff using the tool are able to extract data to create individual student files which can enable personalized interventions, tracking and monitoring of particular gifted and talented students and cohorts. Colleagues with little training and guidance can very simply filter and sort data using a sophisticated set of criteria, and responses have been very positive. Schools have focused on using the tool to improve representation of Somali pupils and others from locally under-represented groups. The tool has also been used by schools to develop a shadow register for a wider group of students who potentially could be gifted and talented, or who are no longer achieving in the top 10%. This group are likely to benefit from a range of effectively targeted interventions such as mentoring, masterclasses and other enrichment opportunities that specifically meet their needs.

Teaching and Learning Strategies

Teaching and Learning Strategies

As demand for specialist EAL resources are most often from new arrivals, there is a real risk that the specific learning needs of gifted and talented students who are advanced learners of English may be overlooked. A common misconception is that the cultural capital and academic language required for successful participation in learning opportunities is simply acquired through the 'normal' learning process. Attainment data for these groups tell us that this is simply not the case.

Teachers need to be able to recognize the distinct needs that advanced learners may have which, if not met, can limit their ability to access challenge. They need to help advanced learners to understand how the learning of language relates to learning in general and both teachers and students need to see how an explicit focus on language development and the acquisition of cultural capital can impact on achievement.

Advanced learners tend to require specific support to access challenge in learning. The REAL Project is working very much from the premise that much of this support can be delivered within everyday classroom learning and that where withdrawal is used it is used explicitly in support of high achievement.

Teachers also need to be able to see how to adapt the best of their own practice so that it can provide stretch and challenge and not just support. The projects outlined in this section show some of the ways in which The REAL Project has engaged with these complex issues to provide more personalized learning for advanced learners.

> This REAL work really fits into the whole gifted and talented agenda. Academic vocabulary could easily be a barrier to those students who could really fly. Being proactive about this kind of vocabulary can speed up the rate of acquisition that particularly EAL and BME students can progress at (Matt Cowing, Science Teacher, Hounslow Manor School).

An advanced bilingual learner is someone who sounds fluent, sounds probably like a native speaker of English. When you look at their writing, it's quite good. But when you look at it closely, there are a number of features of it which show that English isn't their first language, and that they are a long way short of the kind of academic language that they need. And they won't acquire that by osmosis. They will acquire it because you teach it to them explicitly (Graham Smith, Head of Achievement and Diversity, Cambridge Education @ Islington).

Advanced learners of English may have been in the British school system for some time, or be long-term English users who have been educated in English-speaking schools abroad. A substantial body of research indicates that advanced learners tend to have more gaps in their academic vocabulary and handle certain features of writing less confidently for academic purposes than their peers with English as their mother tongue language (EMT). English may be their 'first' language, but they may also speak another language in the home, or they may have few opportunities for formal expression and communication in English beyond the school. Advanced learners may have less grasp of idiomatic speech, or less understanding of literal, figurative or metaphorical language and different genres of English. In relation to academic writing, learners may be unfamiliar with the conventions and expectations of particular genres, such as how a scientific report differs from a summary of a historical event with reference to both language and purpose.

These differences can significantly affect the character and quality of the work of advanced learners when it is compared with a student of similar ability whose mother tongue is English. Individual advanced learners' conversational competence may not be mirrored in their ability to use formal academic language confidently or effectively. They may not have control over the construction and use of more formal registers and writing traditions and often might slip into a more informal tone inappropriate for a particular task. Similarly, these learners may not have strategies in place for organizing and expressing ideas in the ways that school literacy traditions demand. A common feature of their performance is that they often have good topic-level knowledge, but limited capacity to show what they know when answering questions. Their spoken or written answers can take on the characteristics of a list rather than a more well-formed text in the expected genre.

The REAL Project has explored ways in which teachers can respond to these needs through the use of explicit strategies which support advanced learners in overcoming their own challenges with language to play a full part in classroom learning opportunities.

> Getting the top grades for someone of your age – whether you are 11 or 14 or 16 or 18 – can't be done just by knowing the subject really well. You've got to have the academic language that goes with it. We have lots of students who sound fluent in English and are very bright, but their written work is missing big chunks of what the best academic English looks like (Graham Smith, Head of Achievement and Diversity, Cambridge Education @ Islington).

The Academic Word List (Hounslow)

The Academic Word List (AWL) relates to words needed by students to access and understand academic texts. It comprises 570 word families that are not in the most frequent 2000 words of English but which occur reasonably frequently over a very wide range of texts.

> The first 1,000 high frequency words probably account for between 70–75% of individual words in any text. The most frequently used 2,000 words would cover between 75–79% of most if not all texts that students are going to encounter. The 3,000-word level is in theory a threshold at which you should start getting access to authentic texts. By authentic, we mean texts which are

not reading schemes that are graded. The 5,000-word level is a threshold where you have got access to a whole range of texts, and understanding these would be a pre-requisite for doing very well in your GCSEs and A-levels (Manny Vazquez, Joint Head, Hounslow Language Service).

The words are useful for learners studying any curriculum subject and consist of formal vocabulary such as *access, authority, define, environment, assume, criteria, imply*. The list is divided into 10 sub-lists according to frequency of occurrence in texts. The actual size of the list is over 3000 words when one includes the derivatives of the headword, for example *access – accessible, accessibility, inaccessible, accessing*. Secure knowledge of this group of words is an important indicator of word level proficiency, but in addition is a powerful asset in accessing the higher levels of academic tasks at each Key Stage.

The goal of the activity was to establish the students' familiarity with the AWL words and to develop strategies for learning and using those that were unfamiliar. The project compared students' knowledge of these words at the beginning and end of the project. Year 10 students were selected by the G&T coordinator and the Head of Science at one Hounslow school on the basis that they were felt to be underachieving as reflected by their limited use of academic English language and vocabulary.

> This particular group of 570 words . . . cut across all really academic disciplines and subject areas. Interestingly, if you combine the 2,000-word level list with the AWL, students who know both should in theory have access to about 90% of most texts. So there are great gains to be made by consolidating at the 2,000-word level and coupling that with a fairly complete knowledge of the AWL as well (Manny Vazquez, Joint Head, Hounslow Language Service).

The AWL became the focus of a six-session intervention. Students were shown a range of texts which were linked to their science learning. An online vocabulary highlighter tool was used to check for academic words occurring in the text. The students were invited to

- record any words that they were not familiar with;
- look these up in a dictionary;
- write down the meaning;
- check that they understood the meaning back in the context of the text.

They were then introduced to some learning strategies which would help to improve their understanding and use of these academic words. The students were given a final test in the summer term in which they were asked to reflect upon their learning and identify those strategies that had been most useful to them.

Outcomes

This intervention contributed towards almost a third of the target students being moved up a set. They have benefitted from a substantial, measurable increase in their knowledge of this specialist group of words, and an unexpectedly noticeable increase in their motivation as learners. The project has created a set of procedures through which students can take greater control over their vocabulary development. It has enhanced teachers' awareness of the AWL and how language use cuts across subjects. Equally significantly, the students were also able to talk about the impact themselves:

> It's helped me with doing academic words because before, in class when teachers used to explain stuff I didn't really understand it; they used to use all these big words. Sir came and he taught us about the words and how and what they mean and it's helped me in lessons because now I can answer questions and with my homework as well, and in exams I don't have to miss the questions out because it's easier for me to answer (Student, Hounslow).

Literal, figurative and academic language for advanced learners of English (Hounslow)

> Our experience is that these students are barred from their understanding of the curriculum because there are large gaps in their understanding of English. Many are extremely intelligent and are being barred from achieving top grades by this gap (Margot Currie, Assistant Head, Heston Community School).

This activity has been aimed at preparing and familiarizing students with the skills and language range needed to excel in Paper 1 of the Academic Quality Assurance English Language General Certificate in Secondary Education (GCSE) exam. This paper is considered to be one of the most challenging for advanced learners, as it requires students to work with unseen texts.

Higher grades are awarded to those students who can draw and express inferences, make evaluations and comparisons, as well as being able to both recognize and use idioms, metaphor, similes, puns and phrasal verbs. It is additionally dependent on students' ability to draw on their knowledge of society and cultural practices. Part of preparing students for this exam is to heighten their awareness of how language is used effectively in texts to be expressive, to convey emotion and to cause a reaction in the reader. Candidates who gain grade C or above in this paper are able to identify persuasive language features (e.g. emotive language), to use these methods in their own writing, to compare texts and to write in an appropriate style according to purpose.

> It is very important that we bring in strategies and measures that enable mainstream teachers to respond to what may be very gifted students (Manny Vazquez, Joint Head, Hounslow Language Service).

The overall aim was to develop a series of lessons providing an explicit focus on language structures and practices that may be common knowledge (albeit potentially subconscious) to 'native' English speaking students.

The work was trialled in schools with a mixed ability Year 9 group after SATs to encourage teachers to re-evaluate their materials and schemes of work in relation to the implicit language demands of advanced learners. Students were also encouraged to make use of their own English language repertoires, sometimes learned in different cultural environments, in appropriate ways in their current work. The timing of the intervention is important. Achievement at A* at GCSE is dependent on individuals having sufficient time for their skills to mature.

A scheme of work and set of resource materials were produced around the theme of figurative language and football, incorporating a variety of individual, pair and group tasks, peer-evaluation activities and team-teacher modelling of the main task.

> We did a variety of activities with the students, not just text-based. We wanted the students to demonstrate for each other how idioms don't make literal sense, and we wanted them to consciously craft language themselves (Janet Macdonald, English teacher, Heston Community School).

My parents don't say something as typical as 'you hit the nail on its head', cause that's something that would not come into normal conversation with my Mum. You have to have background knowledge about it . . . like a British point of view, and that I don't have (Year 9 Student, Hounslow).

Strategies to increase level 5s for EAL learners in English at Key Stage 2 (Islington)

Over 120 languages are spoken in Islington schools. The largest groups are of Turkish, Kurdish and Bengali (Sylheti) speakers. Traditionally, fewer pupils with EAL have attained level 5 at Key Stage 2 in English than their peers who have EMT. Educators working with EAL students realize that there can be a significant difference between the rates at which these students acquire spoken rather than written English. The academic and technical language that is needed to succeed in the British education system must be taught explicitly – this is the language required to achieve level 5 in English SATs at Key Stage 2. This project sets out to increase the number of EAL students achieving this grade by improving the knowledge base of teachers through focused training, and by encouraging the use of teaching strategies which focus on speaking and listening activities and explicit teaching of language as means of developing writing. It also focuses on supporting and challenging advanced learners within whole class learning, with withdrawal work used principally to support and consolidate high achievement rather than to safeguard basic proficiency. The project initially drew on the work of Lynne Cameron. She analyzed samples of students' written work to identify the types of language structures and textual features used in texts that achieved a level 5, compared to texts that failed to reach this level. What colleagues in Islington found, also in keeping with Cameron's work, was that the work of the advanced learners of English that failed to achieve a level 5 shared similar characteristics in terms of their use of academic English. In looking closely at the students' written work it became clear that familiarity with the requirements of academic writing, such as genre, register and tone, along with their ability to structure texts was a key factor in determining success.

This local research highlighted the need for advanced learners to be made aware of how English is used in different contexts for different purposes to achieve different goals. The response has focused on creating materials and guidance for teachers to engage students in a range of activities designed to raise their awareness to the variety of ways in which English is used, in both speaking and writing, to successfully engage with particular academic tasks and to enable students to be more effective users of academic English.

> [Advanced learners'] cognitive ability is very, very good. And often they'll have strengths in maths, for example. But the only thing really that is holding them back is the fact that they haven't yet got fluency in English. They need that little extra push. One of the main jobs of working with the group is trying to extend their vocabulary so that they're getting that academic language (Helena Blake, Ethnic Minority Achievement Coordinator, Grafton Primary School).

A number of strategies are now in regular use to promote confident and purposeful talk in the classroom. For example, asking students to report back to each other in small groups as well as to the whole class involves a shift in audience and purpose for which students have to change the register of their language, which is often a source of difficulty for advanced learners. This has been largely overcome through the familiarity which students develop for the formal roles they are expected to play, for instance through the use of hot seating or expert groups. These are activities which place the advanced learner in a position where their proficiency in English is challenged. Positive achievement is rewarded through the use of specific praise for use of language as well as in modelling further development.

Significant use is made of partnership teaching in which an EAL specialist teacher works alongside the mainstream classroom teacher in both planning and delivering lessons together. These two roles support the interaction between learners, the technical detail of the content and the use of specific language in context. It allows for a constantly evolving blend of support and challenge to be directed throughout the lesson as well as for specific advice to be understood by the students as relating to language or to the subject/context. It is a rich source of professional development for the class teacher. It is also a clear example of how EAL capacity can be deployed to meet the needs of gifted and talented students, to enable them to access challenge within everyday classroom learning situations and to raise the bar for others too.

Student Voice

Student Voice

The projects in this section share a common goal of encouraging dialogue between students, parents/carers and schools as a means of better understanding the learning environments of gifted and talented students. If students take a cognitive step towards understanding how they learn, they can play a greater role in designing and developing their own education. Through helping them to better understand and take control over their learning, the gaps between their perceptions and teacher expectations can be narrowed.

The tools developed within The REAL Project focus on understanding underachievement of EAL and BME students through accessing the voices of students, parents and teachers. By doing this we have expanded our understanding of underachievement leading to the development of more sensitized and informed interventions and provision through the use of learning logs and other practicable tools. Schools have been able to extract valuable data on student experience, classroom learning and changes in attitudes, in order to more sharply identify needs and to improve practice in the curriculum.

> Students involved in The REAL Project are keeping learning logs, and it has been extremely effective at encouraging students to think about their own learning. The activity also creates a mechanism by which they can discuss their education with their parents at home. It has allowed us to get ahead of the game in terms of understanding our students' learning needs and experiences (Phil Ward, Headteacher, Heston Community School).

It is our belief that by establishing a dialogue between schools, students and parents, students will be better placed to take ownership of their own education. This is because they would be better positioned to reflect on their own learning behaviours and external influences such as their peers, the perceived difficulty of subjects, or teaching styles.

Through the REAL partnership, Haringey and Hounslow have been involved in projects to heighten gifted and talented student's reflection on their learning as well as to identify factors which affect their achievement.

These projects challenge the assumption that students are *passive* recipients of knowledge, and that their success or failure rests with the teacher who is the main 'agent' of learning. Instead, these projects have built on existing practice to develop ways for educators to enable students to become active learners.

In both LAs, gifted and talented students were given a learning log book to fill out on a regular basis, with questions designed to deepen their thinking and to reflect upon what makes a successful lesson and why in some lessons they make little or no progress.

They were prompted by a series of questions designed to encourage personal reflection, such as '*What did you learn this week? What did you enjoy learning this week? What further questions do you have about things you learnt this week?*' In both LAs, this process was complemented with a survey completed by students, parents and staff that sought to reveal attitudes and values to learning (see Parents and Communities section for a more detailed description of this work).

Students for this project were selected on the grounds that they were considered to be gifted and talented but at risk of underachievement. Using prior assessment data, schools were able to identify target students, such as EAL learners achieving significantly less well in English and Humanities than in Science and Maths. Form tutors, mentors and teacher nominations enabled G&T coordinators to identify passive students who were choosing not to engage in gifted and talented enrichment programmes, or those they felt were coasting or disaffected in class.

Over the course of a term, students were given time to complete their log book entries, focusing on the subjects they felt they were making the greatest and least progress in, and why this might have been the case. Haringey students were additionally required to assess their progress against level and grade descriptors for English, Mathematics and Science. The link to assessment raised the value of the discussion and gave a tangible measure of impact.

Outcomes

This process of reflective learning enabled the students freely to record their perceptions of learning in lessons as well as identify teaching practices that impact positively upon their learning and development. The learning logs encourage discussion about learning. Group and one-to-one discussions with teachers encouraged the sharing of concerns that made solutions more practical.

The benefits to the students involved in this project have been wide and varied. The provision of reflective space within which students can think honestly and openly about their experiences of learning has enabled them to take genuine ownership of the process. The open-ended nature of the questions in the logs meant that students tended to be less judgemental in their responses, and through regular conversation learned to become more reflective about their learning and to address the barriers to achievement. Teachers managing the dialogues were also able to support the brokerage of solutions where appropriate.

> I began to see the lessons I was making least progress in were the ones I found most difficult, and consequently as I wasn't enjoying them I put less effort in. But if I was to overcome the difficulties I would have to work even harder in those subjects, because they are important to my future plans (Student, Hounslow).

Through this written record and dialogue with teachers and parents/carers, students began to set their own targets, critically engage with their own learning behaviours and habits and became more actively involved in shaping and determining their own learning.

> The student logs have provided us with absolutely fascinating evidence from the students' perspective. We have gained a wealth of information as to what they consider to be a good lesson. I'm confident that this will make a significant improvement to our teaching and learning (Margot Currie, Assistant Head, Heston Community School).

In Haringey the link with assessment has seen positive effects. In English, on comparing the progress in sub-levels made from Year 8 to Year 9 with the progress made from Key Stage 2 to Year 8, all of the students in the original REAL cohort made better progress once they had started on the learning logs project in Year 8 (six students made three or four sub-levels of progress, and three students made six or more sub-levels of progress). In Science, one student made 10 sub-levels of progress. In the Key Stage 4 cohort, 4 of the original 10 students made better than expected progress from Key Stage 3 to their mock GCSE examinations in English.

School improvement, informing the management of learning

These projects have benefitted the schools just as much as the individual gifted and talented students. The individual logs provided students with the space to give personal feedback on their classroom experience, providing the school with an insight into student's perceptions of good practice. High quality evidence of student voice has been used to support leaders in tackling school improvement priorities. Schools have reported that students who completed reflective learning logs have begun to do something positive to improve their own learning.

> In some cases these student logs have provided significant evidence in which to evaluate and improve the effectiveness of departments (Stefani Shedden, Hounslow G&T Coordinator).

The logs have provided insights into how well lesson content and materials are received by students, and how they feel they could be supported more effectively. This has enabled teachers to plan more personalized support for their classes based on their increasing knowledge of the students.

In Haringey and Hounslow schools, such dialogue with students has enabled whole-school improvement, and in several schools has advanced practice considerably in relation to personalized learning, independent learning and assessment for learning. Schools are developing their own provision in response to the data gathered from these logs, and can pick up patterns and trends to improve upon in their own schools.

At one school, data from student logs were collated by subject and a clear picture emerged of what students felt helped them achieve highly in specific subjects. It became evident that students felt they did well in a particular Science class where they received regular updates of their progress against National Curriculum level descriptors. The use of assessment for learning strategies was highly motivating for students and this was reflected in their results in Science. However, the logs also showed that the same students were doing less well in other subjects. From the logs, details of the Science teacher's classroom strategies were captured and presented across the school to colleagues. This process enabled features of this teacher's effective practice to be disseminated into different subject areas and inform whole-school improvement.

Part of the value of these projects is that it offers schools the opportunity to work with the data themselves and decide, based on their interpretations and local needs, the types of actions and interventions they may plan to undertake. For example, more homework clubs have been introduced at Hounslow Manor School as a result of students' comments in their logs, and at Heston Community School the use of logbooks is now being embedded as an annual project.

G&T coordinators have found the student responses impressive and insightful. The student logs are seen as offering a direct connection between teaching and learning strategies. As one colleague in Hounslow put it, 'this project is to enable, not label' and it is changing the way the schools think about the achievement of all students and moving the conversation away from underachievement.

There have also been unexpected benefits to the projects, such as students talking to their parents more about their learning. By providing a foundation from which a conversation about the school and learning can be built, these logs can help parents to engage further in their children's education.

> The mother of a Year 9 boy in The REAL Project is delighted. Since he has started to keep a learning log, her son has been coming home and talking for the first time about what helps him learn. She thinks it is making a real difference (Margot Currie, Assistant Head, Heston Community School).

Understanding culturally specific gifts and talents (Wolverhampton)

The main focus of the secondary school project in Wolverhampton has been to work with schools and a variety of agencies/professionals – including those working in the community – to explore the ways in which information about in-school and out-of-school talents, interests and achievements are gathered and shared.

This is often an aspect of students' lives that is largely unknown to schools and teachers, but potentially a very rich and informative area. By focusing specifically on identifying community-related gifts and talents in a group of Black Caribbean, Black African and Mixed Heritage young people, the ways in which schools support their gifted and talented students can be informed, and can lead to more personalized learning.

Three working groups have been involved in this project: an established multi-agency group of adults; a group made up of teachers, colleagues from youth services and local community organizations; and a group of approximately 10 students and teaching assistants from local schools. The role of these groups is to generate ideas about what constitute community-related gifts and talents in relation to the target groups.

The student group have been involved in organizing a celebratory event to recognize these community-related gifts and talents. The students are taking responsibility for all aspects of organizing the celebration event, including finding a venue and managing a budget. They have engaged in an extended study project documenting their involvement that gains them accreditation equivalent to AS level and counts towards UCAS points. They also receive a Youth Award Level 3 [Bronze].

The community-related talents identified by the working groups are subject to scrutiny by parents, community representatives and educational professionals, and a questionnaire has been sent to the schools involved seeking students' views about such talents.

Parents and Communities

Parents and Communities

At school level, there is often a lack of clarity in the understanding of what gifted and talented education is. Schools and LAs have reported that this can be even greater amongst those members of the school community who are from BME and/or EAL communities. They add that educators can sometimes assume that parents may not understand the concept of gifted and talented education unless they are from strong educational backgrounds themselves and talk regularly with schools about their children's progress.

Across the REAL partnership we have identified variations in community and cultural attitudes and conceptualizations of giftedness, and working with parents and communities we have tried to establish a shared and accessible understanding. Parental and community engagement is key in all our projects. Where we have worked with parents to develop strategies to enable them to engage with their child's learning and applied positive assumptions the results have been profound.

The notion of the gifted and talented student is not one that easily crosses cultural boundaries. For some communities it can be a threatening idea – they are already marked out in various obvious ways, and then someone comes along and says 'here is another label we want to attach to your child'. But we want to draw people in, not push people away by using terminology that they find a bit frightening. It's a way of saying 'this will really help'. This will mean that your child is able to make real choices about their future. And if they can make it to Oxford, we're going to get them there (Graham Smith, Head of Achievement and Diversity, Cambridge Education @ Islington).

Research has indicated that parental involvement is an important factor related to achievement in primary school, and even that between the ages of 7 and 16 is a more powerful force than family background, size of family and level of parental education. For gifted and talented students, parental support and encouragement at home can provide the impetus for high achievement, and can supplement classroom learning. This can be summarized for our purposes as supporting access to academic challenge.

> Everyone wants the best, not only for our children but for the school, for the community, for the educational system as well (Parent, Hounslow).

Whilst there is generally comprehensive support from most community groups for the academic domain of giftedness, some parent and community groups have been seen to attach lower value to talent. In some cases, resistance is simply due to a concern for future economic implications: traditional academic and scientific qualifications are valued and regarded as a route to academic and financial success and better jobs, whereas some talent domains such as dance and music may not be considered a good basis for a financially rewarding career. In other cases, it has to do with family or community values: dance or drama for example may be judged by some families to be incompatible with the communities' religious, cultural and moral values, particularly for girls.

A key task of The REAL Project has been to highlight ways in which celebrating talents can lead to increased motivation in other areas of learning, and to work with community groups in recognizing culturally relevant and appropriate talents. In Islington, bilingual community officers were supported to develop constructive strategies for engaging with the community's values and culture. These strategies included stressing to parents that if a student is recognized and supported in a talent area this can raise motivation in other areas of learning. It was also emphasized that talent-related success need not necessarily lead to a career or profession, but can lead to wider educational achievement and transferable skills.

Working with parents

The REAL Project has been underpinned by a core belief in the value of listening. Improving parental engagement requires us to spend as much time listening to what is being said as working to improve quality. For the REAL partnership this has involved supporting schools and LAs in developing local solutions to local issues and resisting any temptation to impose a top-down model or to generalize prematurely about what may or may not work. So why work with parents? Simply because their feedback is essential to understanding what is needed and what is effective. Our objectives were

- to strengthen the link between parental involvement and student achievement;
- to reveal or encourage high expectations and aspirations in minority ethnic families;
- to improve understanding of the learning needs of gifted and talented children;
- to address the language needs of both the parent/carer and the child;
- to develop the cultural and social capital of families, the community and the school.

These objectives cannot be met by a single intervention, but at the same time it is neither practical nor necessary to devise comprehensive or top-down approaches which are misdirected or fail to impact by targeting too many issues. What was required were engagement projects which enabled parents to feel included in their children's education.

Our joint projects have addressed the needs of specific communities where appropriate (Islington) or more broadly diverse groups of students from different ethnic groups (Hounslow and Haringey). As a partnership, we have tried to capture the 'authentic voice' of individuals as an intrinsic part of all of the projects: learning first-hand about parents' concerns or expectations changes how schools need to think about the other issues. As a partnership we are finding that it is this dynamic which marks out what is transferable practice from what is merely an interesting idea.

By listening to authentic voices, we have been able to identify clearly the starting points for students, parents and teachers when embarking on these projects, and have thus been able to more effectively evaluate what has been achieved. By providing detailed contextual information and participant evaluations, we have striven to ensure the transferability of the interventions developed. We believe that this will enable other schools and LAs to ask better questions of their own provision.

Pandora's box: parent, student and teacher survey (Hounslow)

A survey of parent, student and teacher attitudes and values to learning has been devised in Hounslow to complement the reflective student log. This REAL project activity set out to explore the views of parents, students and teachers of potential or actual gifted and talented students in relation to:

- *Beliefs, values and attitudes to education.* The similarities and differences between the parent's, student's and teacher's views and ideas in regards to teaching and learning.
- *Perceptions of the student as 'learner'.* How the student is viewed as a learner both in and out of school and by themselves as well.
- *The classroom and homework as learning experiences.* Ideas and attitudes towards the role and effectiveness of work done both in and out of school.
- *Attainment and expectations.* How the student's progress is understood as well as similarities and differences between their and their parent's and teacher's expectations.
- *Agency and power.* The parent's, student's and teacher's ideas about how changes in attainment can be planned and implemented.

By obtaining the three different perspectives from parents, students and teachers we hoped to see where there were areas of agreement and also areas of difference. In addition it has been possible to identify key themes that recur in survey responses (e.g. extra-curricular opportunities and support/ resources for parents).

The challenge for our schools is harnessing parent power so that the parents can work with the schools to achieve the maximum educational outcomes. Many parents want to support their young people, but don't always understand the best way to do that. Schools try very hard to work with parents and young people, and this project is really an effective extension of all those efforts (Stefani Shedden, G&T Coordinator, Hounslow).

A simple checklist was used to target Year 9 and Year 10 students who were either on the gifted and talented register or the shadow register of high achieving students who fall just outside of the top 10%. The student, parent and staff surveys were designed to take only 20–25 minutes to complete. In some cases, the parental questionnaires were translated into a language which parents were familiar with in order to encourage accurate and accessible reflections. In a few cases, a follow-up conversation was undertaken in which the questionnaire was completed over the phone with the parent. This model of enquiry enabled schools to learn more about their students and parents.

Questionnaires have been completed by both parents and teachers of Year 9 students. It was very exciting to get this information back because often at parents' evenings, parents who do not speak English are disadvantaged unless someone will translate for them, and very often that translator is the student. So this gave them an instrument into which they could put their own voice without any other spin on it. It has been wonderful to be able to take into account what parents feel about their children's education, and the Learning Coordinator is working with the information to see how best to generate additional support as well as increasing contact with parents (Margot Currie, Assistant Head, Heston Community School).

The first questionnaires established the baseline for the students' attitudes and feelings about their learning and compared this to their parents and teachers. They were asked to think about instances where they have felt they have made progress, where they felt that they have not and the contributing factors in relation to this.

The project delivered a snapshot view and a longer term reflective account to inform and improve interventions. Some key themes emerged that could improve the outcomes for these students, including more effective use of homework, closer links between home and school, more guidance for parents about how to help their children, improved learning behaviours and more after-school support for learners.

Improving parental capacity to support student achievement (Haringey)

The majority of students at Northumberland Park School in Haringey are from BME backgrounds, and 62% of students speak EAL. The school is above average in size, although its population profile varies each year because a number of students who are new to the country join during the year. As part of The REAL Project, the school conducted a survey of parents of students from a diverse range of ethnic minority backgrounds, all of whom spoke a first language other than English.

Students from BME or EAL backgrounds who had achieved highly at Key Stage 2 and Key Stage 3 but appeared to be subsequently underachieving were chosen for the cohort. Although these students were at risk of not achieving their expected high grades at Key Stage 3 and GCSE, they all had a positive attitude towards school and their learning and felt that their parents could support them to improve on their performance. All the parents of the students invited to participate in the project were introduced to The REAL Project at a preliminary meeting, and were given an opportunity to discuss the contribution that they could make to their child's education.

> The aim was to work in partnership with the Community Learning Manager targeting parents of REAL children and engaging 'hard to reach' families within the local EAL and BME communities. Through The REAL Project parent's programme we wanted to build the capacity of parents to adequately support children's studies (Bianca Greenhalgh, Leading Teacher for G&T, Northumberland Park School).

Engaging gifted learners in a written dialogue with a teacher was intended to be one of a number of strategies for improving achievement. The students were given a weekly reflective journal to write, which parents contributed to, thus reinforcing the importance of involving parents in this dialogue. Parental workshops were then held to address the key themes of gifted education including work on thinking skills and ways to support a high achieving child. Parents' meetings and questionnaires revealed perceived barriers which the school could work to remove and areas of strength to build on.

Other findings indicated that parents mostly had positive attitudes to education, and felt that they were working in partnership with the school. Although students felt that feedback from families was good, they often commented that their parents did not ask to see their homework diaries regularly. Parents as a result of this process were more aware of the impact of their involvement in the learning outcomes for their children.

'Without education there is no light': engaging parents in supporting potentially high achieving Somali students (Islington)

Attainment of Somali students has been a cause of concern in Islington, and as the numbers of Somali students has risen very rapidly – doubled in the last four years – the impact of failure there is on all of our results (Graham Smith, Head of Achievement and Diversity, Cambridge Education @ Islington).

In January 2007, approximately 5% of students in Islington schools reported Somali as their mother tongue language, an estimated 1100 students. Of those students, 80% were eligible for free school meals (double the Islington average). One of the REAL projects supported a cohort of 72 potentially high achieving Somali students from Years 5 and 6.

The 'Somali community' can mean a lot of different things and does not refer to a homogenous group. The parents involved in the project represent differing rural and urban communities and tribal groups within Somalia, with a wide range of educational backgrounds or experiences. Some have been in the United Kingdom for some time, while others are fairly recent arrivals, often from other European and Scandinavian countries as well as directly from troubled areas of Somalia. It is often recognized that the parents of these students have a lack of familiarity with the UK education system, in particular with the idea of parental involvement in education and the concept of gifted and talented.

An initial series of meetings enabled parents to provide input and voice concerns on areas in which they lacked confidence. Some of these areas included

- detailed overviews of the English education system, including National Curriculum levels;
- explanations of the concepts of gifted and talented;
- confirmation of the importance of continuing to use the Somali language and the role that it can play in the development of higher order thinking;

- discussions of some of the social and emotional aspects of learning and the importance of praise and encouragement;
- strategies for increasing communication between home and school, signposting bilingual resources and services for further help and assistance.

The students chosen for this project were identified as higher achievers who could possibly reach level 5 in Key Stage 2 Maths and Science (based on Fisher Family Trust predictions and teacher assessments) with more parental involvement. The students were taken to a local secondary school for help and support in English, maths and Personal, Health and Social Education (PHSE), and the classes operated in both English and Somali. The classes were also attended by some parents/carers in order to bridge the gap of understanding between school and home about talents and abilities. The project sought to engage parents in overcoming potential barriers which might prevent them from helping their children to achieve level 5 and above.

> They work with you until you understand and I am now top of the class in both maths and English thanks to this project (Student, Key Stage 2 Somali project, Islington).

As a result of both the parental classes and the classes they attended with their child, parents have reported an increased understanding of and ability to manage family learning and ways to promote their children's learning in daily contexts. They express a developing interest in understanding the concepts of gifted and talented and have moved to a greater acceptance of the idea that sports and arts activities support their children's personal and academic success. The increased sense of partnership between parents and schools has been echoed in the wider community, where Somali parents record that they feel much more a part of the borough and more willing to participate in the wider school community.

Schools have reported that the project has helped them raise the expectations of Somali students (see Table 4), by better understanding the reasons for the seeming reluctance of parents to get involved in their children's schooling, and creating learning strategies for increasing the partnership between the Somali community and educators.

> About half of the Somali students in the borough actually come to this project, and 85% of all of those who get level 5 come to the project. There is an issue

Table 4 Islington Somali students' achievement (2007 data).

		Number of students	*% getting level 5*
English	REAL Project schools	38	21
	Non-REAL Project schools	40	10
Maths	REAL Project schools	38	18
	Non-REAL Project schools	40	3

here about student voice which people don't normally associate with gifted and talented initiatives. But the gifted kids will tell you what they want, and they did, and we worked with them to provide it (Graham Smith, Head of Achievement and Diversity, Cambridge Education @ Islington).

The most important thing is to work together – the parents and the teachers – to guide the children. Since I have been coming here I have seen the gaps where they need my support as a parent (Parent, Islington).

Engaging parents in supporting potentially high achieving Bangladeshi and Turkish students in numeracy at Key Stage 2 (Islington)

We have learned that people who are learning successfully in two languages do far better than people who are learning successfully in one. Being able to manipulate concepts in two languages gives you insights into those concepts and a grasp of them that you might not get otherwise. For some of our students where English isn't as well developed, if you really want them to get it you have a go at it in their first language first. But for many of them where they have some control in both languages, it is very empowering to be able to learn in both (Graham Smith, Head of Achievement and Diversity, Cambridge Education @ Islington).

Turkish and Bangladeshi students are among the largest of the minority ethnic groups in Islington primary schools, and in several schools at least one group forms 25% of the school roll. The groups are among the lowest performing of Islington's minority groups in mathematics at Key Stage 2 (see Figure 3). This project was therefore undertaken

- because of the consistently lower results in maths of Turkish and Bengali students;

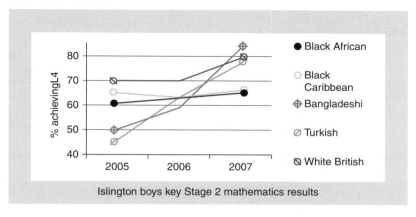

Figure 3   Islington boys Key Stage 2 mathematics results.

- to give encouragement, skills and confidence for parents to support their children at home;
- to give additional support through the use of students' home languages;
- to gain parental participation needed for Key Stage 2 project work.

The target group were the parents of the students identified in four project schools as having the potential to achieve a level 5 in Key Stage 2 SATs, who could do better with more parental support, or whose families had a lack of familiarity with the UK education system. The educational background of the parents appeared to be very mixed, with a range of levels of confidence about their use and understanding of English, the British education system and mathematics taught at Key Stage 2 level in particular.

> It's not always easy getting parents involved. Being culturally and language appropriate makes a huge difference, as sometimes language can be the biggest barrier. There isn't that with this project. This project is about trying to sell to the parents what you're doing – not always just in the context of education. We might just be concentrating on numeracy, but if parents have any other problems and are finding it hard to communicate to the other teachers, these lessons provide the chance for parents to have a productive dialogue with the school (Shamoli Mostafa, Bengali Numeracy Project Tutor, Islington).

In each of the four project schools, Turkish and Bengali speaking teaching assistants were employed to give additional support in classes to targeted

Table 5 Islington students' Key Stage 2 SATs results (2007 data).

		Number of students	% gaining level 4+	% gaining level 5
Turkish/Kurdish students	REAL Project schools	42	81	26
	Non-project schools	81	65	12
Bengali students	REAL Project schools	31	90	26
	Non-project schools	84	77	26

students, and to link the work in class to homework and to the work with parents. They taught a group of parents once a week about the mathematics that their children are learning in school. To complement these classes, a specially trained Turkish or Bengali/Sylheti speaking teaching assistant supported selected students in Year 5 and Year 6 classes during the daily maths sessions using mother tongue language or English as appropriate. Meetings were run for both groups to explain the concept of gifted and talented and the implications for their children both in and outside school (see Table 5).

Attendance data was analyzed to identify any relationship between the level of participation of parents and the level of attainment of the students. Parents were also informally interviewed in their mother tongue language or English to establish whether there had been any shift in their understanding of gifted and talented issues, or any change in their level of participation in school matters generally.

Some parents, they feel a bit scared because they don't know the language, they don't understand what's going on, and maybe they are too embarrassed to ask. But if you are not involved in your child's education, the child is going to say 'well my parents don't care so I'm not going to bother being educated'. For me, these lessons have helped me in the knowledge that I can sit down confidently and say to my child 'this is how we do it (Parent, Turkish class, Islington).

Early-entry Turkish GCSE for Year 6 students and parents (Islington)

Much of the success we have had in Islington in the last five or six years has been through parental engagement. Our experience has been that when you engage parents, standards go up. There are several different components to it. Firstly, if a child sees their parents in school taking an interest in what is going, the children notice and work harder. Second, the parents take back with them things which can really support the child's learning (Graham Smith, Head of Achievement and Diversity, Cambridge Education @ Islington).

The aim of this project has been to work with Turkish students and parents to prepare them both for taking an early-entry GCSE in their home language. Students work with their parents and are supported by bilingual teachers and support staff.

It seems that through their parents' interest and support at home pupils have really flourished. We have also noticed that the children are calmer and more focused. The impact on the children has been amazing. It's touching how much they like their parents to be involved (School, Islington).

The classes have been designed to provide parents and students with a chance to develop their own skills and gain a qualification, and to create a space in which parents and students could support each other during the learning process. Both the parents and students attended the same classes, with an average class size of 20 students. For the parents, the qualification may be relevant to their employment or could facilitate a change in career as well as being a catalyst for a return to education.

It helps their confidence, and their parents' confidence as well. Many parents who came to Turkish GCSE classes managed to get a job, because until then they did not have the confidence. I have heard quite a few of them got jobs or they started going to college (Yüksel Ferit, Turkish GCSE Project Teacher, Islington).

The classes met once a week after school for 1 hour, for 15–20 sessions. During the lessons, conducted in English and Turkish, parents and students engaged in a variety of activities, some of which were explicitly linked to the exam and some of which were more focused on general language use. The classes sought to make links and connections between the exam and curriculum subjects, encouraging students and parents to recognize links across subjects and tasks and encouraging aspirations.

> Being involved in my child's education puts my morale up and it puts her morale up as well. I think if I hadn't been supporting her by coming to school each week, I don't think she would have achieved the standard that she has (Parent, Islington).

In order to successfully complete the exam, candidates were required to work in a range of genres and literacies and the project developed students' literacy in both English and Turkish. The exam is in four parts incorporating: speaking (in the form of an interview in Turkish); listening (to a tape with questions to follow); reading (which is a comprehension exercise); and writing (which involves written questions and two written pieces, often a letter). The demands of the exam are such that the students are learning skills and practices that are well beyond the Year 6 curriculum level which is an invaluable experience and potential resource from which they can draw in their continuing education.

> The effect on self-esteem of having a GCSE at the age of 11 is enormous. So you just removed the barrier. You've taken the glass ceiling away and they can get on with it (Graham Smith, Head of Achievement and Diversity, Cambridge Education @ Islington).
>
> If I can get one GCSE when I'm 11 then I can get loads more when I'm 15!! (Student, Islington)

Conclusions

The foundation of the REAL Project was to share ideas, resources and expertise across schools and LAs. The purposes were to provide stretch and challenge not just support for all the gifted and talented learners. In the process this has led to the development of toolkits, identification procedures and strategies that have enabled the schools to personalize the learning of all of those involved – students, teachers and parents and to meet IQS developed in the gifted and talented area.

We began the REAL partnership with 31 core schools and 6 LAs. By the end of our first year we had the majority of LAs across London seeking involvement. Now at the end of our second year we have expanded to engage with more than 400 schools and 100 LAs nationally.

This level of interest genuinely astonished us and demonstrated that there was a clear need out there. The materials developed across the REAL partnership are starting to be used by schools and LAs nationally to provide a systematic response to helping BME/EAL G&T students, and cultivating innovative and effective practice in identification and provision. By securing a higher quality of support for these learners – especially those at risk of underachieving – the gap between the attainment of these G&T learners and others is beginning to be narrowed.

10

Gifted and Talented Children with Special Educational Needs – Underachievement in Dual and Multiple Exceptionality

Diane Montgomery

Introduction

In the gifted education field twice exceptional, dual or double exceptionality (2E) are terms used to describe those who are intellectually very able (gifted) or who have a talent (a special gift in a performance or skill area) and in addition to this have a special educational need (SEN). This is made complex when children may not demonstrate their 'gifts' and the SEN may be hidden. The likely result is that they perform poorly in school (underachieve). This underachievement (UAch) may bring their performance down to the level of peers so that the giftedness goes undetected.

Dual exceptionality is well known in the SEN field. It is termed co-morbidity. Co-morbidity often occurs in dyslexia when the dyslexic may also show symptoms of attention deficit hyperactivity disorder (ADHD) or Asperger Syndrome (AS). The incidence of co-morbidity is in the region of 30% (Clements, 1966; Duane, 2002). In all three conditions – dyslexia, ADHD and AS there is also a high frequency of the co-occurrence of handwriting coordination difficulties making a multiple exceptionality.

In a set of case studies in a special school Hart (2008) examined the issue of labelling and co-morbidity. Using the checklists provided by specialist organizations for dyslexia, ADHD, Autistic Spectrum Disorders (ASD) and dyspraxia/DCD she found that co-morbidity was strongly prevalent. Dyspraxia was most frequently associated with dyslexia; Asperger with autism,

Able, Gifted and Talented Underachievers, Second Edition   Edited by Diane Montgomery
© 2009 John Wiley & Sons, Ltd

and both dyslexia and dyspraxia with ADHD. Her concern was that with only one need or label identified many of these pupils' needs were going unserved. The fact that some of them might be more able as well had been completely overlooked in their diagnosis.

It is also evident that the specialist organizations producing the checklists tend to include all the symptoms observed in their specialist group rather than just the core or key identifiers and thus they will include indicators of co-morbid symptoms. For example the dyslexia checklists include Developmental Coordination Difficulties (DCD) indicators. Unfortunately, this can mean that only the labelled need 'dyslexia' is given specialist intervention not the handwriting difficulty or the wider range of DCD that may be present.

In addition, if a diagnosis of a difficulty is incomplete such as referring to dyslexia as only a reading difficulty (DfE, 1997) then it is not surprising that subsequent interventions do not remediate the problem and that the National Literacy Strategy has improved reading but not writing (Montgomery, 2008; Tymms, 2004).

SEN is defined in the United Kingdom as a need for educational or other support to enable a pupil to access the mainstream curriculum. The additional resources may be given for learning support, assistive technology, adapting access to the school buildings or providing special education in a specialist environment or within the mainstream. Only since 1999 has some additional funding for special provision been made available for the gifted and talented (DfEE, 1998) since most state-funded grammar school provision was replaced by comprehensive education in the 1970s. Grammar schools were given higher rates of funding and specialist facilities than other secondary schools.

Some problems arising from dual exceptionality

Giftedness with SEN brings about special problems. Students given provision for their dyslexia such as remedial teaching and supportive strategies may be placed in the lowest classes or sets because of their low attainments. This is extremely frustrating for them because then they do not have the stimulation needed to meet or match their high ability. The result of their boredom and frustration as captives in this 'psychic prison' (De Mink, 1995) can be behavioural and emotional problems as well and then they become a multiply exceptional case. At each point the SEN can be the focus for intervention and the high ability is overlooked. The SEN teachers may also not have been trained to identify or make provision for the needs of the more able.

If the high ability is identified and special provision is made then the pupil may not perform well because there may be a lack of teaching skill by gifted education teachers in relation to the SEN.

The ordinary classroom teacher may have little expertise in either area unless the school organizes relevant professional development training and updates.

There may also be the problem of needing dual funding to compensate for the dual needs. It is unlikely that the system is set up to provide this. Funding for one need cannot be allocated to another and double funding for the individual is hard to obtain.

Underachievement and dual exceptionality

A significant number of highly able pupils are never identified as gifted or learning disabled and are at risk from UAch. Estimates of UAch vary from 70% (Whitmore, 1982) to 40% (Gagne, 1995) and to 25% (Stamm, 2004) depending on the criteria used. My observations in 1250 ordinary classrooms suggested that 80% of all pupils in these classes underachieved much of the time (Montgomery, 2002). Those with learning difficulties were particularly vulnerable whatever their level of ability.

Having a special need whilst being highly able frequently conceals or masks the high ability (Baldwin, 2001). This can result in a progressive deterioration in school performance (UAch) and resultant low self-esteem. The frustration and boredom engendered by an inappropriate curriculum can lead to side effects such as social, emotional and behavioural difficulties. These in turn can bring about a cycle of increasing UAch.

Profile of typical underachievers compiled from the studies of Kellmer-Pringle (1970), Whitmore (1982), Butler-Por (1987), Silverman (1989), Wallace (2000) and Montgomery (2000).

- Large gap between oral and written work.
- Failure to complete schoolwork.
- Poor execution of work.
- Persistent dissatisfaction with achievements.
- Avoidance of trying new activities.

- Does not function well in groups.
- Lacks concentration.
- Poor attitudes to school.
- Dislikes drill and memorization.
- Difficulties with peers.
- Low self-image.
- Sets unrealistic goals.
- Satisfactory performance at level of peers.

The underlying theme is an inability or an unwillingness to produce written work of a suitable quality to match the perceived potential. I have argued elsewhere (Montgomery, 2000, 2003) that hidden beneath this profile are two problems – a handwriting coordination difficulty and a spelling problem and a special section later in this chapter is devoted to these issues. There are also the pupils who cannot see the point of writing down what they can remember perfectly well and are not particularly interested in.

The positive side of this picture is that pupils with 2E can be identified because they are likely to be

- inventive and original when motivated;
- quick to learn new concepts;
- very good at posing and solving problems ingeniously;
- good at asking awkward and penetrating questions about everything;
- persevere only when motivated;
- streetwise and full of commonsense wisdom;
- perceptive about people and motives;
- find novel answers to difficult questions or problems.

The difficulty is that IQ tests rarely tap into these capabilities. They test what has been committed to memory during upbringing and education and thus some types of background as discussed in Freeman's chapter, limit performance on IQ tests others facilitate it. In Chapter 1, performance-based assessment was recommended if the curriculum tasks and teaching methodology were appropriately designed – Identification through Appropriate Curriculum Provision (ITAP).

Formal identification in 2E

Schools have 20–22% of pupils on average on their special needs registers and track their progress and offer remedial, supportive, corrective or supplemental interventions. These pupils are to be found across the ability range but this means that overall 78% of pupils are not subject to the same careful review of progress.

Now in the United Kingdom, schools are asked to identify their most able 5–10% and use a variety of methods to do this. This will by no means capture all those with high potential as has already been explained in Chapter 1. We can predict from the normal curve of distribution of ability that approximately 16% will be highly able. Large scale IQ screening surveys show there are always more in fact on the ground than this, so expecting 20% to be highly able (130 IQ and above) is well justified. This omits all those missed by errors of measurement and all those with talent and those who are more able (115–130 IQ) or may have depressed IQ scores because of disabilities. If the trigger for the highest achievement needs only to be 120 IQ (Torrance, 1963) or 125 IQ (Crocker, 1987, p. 172) the pool of additional gifts and talents is very large, but it may still leave out those who are learning disabled and whose disabilities depress the IQ scores and the school attainments. Silverman (1989, 2004) suggested that when there was a learning disability 10 IQ points should be added to the IQ test results when selecting for special gifted education provision.

My research (Montgomery, 1997) showed that 10% of a sample of 300 dyslexics had at least one IQ scale score on Wechsler Intelligence Scale for Children at 130 or above and 34% of the group had full IQs of 120 points or more. The analysis showed that these gifted groups' reading and spelling scores were a year in advance of the rest of the dyslexic group so that they were less likely to be selected for remedial intervention at the earliest age. The chronological age was frequently compared to the reading and spelling performances not the equivalent 'mental age'. The more the bright dyslexics compensated for their disability or concealed it the less likely they were to obtain the help they really needed and this led to progressive UAch as they moved through primary into secondary school and university. Girls too fared worse than boys, they were referred nearly a year later and in the ratio of 1 girl to 5 boys. Recent cohort analyses of spelling showed that the ratio of dyslexic boys to girls was in the order of 1.5 to 1 (Montgomery, 2007) and not 4 to 1 as accepted by the British Dyslexia Association based on Rutter, Tizard and Whitmore (1970) study but compares favourably with his recent analysis (Rutter *et al.*, 2004) where internationally they find a ratio of 1.5 to 1.

Different group patterns in identification of 2E Group 1 (usually identifiable – *discrepant* 2E) – have been identified by discrepancies between high scores on ability tests and low achievements, for example

- high scores on ability tests and low achievement in school subjects or SATs (Standard Attainment Tests);
- markedly discrepant scores on IQ tests between verbal and performance items or within scales but may be performing in class at an average level – depressed scores on the verbal processing tests, for example mental arithmetic, coding, information, digit span (ACID profile) in dyslexia.
- depressed performance scale scores especially coding indicating a handwriting or dyspraxic problem;
- an uneven pattern of high and low achievements across school subjects with only average ability test scores;
- high achievements in out of school or non-school activities, average scores on ability tests and in school subjects.

Group 2 (usually the disability masks the abilities – a *deficit* 2E) have a specific learning difficulty – the ability goes unidentified in the presence of depressed ability test scores for especially in

- dyslexic type difficulties – all sub tests on both scales may be somewhat depressed;
- spelling difficulties – all subtests on both scales may be somewhat depressed;
- dyslexia with gross motor coordination problems, or handwriting difficulties – verbal and performance scale scores are depressed.

Group 3 (usually not identified – a *deceptive* 2E) – ability measures seem to fall within the average but not the gifted range. These tend to be

- pupils with social and behavioural difficulties;
- those with hidden learning difficulties or disabilities not identified;
- daydreamers, uninterested in school, or so called 'lazy' pupils;
- pupils with linguistically and culturally disadvantaged backgrounds.

Because of the limitations of IQ tests in finding the gifted in 2E especially in groups 2 and 3 it is essential to use a wide variety of means such as assessment through performance on real-world tasks – ITAP, authentic assessment; mentoring, grids, self-report and self-referral among others can help us fill out their profiles and track their progress and these have already been outlined in Chapter 1.

The common theme in twice exceptional groups is that many of these gifted and talented pupils are very good orally when they choose to be but are poor at writing ideas or almost anything down at more than an average or even more limited level. Because of this, a special section is devoted to writing at the end of this chapter showing some recent research findings.

Patterns of Special Educational Needs and 2E

There are five main types of difficulty that children with SEN might show and some will have *complex learning difficulties* involving several conditions. Those with giftedness and learning disability are sometimes called Gifted Learning Disabled (GLD) but this abbreviation has already been taken so here they will be referred to as 'GiLD'.

Normal functioning can be expected once a specific learning *difficulty* has been overcome or circumvented and a catch-up programme implemented. In a *disorder* the system is dysfunctional and requires specific training from an early age but even so remains problematic and not normal in function. In each of the five areas the difficulties and disorders will be on a continuum from mild through moderate and severe to profound.

General learning difficulties (GLD) and 2E

GLD is common and occurs on a continuum from mild through moderate to severe and profound. This group is often referred to as 'slow learners'. The core difficulties are problems with memory, language and thinking and these affect development and intellectual functioning across all areas of the curriculum. There are also associated motor coordination difficulties in many cases.

Many of these pupils may write and read adequately but the content of what they write and their general level of comprehension is lower, at their ability level rather than their chronological age level. Others will also have literacy difficulties and underachieve because of this. Thus, while students with GLD may have specific talents they do not appear in the gifted end of the 2E spectrum.

Specific learning difficulties (SpLD) and 2E

SpLD occurs in either or both verbal and non-verbal areas.

(a) Verbal learning difficulties   Developmental Dyslexia – In dyslexia the ability to learn to *both read and spell* is seriously depressed however bright the pupil. Too often the diagnosis is based upon lack of progress in reading and intervention is thus targeted there. The core disability would appear to be a lack of progress in spelling particularly in learning initial sound symbol correspondence and phoneme segmentation (Montgomery, 2007) rather than just a reading difficulty. A good visual memory can conceal the dyslexic difficulties and permit a 'look and say strategy' or pattern recognition approach to be used for reading but at about 8 years when the reading and writing vocabulary needs to widen the difficulties become much clearer. In bright dyslexics this gap may emerge at the age of 6 years (see Figure 1).

Dyslexics will eventually learn to read and write although with considerable effort. Girls more often than boys will persevere and acquire basic literacy skills especially in reading. A specialist dyslexia remedial programme is needed to overcome the difficulties. This needs to be an APSL (alphabetic-phonic-syllabic-linguistic) multisensory programme based on the Gillingham and Stillman (1956) model (e.g. Hickey, 1991 and TRTS (teaching spelling through reading), Cowdery *et al.*, 1994). If the programme is started

Maria aged 5 years 10 months

'I wnt to the Titic Esbtnn
I swo srm thes fom th Titic
And srm thes war reil'

(I went to the Titanic Exhibition, I
saw some things from the Titanic
and some of these were real)
Maria taught herself to read aged 4
and is bilingual in German and
English

Figure 1   Maria aged 5 years 10 months.

towards the end of the Reception Year, the consequences of first level dyslexia may be avoided. First level dyslexia is when the learner is stuck in Frith's (1985) alphabetic stage. Research results show (Montgomery, 2007) that these dyslexics can make at least two years progress *in each year* with an input of two 50 minutes sessions per week – but only if the full lesson plan is followed and especially if its principles are reinforced by the classroom teacher (see Figure 2).

James 8 yrs 6 m (No reading or spelling score at 8 years) just started on TRTS

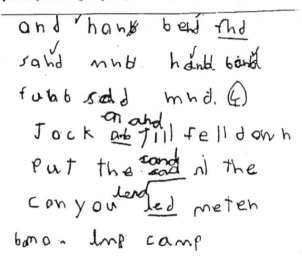

James at 9 yrs 10 m writing from dictation, RA 8 yrs and SA 8 yrs now

Figure 2 James' writing before and after APSL intervention.

He eat him, now I'm no exspert but anemals do behve lick
that, and he did the same to the others but the had a
difrent larws and the Pleos cort him eath is the most
stangest plac Jonow Yors fathly hoblar

• Dear Hoblar (5 mini sessions later)
I fanck you for your letter, I've looked up your animal
consirns and animals on earth have a good reputasn like
Robin Hood, I have beny watching a lat of films and
cartoons and I disagree with you. For example police
dog's save live's and guide dog's help blind people. I'll
meet you at the space

Figure 3   Alex's writing after five mini CPSS lessons for spelling.

However, most bright dyslexics are discovered late and are able to read slowly but write and spell very poorly. They may then need second level intervention with a strategic approach to spelling that will also transfer to reading, see Figure 3 and CPSS (Cognitive Processes Strategies for Spelling) below for details.

What is of major concern is what happens if the problems are not remediated. Miles and Miles (1999) found

> in some cases it seems that the pain can be quite excruciating, but the real costs are to the spirit, the sorrow of observing a child's blank despair, the anguish and alarm when the despair turns to rage (p. 155).
>
> and If the dyslexia is combined with a lack of support in the home or at school and an adverse environment in other ways this is a sure recipe for criminality (p. 160).

Among other studies, Singleton (2006, pp. 119–20) reported on a BDA (British Dyslexia Association) survey in 2004 that found 52% of juvenile offenders in Bradford were dyslexics. The same BDA survey also found that the incidence of dyslexia among the prison population was three to four times that of the general population.

Edwards (1994) was more concerned with the school responses of her dyslexics and found that their emotional responses could be classified under nine headings – truancy/school refusal, psychosomatic pain, isolation/alienation from peers, lack of communication, lack of confidence, self-doubt/denigration of intellect, competitiveness disorders, oversensitivity to criticism and behaviour problems.

With all this to cope with it is not surprising that the dyslexic under-achieves in addition to the problems of achievement created by inappropriate learning environments.

Developmental Dysorthographia – is a specific spelling problem in the presence of adequate or even very good reading skills. It is a common dyslexic condition in gifted students and Maria in Figure 1 is such an example. They may have learned to read self-taught in the pre-school period or began school with a reading difficulty that subsequently cleared up. Some, particularly girls, just work and work at reading and eventually master the skill. The same cannot be said of their spelling. It is often regarded as 'atrocious'. The incidence of dysorthographia is not yet known but appears to be in the order of 10% (Montgomery, 2008) over and above the 4% with severe dyslexia (Rutter, Tizard and Whitmore, 1970; BDA, 2004).

Bright pupils in particular hate rote learning. In school, the most popular spelling correction method they are taught is Look-Cover-Write-Check and to do this five times for each word. Unfortunately it does not work, the dyslexic still misspells the word the next day or the day after. The second most popular strategy is to invent a mnemonic. This is more appealing to the inventive dyslexic but it is a poor strategy, as a new mnemonic has to be invented for every correction and can become a tedious chore with no power to correct more than one misspelling. Rules may be chanted too but once the writing commences they are not applied because the misspelling is already stored in the lexicon and the motor cortex, as well as any new versions. Transfer from what is learned in the remedial tutorial to general classroom work is a major problem.

Strategic approaches to spelling – the Cognitive Processes Strategies for Spelling
It was for the reasons outlined above that a strategic approach to spelling, 12 CPSS were designed and implemented with second level dyslexics beginning with dyslexic teacher education students (Montgomery, 1997, 2007) and then to *second level dyslexics* in schools. Like the APSL programmes it was found to be able to advance the spelling and reading skills by two years in each year with only a few minutes input each day over the period of a term. The essence is to use one of the 12 CPSS 'engage brain' strategies to correct the misspelling in the lexicon in the cerebrum *and* a linked cursive writing strategy to lay down a new memory in the motor memory store in the cerebellum and to link the two. In this manner using a simple protocol the new spelling was given a higher profile in the lexicon and was elicited rather than the incorrect older version. Thus transfer to general writing was

achieved. The students on the programme made the equivalent of two years progress in each year or more.

Derails of the CPSS procedure and format may be found in an Appendix at the end of the chapter before the references section.

(b) Non-verbal learning difficulties　In most cases of NLD there is an associated motor coordination problem (Tanguay, 2002). Typical NLDs are DCD, ADHD and Attention Deficit Disorder (ADD).

Developmental Coordination Difficulties (DCD) – dyspraxia. Dyspraxis is a difficulty with, or an inability to motor plan, or put such a plan into fluent operation after a reasonable period of skill acquisition. There are a range of dyspraxic difficulties from gross motor coordination – a general clumsiness in running and walking, to specific fine motor coordination difficulties in handwriting, bead threading, shoelace tying and buttoning.

Exercise books are filled with scruffy, scrappy work loaded with crossings out and holes. Such pupils are not picked in team games and are frequently seriously bullied even by teachers and become the butt of jokes and blame.

Despite the ungainly behaviour, and perhaps a lack of control of emotional responses, the individual may be highly intelligent trapped in a body that will not do as instructed unless specific training is given. If the writing is legible the DCD is ignored but the pupil is condemned to UAch and is usually poor at spelling and maths (Chesson, McKay and Stephenson, 1991).

Dysgraphia. There is a significant number of pupils who will have handwriting coordination difficulties without gross motor difficulties. Estimates vary from Sassoon's (1990) report of 40% of boys and 25% of girls at age 15, stating that they found writing painful and avoiding it whenever possible. My studies show that the incidence was in the region of 30% in Year 7 (age 11) on a continuum from mild to severe (Montgomery, 2008) with boys 3 to 1 more prone to difficulties than girls. The difficulty appears to be independent of intellectual ability. At the most severe end of the continuum the poorest 1% the numbers of boys and girls were about equal. At the age of 11, growth spurts and general developmental and attitude differences may account for the differences between boys' and girls' writing.

The ability to write neatly secures higher marks despite having poorer content (Soloff, 1973) even though untidy writing from boys is more tolerated.

Young gifted children's thoughts may run much faster than their writing skills can cope with and so they will be criticized too, again content can be ignored and this is very frustrating and can lead to loss of self-esteem.

Writing at speed with reasonable legibility is a difficulty that is given too little attention but it can have a serious effect on school achievement. It results in lower SATs scores and degree classification (Connolly, Dockrell and Barnett, 2005). Roaf (1998) found that pupils who could not write at a speed of 25 words per minute in her 10-minute writing test were those who were failing in all areas of the curriculum using writing. My studies using Allcock's (2001) 20-minute test indicated that the average speed at Year 7 was approximately 13 words per minute, similar to Allcock's survey and poor spelling slowed this speed down by at least 2 words per minute. Boys' speed was 18% slower than girls. Coordination problems did not necessarily affect speed but did hamper legibility. In Year 9, the writing speeds of boys and girls were more similar and spelling problems appeared with nearly equal frequency in boys and girls.

Despite the introduction of laptops a large amount of handwriting still goes on in schools and even laptop use can be slowed by coordination difficulties. Dysgraphia is a hidden SEN and a hidden cause of UAch that needs to be explored further.

Attention deficit hyperactivity disorder   Incidences of ADHD vary from 3–5% in the USA to 1–2% in the United Kingdom with 2–3 boys to 1 girl. The narrower United Kingdom definition leads to the lower incidence (Cooper and Ideus, 1995).

It is not uncommon for very bright children on entry to school to be absorbed by the newness of it all for a week or so and then to become bored by the routine and the sameness and slowness of everything. They begin to leak a nervous energy that has no intellectual outlet and teachers try to over correct and suppress it. These children are soon mislabelled 'hyperactive' and recommended for medication. It is often at this point a desperate parent will consult me for another opinion.

In ADHD the disorder is pervasive, meaning that it is manifested across all lessons and both at home and school. It does not respond to the ordinary management behaviours such as reasoning, ignoring aversive behaviour and punishment.

There are three main symptoms:

Inattention – in behavioural, ocular and postural set.
Hyperactivity – extreme and incessant mobility and restlessness.
Impulsivity – shouting and calling out, cannot take turns.

Overactivity does not always continue into adolescence and may be replaced by underactivity, inertia and lack of motivation.

Terrell and Passenger (2005) describe the classroom profile of pupils with ADHD as follows:

Annoys everybody and cannot help it
Is disliked by others and realises this
Has low self-esteem and often dislikes himself
Is often remorseful after behaving 'badly' saying 'I can't help it' (p. 9)

When the symptoms are present without the hyperactivity the diagnosis is ADD. This condition is frequently overlooked as it can appear as a case of dreaminess, disorganisztion and quiet withdrawal, an easy child to manage in a busy classroom, but little learning takes place. In pre-school, ADD is seen as a pattern of uninhibited curiosity and meddlesomeness. There tends to be continual trial and error learning, wandering away from the guarding adult, rash acceptance of strange adults and proneness to accidents. Studies show that those with hyperactivity are more likely to show aggressive behaviours whilst those without show a sluggish, cognitive tempo. Distinguishing between high energy levels of gifted students that cannot be coped with by mass schooling contexts and ADHD, as a disorder is important. It is best seen in sudden and total concentration on a task of special interest or a computer game that a student with ADHD cannot maintain.

Medication such as Ritalin is often prescribed in ADHD. It may not always calm down the behaviour but can improve concentration temporarily so that students can catch up with schoolwork. It can also depress the gifted child's potential. It should only be a temporary resort until the pupil has been taught coping strategies. It also should not be a first resort, other options need to be tried such as dietary ones.

For example another cause of ADHD may be an allergy to preservatives, and additives in foods such as sausages, soft drinks, and crisps, things that children enjoy. Yet others are allergic to chocolate, cheese, flour or milk protein and an appropriate diet has to be constructed. In the light of this, some schools have replaced sweets and crisps and so on in their tuck shops with fruit, and have found significantly calmer and more attentive behaviour in classes in the afternoons. A calm environment low in distractions and plenty of structured energy consuming activity can be helpful in ADHD.

A third cause of 'ADHD' is suggested by my cases studies and that is that it arises from the frustration, stress and anxiety that result from unremediated dyslexia. The ADHD is triggered by the distress and inability to succeed in school tasks. Once a successful programme is in place the ADHD diminishes.

In a sample of high ability dyslexics, it was found that in 19 out of 20 cases there were distinct signs of emotional or behavioural difficulties recorded in their cases histories by teachers and Ed. Psychs (Montgomery, 1997). In a study of 20 students referred for severe and prolonged behavioural problems and ADHD to a PRU (Pupil Referral Unit) and special school for emotional and behavioural difficulties, Smith (2002) found that one of the students had undiagnosed AS whilst the rest had undiagnosed dyslexic difficulties with reading and spelling skills at least two years below the level expected for their ages.

In a recent study, Pawley (2008) found that 10 boys all in a special school, excluded from mainstream education for behaviour problems and state-mented for ADHD had severe reading and spelling problems, undiagnosed dyslexia. They had all been in the special school for at least 1 year and had made no progress in literacy. When they were put on TRTS (Cowdery *et al.*, 1994) a multisensory APSL specialist dyslexia programme twice a week for 6 months their reading and spelling skills improved by 1.05 and 1.1 years, respectively. Most significantly their behaviour problems diminished in direct proportion to the development of their literacy skills (Rs = + 0.95) as rated on the Connor's Behaviour Rating Scale (2007) and teachers' assessments.

It has to be questioned whether the failure to address their literacy needs earlier using an appropriate programme had resulted in their behaviour problems and unmanageable behaviour in busy classrooms. All the attention was directed to controlling the misbehaviour and caused them to be wrongly labelled as having ADHD. Some of this group were more able but this too had been ignored in the focus on their disruption.

What we tend not to see is the positive side of ADHD. Jaksa (1999) reported cases that manage and use it to advantage such as Phil who insisted that it made him a more exciting speaker, comedian and motivator. He claimed it was a gift, although he admitted that at school, teachers took early retirement when they found he was going to be in their class. Perhaps it is the abnormal environment of classrooms full of confined children that prevents ADHD being used to advantage. A teaching colleague diagnosed with ADHD as an adult found an outlet for his energies doing part time demolition work on building sites.

Physical, sensory and medical difficulties

Students with PSM are in relatively small numbers compared to those with SpLD and SEBD (social, emotional and behavioural difficulties) and the difficulties similarly range from mild through moderate to severe and profound. It is those with severe and profound difficulties whose giftedness so easily goes unobserved whilst their SEN is coped with.

Gifted students with *physical difficulties* such as cerebral palsy and *medical difficulties* such as spina bifida, multiple sclerosis and epilepsies need not only access to the buildings but also to an intellectually challenging curriculum suited to their individual level of ability. It should be the least of the barriers they have to overcome.

Sensory difficulties are the visual and hearing impairments. Measures generally used to aid identification also tend to recognize attainments and not potential (Starr, 2003). Further barriers are that teachers may be reluctant to include children with sensory and physical difficulties in their gifted programmes because they lack experience of working with them and rarely meet them.

Visually impaired gifted students often said that they had to be better than gifted students without disabilities in order to be recognized (Corn, 1986). They share this in common with gifted girls and disadvantaged and minority ethnic groups.

For those with hearing impairment using visual scales of tests and again Raven's Progressive Matrices as the marks of the potential can help identification. In brief, when gifted students with PSM have their special needs catered for their educational needs are much the same as other gifted children.

Social, emotional and behavioural difficulties

SEBD is one of the most common and hidden causes in UAch.

Schlicte-Hiersemensel (2000) recorded the plight of many gifted German pupils who had become behaviourally and emotionally disturbed by their unchallenging mainstream education and Sisk (2000, 2003) described similar results of 'ill-fitting environments' for USA students. McCluskey *et al.* (2003) recorded the same for Canadian students and similar findings were established by Kerry (1983) and Montgomery (1989) in the United Kingdom.

These studies showed that many bright boys and girls found a serious lack of intellectual challenge in the school curriculum and this caused them to become bored and frustrated. They often responded to their frustration and disaffection emotionally and behaviourally by clowning or refusing to do any work at all and engaging in nuisance behaviours. The Confederation of British Industry have regularly reported that significant numbers of their gifted entrepreneurs had failed in school. Others can become 'school averse' and difficult to manage and are excluded or 'resign' from school early. Their talents and abilities go unnoticed. On any one day in English schools over 60 000 non-approved absences are reported (DCFS, 2008).

As well as SEBD caused by a lack of cognitive challenge, there is also a significant number of bright pupils who bring problems with them from dysfunctional or disadvantaging environments (Rutter, 1985; Galloway and Goodwin, 1987; Mongon and Hart, 1989; Cooper, 1999). This makes them unable to easily fit into school routines and demands. Their behaviours range from

acting out – on a continuum from mild attention seeking and continuous chatting to disruption in class; truancy, bullying, wandering, vandalism, lying, theft, arson and violence; to

acting in – usually more anxious pupils, who blame themselves for what is seldom their fault, become fearful of trying anything different, difficult or new. At the extremes they may become isolates, elective mutes, depressed, self-harming or school phobic;

excluded pupils – ten per cent of pupils in PRUs and Centres for SEBD fall into the more able range (Visser and Rayner, 1999);

exclusion and literacy – nineteen out of 20 pupils in some PRUs or excluded from school have literacy difficulties that may have been identified but never addressed (Smith, 2002) because the problem behaviour dominated everyone's mind. Two-thirds of prisoners in gaols have literacy problems and many are illiterate (Pawley, 2008);

dyslexics with SEBD – in my studies who were receiving successful intervention quickly stopped showing behaviour problems and became eager to learn and practice their new skills. As already indicated Pawley's (2008) research found the same. Teachers immediately noticed the change in them. In 90% of the case histories of 500 dyslexics they showed emotional and behavioural difficulties to some degree

(Montgomery, 1995). In extensive case studies, Edwards (1994) found that seven out of eight of her dyslexics were referred for behaviour problems and all had been bullied, some by their teachers.

The bright students with SEBD also showed characteristic patterns of behaviour:

- Claim schoolwork is boring.
- Fear failure or fear success.
- Negativism, refuse to do tasks or obey rules.
- Absent self from school or classes.
- Attention seeking or clowning and calling out.
- Antisocial behaviour, name calling, bullying.
- Problem behaviour and disruption.
- Overassertiveness or oversubmissiveness.
- Fears teachers and school.
- Evades schoolwork.
- Finds plenty of dead time to socialize in lessons.
- Constantly wandering or out of seat.
- Consistently mumbles and grumbles whilst teacher is talking.
- Habitually sings or whistles quietly to annoy others.
- Avoids schoolwork especially writing.
- 'Forgets' homework, gym kit and so on.

Small misdemeanours designed to provoke the teacher and to 'amuse' the other learners can, in hostile or coercive school environments, cause the student quickly to be labelled as a problem and a career in disruption is set in progress. Others are dismissed as the 'class clown'. All of these pupils do respond to the positive management behaviour strategies set out in Chapter 1 especially when the teaching methods and curriculum offer cognitive challenge and stretch as described in the chapters in section one.

Special populations with disorders – Autistic Spectrum Disorders

These pupils have disorders, possibly carried on the genes causing them to have distinct patterns of difficulty in learning. In Autism, AS and Pragmatic Language disorders students have specific difficulties and behavioural rituals that affect their social and communication skills and their perception, language and thinking. It is those with AS who most often have gifts and talents as well other than autistic savants whose exceptional abilities are confined mainly to music, art and number calculations.

Asperger Syndrome   AS was originally thought to be high functioning autism but now the characteristics are more clearly defined and the patterns are different. In AS there is serious impairment in social skills, there are repetitive behaviours and rituals, problems in fantasy and imaginative activities and play, concrete and literal comprehension of speech and a monotonous speech pattern and motor impairment in 50–90% of cases. This latter is in contrast to autism in which there is usually good coordination even gracefulness, but severe impairment in language, perception and social skills. In autism isolated 'gifts' may be found in some 10% such as in musical or artistic ability, or a facility with number calculations such as telling the day of the week in 1754 that was October 4th!

School achievement can be good in AS where the topics command their interest and require a large amount of factual or technical learning. Reading skills are generally good although 90% with AS have writing difficulties (Henderson and Green, 2001). Barber (1996) describes a 15-year-old with AS in mainstream education who was put on an accelerated programme and took GCSEs in Physics and Maths in Year 8 and gained A in both and passed the extension paper in maths. With an enrichment programme he also obtained A* in GCSE (General Certificate in Secondary Education) Biology and A in French. Despite these achievements his behavioural and social skills were a cause of concern. For example when he was asked to do something he did not like he would grumble under his breath, make a fuss look angry and even end up screaming. When he had first joined the school staff reported his frequent interruptions during lessons, inappropriate questions, difficulties in remaining in seat and working in a group. He would not accept that a conversation with member of staff was finished when they had finished it. In Year 9, Barber had to put him on a behaviour management programme to help him with these problems and later a programme of social/life skills to teach him how to take a bus to the local city, visit a shop, use a telephone and prepare a meal otherwise he would not be able to apply for university and cope with life there.

Gifted adults with AS can be highly successful holding important jobs especially if they have good self-care and a placid nature, but they remain socially isolated and idiosyncratic. They appear to lack insight into their own thinking processes, and lack understanding of the perspective of others, a lack of theory of mind, although even this can be improved with specific training.

The child with AS is differentiated from the ordinary gifted according to Neihart (2000) by the following:

- Pedantic seamless speech in which they run on mixing fact and personal detail.
- Low tolerance to change, may ignore class and school routines completely.
- Do not understand humour, understanding is literal.
- Clumsiness in 50–90%.
- Inappropriate affect and lack of insight – may laugh at a funeral.
- Frequently have stereotypic behaviours and rituals.

Early identification of the 'giftedness' may be vocabulary based for they are often hyperlingual but the comprehension shows deficits. In later school years they may be very successful in subjects requiring large amounts of factual material to be recalled. However problems ensue if they are not interested in a subject, and they can make naive and overt criticisms of a teacher's methods and personal attributes that are socially unacceptable.

Their behaviours can also be rigid and resistant to change which brings them into conflict with other children and school staff, so that having been told to sit still and be quiet they continue questioning loudly or get up and walk around, oblivious to the instruction. Some engage in compulsive rituals such as shelf tidying or hand flapping, others are prone to sudden aggressive outbursts, temper tantrums, hyperactivity, anxiety or phobic attacks. They seem to speak what others may only be thinking and know it would be inappropriate to utter. They seem to have no sense that it may be hurtful or disrespectful – the lack of 'theory of mind'.

They are very sensitive to teasing but continually engage in precisely those asocial behaviours that provoke it. A structured approach for AS students is needed in the rules of interaction in conversation, such as to look at the person when they are speaking and only get ready to speak when they signal they are coming to a close by looking away and then looking back. How to 'chat up' a potential girlfriend was high on the 'wants lists' of youths with AS.

The more intelligent these pupils are the better they learn to manage their difficulties especially by adolescence although they need specific and direct step by step training in procedures, school rules and social protocols. They eventually learn to cope with most regular and predictable demands of school but they still need specific instructions for tasks the rest of us learn by experience.

Mild developmental dysphasia/specific language impairment (SLI)

This is a set of language disorders originally termed developmental dysphasia. There are two major areas of deficit either (a) receptive or (b) expressive dysphasia. In receptive difficulties the pupil has difficulty understanding spoken language and in expressive difficulties has problems in organizing and executing speech to explain thought. Receptive difficulties invariably lead to expressive problems but the reverse is not the case.

Children with SLI are slow to learn speak. They may develop no speech by five years of age unless they receive specific pre-school training and their parents also learn to do this. Even so they will have a limited vocabulary, perhaps only 50 words by the age of 7 and lack the syntax to put two words together to indicate their needs or ideas. Most children develop two word utterance by 18 months and gifted children often much earlier than this. Children even with mild SLI find it very difficult to achieve well in schools because of the highly verbal nature of schooling, they may however be exceptionally bright conceptually and perceptually but are unable to demonstrate this except in non-verbal areas. They need from the earliest days in school to be in a nurture group setting that is devoted to promoting speaking and listening skills through specific training strategies (AFASIC, 2008) and the talking curriculum. Again the Raven's Progressive Matrices Test (Raven, 2008) can aid identification of potential ability, even so elements of this test may be mediated by language and so not give the truest estimate.

If children with SLI can draw, design, sing or perform well in another area such as sport they can gain fulfilment, otherwise they can become despairing. Their expressive difficulties often attract bullying.

A learning environment that values different modes of expression and learning such as in the Ruyton school experience in Chapter 6 will help include bright pupils with SLI and help them to achieve well.

Peripheral speech difficulties, stuttering and articulation difficulties   These difficulties can affect pupils across the ability range and make their speech difficult to understand so that peers and teachers lose patience and refuse to listen or cut in and help them find words. Both need speech therapy help and a language-based curriculum to help them learn and then practice speaking clearly. Clear speaking also assists correct spelling. Pupils with these difficulties are frequently bullied so once again a firm positive behaviour management policy is needed to support them with clear guidelines for dealing with the bullying.

In some cases the performance intelligence in SLI may be normal or even high. Art, design and music can all be vehicles for expression of the high ability and they can learn to hold down practical jobs that require minimal linguistic interaction.

Writing and the Hidden Difficulties

In 2005, it became clear even to its authors that the National Literacy Strategy (NLS) introduced in 1998 had still not been entirely successful. It required 1 hour of structured literacy teaching each day in primary schools (as had been the practice before the National Curriculum had been introduced in 1989!). Although 83% of students at 11 years had reached level 4 in reading, the criterion for success, only 63% had met this criterion in writing. In 2006 and 2007, these results only varied by 1% or 2% in each direction. In 2004, Tymms had found there had been little change in writing standards over several decades. He challenged the evidence that literacy had improved as much as the government had claimed. In his analysis of the results he showed that from a low of 48% in 1995, only 60% had achieved level 4 in English by 2004. In 2007, he reported that standards in literacy had remained relatively unchanged since the 1950s.

What is clear from both government and research sources is that pupils' writing is significantly poorer than reading. This is not surprising since it is more difficult to learn and is a much higher order set of skills. Reading is a *recognition skill* where all the words are present and just have to be decoded or matched to stored patterns in the lexicon (memory store for words and meanings). In writing, the writer has to *assemble* the correct spelling using whatever strategies are available or draw it out from the brain's memory store, the lexicon, and then *transcribe* it using fine motor skill. This is a *recall process* involving retrieval and/or reconstruction and transcription processes. In addition a message or composition also has to be constructed.

The processes of coding (spelling) and handwriting coordination fluency and speed underpin the ability to construct good composition. They are the two best early predictors of later success in exams (Graham *et al.*, 1996; Berninger, 2004; Connelly and Hurst, 2001; Connolly, Dockrell and Barnett, 2005). If there are difficulties in spelling and handwriting then the ability to construct good composition is undermined according to these researchers. The difficulties can lead to UAch in school and university subjects.

Many able underachievers are fluent and early readers but develop writing difficulties (Montgomery, 2000). This suggests that reading skill does not automatically transfer to writing as some teaching methods imply and is evidenced in remediation evaluation studies (Montgomery, 2007). It also indicates that there may be a much larger number of pupils with 'dyslexic type' problems affecting spelling and writing but not reading. I have called them 'developmental dysorthographics'.

Bravar (2005) found that 70% of Italian children referred for UAch had writing difficulties. Of these, 47% had poor handwriting and the writing of 23% was illegible but only 6% had actually been referred for writing problems.

In other words, in order to write well in examinations, the higher order executive function, a certain level of fluency and automaticity is needed in the basic skills of handwriting and spelling, the lower order functions. If there are lower order difficulties in transcription the processing power of the brain is deflected to these functions and away from the development of the message. These lower order skills, we know, are deficient in dyslexics and pupils with DCD but their small numbers do not account for the wide range of UAch that we can find in schools unless we are missing many signs of these problems.

The role of DCD in underfunctioning. Between 5% to 10% of the school population are estimated to have DCD. The group includes those with gross motor difficulties and those who have fine coordination difficulties, for example in handwriting. The majority with gross motor difficulties will also have fine motor problems. According to the research 10% or more of pupils have mild handwriting coordination difficulties (Gubbay, 1976; Laszlo, Barstow, Bartrip, 1988; Rubin and Henderson, 1982). Whilst in a survey carried out with 3rd year junior school pupils in Cheshire, Alston (1993) found just over 20% of pupils were not writing well enough for the needs of the secondary school curriculum. In urban schools she found this figure rose to 40%. The Assessment of Performance Unit (APU, 1991) surveyed 2000 pupils at 11 and 15 years and found that 20% of boys and 10% of girls said they hated writing. Twice this number, 60%, said they avoided writing whenever possible.

In children with DCD, Chesson, McKay and Stephenson (1991) found over 50% had had speech therapy, and some of the group were only identified on entry to school. Half their sample were doing well in mathematics but had spelling and handwriting problems that were hampering their progress in school and affecting their self-esteem.

In concrete terms, pupils with handwriting difficulties have difficulty in learning to form letters correctly, placing letters on a line and in producing a neat and legible style on a page at a reasonable speed. When speed was investigated Roaf (1998) found that 25% of secondary school students were unable to write faster than 15 words per minute and these were the pupils who were struggling in all lessons where a lot of writing was required. She also found a close link between self-concept and handwriting presentation. The majority of the slow writers showed difficulties with motor coordination, spelling and letter formation.

Speed in examinations was investigated by Lyth (2004) in relation to the MidYIS additional test. Pupils take this test in Year 8 and go on to take Key Stage 3 exams in Year 9 and GCSEs in Year 11. His results were based upon approximately 15 000 pupils who took MidYIS in 1999 and GCSEs in 2003. The pupils were asked to copy the single same sentence repeatedly for 2 minutes 'I can write clearly and quickly all day long'. They were told their writing must be clear and legible and each sentence must fit exactly onto one line. The results were that the mean number of lines completed was 5.8 with a mean of 112 characters per minute. At 10 words per line this gives an average speed of 29 words per minute. This is a faster rate than that obtained by Roaf but the tasks are radically different. It is easier to write the same sentence rapidly for 2 minutes than for 10 from memory and thinking.

Lyth found that the speed varied from writing 1 line to 13 lines and showed a normal distribution function. Boys' writing speed (5.4 lines) was slower overall than girls (5.7 lines) and showed more variability. State school pupils' writing was slower than that of Independent school pupils (6.0 Boys; 6.3 Girls).

He was able to conclude that generally average ability rises with handwriting speed but this trend breaks down at the extremes. Those with the slowest speeds had ability higher than expected or predicted from the speed

Table 1   Average writing speeds in secondary schools in words per minute (Allcock, 2001).

Year (Chron. age)	Y 7 (12)	Y 8 (13)	Y 9 (14)	Y 10 (15)	Y 11 (16)
Mean speed	13.9	14.6	15.7	16.3	16.9

$N = 2701$.

and at the upper end very high writing speed was associated with lower ability than expected.

The influence of handwriting fluency on compositional quality in later primary and secondary school has been established by Connelly and Hurst (2001), and upon gaining good grades in examinations (Briggs, 1980). Slow handwriting has also been found to constrain the overall performance of undergraduate students in examination essays (Connolly, Dockrell and Barnett, 2005). Thus, the significance of mechanical skills in school achievement must not be underestimated. Over a similar period to Connolly and colleagues I and my MA students have been investigating handwriting and spelling issues in relation to UAch and Allcock's survey was a significant study in this process.

Allcock's (2001) survey (Table 1) was a test of 20 minutes length, in which pupils wrote about their favourite subject. She argued that this was a test that was a better match for what was expected of her pupils in secondary school. She found that a speed of 10.4 words per minute (25% slower than the mean) was severely disabling to their exam results and these pupils needed an extension of their examination time by 25% to be able to do themselves justice. Those who were 40% slower she advised needed an amanuensis.

From the above studies it would appear that there are more pupils with handwriting difficulties than is normally supposed but is the same true of spelling? There were no studies of the incidence of general spelling problems to compare with those with handwriting difficulties and so I began to use Allcock's 20-minute test to collect data from various cohorts in primary and secondary schools to see what would be revealed. This is research in progress.

NB. The two, Year 9 samples come from one specialist school in which the standard of the intakes tend to be higher than the intakes in the Year 5 (2 schools) and Year 7 (3 schools).

Table 2 shows an increasing speed of writing in the cohorts as the pupils grow older and more practised. Coordination difficulties appear to remain

Table 2   Summary of results from Year 5, Year 7 and Year 9 cohorts ($N = 1085$)

YR (N)	Wpm	Co%	F/Co%	Mean sp err%	Dys%	HMI%
5 (137)	9.2	21.7	74.6	9.6	33.9	54.3
7 (576)	13.1	15.6	60.9	10.9	18.7	33.4
9 (372)	18.0	18.7	67.8	8.4	8.3	17.1

Note: N = numbers in the cohorts; Wpm = mean words per minute; Co = percentage with coordination problems; percentage with form/coordination difficulties; mean spelling errors per script; percentages with 'dyslexics' type spelling problems; percentages failing the HMI criterion, for example making five or more errors per script.

stable at around 20% and form difficulties diminish a little as the pupils in secondary school develop more fluency. However, the poor quality of the initial writing teaching continues to hamper the writing in terms of both fluency and legibility (Montgomery, 2008). The mean spelling errors appear to change little over the years suggesting a lack of teaching directed to them however the quality of the errors does change from lower order (articulatory phonics) to higher order (morphemic–linguistic) errors. The 'dyslexic' status was defined as the number of errors per script (e.g. 10 or more per 100 words). These as expected come down markedly between Year 5 and Year 7, but the 33% or one third of the cohorts in Year 7 failing the Her Majesty's Inspectorate (HMI) criterion suggests a problem much bigger than previously identified. Spelling problems slowed down the writing speed more than coordination difficulties for example.

As can be seen in Table 3 pupils from the advantaged area display more fluent handwriting and spelling skills. All should be writing using a joined script, or at least be using a mixed one by this age having obviously been taught print script first. This is a practice that needs to be questioned and cursive introduced from the outset as in many other countries and in the

Table 3   Different writing results from a Year 5 school in an advantaged area compared to one in a disadvantaged area

N	School	Wpm	Co	F/Co	Mean sp err	Dys	HMI
85	A	10.1	12	29	8.8	25.9	42.4
52	B	7.8	19	18	10.6	51.9	66.2

Note: Writing style: joined: 40 A (2 B) mixed: 28 A (22 B) print 17 A (28 B).

United Kingdom in the first half of the twentieth century. Cursive assists fluency particularly in those with writing difficulties.

In the Year 7 cohorts, there were almost double the number of dyslexics traditionally expected and constitute a hidden population of potential underachievers. If we add the one third of pupils who have handwriting difficulties we find that 30–40% of the cohorts have difficulties that could cause them to underachieve in the area of writing. These difficulties have in most cases gone unrecognized. In one of the schools where the Year 7s were set by ability, the top set showed many fewer spelling and handwriting problems. We need to ask if their graduation to Set One is in part due to their good writing skills as Lyth (2004) found.

Gender Differences in the Year 7 Cohorts

The poorest 10% of spellers (and readers) according to the BDA (2004) will be dyslexic independent of ability. Table 4 indicates dyslexia is more common in girls than is supposed – almost equal to boys. When handwriting speed is taken into account then more boys are more disadvantaged at this age than girls.

The Year 7 spelling/writing analysis also showed that the mean speed of the dysorthographics was 14 w.p.m. whilst the speed of dysgraphics was 16 w.p.m. In other words a spelling problem is more disabling than a coordination problem in writing composition when legibility is discounted.

Very few pupils in any of the secondary school cohorts were able to write at a speed fast enough to cope with the school curriculum. In a 20-minute essay, 20 words per minute (rather than Roaf's speed of 25 w.p.m.) seemed an appropriate target speed for the Year 7s. It does suggest that the NLS has had little impact upon improving writing speed and fluency or spelling

Table 4   Gender differences in the poorest 10% of spellers in Year 7 cohort C ($N = 251$)

	Writing speed	Mean sp. err	Gender ratios (girls to boys)
Group A $N = 10$			
Faster writers	14.92 wpm	40.4	2:3
Group B $N = 12$			
Slower writers	7.74 wpm	22.17	1:5

accuracy. It also follows that teachers in the early years of secondary school need to be trained to identify spelling and handwriting difficulties and to intervene within their subject areas.

In GCSEs in the UK boys have been performing less well than girls by about 10%, although at A level this difference tends to disappear, probably as those with difficulties and disaffection leave the school system. The reasons for boy's UAch have been put down to many factors as discussed in the earlier chapters but now we need to consider writing skills and their impact on attainment. Even the use of the computer does not help all pupils; for some are equally slow in using them. Although spellcheckers may support spelling they do not improve reading as improvement in spelling does (Montgomery, 2007) so there are inbuilt disadvantages in technological answers.

Boys have been shown to be more vulnerable to both DCD and dyslexia and these problems may have a wider significance and penetration than just those who are referred for specialist testing and intervention.

Handwriting

The writing speed of boys and girls was significantly different in the cohort analyses described above. The group mean was 13.09 made up of boys 11.79 and girls 14.26. Could this account for the lower achievements of boys in school attainments? Does it account for their better achievements in subjects requiring less writing such as mathematics and science?

The boys overall were slower at writing in all the categories and schools. In the groups who were 25% slower than Allcock's mean speed the ratio of boys to girls was approximately two to one. In the 40% slower category the ratio overall was 5 boys to 1 girl. Boys alone appeared to have the severest writing difficulties, 1% could write at speeds of only 3–5 words per minute.

Spelling

One third of pupils in the cohorts failed the HMI criterion and the ratio of boys' to girls' failure was similar (32.46% boys and 34.34% girls).

Although the ratio of boys to girls in the dyslexic category varied between the cohorts, overall the ratio was 1.2:1 boys to girls, close to Rutter *et al.* (2004) survey figures of 1.5 boys to 1.0 girl. In other words the traditional figure of a 4:1 ratio of dyslexic boys to girls needs to be challenged.

It suggests that girls are not getting their rightful amount of dyslexia provision and their difficulties are being overlooked. This was confirmed in an earlier study where the referral ratio for dyslexia was 5:1 boys to girls and girls were referred a year later than boys with the same level of difficulties (Montgomery, 1997).

Dyslexic difficulties in the Year 7 cohort C a typical community school

At this moment of writing, government funded research at Hull University has shown that of 1300 pupils failing SATs at 7 and 11 years over 50% on further investigation showed 'dyslexic type' difficulties. SATs are written tests and this was where they were first identified. They were then subjected to 'Cognitive Abilities Tests' and showed problems in phonological processing and working memory 'typical of dyslexics'. In ordinary parlance they had failed to develop sufficient knowledge of the sounds and names of the alphabet and synthetic phonics skills necessary for word building. As a secondary function digit span scores (working memory test) were poor. (Koppitz (1977) showed that as reading and spelling improve so does working memory!)

The Hull researchers concluded that a specialist teacher was needed in each state school to address these problems. My research suggests that every primary teacher can easily learn to diagnose the problems starting with analysis of children's emergent writing in Reception. Primary and Secondary English specialists and SENCos can likewise diagnose the problems in the later stages. All of them can amend their teaching methods to deal with the problems leaving the severest cases for the specialist. The specialist must use an appropriate specialist dyslexia APSL programme.

The commonly posited 'dyslexic-type' errors of sequencing or order difficulties, bizarreness, inversions and concatenations in research studies were categories used as shown in Table 5 to trawl through the data from the poorest spellers to see if any errors made would fit the types.

(*NB*. These categories are unhelpful and need to be replaced by those used in CPSS, for example Lower order articulatory-phonemic and Higher order morphemic–linguistic.)

From a total of 670 errors in these 22 poorest spellers' scripts it was not possible to identify more than 8 errors that might qualify as sequencing errors. There were no reversal examples of 'was' for 'saw' or 'on' for 'no'.

Table 5 The 'dyslexic type' errors made by school C 'dyslexics' ($N = 22$)

Sequencing?	Bizarre?	Omissions?	Concatenations?
Bronwe (brown)	Ckach (chase)	Sise (since)	Favote (favourite)
Filed (field)	Takt (chased)	Nity (ninety)	Deiced (decided)
Berdy (buried)	Janjoys (enjoys)	Haging (hanging)	Probl (probably)
Colse (close)	Coicens (cousins)	Enharse (enhance)	
Phonemic – basic			
Biult (built)	Oncl (uncle)	Scapering (scampering)	Inuf (enough)
Nitg (night)	Evetchers (adventures)	Whet (went)	Safen (Southend)
Aronud (around)	Avre (aviary)	Whigs (things)	Coules (colours)
Pepels (peoples)	Haja (hair)	Thand (found)	
Moe			(More)

(This error type reflects a visual approach to spelling and poor grasp of phonics blends rather than a sequencing problem.)

In the bizarre category only the first two words seemed to fit the category but each could be explained on grounds of poor phonic knowledge. For example 'chruck' is often seen for 'truck' in beginning spellers' writing. These poor spellers are being similarly creative (Read, 1986) in their attempts to transcribe their ideas using incomplete phonic knowledge.

In the omissions category only seven examples could be found. Here, we see typical 'dyslexic' and young spellers' errors in which nasals are difficult to identify in articulation for spelling. The nasals 'n' and 'm' nasalify the preceding vowel rather than have an articulatory pattern of their own especially before consonants 'd' and 't'. Pupils with mild pronunciation difficulties might also make these mistakes.

If pupils are taught to syllabify and speak clearly and sub vocalize slowly for spelling then concatenations can be corrected. There were no inversions. The basic phonics errors were typical of beginning spellers attempts to spell – the southern Essex dialect 'safen' for Southend is a classic.

These 'dyslexic' pupils appeared to show the same types of error as the rest of the cohorts but their errors were more frequent with more lower order errors in articulation, syllabification and phonics problems. Their error types seem to me to be of a normal rather than disordered form, similar to errors made by beginning spellers. It would thus be possible to use synthetic phonics teaching and CPSS interventions.

Conclusions

The problems of the education of doubly exceptional children bring into focus two key issues in gifted education – identification and provision. We might ask why do we need to identify them? The answer usually is because we wish to select the most able for some sort of special provision that the ordinary curriculum is not providing. It then becomes important to ask if instead of treating the students as though they are a problem we should look at the other side of the coin and address the ordinary curriculum and its teaching to make it meet most of their needs by differentiation and inclusive teaching. This would ensure that their giftedness would be acknowledged and receive appropriate attention. In addition we need to improve teaching skills in the intervention in learning difficulties, particularly in the area of writing. It would appear that this area has had most attention and least progress has been made because the attention has been ill directed.

We might begin by recognizing that gifted individuals in mass schooling systems are ill served. They need much more freedom and autonomy built into programmes of study with room for creativity and real-world problem solving. In the United Kingdom, schools are being encouraged to do this by personalizing learning and freeing up curriculum time so that 20% of it may be devoted to offering out of school options, master classes, independent projects and so on. This needs to go hand in hand however with reframing the ordinary provision and making it special and more challenging.

The upskilling of teachers needs to begin with enhancing the skills of mainstream teachers so that the everyday provision they offer is more cognitively challenging within the normal classroom. It also needs to allow students to be more participative and be able to choose from a range of response modes to cater for their different talents.

The mainstream teacher also needs better Continuing Professional Development programmes that include knowledge and skills in dual exceptionality so that the learner is not torn between the SEN and the Gifted and Talented provision. The CPD needs to include better knowledge and strategies for behaviour management and how to intervene appropriately on both aspects of written work, the content and the skills.

It also needs to be recognized that the writing curriculum is still widely used as the main response mode in schools and help is needed so that teachers develop kinder attitudes to writing difficulties. They need to be shown how to intervene to support and develop writing skills without creating a problem or 'special' need. They also need to accept a wider range of response modes than writing alone and do all of this in a constructive and positive manner. These five interrelated themes, identification, curriculum, pedagogy, writing, and behaviour policies have been addressed in Chapters 1 and 5 and now in Chapter 10.

Appendix
Cognitive Process Strategies for Spelling

Lower order strategies – articulatory-synthetic phonics

1. *Articulation and pronunciation* – not 'f' for 'th', chimley for chimney, skelington and so on, dialect 'grand' for 'ground', need clear, correct speech for spelling.
2. *Over articulation* – parli-a-ment, gover-n-ment.
3. *Cue articulation* – say it incorrectly Wed-nes-day, Feb-ru-ary.
4. *Syllabification* – break it down into syllables or beats in the word, favrite/fa-vour-ite, intresting/in-ter-est–ing.
5. *Phonics* – try to get a basic skeleton of the sound of the word – sine for sign, wen for when, tung for tongue.
6. *Rules* – for example 'i before e except after c', and the l-f-s rule – double l-f-and s after a short vowel full, off, puss (make a sentence for the seven exceptions yes, if, gas, bus and so on).

Higher order strategies – morphemic–linguistics dictionary work helps here

7. *Origin* – the word's root in another modern foreign language can help, or its origin in a past language, for example op/port/unity.
8. *Linguistics* – basic syllable structures (cvc, ccvvce and so on, and open or closed) and the four suffixing rules – ADD DOUBLE, DROP, CHANGE govern most word misspellings.

9. *Baseword/family* bomb, bombing, bombardment; sign signal, signature, signing.
10. *Meaning* – se-pare, to separate to pare or part.
11. *Analogy* – it is like braggart helps spell braggadocio.
12. *Funnies* – 'cess pit' helped me remember how spell 'necessary'.

Homophones – words which sound the same – there/their, to/too/two are the last to disappear and respond best to the meaning strategy.
Procedure

1. Ask pupils to *choose two misspellings* they want to learn to correct.
2. Look up each correct spelling in a *dictionary*, plus meaning origin and pronunciation.
3. Draw a *ring round* the area of error – usually only one letter.
4. Select one *best fit CPSS* and talk it through with the pupil.
5. Find a second or *reserve strategy* or perhaps a 'funny' if possible.
6. Pupil now writes the spelling correctly *THREE* times from memory in *FULL FLOWING CURSIVE* saying the names of the letters as they are written – Simultaneous Oral Spelling. (Copyright: D. Montgomery, 2007).

(Montgomery (1997) *Developmental Spelling Handbook*, LDRP, Maldon)

References

APU (Assessment of Performance Unit) (1991) *Assessment of Writing Skills*, Further Education Unit, London.

AFASIC (2008) *Association For All Speech Impaired Children Information Booklet*, AFASIC, London.

Allcock, P. (2001) The importance of handwriting skills in Keystage 3 and GCSE Examinations of more able pupils. *Educating Able Children*, **5** (1), 23–5.

Alston, J. (1993) *Assessing and Promoting Handwriting Skills*, NASEN, Stafford.

Baldwin, A.Y. (2001) The different masks of giftedness, in *Proceedings of the 13th Biennial Conference of the World Council for Gifted and Talented Children* (ed. B. Clarke), WCGTC, CDRom, Istanbul, August 2–9, 1999.

Barber, C. (1996) The integration of a very able pupil with Asperger Syndrome into mainstream school. *British Journal of Special Education*, **23** (1), 19–24.

BDA (2004) www.bda.org.uk/ April 2006.

Berninger, V.W. (2004) *The Role of Mechanics in Composing of Elementary Students.* A review of research and intervention Keynote: Annual DCD Conference, Oxford, April.

Bravar, L. (2005) Studying handwriting: an Italian experience *6th International DCD Conference*, Trieste May.

Briggs, D. (1980) A study of the influence of handwriting upon grades in examination scripts. *Educational Review*, **32** 185–83.

Butler-Por, N. (1987) *Underachievers in Schools: Issues and Interventions*, Wiley, London.

Chesson, R., McKay, C. and Stephenson, E. (1991) The consequences of motor/ learning difficulties in school age children and their teachers: some parental views. *Support for Learning*, **6** (4), 172–7.

Clements, S.D. (1966) *National Project on Minimal Brain Dysfunction in Children – Terminology and Identification Monograph No 3 Public Health Service Publication No 1415*, Government Printing Office, Washington DC.

Connelly, V. and Hurst, G. (2001) The influence of handwriting fluency on writing quality in later primary and early secondary education. *Handwriting Today*, **2**, 50–7.

Connolly, V., Dockrell, J. and Barnett, A. (2005) The slow handwriting of undergraduate students constrains the overall performance in exam essays. *Educational Psychology*, **25** (1), 99–109.

Connor, M. (2007) *Connor's Behaviour Rating Scale*, Pearson Assessment, Oxford.

Cooper, P. (ed.) (1999) *Understanding and Supporting Children with Emotional and Behavioural Difficulties*, Jessica Kingsley, London.

Cooper, P. and Ideus, K. (1995) Is attention deficit hyperactivity disorder a Trojan horse? *Support for Learning*, **10** (1), 29–34.

Corn, A. (1986) Gifted students who have a visual difficulty. Can we meet their educational needs? *Education of the Visually Handicapped*, **18** (2), 71–84.

Cowdery, L.L., Montgomery, D., Morse, P. and Prince-Bruce, M. (1994) *Teaching Reading through Spelling (TRTS)*, TRTS Publishing, Wrexham.

Crocker, A.C. (1987) Underachieving, gifted working class boys: Are they wrongly labelled underachieving? *Educational Studies*, **13** (2), 169–78.

DCFS (2008) *Pupil Absences in Schools in England, Including Pupil Characteristics, 2006/7 National Statistics First Release 26th February*, DfES, London.

De Mink, F. (1995) High ability students in higher education, in *Nurturing Talent: Individual Needs and Social Ability Volume 1* (eds M.W. Katzko and F.J. Monks), Van Gorcum, Assen, The Netherlands.

DfE (1997) *Excellence for All Children: Meeting Special Educational Needs*, The Stationery Office, London.

DfEE (1998) *The National Literacy Strategy: Guidance for Teachers*, The Stationery Office, London.

Duane, D. (2002) The Neurology of NLD Keynote Lecture. Dyslexia Conference on Policy into Practice Uppsala, Sweden, August 14–16.

Edwards, J. (1994) *The Scars of Dyslexia*, Cassell, London.

Frith, U. (1985) Beneath the surface of developmental dyslexia, in *Surface Dyslexia* (eds K. Patterson and M. Coltheart), Routledge and Kegan Paul, London.

Gagne, F. (1995) Learning about the nature of gifts and talents through peer and teacher nomination, in *Nurturing Talent: Individual Needs and Social Ability Volume 1* (eds M.W. Katzko and F.J. Monks), Van Gorcum, Assen, The Netherlands.

Galloway, D. and Goodwin, C. (1987) *The Education of Disturbing Children*, Longman, London.

Gillingham, A. and Stillman, B. (1956) *Remedial Training for Children with Specific Disability in reading, Spelling and Penmanship*, Sackett and Williams, New York.

Graham, S., Berninger, V. W., Abbott, R.D., *et al.* (1996) The role of mechanics in composing of elementary students: a new methodological approach. *Journal of Educational Psychology*, **92** (4) 70–182.

Gubbay, S.S. (1976) *The Clumsy Child*, W.B. Saunders, London.

Hart, D. (2008) Should SEN be seen as separate labelled obstacles or one continuum?MA SpLD Dissertation, *Middlesex University, London.*

Henderson, S.E. and Green, D. (2001) Handwriting problems in children with Asperger Syndrome. *Handwriting Today*, **2**, 65–71.

Hickey, K. (1991) *Dyslexia: A Language Training Course*, 2nd edn (eds J. Augur and S. Briggs), Whurr, London.

Jaksa, P. (1999) The Flowers and the Thorns, FOCUS Reprint Newsletter of the National ADDA, pp. 1–4, www.adda.org.com September 1999.

Kellmer-Pringle, M. (1970) *Able Misfits*, Longman, London.

Kerry, T. (1983) *Finding and Helping the Able Child*, Croom Helm, London.

Koppitz, E.M. (1977) *The Visual Aural Digit Span Test*, Grune and Stratton, New York.

Laszlo, M., Barstow, P. and Bartrip, P. (1988) A new approach to perceptuomotor dysfunction, previously called 'clumsiness'. *Support for Learning*, **3**, 35–40.

Lyth, A. (2004) Handwriting speed an aid in examination success?*Handwriting Today*, **3**, 30–35.

McCluskey, K.W., Baker, P.A., Bergsgaard, M. and McCluskey, A.L.A. (2003) Interventions with talented at-risk populations with emotional and behavioural difficulties, in *Gifted and Talented with SEN: Double Exceptionality* (ed. D. Montgomery), David Fulton, London, pp. 168–85.

Miles, T.R. and Miles, E. (1999) *Dyslexia 100 Years on*, 2nd edn, Open University, Buckingham.

Mongon, D. and Hart, S. (1989) *Improving Classroom Behaviour: New Directions for Teachers and Learners*, Cassell, London.

Montgomery, D. (1989) *Managing Behaviour Problems*, Hodder and Stoughton, Sevenoaks.

Montgomery, D. (1995) Social abilities in highly able disabled learners and the consequences for remediation, in *Nurturing Talent: Individual Needs and Social Ability Volume 1* (eds M.W. Katzko and F.J. Monks), Van Gorcum, Assen, The Netherlands, pp. 226–38.

Montgomery, D. (1997) *Spelling: Remedial Strategies*, Cassell, London.

Montgomery, D. (ed.) (2000) *Able Underachievers*, Whurr, London.

Montgomery, D. (2002) *Helping Teachers Improve through Classroom Observation*, 2nd edn, David Fulton, London.

Montgomery, D. (ed.) (2003) *Gifted and Talented with Special Educational Needs: Double Exceptionality*, David Fulton, London.

Montgomery, D. (2007) *Spelling, Handwriting and Dyslexia*, Routledge, London.

Montgomery, D. (2008) Cohort analysis of writing in year 7 after 2, 4, and 7 years of the National Literacy Strategy. *Support for Learning*, **23** (1), 3–11.

Neihart, M. (2000) Gifted children with Asperger's Syndrome. *Gifted Child Quarterly*, **44** (4), 222–30.

Pawley, J. (2008) Dyslexia the hidden trigger?MA SpLD Dissertation, Middlesex University, London.

Raven, J.C. (2008) *Raven's Progressive Matrices*, Harcourt Assessment, London.

Read, C. (1986) *Children's Creative Spelling*, Routledge and Kegan Paul, London.

Roaf, C. (1998) Slow hand. A secondary school survey of handwriting speed and legibility. *Support for Learning*, **13** (1), 39–42.

Rubin, N. and Henderson, S.E. (1982) Two sides of the same coin. Variations in teaching methods and failure to learn to write. *Special Education*, **9** (4) 14–18.

Rutter, M.L. (1985) *Helping Troubled Children*, 2nd edn, Penguin, Harmondsworth.

Rutter, M.L., Caspi, A., Fergusson, D. *et al.* (2004) Sex differences in developmental reading disability. *Journal of the American Medical Association*, **291–299** (16) 2007–12.

Rutter, M.L., Tizard, J. and Whitmore, K. (eds) (1970) *Education, Health and Behaviour*, Longman, London.

Sassoon, R. (1990) *Handwriting: A New Perspective*, Stanley Thornes, Cheltenham.

Schlicte-Hiersemensel, B. (2000) The psychodynamics of psychological and behavioural difficulties of highly able children: experiences from a psychotherapeutic practice, in *Able Underachievers* (ed. D. Montgomery), Whurr, London, pp. 52–61.

Silverman, L.K. (1989) Invisible gifts, invisible handicaps. *Roeper Review*, **12** (1), 37–42.

Silverman, L.K. (2004) *Poor Handwriting: A Major Cause of Underachievement*, http://www.visualspatial.org/Publications/Article%20List/Poor_Handwriting. htm (accessed 12 March 2004).

Singleton, C. (2006) Dyslexia and youth offending, in *The Dyslexia Handbook* (eds S. Tresman and A. Cooke), The British Dyslexia Association, Reading, pp. 117–21.

Sisk, D. (2000) Overcoming underachievement of gifted and talented students, in *Able Underachievers* (ed. D. Montgomery), Whurr, London, pp. 120–49.

Sisk, D. (2003) Gifted with behaviour disorders: marching to a different drummer, in *Gifted and Talented Children with SEN* (ed. D. Montgomery), David Fulton, London, pp. 131–54.

Smith, L.J. (2002) An investigation of children having EBD with dyslexic type difficulties in special schools and one pupil referral unit. MA SpLD Dissertation, Middlesex University, London.

Soloff, S. (1973) The effect of non content factors on the grading of essays. *Graduate Research in Education and Related Disciplines*, **6** (2), 44–54.

Stamm, M. (2004) Looking at long term effects of early reading and numeracy ability: a glance at the phenomenon of giftedness. *Gifted and Talented International*, **18** (1), 7–16.

Starr, R. (2003) Show me the light, I can't see how bright I am: gifted students with visual impairment, in *Gifted and Talented Children with Special Educational Needs* (ed. D. Montgomery), NACE/David Fulton, London, pp. 93–109.

Tanguay, F.B. (2002) *Nonverbal Learning Difficulties at School*, Jessica Kingsley, London.

Terrell, C. and Passenger, T. (2005) *Understanding ADHD, Autism, Dyslexia and Dyspraxia*, Family Doctor Publications, Dorset.

Torrance, E.P. (1963) *Education and the Creative Potential*, University of Minnesota Press, Minneapolis.

Tymms, P. (2004) Why This Man Scares Ruth Kelly, Article by Kenneth Mansell, *Times Educational Supplement*, 28 August, p. 9.

Visser, J. and Rayner, S. (1999) *Emotional and Behavioural Difficulties, A Reader*, Q. Ed., Birmingham.

Wallace, B. (2000) *Teaching the Very Able Child*, David Fulton, London.

Whitmore, J.R. (1982) *Giftedness, Conflict and Underachievement*, Allyn and Bacon, Boston.

11

Using Assistive Technologies to Address the Written Expression Needs of the Twice-exceptional Student

William F. Morrison, Tara Jeffs and Mary G. Rizza

Introduction

Programmes for students with learning disabilities often include some component of assistive technology. Technology is also used to enhance the experience for students in programmes for the gifted. The use of technology, assistive or otherwise, with twice-exceptional students is an area of need that has yet to be fully explored. This chapter reviews the literature on the use of assistive technology for students with disabilities, making the case for the use of this strategy with students who are twice exceptional. Of particular interest is the infusion of technology on instruction for students with written expression disabilities. Specific strategies and technologies will be provided to assist educators in differentiating the curriculum in the writing process for the twice-exceptional student.

It is generally accepted that the term twice exceptional is used to describe students who have or show potential for giftedness in one or more areas and who also display academic difficulties consistent with a documented area of disability. As such, the twice-exceptional student must navigate the complex environments of school in three different classrooms, regular, gifted and special education. Paradoxically, they often fit into none of these spheres and, although we can identify these students, programmes for addressing their unique needs are scant. Programmes for students with learning disabilities, are well defined and often include some component of assistive technology. Technology infusion is also a technique long used to enhance the experience

Able, Gifted and Talented Underachievers, Second Edition   Edited by Diane Montgomery
© 2009 John Wiley & Sons, Ltd

for students in programmes for the gifted. The use of technology, assistive or otherwise, with twice-exceptional students is an area of need that has yet to be addressed (NAGC, 1998). The purpose of this chapter is to identify the needs of the twice-exceptional student and explore assistive technology options that address those needs.

Specifically, we will examine how the use of assistive technology can be used to address the needs of the twice-exceptional student in the area of written expression. Beginning with a review of identification issues related to the twice exceptional, this article will focus on a discussion of the assistive technology tools available for educators who wish to infuse technology into the writing process and meet the needs of this unique population.

Identification

Students who are twice exceptional, are well served only when their learning needs are accurately defined. Similarly, intervention is only effective when appropriately applied. Until we identify students' abilities and disabilities, can we design a programme that appropriately serves their needs. Identification, therefore, continues to be the primary reason for the difficulties in serving students who are twice exceptional because this unique population of students may not adhere to a prescribed pattern for behaviour (Baum and Owen, 2003). Understanding that students can have both gifts and disabilities is the cornerstone for helping these students succeed. Translating this understanding into success building programmes, however, requires additional information about how these students learn, and most importantly, what resources are available to aid in their learning (Baum and Owen, 2003; Brody and Mills, 2004; Nielsen *et al.*, 1993). To this end, child-find efforts on the behalf of the twice exceptional should begin by tracking progress of identified students in both gifted and special education programmes. Twice-exceptional students who are first identified as gifted will show any of a variety of signs that a specific disability is present. In some cases, there is a sudden shift in grades that indicates the disability resulting from increased academic demand. For average students, we notice problems in third or fourth grade when requirements change. The twice-exceptional students, however, can rely on advanced abilities to self-remediate and are able to sustain achievement sometimes until fifth or sixth grade. Students with learning disabilities may show signs of giftedness in school when permitted to work in areas of talent. However, the concern of most special education programmes is on remediation and students are rarely given the chance to work on challenging material. For this reason, it is crucial that schools provide opportunities for enrichment to all students.

Securing Services for Dual Exceptionality

For the student who is identified first with a learning disability, securing services in the gifted area may be problematic. One issue is teacher attitudes toward the twice exceptional. Researchers have found that teacher referrals for gifted programmes are biased against students with disabilities or learning differences (Bianco, 2005; Cline and Hedgeman, 2001; Siegle and Powell, 2004). Another difficulty is that students in special education programmes may not be exposed to activities that would highlight their talent areas. Next, twice-exceptional students can be hard to identify because their disabilities mask their abilities. These students appear to be functioning in the normal range but are discovered when either a special talent is revealed or a problem arises. Waldron and Saphire (1990) warn that this is the danger in using IQ scores to identify twice-exceptional students, their disabilities may be suppressing the test scores. The final category of twice-exceptional student identified by Baum and Owen (2003) is the underachieving student. Many gifted students with disabilities are able to contend with lower level work, it is only when the rigours of their academic programme increase that their disability area becomes apparent. For many of these students the cycle of underachievement has already begun and they are not able to fully understand the true reasons for their difficulties. Again teachers may be confused that a previously high achieving student would have difficulties and misdiagnose the problem as underachievement. Understanding that students can have both gifts and disabilities is the cornerstone for success. Translating this understanding into effective programmes, however, requires additional information about how these students learn (Baum and Owen, 2003; Nielsen *et al.*, 1993). Twice-exceptional students require an educational programme that includes both remediation and enrichment. A comprehensive plan must take into account the student's individual patterns of strengths and weaknesses, addressing both a need for skill support and for challenging content. The twice-exceptional student is one who developed a set of coping strategies for learning, the key is to uncover these and insure they are working in a manner that maximizes potential.

Research investigating the needs of the twice exceptional advocates for curriculum and experiences that provide skill development within the context of appropriate challenge (Baum and Owen, 2003; Baum, Cooper and Neu, 2001; Robinson, 1999). Baum, Cooper and Neu (2001) further describe a concept called dual differentiation, which is no more than a method for providing services that address both the need for challenge and for skill acquisition. Service models specifically designed to meet the needs of the twice exceptional often include provisions for remediation but emphasize the need for challenging curriculum that capitalizes on student strengths (Baum, Cooper and Neu, 2001; Nielsen and Higgins, 2005; Weinfeld *et al.*, 2002, 2005). All too often programmes for students with disabilities focus primarily on skill acquisition and remediation of deficits. Conversely, programmes for gifted students generally include provisions to meet the advanced cognitive capabilities via advanced or accelerated content and skills. Finding the balance between remediation and enrichment is difficult, leaving the student to struggle in a programme that may not meet either need. Programmes should be designed using a continuum of services and flexible enough to address the nuances of the dual diagnosis. Teaching skills within a problem-based learning environment, allowing for choice in activity, and providing mentoring are all common components to programmes (Coleman, 2005; Nielsen, 2002; Shevitz *et al.*, 2003).

The use of technology in programmes for the twice exceptional is also recommended but only to the extent that it is widely used with other students. It is our contention that technology is an important component to any programme for the twice exceptional because it can help students develop coping strategies to deal with various learning differences. Assistive technology is a common intervention provided to students with disabilities and generally varies depending on student need. Within gifted education, the use of computers and technology is concentrated on curricular applications and activities that extend learning experiences of the students. Siegle (2004) contends that the very goals of gifted education to provide increasingly more complex, faster paced information and skill acquisition mirrors that of technology literacy. Use of technology in classrooms has increased exponentially in the past few decades as a means for keeping up with the ever burgeoning infusion of technology in everyday life. Students today are literate individuals who are at ease in technologically rich environments, using native skills like critical and creative thinking to enhance their experiences online. Keeping pace with technology literacy trends is vital to success in all educational programmes but more so for gifted programmes because gifted students are typically those who are innovative users of technology.

It will be shown that twice-exceptional students can benefit most from technology infusion that promotes skill building within an environment that is stimulating and engaging, thus meeting their need for challenge. Since the use of technology is inherently innovative, the focus on remediation skills will become less apparent but should never be overshadowed by the glamour of the technology. The traditional purpose of assistive technology is to provide support to students with disabilities, the traditional purpose of using technology in gifted education is to capitalize on student ability through innovation. The use of technology, assistive or otherwise, with the twice exceptional should encompass both purposes. However, technology is a tool that is a means to an end and not an end in and of itself. The infusion of technology therefore should be organic to the programme and above all provide support to students based in individual need.

Universal design for learning

Mastering academic content and obtaining essential writing skills is often viewed as the sole responsibility of the student and not within the teaching paradigm or learning environment. McDonald and Riendaeu (cited in Strobel *et al.*, 2007) state that 'Learning Diversity' is where individual differences are not only expected, but celebrated within the classroom. This is the overall concept of universal design for learning (UDL). UDL promotes multiple ways for learners to access, engage and express the learning content. The central focus of UDL is to promote the planning and designing of classrooms that provide learning activities, curricular materials and learning technologies that are flexible enough to accommodate the unique learning styles of a wide range of students (Rose, 2000). Developing such learning environments, however, requires additional background knowledge of successful practices in the specific area of remediation, in this case written expression, and assistive technology.

Writing process for the student with LD

Difficulty in written expression is one of the most significant problems experienced by children identified with learning disabilities (LD) (Lange *et al.*, 2006; Lindstrom, 2007; Vaughn, Gersten and Chard, 2000; Walker, Shippen and Alberto, 2005). In comparison to normally achieving peers, students with LD tend to produce a shorter, less coherent and often less refined writing product as a result of the inability to generate ideas, organize text and apply metacognitive skills (McAlister, Nelson and Bahr, 1999; Walker, Shippen and Alberto, 2005). Students with disabilities make considerably more spelling, capitalization and punctuation errors; commonly referred to as writing mechanics (Graham, Harris and Larsen, 2001). MacArthur (1999) states 'problems with writing mechanics interfere with higher level composing processes and affect both the quantity and overall quality of writing' (p. 170). For some students with LD, the physical demand of handwriting produces a slow and less legible writing product (Graham and Weintraub, 1996; Saddler *et al.*, 2004).

Writing process for the twice-exceptional student

Problems related to the writing process for the twice-exceptional student have been well documented in the literature and mirror, to a large extent, those of the student with a learning disability. Noticeably different for the gifted and talented (GT) student with LD is the increased discrepancy between performance and achievement. Current problems identified in the literature include limited spelling ability (Baum, Cooper and Neu, 2001; Bireley, Languis and Williamson, 1992; Hishinuma and Tadaki, 1996), poor handwriting (Baum, Cooper and Neu, 2001), problems with organization skills (Baum, Cooper and Neu, 2001; Waldron and Saphire, 1990) and visual perception or motor deficit (Bireley, Languis and Williamson, 1992). To aid the twice-exceptional student in the writing process researchers have consistently recommended the use of computers and assistive technologies.

Assistive technology

Currently, federal law in the United States requires that every individual education plan written for students with disabilities take into account the assistive technology needs of the student. A common adaptation has been computer-enhanced instruction, which runs along a continuum from very simple spell check programmes to more complex screen-text readers. The research on assistive technology involving students with disabilities is replete with examples of successful implementation. Similarly, researchers addressing the needs of the GT/LD student repeatedly called for the inclusion of technology and software to meet their needs as well (Imbeau, 1999). Such recommendations of technology generally address the need for advanced thinking skills and overall challenge commonly expressed by gifted students. Higgins and Boone (1996) stress that the key to selecting effective technology is making the right match between the technologies, commonly faced challenges of the individual and the requirements needed for successful implementation.

Assistive technology is a natural fit for the twice-exceptional student because the instruction can be easily adapted to meet the needs for remediation and challenge. According to Lewis (2000) the two fundamental purposes of assistive technology are that is can help counterbalance a disability with a strength area, and provide a different avenue for performing a task so as to compensate for the disability. It is through assistive technology and instructional accommodations that learning becomes accessible because of the natural differentiation it affords. Technology-based learning activities facilitate active participation and can be easily altered in content, process and product thus increasing chances at success for the twice-exceptional student.

While researchers have consistently voiced and recommended the use of assistive technology to aid in the writing processes for the GT/LD student, a review of the extant literature found these recommendations, for the most part, have been limited to simple word processing tools. The following section will introduce assistive technology tools and provide a brief description of each tool that can be used in all phases of the writing process. Table 1identifies common writing difficulties in each phase of the writing process: prewriting, writing revision, editing and publishing and gives suggestions of commercially available assistive technology tools.

Assistive Technology Tools

Prewriting skills

Graphic-based word processors   Graphic-based word processors provide a fun and exciting manipulative writing environment that puts students in control of graphics, animations and sound effects that can spark imagination and make writing fun and motivating. Students initially brainstorm writing ideas and develop rich details of their story through the power of graphics. When using a graphic-based word processor, students select supporting pictures to tell their story. Through the ownership of planning and selecting graphics, students begin to establish writing details. As a result a more in-depth story or writing product is developed. Within graphic-based word processors, features such as spell checkers, voice recorders and text readers enable students to bypass weaknesses when working with text. Graphic-based word processors minimize the fear or intimidation of the written word and enable the creative side of the student to flourish and generate content.

Voice recognition software   For the student that can 'think aloud' and share his/her thoughts verbally but has difficulty in expressing these thoughts in writing; voice recognition can provide speed and productivity to the writing process. Although voice recognition requires mental planning and a different way of thinking, if shown appropriate metacognitive strategies, an individual can be very productive in the writing process. When using voice recognition, the student speaks clearly and distinctly into a microphone, as a result the software programme types what is spoken. Advancements in computer technology have increased the effectiveness and use of speech recognition software. The most common type of speech recognition soft-ware is continuous speech. Continuous speech allows the user to speak naturally, using phrases or sentences, thus can be quite useful for the stu-dent whose cognitive processing and oral expression ability exceeds written expression skills as in the case for some twice-exceptional students. Advan-tages of speech recognition for the GT/LD student include the generation of text quickly and accurately. Additional advantages includes the use of strong verbal skills by the users to achieve success in writing tasks that normally would be unsuccessful due to the inability to bypass weak written lan-guage/spelling skills (De La Paz, 1999; Hartley, Soto and Pennebaker, 2003).

Text-to-speech   Text-to-speech software allows students to research and ex-plore text on the Internet or in an electronic text file. The software reads aloud the text on the computer screen allowing students reading below grade level to independently research and gather information. Text-to-speech pro-grammes support writing through the use of visual and auditory stimuli. The primary function of text-to-speech software is to convert text to speech output, allowing the reader to use his or her auditory skills as well as visual skills. In essence, text-to-speech programmes enable the user to see text that is displayed on a computer screen as it is simultaneously spoken. Text-to-speech software provides many options and features. Universal text readers perform text reading in many computer applications, therefore, completing tasks such as researching on the Internet, reading email and writing and editing a report with greater ease. Many text-to-speech programmes offer valuable tools such as audible spell checking, voice notes, highlighting features and invaluable electronic dictionaries.

Writing skills

Talking word processors Talking word processors allow a student to hear what he/she is typing or creating in text within the specific talking word processing software programme. Using the text-to-speech capabilities mentioned above enables the text to be read back to the student by word, sentence or paragraph. Generally, talking word processors are more limited in features than text-to-speech programmes in that the user can only manipulate and have text spoken that was created and saved within the talking word processor programme itself. Consequently, the versatility of reading electronic text files produced in a variety of software application programmes is limited. In most cases, talking word processors provide students with the basic features of a word processing programme (offering a grammar and spell checker) along with the capability to type text and have it highlighted and read back to them.

Software with highlighting and speech capabilities Highlighting and scanning software allows the user to manipulate text in all forms. Papers, worksheets and articles can be scanned in and the text can be manipulated by the student. The student can highlight in different colours main ideas and supporting details. Writing and editing his/her work becomes easier through the use of visual and auditory feedback. This allows both auditory and visual learners to build on their strengths and minimize their weaknesses when approaching the writing process.

Software features combining the use of a scanner and optical character recognition technology is used to convert printed text into electronic text. This feature prepares the printed materials to be read aloud, underlined, highlighted and manipulated by the learner. Research supports the practice of using software with highlighting and speech capabilities to provide the student with support in word recognition and vocabulary difficulties (Lange *et al.*, 2006; Montali and Lewandowski, 1996; Wepner, 1990/1991/1991). Software programmes with highlighting and speech capabilities may benefit twice-exceptional students by providing them with a multi-modal approach to writing along with customizable options to enhance study skills. In addition, selection of text can be differentiated to include more complex source material that meets the student's need for higher level content.

Word prediction software   Word prediction software provides students with a list of word choices as they begin to write. These word choices are provided through the prediction of spelling or sentence syntax structure. Students can select the appropriate words through auditory or visual recognition. Word prediction allows students to express ideas in their writing without getting bogged down with spelling and vocabulary, thus allowing ideas to flow freely and smoothly. Such software can benefit GT/LD students by providing features that reduce the amount of energy spent on the writing format. Features such as automatic spacing, capitalization, grammatical accuracy, spelling and sentence structure ease the demands of writing and increase overall writing productivity. Research has shown that word prediction can improve the quality and quantity of writing for students with disabilities (Graham, Harris and Larsen, 2001; Lewis *et al.*, 1998; MacArthur, 1999). For the twice-exceptional student whose cognitive processes of information is quicker than their ability to produce information in written form, these programmes offer options for fluency and accuracy.

Mind mapping/outlining software   Graphic organizers, concept maps and outlines have been used in the learning process for over two decades. Mind mapping and outlining software programmes provide students with electronic visual learning tools that are powerful in assisting students in maintaining focus on a topic, developing ideas and creating clear and concise relationships between various types of information. Students and teachers can use outlining and concept mapping software to enhance the overall structure and quality of their writing. The power of such tools is obvious when the learner creates the mapping of a new concept and constructs a meaningful conceptual framework for which learning can take place (Boone *et al.*, 2006; Lenz, Adams and Bulgren, 2007).

   Mind mapping software can be beneficial for the twice-exceptional student for it provides a manipulative and customizable shell or holding place to collect, organize and interact with information often needed to complete writing activities. These programmes also offer assistance to students with organizational problems who have advanced ideas and complex story structure. Having ideas presented in a visual format also helps the student conceptualize the material at a higher level within a concrete structure.

Structured writing software   Structured writing programmes provide the student with writing formats, templates and prompts to organize thoughts and ideas into a professional looking writing product. Students are guided through the various steps required to complete specific writing tasks (i.e. research papers, journals, poems, reports and newsletters). Most structured writing software programmes incorporate the five stages of the writing process into fun and motivating activities. These provide students with the opportunity to plan their writing project to meet a specific purpose and create a written product that meets this need.

Revision skills

MS Office tools   Microsoft Office tools allow students to build writing skills in addition to providing feedback and ideas to other students' writing products. The find and replace feature (found under edit on the tool bar) provides students with a handy tool to build vocabulary. Students with limited vocabulary tend to use the same words over and over. The find and replace feature allows students to find the overused word and replace with a new, perhaps more descriptive word.

The track changes feature (found under tools on the tool bar) allows students to become writing editors. Students can exchange writing files and share edits visually. Students can suggest the deletion and addition of words, provide proper punctuation and other writing conventions through software features that create visual markings such as strikethroughs, bolding and text colour change.

The insert comments feature (found under insert on the tool bar) provides an opportunity for the writer to get visual and auditory feedback from their readers. As readers peruse the writing sample they can leave electronic sticky notes with ideas and comments for the author. These comments can be inserted through text or speech allowing students to express feedback in the mode that they feel most comfortable.

Within all these Microsoft Office tools, the writer has the opportunity to accept or delete the feedback of their readers, thus providing an opportunity of decision making and choice in using feedback from student editors and their audience in the writing process. Find and replace, track changes and comment features enable readers and writers alike a convenient way to communicate and provide timely feedback.

Editing skills

Grammar and spell checkers   Grammar and spell checkers provide students with tools that offer automatic visual cues for spelling, capitalization and grammar corrections. By providing such tools the learner can build their repertoire of writing conventions. For students with spelling difficulties the spelling checker provides them with an opportunity to recognize and select the correct spelling of a word from a list of words suggested. The advancement in word processing features; such as the auto correct capabilities can self-adjust the combination of letters when typed incorrectly to form the correct word (i.e. wehn is automatically changed to when) with no effort from the writer. In addition to spelling corrections students are also provided with grammar suggestions. The student is given a visual cue (colourful underlining) indicating that the grammar of a sentence needs attention. The student can then look at the provided suggestions to decide what action needs to be taken. Grammar and spell checkers are at the students' fingertips and provide the tools needed for fundamental writing.

Publishing skills

Multimedia software   Multimedia software brings writing to life for students. Students create writing products (i.e. electronic stories, presentations, videos or slideshows) that demonstrate the complexity and depth of their thoughts within the writing process. Multimedia is one avenue teachers can help children connect their specific perspectives and ways of expressing themselves to a common curriculum (Daiute and Morse, 1994). Students are motivated to engage in the writing process by the outcome of a professional looking final product.

Table 1 identifies potential writing difficulties for the twice-exceptional student in the prewriting, writing, revision, editing and publishing phases of the writing process. Suggestions of commercially available assistive technology tools are listed and suggested implementation ideas are provided.

Table 1 Assistive technology applied to the writing process

Writing difficulties	Assistive technologies	Implementation ideas
Prewriting skills		
Generating writing ideas/ topics	Graphic-based word processors Imagination Express StoryBook Weaver Deluxe Clicker5	Provide students with story starters or theme ideas for writing or better yet, have students create stories from everyday meaningful experiences. For students that absolutely dislike writing, provide structure when using the graphic-based word processor by guiding the student to create one page of graphics and text before moving on to the next page of graphics. This eliminates a story or book of just graphics with little or no text
Expressing ideas and background knowledge Writing skills are inconsistent with verbal abilities	Voice recognition software Dragon Naturally Speaking IBM Via Voice Windows Vista Voice Recognition	Provide the learner with both online and offline supports. For example plan and map out ideas first in mind mapping software. Index cards and other paper pencil strategies can be used to assist the student in speaking aloud their ideas and thoughts. Developing critical editing skills is essential since voice recognition software rarely misspells a word. Caution – do not assume that a student can use voice recognition independently the first time out of the box. Talking into a computer is easy but actually writing for a purpose takes planning and practice

(*Continued*)

Table 1 (*Continued*)

Writing difficulties	Assistive technologies	Implementation ideas
Exploring motivational topics and interests	Text-to-speech programmes Kurzweil 3000 textHELP: Read and Write ReadPlease eReader WordQ	When using text-to-speech programmes to research resources on the Internet, plan ahead and work with the student to select and bookmark informative sites. Students can use the text-to-speech programmes to read pages of text that normally they would have avoided if reading on their own. After the student has found the desired information demonstrate how to cut and paste, and summarize information found on the Internet. This is a great time to encourage proper citation of others work
Writing skills		
Developing the main idea and supporting details	Talking word processors WriteOutloud Clicker 5 eReader Type and Talk Read, Write and Type WordQ	Talking word processors can be used for any purpose of writing. One fun idea is students plan and create an invention. They first must develop and map out the main idea of the invention and then add supporting details. They can write up their information as a magazine advertisement or as a patent office report or any other useful format. In any case student can use talking word processors to generate the text while the ideas keep flowing

Table 1   (*Continued*)

Writing difficulties	Assistive technologies	Implementation ideas
	Software with highlighting and speech capabilities	Reinforce student vocabulary and study skills by using software with highlighting and speech capabilities.
	Kurzweil 3000 textHELP Clicker 5 WordQ	Students can build essential study habits by using the electronic tools to manipulate their writing ideas. Imagine students creating electronic note cards that guide the students through writing research papers or large reports. Through such an activity students can systematically collect facts and information on their writing topic
Demonstrating correct Semantic and syntactic structure used in predicting words	Word prediction software CoWriter textHELP Read and Write WordQ	One activity to introduce the support of word prediction for writing is to interview the students (one-on-one) about things that are interesting and motivating to them. As they talk, write down specific vocabulary that is used and is unique to their communication style. Take a minute to customize the dictionary within the word predication programme, to add the list of vocabulary words noted during the interview. The next step is to ask the students to start writing with the word prediction programme simply by remembering all the words that were said in the interview.

(*Continued*)

Table 1   (*Continued*)

Writing difficulties	Assistive technologies	Implementation ideas
		With the support of the word prediction, students will see their ideas begin to formulate as the words are predicated and shown on the screen. With the needed support students are on their way to writing those wonderful ideas down
Organizing text	Mind mapping/ outlining software	Those common paper strategies such as K-W-H-L charts, comparison and contrast activities, literacy webs or VENN diagrams are already pre-made templates in common mind mapping software. Have students create storyboards, writing maps, when creating a web page, multimedia slide show or electronic book
	Inspiration/ Kidspiration DraftBuilder Writers Block	
	Structured writing software	
	Ultimate Writing Creativity Center The Amazing Writing Machine Student Writing and Research Center	Students will find that structured writing software enables them to write with a purposeful outcome through desktop publishing. GT/LD students may enjoy exploring the software templates to create interesting newsletters, postcards or a variety of other products. One writing activity that students can do is to create a postcard from their state

Table 1   (*Continued*)

Writing difficulties	Assistive technologies	Implementation ideas
Revising skills		
Identifying awkward sentence structure and expanding vocabulary choices	MS office tools Find and replace Track changes Insert comments Kurzweil 3000 highlighting tools textHELP Read and Write study tools	A fun and powerful writing activity is called Progressive Writing. This programme allows multiple authors to add to and delete from a writing sample by having students write a sentence, paragraph or page (depending on grade/ability/motivation level and allowed time for the activity) and save their work on a disk. After saving their work instruct students to pass it onto the next student in the team or class. Students then examine and critique the writing product and provide revising feedback through the track changes, comments and find and replace tools in Microsoft Office. Their feedback is then saved and the writing file is returned to the original author for reviewing. At this point, the author can decide to accept or reject the changes. If helpful the file can be passed on again for further ideas and feedback
Editing skills		
Writing mechanics (i.e. spelling capitalization/ punctuation)	Grammar and spell checkers Spell checkers, Language Master	Provide students with an opportunity to become authors and have them submit their story for a class publication.

(*Continued*)

Table 1   *(Continued)*

Writing difficulties	Assistive technologies	Implementation ideas
	Kurzweil 3000 highlighting tools textHELP Read and Write study tools	Through this submission students can learn not only the importance of the editing stage but also gain an understanding of how to get their work published. Student editors review the writings submitted and provide edits and feedback needed to make the product ready for publication
Publishing skills		
	Multimedia software PowerPoint Hyper studio Visual communicator Kid Pix Clicker5 Blogs, wikkis, digital storytelling	Endless opportunities are available through multimedia. Students can become storytellers, filmmakers, TV newscasters or scientist and researchers sharing interactive research reports. Multimedia projects can provide students with a variety of opportunities to plan, organize, apply and reflect on knowledge and skills learned in a study unit. Such efforts produce a showcase of learning artefacts to include in a writer's portfolio

Innovative Technologies for Writing

Today's learners are often referred to as Digital Children, The Net Generation, or Millennials due to their perceptions and use of technology. They have grown up in a technology-rich world. They are exposed to and comfortable with technology that is transparent to them and a completely accepted part of their lives (Perterson-Karlan and Parette, 2005).

Student success can be achieved through careful planning and designing of the learning environment. Providing access to innovative learning technologies can be the catalyst for actively engaging students in the writing process. Technology provides the twice-exceptional student with an environment for writing that encourages collaboration, problem solving, role playing and the development of critical thinking skills. Innovative technologies that are currently being used in the writing process include: (a) interactive white boards, (b) blogs, wikis, text messaging, (c)digital story telling and the use of (d) MP3 files or podcasting to name just a few. Such technology enables students to acquire new knowledge through authentic learning experiences.

Interactive whiteboards are becoming increasingly popular in the classroom. The touch screen capability eliminates the need for a mouse and/or keyboard. Interactive white boards impact the writing task by increasing engagement and motivation. In addition to engaging in active discussion, this learning tool enables the twice-exceptional student to physically interact and manipulate writing ideas and concepts.

Blogs provide twice-exceptional students with the opportunity to create a personal web-based writing space. Such space can be very motivating because students have an anytime, anywhere writing platform that publishes their research, creative writings and opinions and allows the student to practice essential writing principles and conventions. Additionally motivating is the fact that there is an audience that is able to read and react to their digital print. It is estimated today that there are over 27 million blogs. Within the classroom, blogs can provide an opportunity for collaboration, peer mentoring and an active place to house student productivity and writing artefacts.

Wiki technology is a web-based writing tool that enables multiple users to work together on the same document or content. It provides an easy to use interface where each user can add, remove or edit content in a seamless manner. Wikis can be very powerful in the classroom by allowing the twice-exceptional student to approach a topic and participate in an online collaborative creation. Students are able to engage in the evolution of a project by writing, editing and practicing online writing skills.

Text messaging or instant messaging provides students with just-in-time learning resources, information or mentoring. This just-in-time media can provide students with a go anywhere/learn anywhere tool. In the United States, over 200 000 children (ages 5–9) and 7 million children (ages 10–14) carry cell phones (Dodds and Manson, 2005). Students are text messaging and quizzing one another, one question at a time, in a trivia type format on important information needed for tests and projects preparation.

Digital storytelling combines the art of telling stories with a variety of multimedia tools. Photos, soundtracks, drawings, animation and web publishing are used to communicate and express personal reflection. In the classroom, digital storytelling is effective in introducing, new material and guiding students to research and transform their thoughts and feelings on a specific topic. This powerful learning medium allows the student to be in control of the content and plan and create interesting stories. A written script transforms into a digitized product. Digital storytelling appeals to diverse learning styles and at the same time build essential writing and communication skills.

Podcasting is a term resulting from the Apple Computer Corporation's iPod. The iPod is a portable digital audio player that allows the user to download digital audio files (most commonly in MP3 format). Today there are many different kinds of MP3 players and Podcasting has gone beyond the single Apple Computer device. Podcasting is enabling education to become portable thus promoting that learning should occur anywhere and anytime. The simple, easy to use, affordable technology used for podcasting, allows twice-exceptional students to record writing content, field observations, interviews and reflections.

Classroom teachers are discovering the power of the spoken word in the writing process. Podcasts support different learners and learning styles (i.e. auditory learners and English language learners) and provide multiple means of representing written content. Implementing podcasts into the classroom brings pop culture into education. Students are already familiar with such technology-based entertainments systems and embrace technology in the learning process. Most often the twice-exceptional students on their own integrate this technology to their academic advantage.

Conclusion

The technologies discussed in this chapter, while specifically applied to the writing process, are not unique to this one content area. These technologies should be viewed as tools for the classroom in all areas. The overall concept is to provide advanced level content to meet the needs for higher order thinking yet still provide concrete skill training in areas that pose problems for the student. These are students who have the ability to think at an advanced level, deal with concepts that are abstract yet have processing problems that interfere with their ability to work at the level commensurate with their potential. Unlocking that potential is the key to success and should be the ultimate goal of programming for the twice-exceptional student.

References

Baum, S.M., Cooper, C.R. and Neu, T.W. (2001) Dual differentiation: an approach for meeting the curricular needs of gifted students with learning disabilities. *Psychology in the Schools,* **38**, 477–90.

Baum, S. and Owen, S. (2003) *To be Gifted and Learning Disabled: Strategies for Helping Bright Students with LD, ADHD, and more,* Creative Learning Press, Mansfield Center, CT.

Bianco, M. (2005) The effects of disability labels on special education and general education teachers' referrals for gifted programs. *Learning Disability Quarterly,* **28**, 285–93.

Bireley, B., Languis, M. and Williamson, T. (1992) Physiological uniqueness: A new perspective of the learning disabled/gifted child. *Roeper Review,* **15**, 100–7.

Boone, R.T., Burke, M.D., Fore, C. and Spencer, V. (2006) The impact of cognitive organizers and technology-based practices on student success in secondary social studies classrooms. *Journal of Special Education Technology* 2, 5–11.

Brody, L.E. and Mills, C.J. (2004) Linking assessment and diagnosis to intervention for gifted students with learning disabilities, in *Students with both Gifts and Learning Disabilities: Identification, Assessment, and Outcomes* (eds T.M. Newman and R.J. Sternberg), Kluwer Academic/Plenum Publishers, New York, pp. 73–94.

Cline, S. and Hedgeman, K. (2001) Gifted children with disabilities. *Gifted Child Today,* **24**, 16–24.

Coleman, M.R. (2005) Academic strategies that work for gifted students with learning disabilities. *Teaching Exceptional Children,* **38**, 28–32.

Daiute, C. and Morse, F. (1994) Access to knowledge and expression: Multimedia writing tools for students with diverse needs and strengths. *Journal of Special Education,* **12**, 221–256.

De La Paz, S. (1999) Composing via dictation and speech recognition systems: Compensatory technology for students with learning disabilities. *Learning Disabilities Quarterly,* **22**, 173–82.

Dodds, R. and Manson, C.Y. (2005) Cell phones and PDA's hit k-6. *Education Digest: Essential Readings Condensed for Quick Review,* **70**, 52–53.

Graham, S., Harris, K.R. and Larsen, L. (2001) Prevention and intervention of writing difficulties for students with learning disabilities. *Learning Disabilities Research and Practice*, **16**, 74–84.

Graham, S. and Weintraub, N. (1996) A review of handwriting research: Progress and prospects from 1980 to 1994. *Educational Psychology Review*, **8**, 7–87.

Hartley, J., Soto, E. and Pennebaker, J. (2003) Speaking versus typing: a case study of the effects of using voice-recognition software on academic correspondence. *British Journal of Educational Technology*, **34**, 5–16.

Higgins, K. and Boone, R. (1996) Special series on technology: an introduction. *Journal of Learning Disabilities*, **29**, 340–3.

Hishinuma, E. and Tadaki, S. (1996) Addressing diversity of the gifted/at risk: characteristics for identification. *Gifted Child Today*, **19**, 20–5, 28–9, 45, 50.

Imbeau, M.B. (1999) A century of gifted education: a reflection of who and what made a difference. *Gifted Child Today*, **22**, 40–3.

Lange, A.A., McPhillips, M., Mulhern, G. and Wylie, J. (2006) Assistive software tools for secondary-level students with literacy difficulties. *Journal of Special Education Technology*, **21**, 13–21.

Lenz, K., Adams, G.L., Bulgren, J.A. *et al.* (2007) Effects of curriculum maps and guiding questions on the test performance of adolescents with learning disabilities. *Learning Disability Quarterly*, **30**, 235–44.

Lewis, R.B. (2000) Musings on technology and learning disabilities on the occasion of the new millennium. *Journal of Special Education Technology*, **15**, 5–12.

Lewis, R.B., Graves, A.W., Ashton, T.M. and Kieley, C.L. (1998) Word processing tools for students with learning disabilities: A comparison of strategies to increase text entry speed. *Learning Disabilities Research and Practice*, **13**, 95–108.

Lindstrom, J.H. (2007) Determining appropriate accommodations for postsecondary students with reading and written expression disorders. *Learning Disabilities Research and Practice*, **22**, 229–36.

MacArthur, C.A. (1999) Overcoming barriers to writing: Computer support for basic writing skills. *Reading and Writing Quarterly*, **15**, 169–92.

McAlister, K.M., Nelson, N.W. and Bahr, C.M. (1999) Perceptions of students with language and learning disabilities about writing process instruction. *Learning Disabilities Research & Practice*, **14**, 159–72.

Montali, J. and Lewandowski, L. (1996) Bimodal reading: Benefits of a talking computer for average and less skilled readers. *Journal of Learning Disabilities*, **29**, 271–9.

National Association for Gifted Children. (1998) *Students with Concomitant Gifts and Learning Disabilities*, Author, Washington, DC.

Nielsen, M.E. (2002) Gifted students with learning disabilities: Recommendations for identification and programming. *Exceptionality*, **10**, 93–111.

Nielsen, M.E. and Higgins, L.D. (2005) The eye of the story: Services and programs for twice-exceptional learners. *Teaching Exceptional Children*, **38**, 8–15.

Nielsen, M.E., Higgins, L.D., Hammond, A.E. and Williams, R.A. (1993) Gifted children with disabilities. *Gifted Child Today*, **16**, 9–12.

Peterson-Karlan, G.R. and Parette, P. (2005) Millennial students with mild disabilities and emerging assistive technology trends. *Journal of Special Education Technology*, **20**, 27–38.

Robinson, S.M. (1999) Meeting the needs of students who are gifted and have learning disabilities. *Intervention in School and Clinic*, **34**, 195–205.

Rose, D. (2000) Universal design for learning. *Journal of Special Education Technology*, **15**, 67–70.

Saddler, B., Moran, S., Graham, S. and Harris, K. (2004) Preventing writing difficulties: The effects of planning strategy instruction on the writing performance of struggling writers. *Exceptionality*, **12**, 3–17.

Siegle, D. (2004) The merging of literacy and technology in the 21st century: A bonus for gifted education. *Gifted Child Today*, **27**, 32–5.

Siegle, D. and Powell, T (2004) Exploring teacher biases when nominating students for gifted programs. *Gifted Child Quarterly*, **48**, 21–9.

Shevitz, B., Weinfeld, R., Jeweler, S. and Barnes-Robinson, L. (2003) Mentoring empowers gifted/learning disabled students to soar. *Roeper Review*, **26**, 37–40.

Strobel, W., Arthanat, S., Bauer, S. and Flagg, J. (2007) *Universal Design for Learning: Critical Need Areas for People with Learning Disabilities*. Assistive Technology Outcomes and Benefits, http://www.atia.org/files/public/atobvol4iss1-articlesix.pdf (accessed January 14, 2008).

Vaughn, S., Gersten, R. and Chard, D. (2000) The underlying message in LD intervention research: Findings from research syntheses. *Exceptional Children*, **67**, 99–114.

Waldron, K.A. and Saphire, D.G. (1990) An analysis of factors for gifted students with learning disabilities. *Journal of Learning Disabilities*, **23**, 491–8.

Walker, B., Shippen, M.E., Alberto, P. *et al.* (2005) Using the expressive writing program to improve the writing of high school students with learning disabilities. *Learning Disabilities Research and Practice*, **20**, 175–83.

Weinfeld, R., Barnes-Robinson, L., Jeweler, S. and Shevitz, B. (2002) Academic programs for gifted and talented/learning disabled students. *Roeper Review*, **24**, 226–33.

Weinfeld, R., Barnes-Robinson, L., Jeweler, S. and Shevitz, B. (2005) What we have learned: Experiences in providing adaptations and accommodations for gifted and talented students with learning disabilities. *Teaching Exceptional Children*, **38**, 48–54.

Wepner, S.B. (1990/1991) Computers, reading software, and at-risk eight graders. *Journal of Reading*, **34**, 264–8.

12

Case Studies of Three Schools Tackling Underachievement

Diane Montgomery

Introduction

There are two kinds of objective forms of data that can be collected in a research project. It is either nomothetic, dealing with numbers of cases or idiopathic, dealing with the individual. Nomothetic studies focus on general laws and descriptive statements that summarize a group but may not describe any single member, for instance a mass survey. Idiopathic studies deal with what is unique and particular to an individual case, for instance a school, a class or an individual person. Case study was originally a clinical approach used in medicine and social work clinics. The method was frequently used as a teaching method, as part of professional development in a number of careers, and has gradually spread to other disciplines as the value of it has been recognized.

It became popular in business studies courses and as case studies of organizations and in teaching linked to observational methods. For example, a puzzling sample of child's behaviour in an observation session or in a test can become more meaningful when we learn other facts about him or her through a case study. It is not possible to study the whole child, but it is a desirable aim.

Case study has only been used as a research tool in education in recent decades. Case study method is a systematic way of looking at events, collecting data, analyzing the information and reporting the result. It can lead to a sharpened understanding of why something happened as it did, and what might be useful to look at more intensively in future research. Case

Able, Gifted and Talented Underachievers, Second Edition   Edited by Diane Montgomery
© 2009 John Wiley & Sons, Ltd

studies are used both to gather information, to form hypotheses and to give hypotheses a preliminary test.

> Case study methodologies are an important tool that provide a comprehensive picture of any issue which could be a complex one. Case study also helps to extend experience or add strength to what is already known through previous research. Case studies emphasise detailed contextual analysis of a limited number of events or conditions. Researchers have used case study for a number of disciplines (Flyvbjerg, 2006, p. 219).

Any or all methods of data gathering, from testing to interviewing, can be used in case studies. Qualitative case study research takes a holistic perspective to try to gain an in-depth understanding of the situation and its meaning for those involved. There is an interest in processes rather than outcomes. The context is important rather than a specific variable (Soy, 1997).

Case study is appropriate when the researcher is focusing on the 'how' and 'why' questions. It is a preferred method when the researcher has little control over events, and when the focus is on a contemporary issue in a real-life context. It is a *method of choice when the researcher aims to create new knowledge.*

It is necessary to write this preamble in the current educational climate for government ministers have discovered Randomized Control Trials, and have reified these as the 'gold standard' for research in education. This is despite the fact that classroom and school research in real time and real life does not easily lend itself to the narrow constraints of single variable manipulations or controlling the settings. Mass education in all its forms is still not to be compared with a chemistry research design of a factory input-output analysis. Quite a lot of history and experience lies between an input and an output even in a reception class pupil.

The case studies of 12 schools undertaken in the NACE/London Gifted and Talented Research Project led by Belle Wallace *et al.* (2008) are extremely informative about how schools lifted underachievement. They provide many guidelines that other schools can follow to raise their performance.

In this chapter, I have included a comparative analysis of the two primary schools that I visited for the NACE Research project during 2006–2007, and have added data from another school that won the NACE Challenge Award in 2007. It was remarkable how many features the three schools shared in common, although they were in extraordinarily different situations. Not only did they meet many of the institutional quality standards for personalizing learning in the inner ring: extension and enrichment in the curriculum, effective teaching and learning and assessment for learning, but also in relation to the outer ring.

Reasons for choosing to focus on three primary schools

Terman (1930) and his researchers surveyed 100 000 Californian pupils between the ages of 7 and 11, and found that without appropriate training they missed 50% of the gifted pupils that Terman could identify by IQ testing. Although in the United Kingdom today, most teachers do have training in identification and provision, and we know that even IQ tests will not identify all the gifted, it is interesting to see which groups his research showed were missed.

According to Terman, they fell into three broad categories:

- Children from lower socio-economic families, whose parents only attended school for the minimum period required.
- Girls who tended to be more conforming, and would work quietly even when bored.
- The youngest children in the class, who had been late entrants in the school year – the 'summer' children.

As can be seen from the chapters in this section, the position has not radically changed even when we do train teachers; these children will still tend to be overlooked by some.

Many studies over time have shown the powerful effect of teacher expectation on pupil performance (Jackson, 1986; Rosenthal and Jacobson, 1967; Nash, 1973; Murphy, 1974; Crocker and Cheeseman, 1988; Good and Brophy, 1977). Butler-Por (1993), in addition, drew attention to the effect of parental expectation or lack of it in underachievement of gifted girls. Volume one of this book (Montgomery, 2000) and now this edition summarize the factors contributing to underachievement, and one of these is the expectation of teachers, parents and children themselves. Of particular concern here is the expectation of teachers, because it can change that of both parents and their children.

Paule (2006) explains that teachers usually espouse the values of the dominant culture, and children who do not display these values are in turn not considered to be gifted. Children have to learn to be adept at interpreting and participating in dominant school and class cultures. Those who do this early on are more likely to be offered more challenge than the rest, and those that do not are less likely to be stretched. Hollingworth (1942) showed that once a pattern of underachievement had set in, it was very difficult to reverse it.

Brophy and Good (1970) and Good and Brophy (1977) researches showed that a positive self-image develops partly from being successful and partly from being seen as successful by others, particularly significant others such as teachers. This belief tends to remain with us throughout school, and after school into work unless conflicting new evidence comes upon us.

Pupils can successfully rate their peers (Gagne, 1995) on the basis of ability, and such ratings are consistent with that of their teachers (Nash, 1973). Cheeseman (1986; cited in Crocker and Cheeseman 1988, p. 108) found that her infant school pupils could do this by the age of six. They learned to rate their peers in the way the teacher did in their first 2 years in school.

Therefore, the way the infant school or infant years are organized and construct their pupils' expectations and successes, will define their careers and successes in later school and beyond to an important degree. These infant years can be the key to achieving potential and to equity, if teachers are sensitive to differences and needs and are highly skilled.

To emphasize the point, I will describe an experience of a reception class child observed some years ago but never forgotten. She had been 2 weeks in the class and they were learning phonics and practising writing letters with a similar pattern whilst saying their sounds. They wrote a line of Ls in their writing books (no ligatures in this school) – l l l l l l l l l.

Next, they learnt the sound 't' and were shown how to make the line down again and cross the T – t t t t t t t t.

'Angie' is doing well, making her letters, tongue stuck out as she worked. She completes several wobbly Ts and sits back and smiles at her friends, they have all finished too and all are smiling and satisfied.

Now, the teacher decides they have done so well as she makes a quick circuit to check that they will learn just one more shape for today – they will learn to sound and write F. 'It goes up and over and stop and cross', she demonstrates, they make the movements in the air, now they write it in their books – f f f f f.

That is, all except Angie. She starts and the pencil simply gets stuck at the overhang, she tries again, and again and each time the same thing happens. She becomes fixated and the wobbles become worse. By now her mouth is in a richtus grin, and the mouth is white all round and perspiring, her cheeks flame and her eyes fill with tears. She squints at her friends and sees them happily making their perfect Fs. With one huge effort she lifts the pencil and scribbles in rage across the paper making a hole and crumpling it.

From that session, her originally good behaviour deteriorated. She frequently roamed the classroom upsetting other children, and avoided any activities that might lead to writing. Her teacher was concerned at the deterioration in behaviour and wondered if the challenge of learning was as yet too much for her, especially as the background from which she came was a disadvantaged one.

I still grieve for Angie.

The Case Studies: Contextual Information

School A

The school is on the outskirts of an attractive Kent village. Open fields and hills lie behind the school, which is about 10 miles within the bounds of the southern M25.

It is a mixed one-form entry community school in the London Borough of Bromley. There is phased entry into the reception year with new pupils starting in each term. There are 210 pupils on roll and 8 members of full time staff in addition to the head teacher. The pupils' age range is from 4 to 11 years. The size of the school is typical of most primary schools nationally, and there are roughly equal numbers of boys and girls.

The school moved to new premises in 1984, and because of falling rolls the village infant and junior schools were merged. In 2005, two new classrooms and an Information and Communication Technology (ICT) suite were added as well as improvements to the existing facilities. A new outside adventure playground was developed for the foundation stage children.

Most of the pupils live within 2 miles of the school. The immediate area is mainly private residential housing consisting of terraced cottages or large detached properties. The number of pupils on the special needs register at school action/plus is above the national average at 25.4%, and the percentage of pupils with statements is 1.8%. The pupils' special needs are mainly in the area of SEBD and speech and communication difficulties; 3.8% of pupils have English as an additional language, and 10.7% of the pupils come from minority ethnic backgrounds.

On entry to the school, the pupils' attainment is wide ranging but broadly average overall. They come from homes that are socio-economically diverse, and only 4.1% are eligible for free school meals.

The school has no nursery provision, but is fed by approximately 10 different providers including all day care, play groups and a Montessori nursery. In 2005, all the reception pupils had previously attended a nursery provision. However, not all the children joining the school have experienced the Foundation Stage programme or have been assessed against the Foundation Stage profile.

Mobility at 10.4% is evident in the junior stage as families move to larger accommodation, and smaller family units move in raising the class sizes in years 5 and 6 above 30. The school is oversubscribed in the infant sector, and there is a waiting list. Attendance is slightly below the national average.

The school is recognized in the OFSTED inspection report of May 2004 as an increasingly effective school with standards in English, mathematics and science at the end of year 6, well above national averages. The school has received a range of awards such as Activemark (2005), Healthy School Award (2005), SEED Challenge (2004) for improvement and expansion to the building, Investors in People (re issued in 2006), Environment Awards (2006) Kent and National winners of grow a sunflower competition. It is an accredited partnership training school with the University of Greenwich.

School B

The school is an imposing three-storey Victorian edifice set in the London Borough of Islington. It has green tiled interiors and stone stairs once with separate boys' and girls' entrances. The school now has a modern entrance area, and is attached to and opposite a row of elegant white fronted regency style dwellings. It is in a quiet area, in a corner behind two main roads with pubs, cafes and restaurants giving a village feel to it.

It is an inner city community primary school for some 450 children from 3 years 6 months to 11-years-old. The school serves a very diverse community in the centre of a shopping and business area, and the school population reflects this with a rich ethnic mix.

The school grounds are extensive with a large hard surfaced play and sports area, a quiet garden with trees and a wild and formal garden including a large pond. In addition, the nursery and reception classrooms lead out to their own secure play areas. There is a computer suite, a large community sports hall and a school library.

The school serves an area whose socio-economic circumstances are much lower than usually found. More than half the pupils are entitled to free school meals, and a similar proportion have learning and emotional difficulties with high numbers of children experiencing language and communication needs. Slightly more than half the pupils are from ethnic minority backgrounds, the largest groups being Black African and Caribbean. Three-fifths of the pupils have a first language that is not English, predominantly Turkish, then Somali, Bengali, Spanish and Italian. All school signs are in the three main languages of the school – English, Turkish and Bengali, and translators and translations are widely available including Spanish and Italian.

Attainment on entry to the school is well below the national average. There is also high mobility (over 50% in Year 6). Despite this, the school was identified in its latest OFSTED inspection report (October 2005) as 'an exceptional school. The individual child is at the centre of all it does.' It was assessed as 'outstanding' in all areas, for although the pupils enter the school with very low achievements, by the end of Year 6 their standards are above average in English, well above average in mathematics and high in science.

The school was a former Beacon school; it has Investors in People accreditation, holds the Quality in Study Support award and the Arts Mark Gold award, and in addition is a member of the Creative Partnerships for London East.

School C

The school is set in a town in the flatlands of southern Essex. It is a community school for 3 to 11-year-old, and is surrounded by an estate of suburban white rendered council-type houses. It is an area where many families experience considerable social and economic disadvantage. Because of declining birthrates, the school has falling rolls and the infant and junior schools were merged in 2004.

The number eligible for free school meals is double the national average, and pupil turnover is very high in an area of transient population. Attainment on entry is also falling year by year, and is currently well below the national expected average for 3-year-olds.

Most of the pupils are of white British heritage, and only a few have English as an additional language. There are an average number of pupils with special educational needs or learning difficulties, and a small number are statemented.

In the school's OFSTED report (2005), it was found that the school had a good curriculum and improving standards, and the staff was good at finding ways for the pupils to succeed. The nursery and reception provision was effective and stimulating. Good progress was being made in mathematics and English, although writing needed further attention. Standards were below average by the end of Year 6, because of the high pupil mobility.

In 2007, the school had won the NACE Challenge award, which meant that the criteria for this had been well met (see appendix to this chapter). The evaluators' report stated that, 'At this school there is a richness of opportunity whereby children develop the confidence to try something new and where gifts and talents are discovered and fostered'. The school vision of being '. . . a community. . . where true potential is recognized and developed, is embedded in the practice seen.' 'Lessons are stimulating and challenging in the tasks set with many opportunities for pupils to articulate their understanding, self-assess and take responsibility for their own learning.'

Pupils were supportive of each other and said they enjoyed learning because, "We learn how we like – we can be independent if we want. I like the challenges, set my own targets and talk to my teacher about it.'

Parents appreciated the culture of celebration of effort and achievement, and said that their children felt valued and were proud of their achievements.

The Common Characteristics of the Three Schools

Identification procedures

All the schools used a range of identification procedures. The identification of the more able pupils took place by both qualitative and quantitative procedures. A comprehensive picture is built up of each child's progress and performance by a rigorous process including the use of hard data from entry profiles, SATs, NC levels, continuous assessment, national and school-based tests, careful record keeping and collation of evidence including samples of pupils' work, discussion with colleagues and parents and the use of tracker packages. There is also school-based monitoring and lesson observation.

They also used a trio from the assessment coordinator, G and T coordinator or the SENCo, with class teacher and head teacher to analyze the learning outcomes for identified pupils and set targets for them. The outcomes were monitored by gender, ethnicity, special educational needs and stages of language acquisition.

The strong commitment to extending the opportunities for all pupils enables pupils with special ability and talent, who may not have been observed in the normal curriculum, to be identified.

General ethos of the schools

In each one, the children were moving around the school in a purposeful manner talking quietly. The teachers' voices were quietly spoken as they lead or follow their classes. All was orderly and self-controlled. There was no rushing, pushing and shouting.

The children dealt with visitors in an easy and polite manner. They talked openly and pleasantly, and had a good measure of interested curiosity. They enthused about their school and their teachers and current work they were engaged upon. Philosophy for children was going down very well, as were master classes in art and dance and drama, choir and orchestra, French lessons, 'brain club', skills academy and many more.

Each school was viewed by the children, parents and the staff as 'the family', there was an easy, welcoming and good relationship between them all. Each was accorded proper respect.

The curriculum

All the schools were committed to making inclusive provision, whilst at the same time providing the widest range of opportunities so that no pupil and no talent would be left out. In evidence were all the seven levels of curriculum provision described in Chapter 5. Distance learning was being provided through ICT and web-based learning opportunities that could be adapted at any point to meet the very advanced needs of some learners.

The ICT provision in each of the schools was of a high standard and quality with whiteboards in every classroom and well-equipped ICT suites.

The mainstream curriculum provision was backed by an extensive range of lunchtime, after hours, and out of school clubs and specialist local learning opportunities. Specialist sports coaches, ICT experts, experts in science and the performing arts and in art and culture were all in evidence at some point in the school calendar. All three had excellent early years provision.

All effective primary schools place an emphasis upon the arts subjects to achieve a balance in the curriculum and respond to talent, these three schools went further as there was a resplendent display and celebration of success in the arts and the performing arts. They went to great lengths to foster all talents, recruiting expertise from every source they could find and it had paid great dividends for the pupils.

One school participated in the annual 'take one picture' competition, and the artwork produced was of such a high standard that the school became a competitor on the annual 'take one picture' event and got through to be one of a small number of schools in the country to display their work at the National Gallery, in the children's section. The 'family' was very proud of this!

The more talented artists among the children in this school also worked with the art coordinator in weekly master classes. In the visit week, this involved the close observation and fine drawing of found objects, one seashell. There were also creative partnerships and resident artists who came in to work with the children. This was evidenced in the huge numbers of two and three-dimensional displays of all kinds to be seen. Most recently they had made African masks, and both girls and boys talked excitedly about the experience and the drums. In another of the schools, the art coordinators ran master classes based on the style of the apprenticeship system of the great painters, and the walls were covered with 'Lowrys', 'Matisses', 'Cezannes' as they worked on composition and style. They were so good that they would grace any company boardroom or heritage building.

In dance, one school had recruited a professional male dancer as instructor, and had set up boys' dance as a regular part of the curriculum as well as mixed dance classes with some fine performances including 'Billy Elliott' as a result.

Drama was a strong component in the curriculum of all the schools, as well as related classes from writers in residence and college experts linking drama and writing in master classes for the pupils on the G and T register. Those still working on the literacy hour levels had their own specialist enrichment lessons.

Music was another area of talent in which no child was left out. There were opportunities to join the choir, singing for the elderly, joining local choirs and this could lead on further. In one school, LSO musicians came to teach Gamelan and identify pupils with musical ability. Trained opera performers came to run opera classes based upon fairy stories leading to an annual cross-curricular inter schools opera project in preparation for a final performance. One of the pupils interviewed had taken a leading role and proved to be uniquely talented to the delight of all his friends and the general audience.

Another of the schools by involving LEA experts and the local community had introduced 70% of its pupils to playing a musical instrument and a range of violin, cello, clarinet and brass lessons took place as well as orchestra practice.

One of the schools was twinned with a school in Shanghai, and the pupils were looking forward with great excitement to a China week.

With all of these initiatives, the pupils were assured that if they had a desire to learn something a way would be found for them to do it, no stone would be left unturned.

Effective Teaching and Learning

Through the differentiation, extension and enrichment strategies in lessons, teachers were able to use curriculum-based identification findings to extend the pupils' range of skills and develop further the cognitive stretch in targeting thinking and questioning skills.

Each school was complimented in the OFSTED reports on its high quality or excellent and stimulating provision in the nursery and infant years. It also was characteristic that each school used a specific programme for teaching phonics in the early years. Two used 'Jolly Phonics', and the third used Ruth Miskin's reading programme. Both provide a firm and incremental structure to the learning that has been shown to improve reading and writing performance above the levels achieved in the National Literacy Strategy. One school had only recently introduced Jolly Phonics, and had seen a most marked improvement in the pupils' literacy achievements. The school using Miskin's approach found that the pupils gained three levels more than previous teaching had achieved.

In the inner city school – 'The many pupils at an early stage of learning English grasp the basic skills quickly, and achieve extremely well because provision is exceedingly effective' (OFSTED, 2005). Family literacy sessions were held 2 mornings a week for reception children and parents/carers. 'Patch' meetings were held in three languages and allowed parents/carers of children in the nursery, reception and years 1 and 2 to observe a literacy lesson by a group of children, and discuss the way the school and home can work together to improve reading in the early years.

Assessment for Learning

Through effective planning, assessment and record keeping and liaison with the children's previous teachers, where possible, they establish what the pupils have previously done to prevent repetition. They then provide challenges through high quality tasks and plan work, so that there is always differentiated work and extension material available. By assessing performance on these tasks, it is then possible to set individual more challenging targets and individual homework. Study skills are also taught.

The pupils are allowed to make choices about and to organize their own work. They are expected to carry out, unaided, tasks that stretch their capabilities, and help develop their abilities to evaluate and check their work. Pupils set their own targets in upper junior classes, and monitor their own progress through self-assessment and marking each other's work.

The OFSTED reports found that the assessment techniques were used very effectively by most of the teachers. There was a rigorous analysis of data that correctly showed that different groups of pupils make equally outstanding progress, including those from ethnic minority backgrounds.

The pupil review process enabled all aspects of each child's progress and attainment to be considered, and ideas shared and action taken to intervene as necessary. This process also engaged staff in a continuous cycle of self-reflection and development. This was supported by team teaching and teaching partners in one of the schools.

The inner city school was particularly strong in its pupil review process, which took place termly between headteacher, class teacher and SENCo. For example, they discussed 'V' V, all agreed was a 'star', forthright and stubborn and they laughed fondly. She already goes to the A. Study Centre on Thursday mornings and was in the G and T group. Her literacy work was regarded as outstanding, and it was at first decided to start a writers' club for her and pupils like her in Year 5. Then, it was considered whether she might move into the Year 6 writers' group. When another pupil D., a friend, was also considered capable of joining her, this was the action decided so they would have each other for support amongst the Year 6.

The pupils' voice

In each of the schools the pupils had a strong voice. There were buddy systems, playground play leaders, mentors, and a system of class representatives and very active schools councils that contributed to school decision making and policy.

They had a good knowledge of their schools, and were very appreciative of what it offered and how included they felt in all its activities and aspirations. They had very positive views of the curriculum, the teaching and the staff. 'They listen to us do not shout at us.' 'When we don't understand they explain it again.'

The parents

The parents held the schools in high regard. They were very happy with the way the schools were being led. They were very supportive and well informed. This was certainly true in 2006–2007 of the Governors and parents met and interviewed, they like the pupils spoke animatedly and knowledgeably about their schools and the learning experiences on offer. They too contributed their time and expertise.

Community

There was good liaison between the schools and their local communities.

There is a genuine commitment to the local community, and a wide range of contacts were fostered. For example, a biennial business project developed pupils' understanding of the wider world, economic well-being and strengthened links with the businesses and community members; a project with a local architect to bring alive the history and culture of their high street using a variety of modern technology and media; the outdoor classroom project using local knowledge and expertise; partnership projects with local secondary schools, study centres and universities in science, maths and ICT; initiatives with local organizations to raise achievements in sport; work placements in years 5 and 6 in one school; brain gym and so on.

The staff

The schools were blessed with leaders of the highest quality who were innovative, intelligent and hard working. They had bound their staff of teachers and support staff into a team. The team was fully engaged in continual and continuing staff development to capture any skills and knowledge that might improve their teaching and learning for the children. They were very active in pursuit of supplementary funding and networking.

Conclusions

It is the strong developmental approach by expert practitioners in the early years in the three schools that clearly underpins and provides the right foundation for what happens in the later years. When children can read and write fluently, they can use these skills to learn how to learn more. All three schools were able to promote language and literacy skills earlier, helping pupils to become fluent in their use more quickly setting them free to achieve more in the wider curriculum.

In the junior stage, the opportunities for learning opened even more widely than usual using a range of differentiation, acceleration, extension and enrichment approaches. Within the classrooms, this usually began with differentiation of the standard curriculum. There were so many out of school and after school and community activities that you might wonder when they slept. The places were hives of industry, imagination and creativity. Each was a living, learning community committed to personalizing learning and lifelong learning.

Although Skelton, Francis and Valkanova (2007) found that the major barriers to achievement were now disadvantage and low socio-economic status rather than gender or ethnicity at Key Stage 2, these three case studies show how schools that have high quality leadership and good teachers working as a team, knowledgeable about teaching and learning effectively, can make a difference.

It is good to be able to end on a positive note, Harry Passow would be pleased.

Epilogue

Looking forward, I should like to see more investment in primary education and CPD to bring all schools up to the levels seen here.

Although, the case studies from the NACE research also showed how 6 secondary schools were effective in addressing underachievement, I should like to see that sector changed. Changed from mainly huge 11–18 collossi, and reverting to 11 to 16 secondary schools that could be much smaller and more pupil friendly with 650–800 pupils.

The reasons for this is that smaller family friendly units where everyone knows each other and every one is known can help alleviate the disaffection and anomie induced in some large institutions, and provide the family support that is needed in an environment of increasing family breakdown and discord.

From 16 pupils could then be accommodated in high schools and colleges helping them make the transition to a more adult orientated education and training.

Each transition could thus also be made less traumatic. All of the effective schools had to spend considerable time, effort and materials on preparing their pupils for transition.

Appendix

The NACE challenge award

The challenge award is given by the National Association for Able Children in Education, a leading educational organization and registered charity established for 25 years. The challenge award is a framework for continuous audit, planning and development by the whole school. Schools that meet the criteria of the 10 elements of the framework and show continuing commitment to provision for able pupils may choose to apply for assessment and accreditation for the award.

(a) Schools are in a position to achieve the award because they
   - have chosen a whole-school focus on provision for the able pupils to raise standards for all;

- are working as a whole-school to audit, plan and develop provision;
- are gathering evidence of effective practice against the criteria of the 10 elements;
- are using the Supportive Documents, particularly, 'What is Good teaching' and 'What is Good Work', to teacher self evaluate and monitor the challenge in teaching and learning;
- are working in clusters, networks and regions to develop and disseminate practice against the 10 elements.

(b) Prepare for the annual conversation because they
- are using the map which relates to the challenge award and quality standards;
- have their evidence of effective provision collated in the challenge award file against the 10 elements plus their action plan (NACE, 2005).

References

Brophy, J.E. and Good, T.L. (1970) Teachers' communication of differential expectations from children's classroom performance. *Journal of Educational Psychology*, **65**, 365–74.

Butler-Por, N. (1993) Underachieving and gifted students, in *International Handbook of Research and Development of Giftedness and Talent* (eds K.A. Heller, F.J. Monks and A.H. Passow), Pergamon, Oxford, pp. 648–68.

Crocker, A.C. and Cheeseman, R.C. (1988) The ability of young children to rank themselves for academic ability. *Educational Studies*, **14**, 105–10.

Flyvberg, B. (2006) Five misunderstandings about case study research. *Qualitative Inquiry*, **12** (2), 219–45.

Gagne, F. (1995) Learning about the nature of gifts and talents through peer and teacher nomination, in *Nurturing Talent* (eds K.M. Katzko and F.J. Monks), Van Gorcum, Assen, pp. 20–30.

Good, T.L. and Brophy, J.E. (1977) *Educational Psychology: A Realistic Approach*, Holt, Rinehart and Winston, New York, pp. 380–4.

Hollingworth, L. (1942) *Children Above 180 IQ*, World Books, New York.

Jackson, P.W. (1986) *Life in Classrooms*, Holt Rinehart and Winston, New York.

Montgomery, D. (ed.) (2000) *Able Underachievers*, Whurr, London.

Murphy, J. (1974) Teacher expectations and working class underachievement. *British Journal of Sociology*, **25**, 323–44.

Nash, R. (1973) *Classrooms Observed: The Teacher's Perception and the Pupil's Performance*, Routledge, Kegan Paul, London.

Paule, M. (2006) *Understanding Underachievement: Some Questions to Ask, Things to Think About and Things to do*, Oxford Brookes University/Westminster Institute pamphlet, Oxford.

Rosenthal, R. and Jacobsen, L. (1967) *Pygmalion in the Classroom*, Holt Rinehart and Winston, New York.

Skelton, C., Francis, B. and Valkanova, Y. (2007) *Breaking Down the Stereo-types. Gender and Achievement in Schools*, Equal Opportunities Commission, London.

Soy, S.K. (1997) The case study as research method, p. 1, www.gslis.utex.edu (accessed August 2007).

Terman, L. (1930) *The Promise of Youth*, Harrap, London.

Wallace, B., Fittler, S., Leyden, S. *et al.* (2008) *Raising the Achievement of Able, Gifted and Talented Pupils within an Inclusive Setting*, NACE/London Gifted and Talented, Oxford.

Index

ability
  checklists 28
  testing 22–6
absences 281
academic
  English 239–44
  writing 239–40, 243
Academic Word List (AWL) 239–42
acceleration 156
accelerated learning (AL) 129
access issues 225
achievement
  barriers 247
  boys 210
  motivation 209
action research 65, 95, 97–8, 101,
    104, 203
activating children's thinking skills
    (ACTS) 130, 131
active learners 246
additive bilingual 64
advanced learners of English 237–9
affective codes 172
affirmation 161
A-level gender gap 202
Allcock, P. 30
alphabetic-phonic-syllabic-linguistic
    (APSL) 272, 273, 275

Alston, J. 287
Amrein, A.L. 103
analytic
  strategies 173, 174
  logic 204
anxiety 162
Arnold, R. 208, 211
Arnot, M. 202
autistic spectrum disorders
    (ASD) 265–6, 282–5
Asperger syndrome (AS) 283–5
assessment 14–18
  of abilities 104
  authentic 29, 271
  criterion-referenced 14
  diagnostic 27–8
  formative 12, 14–15
  for learning (AfL) 14, 146–8, 248
  performance 271
  process 232–3
Assessment of Performance Unit
    (APU) 287–8
assistive technologies 309–22
  editing skills 311, 314, 319–20
  organising 312–13
  prewriting 309–10
  publishing 314, 320
  writing 315–20

Association For All Speech Impaired
Children (AFASIC) 285
asynchronous development 163
at risk groups 225, 236, 246
attachment 51
attainment testing 26–7
reading and spelling 26–7
SATs 26
attention deficit disorder
(ADD) 276, 278
attention deficit hyperactivity disorder
(ADHD) 265–6, 277
creativity 277
diet 278
incidence of 277
medication 278
profile of 278
symptoms 277–8
attitudes
anti-school 208–9
gender 209
survey 246
Ausubel, D.P. 144
authentic
texts 239–40,
voice 252, 253
avoidance 190

Baddeley, A.D. 169
Baldwin, A.Y. 267
Bath MA programmes 87, 91
Bangladeshi REAL project 258–62
Barber, C. 283
barriers to achievement 247
model 8
basic literacy 42
Baum, S.M. 4, 306, 308
behaviour
checklist 28
control 146
for learning 121
Benbow, C.P. 205

Berliner, D.C. 103
bias 205
IQ items 205
marking 205
test taking 205
Biddulph, S. 204, 209
Biesta, G.J.J. 94, 101–3
Biggs, J.E. 137
big picture 130, 147
Birch, H.G. 28
Black, P. 203
Black Country Children's Services
Improvement Partnership
(BCCSIP) 225, 227–8
black and minority ethnic
(BME) 220
blogs 321
Bloom, B.S. 128, 148
evaluation criteria 148
Borkowski, J.E. 68
boys' achievement 7
Bravar, L. 287
Brazilian study 47–8
Brereton, C. 4
bridging 130
Brown, Gordon, PM 219

Campione, J.C. 68
career issues 194
case study
examples 331–40
method 327–8
castle building problem 141–2
'catch them being good' (CBG) 17,
21
CATE 114
Caudill, G. 216
challenge 193, 225, 238
changing teaching 160
characteristics of UAch 159–60
checklists 6, 28, 35–6
Chess, S. 28

Chesson, R. 288
child
  deprivation 52–3
  prostitutes 52
  soldiers 52
  workers 52
choice 306
class 207
  clown 29, 282
  control 16–21
classroom observation 32
coaching 112
coasting 29, 249
coercive schools 282
codes
  learning 169, 170–2
  example 175–7
cognitive
  activity 103
  challenge 11–13, 25, 127–8, 262,
    282, 295, 306, 337
  curriculum 127–46
  development 123
  process methods 125, 134–46,
    274, 296–7
  skills 26, 103, 125
  styles 171, 204
cognitive acceleration through science
    education (CASE) 13
cognitive process strategies for spelling
    (CPSS) 274, 296–7
Cognitive Research Trust
    (CoRT) 129
collaborative learning 126, 144–5
Collins, W.A. 51
combating boys' UAch 213–15
common indicators of UAch 6
co-morbidity 256–6
communities
  learning 181
  liaison 339
competent language development 45

competition 190
complex learning difficulties 271
compulsory schooling 43
concept
  classification 137
  completion 137–8
  mapping 137
conceptual gap 46
Confederation of British Industry
    (CBI) 281
conforming 190, 208
Connelly, V. 287
Connor's Behaviour Rating Scale 279
constructivist learning 65, 122, 127,
    135, 136
  theory 4, 112
continuing professional development
    (CPD) 76, 267, 295, 340
Cooley, D. 195
Coutts, L.M. 208
creativity 11–13
  thinking 307
  training 131
critical
  friends 226, 229
  thinking theory 122, 134, 307
Crocker, A.C. 269
Cropley, A. 131, 204–5
Csikszentmihalyi, M. 209
cultures 15–16
cultural
  capital 231, 249, 250–3
  context and literacy 42–3
  disadvantage 50
  influence 51
  perceptual learning 50
  programming 168
  toxins 47
curiosity 55
curriculum 231, 241, 247, 249, 254
  based identification 29–30
  cognitive 137–46

curriculum (*cont'd*)
  developmental writing   125
  hidden   133, 210
  and pedagogy   36
  seven levels of provision   117
  talking   125–6

developmental coordination
    difficulties (DCD)   266
de Bono, E.   129
de Alencar, E.M.L.S.   139
De Corte, E.   124, 136
deep learning   112, 115, 136, 142–4
definition of UAch   3–8
deprived children   52–3
Desforges, C.   8, 65, 112, 127, 136,
    166
developmental PCI (positive cognitive
    intervention)   15, 18
diagnostic tests   27–8
didactics   13, 115, 122
differentiation   116–17, 119, 303,
    338
  developmental   134
  dual   306
  model   114–15
differently cultured   43
digital
  children   320
  story telling   321–2
disadvantage
  cultural   43, 45, 50
  educational   221
  language   45
dialectics   104, 105, 174
disaffected
  boys   79
  children   125, 145
DISCOVER   82
discrepancy IQ scores   22
diversity   220
dominant culture   329–30

Downes, P.   208
Dracup, T.   118
Dromi, E.   64
dual exceptionalities   270–1
Dweck, C.S.   91, 100, 104, 208
dynamic interactions   16–21
dyslexia   265–6, 273
  first level   273
  girls   269
  ratios   249–70
  second level   274
  spelling error analysis   294

Economic and Social Research
    Council (ESRC)   88
editing skills software   311, 314,
    319–20
educational relationships   93–4
Edwards, J.   274
effective teaching and learning   120,
    122–46, 136, 156–7, 337
Eisner, E.   87
electronic
  appliances   55
  gap   42
  literacy   42–3
Elwood, J.   202
emotional literacy   211
emotive language   186
'engage brain' strategies   13, 275–6
English
  acquisition rate   236
  as an additional language
      (EAL)   11
  mother tongue (EMT)   243
  national curriculum (NC)   105
episodic code   171
epistemology   97, 99
Equal Opportunities
    Commission   188
Essex Curriculum Enrichment
    Materials   141

ethical space   102
evaluation   91
   criteria   148–9
   and marking   147
Every Child Matters   82, 104, 188,
   225
evidence-based practice   88–9
Excellence in Cities   118
expectations
   parent   205, 329
   pupil   329
   teacher   329–30
extension and enrichment   114–15,
   117
external factors in UAch   11–16
   barriers in   192

facilitation of learning   140
failing boys   202–3
family literacy sessions   337
Farmer, D.   165
feedback   167, 168, 252
   on language   45
females' language development
   44
Fennema, E.   195
Feuerstein, R.   142
flexible curriculum   121
   thinking   48–9
'Flynn effect'   54
Fogelman, K.   52
'foreigners'   53
formal teaching   174
   see also didactics
formative assessment   11, 15, 119
Formby, C.   89
Francis, B.   186, 187
Freeman's comparative study   48–9,
   52, 197, 203
Freire, P.   60, 61, 63, 67
frontloaded learning   135, 180
Fullerton study   44

Gagne, F.   125, 140
Gagne, R.   26
Gallagher, J.   140, 155
games and simulations   142
gap
   conceptual   46
   gender   186–8, 196
Gavin, M.K.   196
G&T (gifted and talented)
   quality standards   225
   register   254
   shadow register   254
gender
   differences   203–6
   gap   186–8, 196
   and maths   172
   stereotypes   186, 192, 193, 195
   support tactics   197
gender-biased IQ items   203, 205
   marking   203, 205, 212
general learning difficulties
   (GLD)   271
Gibbs, G.   124, 143
gifted girls profile   190–1
'gifts'   85, 91, 107
Gilborn, D.   220–1
Gilligan, C.   188
Ginott, H.   88
Gipps, C.   91
glass ceiling   203, 262
goal orientated learning   166
'gold standard'   328
'good' teaching   124
   see also effective teaching and
   learning
Gottfried, A.E.   44
Gottfried, A.W.   44
Gradgrind   122
Graham, S.   308, 312
grammar checkers   314
grammar school education   119, 246
   see also didactics

graphic word processors 309–10
grids 30–2
group work 164
  see also collaborative learning
Gunnar, M.R. 51
gypsies 53

Hallam, S. 115–17, 146
handwriting
  difficulties 266, 268
  gender and 288, 294
  legibility 277
  speed 272, 277, 286–7, 288–91
  untidy 276
Haringey REAL project 246, 247,
    252, 255, 256–8
  Greenhalgh, B. 255
  Shedden, S. 226, 248, 253–4
Hartog, M. 87–8
Hibbert, A. 52
hidden curriculum 133
high level thinking 45
high stakes tests 91, 103
higher order thinking 140
highlighting processors 311–12, 317
highly able, language
    development 44–5
holistic strategies 173–4
home reading 46
homework clubs 249
hot seating 244
Hounslow REAL project 241, 242–3,
    247, 249, 251, 254
  curriculum 241
  Macdonald, J. 242
  Smith, G. 231, 239, 256, 258
  Vasquez, M. 240, 242
  Ward, P. 245
Howe, M.J.A. 98
Hughes, M. 45
Hull study 293
Hundeide, K. 54
Hymer, B. 91, 96–7

identification
  dual exceptionality 270–1,
    304
  informal 29–30
  instruments 22–4
identification through appropriate
    provision (ITAP) 6, 117, 268,
    271
immigrants 53
incidence of G&T/UAch 267
inclusion 82, 91, 96–7, 116, 146, 163,
    225, 243, 251
  approaches 249
  developing practice 96–102
  and teaching 134, 295
influences, cultural 51
infusion 130
  of technology 303, 304, 306,
    307
innovative technologies 320–2
input differentiation 119
insatiable readers 46
intellectual skills 25
intelligence testing, 22–8
  bias 205, 268
  issues 23–4
  IQ use 119, 305, 328
  models 22–3
  problems 24–5
  tests 109 119
  validity 23–4
internal barriers 190–2
  factors in UAch 8–11
international comparisons 120
intrinsic motivation 124, 126, 127,
    140, 145
Islington REAL project 226, 243–4,
    251–2, 256–62
  Blake, H. 244
  Ferit, Y. 261
  Mostafa, S. 259
  Smith, G. 226, 231, 238, 239, 251,
    256, 258, 261, 262

Jaksa, P. 279
Joad, C.E.M. 210
Jolly Phonics 337
journal, reflective 255

Keele survey 268
Kellet, M. 93
Kelly, G. 12, 140
Kemmis, S. 65
Kerr, B. 189
Key Stage 2 learners 243
Kimbell, M. 185
kinaesthetic codes 172
Kings College 229
KwaZulu/Natal 60, 61–3, 65
  causes of UAch 62–4
  problems 70
  TASC results 75

labelling 265
language
  development 43, 63, 64
  and literacy skills 211–12
learning 102, 166
  codes 51, 161, 169, 171–4
  communities 181
  constructivist 65
  cycles 130
  deep 112, 115
  disabilities 163
  diversity 307
  effective 156–7
  frontloaded 135
  interactions 161–2
  intra-learner dimensions
    167
  lifelong 43, 65, 129, 340
  logic 104–5
  logs 243–6, 248
  metaphor 170
  methods 177
  models of 165, 167
  motivation to 160

numbers 46
outcomes 130, 146, 160
principles 180–1
to read 45–6
reflective 131–3, 246–7
social basis of 167–9
styles 160–1
surface 115
theories of 158, 165–6
uneven development in 163
universals design 307
Levinas, E. 102
Lewis, M. 50
Leyden, S. 209
listening 292
literacy 41–3, 53
  and culture 50–1
  electronic 41–3
  family 43
  feedback 45
  and women 53–4
living theory 90, 94–105
lockstep cohorts 121
locus of control 10, 65, 190, 191
Lyth, A. 288

Maker, J.C. 82
management, monitoring and
    maintenance (3Ms) 18–21
marking biases 205, 212
Marton, F. 142
masked abilities 237, 305
Maslow, A. 66
master classes 237
maths phobia 47
McBeath, J. 100
McCluskey, K.W. 280–1
McLeod, J. 204–5
mediation 142
medication (Ritalin) 278
mentoring 33, 196, 237, 271, 306,
    321
metacognition 45, 68–9, 174, 308

metacognitive
  skills   134
  strategies   310
metaphor for learning   169, 170
methods, teaching   125
Michalson, L.   50
Microsoft Office tools   313–14
Middlesex MA programmes   137,
  147
Miles, E.   24, 274
Miles, T.R.   24, 274
mind mapping tools   312–13
Miskin, R.   337
mismatches   178–9
missing cohort   221–2
mixed ability   114, 115, 120, 146
model
  of curriculum differentiation
    115
  of learning   165
  of teaching   113–14
modelling by teachers   129
monitoring   179, 231
Montgomery, D.   5, 7, 16–21, 276,
  293
MP3   321, 322
mothers' emotions   51
mother tongue assessment   233–4
motivation   9, 113, 129, 160
  achievement   207
  intrinsic   124, 126
Mounter, J.   91, 92–4, 101, 104, 106
multicultural society   219
multidimensional assessment   35
multimedia software   314, 320
multiple exceptionalities   266
Murray, Y.P.   99–100

NACE (National Association for Able
  Children in Education) Challenge
  Award   341–2
  Research project   13, 328
Nation's 1000 word list   233

National Strategies   90, 91, 118–19,
  266, 275, 286
new arrivals (EAL)   232–3
new millennium   122–3
number learning   46
Nunes, T.   47–8
nurture groups   33–4
nurturing qualities   191

Open University   229
oral expression and print   41
outcomes for learners   103, 160, 258

Paivio, A.   171
Papert, S.   46–7
parent(s)
  expectations   205–6, 337–8
  voice   34, 339
  working with   252–3, 255–6, 337–8
Passenger, T.   278
passive students   246
Passow, H.   123, 201, 340
'passport project'   235
Paul, R.W.   122
Pawley, J.   279
peer mentoring   34, 321
perfectionism   164, 191
performance
  appraisal   147
  based assessment   29
personalised learning (PL)   119, 120,
  127, 133, 182, 193, 238, 248, 249,
  329, 340
physical, sensory and medical
  difficulties (PSM)   180
Pickering, J.   204, 207
podcasting   321, 322
Pollard, A.   132–3
positive
  approaches to behaviour   16–19,
    125, 286
  class control   16–21
  school ethos   146

positive cognitive intervention
    (PCI) 17–18, 127, 134, 146
praise
    too much 193–4
    value of 257
    see also 'catch them being good'
        (CBG)
pre-writing software 309–11
problem
    based learning (PBL) 140, 306
    solving skills 49–50, 55
    software 321
process based teaching
        methods 113–15, 117
product based teaching 114, 115
    see also didactics
professional training 112
proportional logic 104
psychological barriers 190–2
publishing software 314, 320
pupil
    case examples 330–1, 338
    rating 330, 331
    voice 35, 92
purposeful talk 244

qualities 191
quality assurance 229, 230
    institutional standards 231
questioning skills 337
QUIFF 93

race 147
    inequality 221–2
Radford, J. 44
raising achievement 213–15
Ramos, M.B. 60, 61
Raven's Progressive Matrices 22, 54,
        280, 286
Rayner, A. 97
reading
    and context 42–3
    gap 202

learning to read 45–6
    skill 286
    and understanding 46, 53
    and women 53–4
real problem solving 17
Realizing Equality and Achievement
        for Learners (REAL)
    Project 219–63
    outcomes 241–2, 258
    partnerships 226–8
reception learning 144
recoding example 175–7
reflection
    feedback 112
    journal 253
    on learning 131–2, 246–8
    learning logs 245–6, 248
    questions 246
reframing
    curriculum provision 295
    teaching 125
regulating learning 174
Reis, S.M. 196
remediation 305, 306, 307
    see also cognitive process strategies
        for spelling (CPSS)
representativeness 231
revising software 313–14, 319
Roaf, C. 277, 288
role(s) 209
    change 113
    models 193, 206, 207, 208
roots of thinking 49–50
Rowe's study 46
Ruddick, S. 89
rhythmic code 172

Sadler, K. 209
Saljo, R. 142
Sandwell REAL project 235–8
    passport project 235
Saphire, D.G. 305
SATs 26

scaffolds   139
schemas   139
Schlicte-Hiersemensel, B.   280–1
Schneider, F.W.   208
Schon, D.   97
Schools Council, The   33, 112
school   339
  averse   281
  improvement   248–9
  refusal   162
scripts, learning   123, 146
self
  esteem   63, 65, 127, 188, 190
  image   63, 65, 330
  instruction   174
  theory of   100
setting by ability   221
shadow G&T register   254
shadowing   32–3
Silverman, L.K.   269
Singleton, C.   274
Skelton, C.   188, 195, 196, 203
skills
  cognitive   103
  intellectual   102
Skuse, A.   90
social
  basis of learning   167–9
  class   188, 189
  context   226
  engineering   118
  influence   51
  isolate   168
  justice   219
  values   51
social, emotional and behavioural
    difficulties (SEBD)   279, 280–2
Somali students REAL project
    256–8
spatial strengths   165
special educational needs
    (SEN)   10–11, 79, 114–15, 266

specific language impairment
    (SLI)   285
spelling
  correction   275
  problem   268
  strategies   275–6, 296–7
specific learning difficulties (SpLD)
    and 2E   272
stable families   51
standards   119
Stanley, J.R.   205
stereotypes   186, 192, 193, 195, 203,
    210
Sternberg, R.   66, 103–4
  sub-theories of intelligence
    68
Stewart, W.J.   204
strategic approaches
  to identification   30–2
  to spelling   274
street children   47–8
stretch and challenge   226
  see also challenge
structure of observed learning
    outcomes (SOLO)   137
student voice   245–9
study skills   134–8
subject nominations   231
summative assessment   14
surface learning   115, 142, 143
Supplee, P.L.   201, 210
SureStart   130
synthetic strategies   173, 174,
    175

2E   265–72
3Ms (management, monitoring and
    maintenance)   18–21
tactical lesson plans (TLP)   21
talents   85, 91, 107, 156, 189–90, 191,
    220, 308
talking word processors   311, 316

teacher
  attitudes 305
  education 144, 156–8, 243
  expectations 163, 329–30
  reflection 338; *see also* learning,
    reflective
  retraining 157–8
Teacher Training Agency (TTA)
  114
teaching 123
  effective methods 146
  'good' 124, 125–45
  reframing 125
  team 338
  thinking skills 128–9
  traditional methods 134–5; *see*
    also didactics
teaching reading through spelling
  (TRTS) 279
technology
  assistive 309–22
  infusion 303, 304, 306–7
  strategies 163
Terman, L.M. 204
Terrell, C. 278
test
  instruments 22–28
  taking biases 205
  validity 23–4
text
  messaging 321–2
  to speech processors 310–11
theory(ies)
  of learning 158, 165–6
  of mind 284
thinking
  codes 171
  critical theory 122
  cultural disadvantage 50
  flexible 48–9
  new style 54–5
  roots of 49–50

skills 49–50, 119, 255
space 169
Thinking Actively in a Social Context
  (TASC) project 29, 65–82, 92,
  97–8
  extended framework 71–4
  knot 99, 101
  learning principles 69
  lesson planning 77–8
  problem solving processes
    69–70
  results 73
  UK results 79–82
  wheel 71, 78
Thomas, A. 28
Tizard, B. 45
Torrance, E.P. 269
tracking progress 304
traits 23
Trends in International Mathematics
  and Science Study (TIMSS)
  119
truanting 52
Turkish students REAL
  project 258–62
Turks 53
Tymms, P. 264, 286
typologies 29

UK education scene 75–6
underachievement (UAch)
  checklists 28, 35, 267–8
  factors, external 11–16
  factors, internal 8–11
  model 8
under-representation 220–1
  of minority groups 222–3

validity of tests 23–4
values 86, 103, 104–7
Van Tassell-Baska, J. 205
Vasilyuk, F. 95–6

verbal learning difficulties 272–6
verbal-linguistic codes 171
verbalising 179
visual imagery codes 171
voice recognition software 310, 315
Voigt, J. 167
Vygotsky, L.S. 50, 63, 66, 129

Waldron, K.A. 305
Wallace, B. 13, 29, 91, 94, 97–8, 130
Waters, E. 51
Whitmore, J.R. 7
Wilgosh, L. 185
Wiliam, D. 203
wikis 321

Wechsler Intelligence Scale for
    Children (WISC) 23–4, 27
Within-learner differences 169–70
Wolverhampton REAL project 227,
    229, 249–50
women, family health and
    reading 53–4
working memory 293
writing
    difficulties 286–91, 308; *see also*
        handwriting
    skills processors 311–14, 316–20
    test 30
word prediction processors 312,
    317–18